The Community, the Family
and the Saint

D0139983

International Medieval Research
Selected Proceedings of the International Medieval Congress
University of Leeds

International Medieval Research

The Community, the Family and the Saint

Patterns of Power in Early Medieval Europe

Selected Proceedings of the
International Medieval Congress
University of Leeds
4-7 July 1994, 10-13 July 1995

edited by
Joyce Hill and Mary Swan

Turnhout, Brepols
1998

Articles appearing in this volume are indexed in
"International Medieval Bibliography"

© 1998 – BREPOLS
Printed in Belgium
D/1998/0095/55
ISBN 2-503-50668-2

Contents

I COMMUNITY AND FAMILY

II SAINTS

III POWER

IV DEATH, BURIAL AND COMMEMORATION

Preface

The majority of the papers in this volume were originally presented at the first two meetings of the International Medieval Congress, in 1994 and 1995. The IMC is now annually established at the University of Leeds as the largest European congress on Medieval Studies. We should like to thank our colleagues and all the participants who have done so much to make it a success, and in particular the contributors to this volume, whose essays are indicative of the range and quality of the work presented each year in the sessions devoted to the study of early medieval Europe.

We also owe a debt of gratitude to Paul Fouracre and Mayke de Jong for their specialist advice, and to those who have assisted in the practical production of the volume: Amanda Banton, Sue Clarke and especially Suzanne Paul. Our readers worked swiftly and meticulously, and their insight and generosity made our work much easier. The cover illustration of an eighth-century Anglo-Saxon sculpture fragment in Otley Parish Church near Leeds is taken from a photograph by Paul Barnwell, supplied to us by Ian Wood. We are grateful to the Parochial Church Council for permission to use this illustration on the cover.

In order to standardise work on the wide range of topics covered by the papers in this volume, the contributors have kindly reshaped their papers from oral presentations to written essays, and have followed the editorial policy of foregrounding original textual material in the main body of each paper wherever appropriate, and of providing full translations to support this. They have made our task as editors enjoyable, and we are very grateful to them for their cooperation throughout in our efforts to produce for a wide readership a uniform and accessible volume covering such a diversity of specialist fields.

Joyce Hill and Mary Swan
Leeds, May 1998

Introduction

Since the establishment of the Leeds International Medieval Congress in 1994, the study of early medieval Europe has been strongly represented year by year. One of the notable characteristics of work in this period has always been its interdisciplinarity: work on any one type of evidence is commonly set in a broader context, and scholars in a range of disciplines engage in fruitful dialogues with each other across the traditional subject boundaries. It was immediately evident to the series editors of International Medieval Research that one of the early IMR volumes should be devoted to this vigorous area in medieval studies. *The Community, the Family and the Saint* is the outcome, its twenty-two essays being chosen for their varied but complementary approaches to the investigation of the organising forces of social identity and power in early medieval Europe. At the same time, the contributors' exploitation of such a rich array of primary materials – literary and historical texts, and artefacts and archaeological evidence from a wide geographical area, ranging in time from the early Celtic world to the emerging city states of twelfth-century Italy – is a powerful testimony both to the diversity of work currently being undertaken and to its essential interdisciplinarity.

The essays are grouped into four sections which reflect the nexus of power in the early Middle Ages. The title of the first section, 'Community and Family', reflects the growing awareness that categories of social organisation operate differently in the early Middle Ages from those in the modern world, the family, as we understand it, being just one of a number of important social groupings alongside monastic, racial, civic, genealogical and ideological communities which contribute to the organisation of society and the construction of identities. In the opening essay Mary Alberi takes the larger view of the community in examining Alcuin's concept of the *Imperium christianum* and uses Alcuin's letters and other writings to show how he offered correction and guidance to Charlemagne on the exercise of imperial power. Stefan

Brink, with a more northerly focus, investigates the connections between Church and society in the formation of the Scandinavian parish. In charting the progress of Christianisation and state-formation, he addresses the question of whether the word *sokn* (parish) and the concept it denotes originated in England and were transferred to Scandinavia as a result of the Viking settlement of England in the ninth and tenth centuries, or whether they originated in Scandinavia. The Italian communes of the Middle Ages and their relationship with imperial power are the subject of Edward Coleman's study. He shows how literary texts highlight important elements in the construction of civic identity and how the cult of the patron saint of a city becomes the spiritual focus of civic life. Matthew Ellis also explores civic life in this period, this time in Rome. He charts the ways in which civic power is administered in the twelfth century through families, and how clientage and kinship constitute important links in social power networks. By tracing the interconnection of three kinship groups, Ellis shows how minor families, which are often invisible or anonymous in narrative sources, show up in legal documents and cartularies as vital power-brokers. Tribal groupings in the earlier period are the subject of Harald Kleinschmidt's essay, which surveys the range of factors which may constitute a *gens* and, using Bede's references to the Geuissae as an example, investigates the ways in which changes in the name of a *gens* may indicate changes in concept in the seventh and eighth centuries. Commonly accepted views of a later social change – the modification of family structures and kinship systems believed to have taken place in the twelfth century – are critiqued by Pauline Stafford. She uncovers some of the undeclared ideologies which shape documentary sources and the interaction of individuals, families and external factors and shows how one can arrive at a more nuanced interpretation of social change and its effects on definitions of kinship, especially as it pertains to women and their status; different kinship systems may coexist, and may be used in different circumstances. The female community of Gandersheim and its relationship to the communities of women created in the writings of Hrotsvitha are examined by Lisa Weston. She shows Hrotsvitha redefining female community and secular and spiritual marriage in her challenges to Terence in her dramatic works.

Saints and their cults are of central importance in the construction and articulation of early medieval power complexes and for this reason they form the focus of the second section, 'Saints'. The power associated with saints is both secular and spiritual, and the intersection of these two spheres is often achieved through the spiritual and ideological qualities of individual saints and their cults. The secular and social aspects of sanctity are examined by Mayke de Jong with reference to Ekkehard's *Life* of Iso of St Gall as an expression of social regulation. The penance which Ekkehard describes Iso's parents being instructed to carry out for their sin of having sexual intercourse in Lent is an example of the power of the Church to legitimise ritual innovation and of the involvement of the community in new rituals which serve as markers of saintly potential. David Pelteret's focus is accounts of the Life of St Wilfrid and what can be discerned from them about Wilfrid's interpretation of the role of a bishop. He shows how regional social institutions play a part in shaping the episcopacy and how Wilfrid's career is modelled upon the secular lord as well as a range of episcopal examples. Hedwig Röckelein uses accounts of miracles and translations from early medieval Saxony to examine the factors which determine a saint's sphere of influence and to discuss definitions of geographical mobility in pilgrimages with particular reference to the involvement of women.

The third section is entitled 'Power'. Under this heading are grouped papers which address this issue directly and so interconnect with many of the threads of discussion already established in the volume, including religion, sanctity, government and the intersection of the spiritual and the mysterious. One notable recurrent element in these studies is that mystery and mystification are very important elements in the construction and maintenance of power. Philippe Depreux studies the presentation of Louis the Pious and of a programme of government in Ermold's *Elegiacum Carmen*, which emphasises the importance of *ordo*, the relationship between faith and royal power, and that between ideology, rulership and literature. The power of ecclesiastical and lay courts to judge marital affairs is

explored by Karl Heidecker in his study of the case of the divorce of
King Lothar II. He shows how episcopal and royal power overlap in
this instance, and he charts a change in ecclesiastical attitudes to
legal marriage in the mid-ninth century. The power of the law is also
the subject of Sarah Larratt Keefer's essay, which examines the
ways in which spiritual, physiological and psychological factors
combine to give a judicial ordeal its power, with reference to the
ordeal of *corsnæd*, referred to in texts from Anglo-Saxon England.
She examines evidence for the precise legal practice which this
involves and edits and translates one version of a *Corsnæd* liturgy.
Social power is the subject of Joaquín Martínez Pizarro's study of a
ninth-century account of the murder of the inhabitants of one
quarter of Ravenna by those of another quarter. In the examination
of the text, he shows how it foregrounds collectives of people –
crowds, neighbourhood groups and families – and exploits images
of division, conspiracy and ritual in order finally to promote the
unification of a community. Rob Meens poses questions about the
information on actual behaviour which can be deduced from literary
sources referring to magical practices and in the course of his
discussion reveals the strong connection established in such texts
between impurity and power. Like Mayke de Jong's essay in the
section on saints, this is a striking contrast with the relationship
between purity and power so often established in hagiography and
an important reminder of the power of opposites and extremes in
social practices and spiritual beliefs. Patricia Skinner's study of
healthcare in Southern Italy shows the tensions between medicine
and popular religious belief. Both *medici* and clergy have a
relatively high social status and in the hagiographical texts which
are the focus of this essay we can see clearly their professional and
financial rivalry in the competition to treat physical suffering. Legal
power is addressed again by Martina Stein-Wilkeshuis, who
investigates the evidence for Scandinavian influence on a tenth-
century Rus'-Greek commercial treaty. By juxtaposing the treaty
with a range of Scandinavian legal articles on the publication of
offences, the role of witnesses, proof and revenge, she is able to
point to a number of similarities in basic legal principles in
Scandinavian material and the Rus'-Greek treaty.

The final section, 'Death, Burial and Commemoration', draws together the volume's main themes of social and religious organisation and the definition of communities. Representations of death, burial and commemoration are expressions of the status and the power both of the individual and of the group to which he or she belongs, as well as being a means by which, through collective ritual, a community reinforces its own identity in part through mystification. The social, ritualised conventions which are established to deal with death, burial and commemoration are at once markers of closure and of perpetuation. Guy Halsall explores the way in which social information is stored and transformed through burial rituals and ritual language in Merovingian society. Using the example of grave-goods, he shows how cosmology is defined and redefined through ritual, and how grave-goods mark social status and are an indication of insecure power. Commemoration practices in early medieval western Britain are the focus of Mark Handley's essay, which examines surviving inscribed stones from this area. Handley argues that the inscriptions develop a function close to that of charters and that they can thus be used as a source of socio-economic data. The use of some standing stones as boundary markers reveals their links to the social structures involved in landholding and to the proclamation of power which they articulate. The ways in which judicial procedures can act as expressions of the relationship between the living, the dying and the dead are explored by Dominic Janes in his study of the symbolic gift of a bequest as a publicly witnessed event. In the volume's second essay on inscribed stones, Bertil Nilsson investigates Viking activity in England in the first half of the eleventh century through runic memorials in Sweden which refer to journeys to England made by the people they commemorate. These memorials provide evidence of the impact of Christianisation and the enhancement of social status apparently provided by travelling to England. In the third essay to take inscribed stones as its focus, Mark Redknap traces work done by Victor Erle Nash-Williams and other scholars in more recent years to conserve and record inscribed stones from Early Medieval Wales. He shows how Nash-Williams' scheme of classification and chronology have influenced the understanding of the inscribed stones and what they might reveal about the population of early Christian Wales. This final essay thus offers an important reminder about how our perception and interpretation of patterns of power in early medieval Europe are shaped by the work of earlier scholars. We are therefore made aware not only of the importance of interpreting the ideologies which formed and informed the written materials and the artefacts surviving from early Medieval Europe, but also of how our understanding of that material is determined by the work of others.

Joyce Hill and Mary Swan

Abbreviations

AASS	Acta Sanctorum.
ASRSP	*Archivio della Società Romana di storia patria.*
CIH	D. A. Binchy ed., *Corpus Iuris Hibernici* (Dublin, 1978).
CIIC	R. A. S. Macalister, *Corpus Inscriptionum Insularum Celticarum* (Dublin, 1945/49).
CCSL	Corpus Christianorum Series Latina.
ECMW	V. E. Nash-Williams, *The Early Christian Monuments of Wales* (Cardiff, 1950).
FSI	Fonti per la Storia d'Italia, (various editors), (Rome, 1887-).
MGH	Monumenta Germaniae Historica.
Dip. reg. et imp. Ger.	Diplomata regum et imperatorum Germaniae.
Epp. Kar. Aev.	Epistolae Karolini Aevi.
LNG	Leges nationum Germanicarum.
SRG (in us. schol.)	Scriptores rerum Germanicarum in usum scholarum separatim editi.
SRG Nova ser.	Scriptores rerum Germanicarum Nova series.
SRL	Scriptores rerum Langobardicarum et Italicarum saec. VI-IX.
SRM	Scriptores rerum Merovingicarum.
SS	Scriptores (in folio).
PL	Patrologia cursus completus ... series latina, ed. J. P. Migne, 221 vols (Paris, 1844-64).
RCAHM	Royal Commission on Ancient and Historic Monuments.
RIS[1]	Rerum Italicarum Scriptores, ed. L. A. Muratori, 28 vols (Milan, 1723-51).
RIS[2]	Rerum Italicarum Scriptores, ed. G. Carducci and V. Fiorini (Rome, 1900-).

I   COMMUNITY

The Evolution of Alcuin's Concept of the *Imperium christianum*

Mary Alberi

The earliest evidence for Alcuin's concept of empire appears in his *Vita Willibrordi* and letters on the conversion of the Avars.[1] Alcuin wrote the *Vita Willibrordi* at the request of his kinsman, Beornrad of Echternach, sometime between 785 and 797. The *Vita* reflects the kinship of both men to Willibrord and the monastery's ties to the Carolingian dynasty.[2] In 796 or 797, on his own initiative, Alcuin wrote a series of letters to men deeply involved in the Avar war and mission: Paulinus of Aquileia, Arn of Salzburg, Charlemagne, and Charlemagne's treasurer, Megenfrid.[3] In spite of different origins

---

[1] Alcuin, *Vita Willibrordi archiepiscopi Traiectensis*, ed. W. Levison, MGH SRM 7 (Hanover and Leipzig, 1920), pp. 81-141. See I. Deug-Su, *L'opera agiografica di Alcuino* (Spoleto, 1983), pp. 31-71; and W. Berschin, *Biographie und Epochenstil im lateinische Mittelalter*, 3 vols, Quellen und Untersuchungen zur lateinischen Philologie des Mittelalters 8, 9, 10 (Stuttgart, 1986-1991), 3:113-39.

[2] A. Angenendt, "Willibrord im Dienst der Karolinger", *Annalen des historischen Vereins für den Niederrhein* 175 (1973), 63-113; and H.-J. Reischmann, ed. and trans., *Willibrord – Apostel der Freisen: Seine Vita nach Alkuin und Thiofred* (Sigmaringendorf, 1989), pp. 20-22.

[3] Alcuin, *Epistolae* 99, ed. E. Dümmler, MGH Epistolae 4, Epp. Kar. Aev. 2 (Berlin, 1895), pp. 143-44; *Ep.* 107, MGH Epp. Kar. Aev. 2:153-54; *Ep.* 110, MGH Epp. Kar. Aev. 2:156-59; *Ep.* 111, MGH Epp. Kar. Aev. 2:159-62; *Ep.* 112, MGH Epp. Kar. Aev. 2:162-63; and *Ep.* 113, MGH Epp. Kar. Aev.

and genres, both the *Vita* and the letters try to answer the same question: how could the hegemony of the Carolingians promote the church's mission to convert the nations before the Last Judgement? This question weighed upon Alcuin in the 790s because of the apparent failure of Charlemagne's policy of forced conversion in Saxony, the involvement of Frisians and Saxons in the rebellions of 792/793, and finally, the Carolingian triumph over the pagan Avars in 795/796.

The *Vita Willibrordi* counters Charlemagne's harsh policies in Saxony with an idealised history of the early Carolingian *imperium* and Willibrord's mission in northern Francia and Frisia.[4] Alcuin derived his concept of the Carolingian *imperium* from Anglo-Latin literature. In his *Historia ecclesiastica*, Bede frequently describes a king's lordship over *regna* he had conquered as an *imperium*.[5] Bede also designates Pepin's rule over Frisia as *imperium*. Bede's definition of *imperium* later influenced Willibald's *Vita Bonifatii*, in which the establishment of Charles Martel's military *imperium* precedes the conversion of the Frisians. Both Bede and Willibald influenced Alcuin.[6] In Alcuin's *Vita Willibrordi*, Carolingian *duces* bring the Frisians under their *imperium* and protect Willibrord as he converts them to Christianity. Submission to Carolingian lordship

---

2:163-66. For the Avars, see W. Pohl, *Die Awaren: Ein Steppenvolk in Mitteleuropa, 567-822 n. Chr.* (Munich, 1988), pp. 308-22; and C. Bowlus, *Franks, Moravians, and Magyars: The Struggle for the Middle Danube, 788-907*, Middle Ages Series (Philadelphia, 1995), pp. 46-60.

[4] For Alcuin's treatment of historical events, see W. Levison, "Die Quellen zur Geschichte des hl. Willibrord", in *Aus rheinischer und fränkischen Frühzeit: Ausgewählte Aufsätze* (Düsseldorf, 1948), pp. 304-13; and J. Schroeder, "Willibrord – Erzbischof von Utrecht oder Abt von Echternach?" *Hémecht* 42 (1990), 137-46.

[5] S. Fanning, "Bede, *Imperium*, and the Bretwaldas", *Speculum* 66 (1991), 15-22.

[6] U. Nonn, "Das Bild Karl Martells in den lateinischen Quellen vornehmlich des 8. und 9. Jahrhunderts", *Frühmittelalterliche Studien* 4 (1970), 79-82; and J. Nelson, "Kingship and Empire in the Carolingian World", in *Carolingian Culture: Emulation and Innovation*, ed. R. McKitterick (Cambridge, 1994), pp. 52-87 (p. 69).

and baptism unite all the "electos a Deo populos regni Francorum".[7]
Other Carolingian authors shared Alcuin's perspective on the
sources of Frankish unity. For example, according to Einhard, the
Saxons converted to Christianity and were united with the Franks as
"one people" after they accepted Charlemagne's lordship:

> Eaque conditione a rege proposita et ab illis
> suscepta ... bellum constat esse finitum ut, abiecto
> daemonum cultu et relictis patriis caerimoniis,
> Christianae fidei atque religionis sacramenta
> susciperent et Francis adunati unus cum eis
> populus efficerentur.[8]

According to Alcuin, the lordship of Pepin II and Charles
Martel enabled Willibrord to perform his *ministerium euangelicae
praedicationis* among pagan Franks and Frisians.[9] The *dux
Francorum* Pepin sends Willibrord to preach among the pagan
Franks who live "intra terminos regni sui".[10] Later, Pepin sends
Willibrord to Rome to be consecrated bishop by Pope Sergius II,
"quatenus apostolica benedictione et iussione suscepta, maiori ab eo
missus fiducia roboratus in opus euangelii reverteretur".[11] When

---

[7] Alcuin, *Vita Willibrordi*, p. 124, lines 3-4: "the peoples chosen by God
for salvation". For the unity of diverse *populi* in the *regnum Francorum*, see P.
Fouracre, "Frankish Gaul to 814", in *The New Cambridge Medieval History,
Vol. 2: c. 700-c. 900*, ed. R. McKitterick (Cambridge, 1995), pp. 85-109; and J.
Nelson, "Kingship and Royal Government", in *New Cambridge Medieval
History, Vol. 2*, pp. 383-430.

[8] Einhard, *Vita Karoli Magni*, ed. O. Holder-Egger, MGH SRG (in us.
schol.) (Hanover, 1911; repr. 1927), chap. 7, p. 10, lines 25-30: "The war was
ended ... when the king proposed his conditions and the Saxons agreed, that,
after casting away the cult of demons and abandoning their father's religious
ceremonies, they should take up the sacraments of the Christian faith and cult;
and, united with the Franks, be made one people with them".

[9] On the "service [to God] of preaching the Gospel" in this *Vita*, see
Deug-Su, *L'opera agiografica*, p. 63.

[10] Alcuin, *Vita Willibrordi*, p. 121, line 3: "within the boundaries of his
kingdom".

[11] Alcuin, *Vita Willibrordi*, p. 121, lines 13-15: "so that, after receiving an
apostolic blessing and command, and strengthened by the greater confidence of
having been sent by him, Willibrord might return to the work of preaching the
Gospel".

Willibrord returns, Pepin sends him back to the northern part of the Frankish kingdom. Ordaining priests, building churches, and founding monasteries, Willibrord completes the conversion of the Franks, the "novus Dei populus".[12]

After Pepin's death:

> Contigit ... Pippinum ducem Francorum diem
> obire et filium eius Carolum regno patris potiri.
> Qui multas gentes sceptris adiecit Francorum, inter
> quas etiam cum triumphi gloria Fresiam, devicto
> Rabbodo, paterno superaddidit imperio.[13]

Following his Anglo-Latin models, Alcuin introduces the concept of *imperium* to describe a specific type of *regnum*, which unites several *populi* under the hegemony of one ruler.[14] Already a *dux* commanding the Franks and the *populi* subject to them, Charles Martel brings the Frisians under the *imperium* established by his father. Here *imperium* designates Carolingian rule over the Frisians, the "gladio adquisitam gentem" (1 Peter 2.9).[15] The Carolingian "sword" protects Willibrord's mission, and together, both "sword" and mission serve God's purposes within salvation history. Accordingly, Charles Martel gives Willibrord Utrecht, the episcopal see from which he organises the Frisian church. Protected by the warlike *dux*, the saintly bishop seals the unification of the Frisians with the *regnum Francorum* through baptism. Afterwards, Willibrord sanctifies the civic life of the Frisians, now the baptised "filii Dei viventis" through his preaching and ecclesiastical foundations.[16] As he sows God's word and reaps the harvest of the

---

[12] Alcuin, *Vita Willibrordi*, p. 123, lines 1-12; and p. 126, line 4 to p. 127, line 4; with "God's new people" at p. 127, line 1.

[13] Alcuin, *Vita Willibrordi*, p. 127, lines 5-8: "It happened that ... Pepin, duke of the Franks, died and his son Charles succeeded to his father's kingdom. Charles added many peoples to the kingdom of the Franks. And also among those, he added Frisia to his paternal empire with triumphant glory, after defeating Radbod".

[14] Fanning, "Bede, *Imperium*, and the Bretwaldas", pp. 10-14, and p. 19.

[15] Alcuin, *Vita Willibrordi*, p. 127, line 10: "the people acquired by the sword".

[16] Alcuin, *Vita Willibrordi*, p. 127, line 14: "the sons of the living God", a citation of Hosea 1.10 and Romans 9.25.

elect in Frisia, Willibrord gives the Carolingian *imperium* eschatological significance.[17]

Alcuin insists that laymen must assist preachers like Willibrord as they go about God's work in the last days. In one of the *Vita*'s miracle stories, Willibrord, on his way to preach to the Frisians, rests his horses in the meadow of a proud rich man. When the rich man objects, Willibrord explains that he has stopped out of necessity on his way to preach the Gospel, whose rewards the rich man may share if he receives Willibrord kindly. Willibrord reminds the rich man of Christ's promise that whoever receives his disciples will receive him (Matthew 10.40). The rich man, however, refuses Willibrord's request, and suffers unquenchable thirst for a year, until the saint pardons him.[18] Unlike this proud rich man, Pepin and Charles Martel receive Willibrord, and through him, Christ, with honour. God rewards them for their support of Willibrord's work with a more glorious *imperium*.

Another miracle story emphasises the glory of a Carolingian *imperium* dedicated to defending the church against pagans and preaching to baptised Christians. When Charles Martel brings his son, Pepin III, to Willibrord for baptism, the saint prophesies that the infant will be greater than all the earlier "dukes" of the Franks. Symbolising Pepin's future consecration as king, this baptism confirms the election of the Carolingians and the Franks.[19] The election that takes place in the *Vita Willibrordi* focuses especially on Pepin, his son Charlemagne, the Franks, the monks of Echternach, and Alcuin himself. Together, they create what Alcuin calls "our empire", as Willibrord's prophecy is fulfilled. As an adult, Pepin "terminos nostri dilatavit imperii ... christianam in

---

[17] For an example of the *Vita*'s many references to sowing and reaping, see Alcuin, *Vita Willibrordi*, p. 119, lines 15-16; and p. 121, lines 3-6. On the harvest of the elect, see Gregory, *Moralia in Job*, ed. M. Adriaen, CCSL 143, 143A, 143B (Turnhout, 1975-85), 143B:1373-74.

[18] Alcuin, *Vita Willibrordi*, p. 131, line 6 to p. 132, line 4.

[19] E. Ewig, "Zum christlichen Königsgedanken im Frühmittelalter", in *Spätantikes und fränkisches Galliens: Gesammelte Schriften (1952-1973)*, ed. H. Astma, Beiheft der Francia 3/1 and 3/2 (Munich and Zurich, 1976-79), 3/1:42-43.

regno suo propagavit relegionem, vel ... pro defensione sanctae Dei ecclesiae apud extraneos exercuit gentes".[20] Moreover, this Pepin was "patrem huius nobilissimi Caroli, qui modo cum triumphis maximis et omni dignitate gloriosissime Francorum regit imperium".[21]

How could Alcuin, an Englishman writing for a monastic community with a strong Insular presence, identify the Frankish *imperium* as "ours"?[22] In one of his letters, Alcuin explains that baptism arms every Christian with the spiritual weapons of the *miles Christi* and imposes on every Christian the duty to preach to others.[23] The Carolingian *imperium* united many Christian *populi* under a single lord dedicated to the conversion of the nations before the Last Judgement. Alcuin believed this *imperium* enabled every Christian to fulfil the obligation imposed on him in baptism, to preach to other baptised Christians and to pagans "acquired by the sword". Furthermore, in the *Vita Willibrordi*'s story of Pepin's baptism, Alcuin placed the Carolingians and the Franks under Willibrord's patronage. The Carolingians are bound by their personal relationship with the saint to follow his model of evangelisation.[24] Alcuin portrays Willibrord as an ideal missionary,

---

[20] Alcuin, *Vita Willibrordi*, p. 134, lines 2-5: "[Pepin] ... enlarged the frontiers of our empire ... extended Christianity within his kingdom, and ... worked for the defence of God's church against foreign nations". See H. H. Anton, *Fürstenspiegel und Herrscherethos in der Karolingerzeit*, Bonner historische Forschungen 32 (Bonn, 1968), p. 98, note 117 on the phrase "dilatare fines".

[21] Alcuin, *Vita Willibrordi*, p. 133, lines 18-19: "the father of this most noble Charles who now rules the empire of the Franks with the greatest triumphs and every dignity most gloriously".

[22] On Echternach and its Insular traditions, see N. Netzer, *Cultural Interplay in the Eighth Century: The Trier Gospels and the Making of the Scriptorium at Echternach*, Cambridge Studies in Palaeography and Codicology 3 (Cambridge, 1993), pp. 4-11, 34-41.

[23] *Ep.* 134, MGH Epp. Kar. Aev. 2:202, line 18 to p. 203, line 6.

[24] On the personal nature of this bond, see Angenendt, "Willibrord im Dienste der Karolinger", pp. 63-66; and his "Taufe und Politik im frühen Mittelalter", *Frühmittelalterliche Studien* 7 (1973), 145-51.

whose preaching embodies apostolic *caritas* and a desire for an eternal reward.

Reflecting Echternach's Insular traditions, Alcuin's *Vita Willibrordi* remained faithful to concepts of empire found in eighth century Anglo-Latin authors. But this imperial ideal proved unsatisfactory in 796/797, when Alcuin confronted the problem of the Avar mission. His anxieties over the possible failure of another mission compelled Alcuin to reformulate his concept of empire. In addition, Charlemagne's dominance blurred the distinction between worldly and spiritual powers which Alcuin maintained in the *Vita Willibrordi* and elsewhere.[25] Alcuin feared that Charlemagne and his advisers at court would subordinate the church's mission to the selfish aggrandisement of their power.[26] As a result, Alcuin decided to write a series of letters preaching to his powerful friends at court about the proper conduct of the Avar mission and the exaltation of imperial power through service to Christ. In these letters, Alcuin acknowledged Charlemagne's lordship over the *populus christianus*, while challenging him to avoid the besetting sins of imperialism, love of domination and greed.[27] Alcuin appealed to patristic authority to correct an ambitious king and clergy who had conducted the Saxon mission and were about to begin the mission to the Avars without regard for the *ministerium euangelicae praedicationis* exemplified in saintly bishops like Willibrord.

Indeed, Alcuin believed Charlemagne had allowed his clergy to damage the mission in Saxony.[28] The Saxons rejected Christianity

---

[25] Anton, *Fürstenspiegel und Herrscherethos*, pp. 123-30.

[26] On Charlemagne's policy of asserting his lordship in these years, see M. Becher, *Eid und Herrschaft: Untersuchungen zum Herrscherethos Karls des Grossen*, Vorträge und Forschungen, Sonderband 39 (Sigmaringen, 1993), pp. 74-77 and 191-216.

[27] The source of Alcuin's concerns about imperialism may be seen in Augustine's *De civitate Dei*. See, for example *De civitate Dei*, ed. B. Dombart and A. Kalb, CCSL 47, 48 (Turnhout, 1955), 47:142-46.

[28] A. Hauck, *Kirchengeschichte Deutschlands*, 8th ed., 6 vols (Berlin, 1954), 2:371-424; H.-D. Kahl, "Karl der Grosse und die Sachsen: Stufen und Motiv einer historischen 'Eskalation'", in *Politik, Gesellschaft, Geschichts-schreibung: Giessener Festgabe für Frantisek Graus zum 60. Geburtstag*, ed. H. Ludat and R. C. Schwinges, Beihefte zum Archiv für Kulturgeschichte 18

because of the Frankish clergy's insistent demand for tithes and the imposition of harsh punishments for minor offences.[29] Alcuin accuses Frankish clerics involved in the Saxon mission of greed and ambition.[30] He reproaches "sacerdotes Christi, qui habent parochias et honores saeculi, et gradus ministerii non volunt habere ... Nunc ... alius laborat pro mercede perpetua; illi vero pro saeculari honore. Privati vero sunt ... potestate ligandi et solvendi".[31] Lamenting such behaviour, Alcuin concludes that Charlemagne's lack of honest helpers is a symptom of "the dangerous times of this last age" (2 Timothy 3.1): "Cui omnis bonitas et potentia ad benefaciendum sufficit, nisi unum tantummodo propter tempora periculosa huius saeculi: quod rariores habet adiutores in opere Domini quam necesse sit".[32]

Alcuin worried that the selfish interests of such priests would influence Charlemagne, who believed that renunciation of the devil and submission to baptism sufficed for genuine conversion.[33] In response, Alcuin based his own plan for the church's mission on

(Cologne and Vienna, 1982), pp. 49-130; and E. J. Goldberg, "Popular Revolt, Dynastic Politics, and Aristocratic Factionalism in the Early Middle Ages: The Saxon *Stellinga* Reconsidered", *Speculum* 70 (1995), 472-80.

[29] *Ep.* 107, MGH Epp. Kar. Aev. 2:154, lines 16-20; *Ep.* 110, MGH Epp. Kar. Aev. 2:158, lines 4-14; *Ep.* 111, MGH Epp. Kar. Aev. 2:161, lines 5-7. In 799, Alcuin was still urging Charlemagne to give the Saxons some relief from tithes: *Ep.* 174, MGH Epp. Kar. Aev. 2:289, lines 6-9.

[30] *Ep.* 112, MGH. Epp. Kar. Aev. 2:162, line 31.

[31] *Ep.* 111, MGH Epp. Kar. Aev. 2:161, lines 26-31: "Christ's priests, who have parishes and worldly offices, and do not want to have the ecclesiastical dignity of pastoral care ... Now another works for eternal reward; but they strive for worldly office. In truth, they have been deprived of the power of binding and loosing".

[32] *Ep.* 111, MGH Epp. Kar. Aev. 2:161, lines 15-17: "All [Charlemagne's] goodness and power suffice for doing well, except for one thing only, on account of the dangerous times of this world age: that he has fewer helpers in doing the Lord's work than is necessary".

[33] For Charlemagne's views, see K. Hauck, *Karolingische Taufpfalzen im Spiegel hofnaher Dichtung*, Nachrichten der Akademie der Wissenschaften in Göttingen, Philologisch-historisch Klasse 1 (Göttingen, 1985), pp. 43-44.

biblical and patristic authority.[34] First, priests must instruct converts, for baptism has no effect where faith is lacking. After baptism, instruction in the Gospel will guide the convert toward moral perfection.[35] In fact, Alcuin's letter to Charlemagne attempts to bring about a deeper, more spiritual form of conversion in the Frankish king and his officials by instructing them in the Gospel precepts which should guide the performance of their *ministerium*, or service to God in the *christianitatis regnum*.[36]

Alcuin introduced the *christianitatis regnum* in a formal letter written to Charlemagne, "rex Germaniae Galliae atque Italiae", and the Frankish clergy.[37] In language recalling the *Vita Willibrordi*, Alcuin affirms God's role in the creation of the *christianitatis regnum*:

> Gloria et laus ... Patri et ... Iesu Christo, quia in
> gratia sancti Spiritus – per devotionem et
> ministerium sanctae fidei et bonae voluntatis
> vestrae – christianitatis regnum atque agnitionem

[34] R. E. Sullivan, "The Carolingian Missionary and the Pagan", *Speculum* 28 (1953), 705-40; and his "Carolingian Missionary Theories", *Catholic Historical Review* 42 (1956), 277-80; J.-P. Bouhot, "Alcuin et le 'De catechizandis rudibus' de saint Augustin", *Recherches augustiniennes* 15 (1980), 176-240; and P. Cramer, *Baptism and Change in the Early Middle Ages, c. 200-c. 1150*, Cambridge Studies in Medieval Life and Thought (Cambridge, 1993), pp. 185-95.

[35] *Ep.* 110, MGH Epp. Kar. Aev. 2:159, lines 10-13.

[36] On this phrase and a later variant, *imperium christianum*, see G. Tellenbach, "Römischer und christlicher Reichsgedanke in der Liturgie des frühen Mittelalters", *Sitzungberichte der Heidelberger Akademie der Wissenschaften*, Philosophisch-historische Klasse 25 (1934/35), 17-36; H. Beumann, "Nomen Imperatoris: Studien zur Kaiseridee Karls des Grossen", *Historische Zeitschrift* 185 (1958), 37-39; and Ewig, "Zum christlichen Königsgedanken", pp. 53-71. On *ministerium* as personal service, see K. Bosl, "Vorstufen der deutschen Königsdienstmannschaft", in Bosl, *Frühformen der Gesellschaft im mittelalterlichen Europa: Ausgewählte Beiträge zu einer Strukturanalyse der mittelalterlichen Welt* (Munich, 1964), pp. 232-55. On Charlemagne's davidic monarchy and the royal *ministerium*, see Anton, *Fürstenspiegel und Herrscherethos*, pp. 105-20, 198-209 and 406-15.

[37] *Ep.* 110, MGH Epp. Kar. Aev. 2:157, lines 1-2: "king of Germany, Gaul, and Italy".

> veri Dei dilatavit, et plurimos longe lateque
> populos ab erroribus impietatis in viam veritatis
> deduxit.[38]

Like a saintly bishop, Charlemagne will lead a procession of people
converted from pagan idolatry through his care before God's
tribunal on Judgement Day.[39] In order to attain this ultimate imperial
glory, however, Charlemagne's *ministerium* now requires him to
choose missionaries who will follow Paul's example of
evangelisation without thought of material gain.[40]

A second letter written at the same time to Megenfrid the
treasurer expands upon the requirements of the layman's
ministerium in the *christianitatis regnum*. Alcuin describes the
proper administration of office within this kingdom according to the
parable of the talents (Matthew 25.14-30 and Luke 19.12-27).
Although usually interpreted as an allegory on the cleric's duty to
preach, in this case Alcuin applies the parable to laymen:[41]

> Sed unicuique pensandum est, in quo gradu
> statuisset eum Deus et quo talento ditasset eum.
> Non enim solis episcopis vel presbyteris pecuniam
> suam tradidit Dominus ad multiplicandum, sed
> omni dignitati et gradui talenta bonae operationis
> tradidit, ut datam sibi gratiam fideliter
> amministrare studeat et conservis suis erogare
> contendat. Alius est, qui talentum praedicationis
> accipit; alius sapientiae; alius divitiarum; alius
> cuiuslibet amministrationis, quidam forte alicuius

---

[38] *Ep.* 110, MGH Epp. Kar. Aev. 2:157, lines 5-8: "Glory and praise ... to
the Father and ... to Jesus Christ, since in the grace of the Holy Spirit – through
obedient preaching of the holy faith and your good will – he has enlarged the
kingdom of Christianity and the knowledge of the true God, and has led very
many peoples from far and wide away from the errors of disbelief into the way
of truth".

[39] *Ep.* 110, MGH Epp. Kar. Aev. 2:157, lines 8-12. Compare this with
Alcuin, *Adhortatio ad imitandas virtutes sancti Vedasti*, PL 101, col. 679A,
where Vaast will lead his monks "ante tribunal summi judicis in die ultimo".

[40] *Ep.* 111, MGH Epp. Kar. Aev. 2:160, line 25 to p. 161, line 4.

[41] See Deug-Su, *L'opera agiografica*, p. 70, for citations in Alcuin's
letters.

> artificii donum a Deo, horum omnium bonorum
> dispensatore. Et in his omnibus fides et devotio
> spectanda est, ut fideliter laboret et viriliter sui
> domini pecuniam multiplicare satagat.[42]

Alcuin relies on Gregory the Great and Augustine for his reading of this parable. Gregory interprets the talents according to 1 Corinthians 12.4-14, where Paul comments on the diverse gifts the Spirit has given to each member of Christ's mystical body for the general good. Gregory urges each one to "pay out", to benefit others, according to his spiritual gift before facing judgement.[43] Like Gregory, Alcuin sees the talents as spiritual gifts from God, but he considers these gifts the means of performing a *ministerium* faithfully within Christ's *regnum*.[44] Alcuin borrowed the idea that the administration of the talents pertains to the layman's office from Augustine's sermon on Matthew 25.24:

> Sed etiam ad vos nolite existimare non pertinere
> erogationem. Non potestis erogare de isto loco
> superiore, sed potestis ubicumque estis ...
> Episcopus inde appellatus est, quia superintendit,
> quia intendendo curat. Unusquisque ergo in domo
> sua, si caput est domui suae, debet ad eum
> pertinere episcopatus officium, quomodo sui
> credant, ne aliqui in haeresim incurrant ... Haec si

---

[42] *Ep.* 111, MGH Epp. Kar. Aev. 2:160, lines 1-10: "But each one must consider in what rank God has placed him and with what talent he has enriched him. For the Lord has handed over his money not only to bishops or priests for increasing, but has also handed over the talents of good work to every office and rank, so that each may strive to manage faithfully the mark of favour granted to him and may exert himself to pay out to each one's fellow servants. One has received the talent of preaching, another the talent of wisdom, another the talent of riches, another the talent of some craft, perhaps the gift of some skill given by God, the granter of all these goods. And in all these, each one must bear in mind good faith and devotion, so that each one may labour faithfully and manfully to multiply the money of his lord".

[43] Gregory, *Homelia* 9, PL 76, cols 1105-09.

[44] F.-C. Scheibe, "Geschichtsbild, Zeitbewusstsein und Reformwille bei Alcuin", *Archiv für Kulturgeschichte* 41 (1959), 42-43.

> facitis,   erogatis: pigri   servi   non   eritis,
> damnationem tam detestandam non timebitis.[45]

Alcuin thought of the kingdom as one great household under the king's supervision.[46] Within this household, all members have their duties and functions, united in a single *corpus* or "body politic".[47] Charlemagne should teach and admonish his "assistants" wisely, while officials like Megenfrid owe their king good advice, willing obedience, and virtuous behaviour:

> Hos [adiutores] erudiat, ammoneat, et doceat
> secundum sapientiam sibi a Deo datam. Et tu
> fidelissime dispensator thesaurorum et servator
> consiliorum et adiutor devotus, viriliter fac
> voluntatem illius. Esto in consilio suavis et in
> opere strenuus.[48]

Thus Alcuin urges Megenfrid to obey Christ's command (Matthew 9.35-38) and advise Charlemagne, "dominum messis ... ut mittat operarios in messem suam; quatenus illis dicat rogatus, sicut suus proprius protector et unicus amator Christus deus dixit

---

[45] Augustine, *Sermo* 94, PL 38, cols 580-81: "But, truly, do not suppose that this paying out [of the talents] does not pertain to you. You are not able to pay out from this high place, but you can from wherever you are ... Whence a bishop is named, because he has oversight, since he governs by paying attention. Each one, therefore, in his own household, if he is head of his household, ought to refer the office of bishop to himself, how the members of his household believe, lest any fall into heresy ... If you do this, you pay out; you will not be lazy servants, you will not fear a condemnation so detestable".

[46] J. Fried, "Der karolingische Herrschaftsverband im 9 Jh. zwischen 'Kirche' und 'Königshaus'", *Historische Zeitschrift* 235 (1982), 22-39.

[47] For these concepts in Louis the Pious' reign, see O. Guillot, "Une *ordinatio* méconnue: Le Capitulaire de 823-825", in *Charlemagne's Heir: New Perspectives on the Reign of Louis the Pious (814-840)*, ed. P. Godman and R. Collins (Oxford, 1990), pp. 455-86.

[48] *Ep.* 111, MGH Epp. Kar. Aev. 2:161, lines 18-21: "He [Charlemagne] should instruct, admonish, and teach his assistants according to the wisdom given to him by God. And you [Megenfrid], steward of the treasury and preserver of good counsel and devoted helper, do his will manfully. In counsel be agreeable and in performance energetic".

discipulis suis: 'Ite, ecce ego mitte vos'" (Luke 10.3).[49] The parable of the vineyard (Matthew 20.1-16) provides another lesson on Charlemagne's duty to administer the church wisely, for, "ipsius potestas et dispensatio vineae Christi, id est ecclesiarum Dei".[50] In his letters to Charlemagne and Megenfrid, Alcuin defines Charlemagne's *ministerium* as the duty to order all of Christian society into one body politic, and to administer his special talent, wisdom, to effect the salvation of many peoples. Significantly, Alcuin attributes to Charlemagne roles previously reserved to Willibrord and even Christ himself in the *Vita Willibrordi*. Charlemagne governs the *christianitatis regnum,* a universal empire which turns all baptised Christians toward Christ's service and the harvesting of the elect before the Last Judgement.[51]

Alcuin remains constant in giving highest priority to the church's mission among the pagans. Nevertheless, his letters on the Avar mission modify the *Vita Willibrordi*'s concept of an empire defined as the military hegemony of the Carolingian dynasty and Frankish *populus*. The *christianitatis regnum* or *imperium christianum* unites the *populus christianus*, the baptised "sons of God", in an empire which transcends nationality (Galatians 3.27-28), ostensibly diminishing the elite status of the Frankish *populus*

[49] *Ep.* 111, MGH Epp. Kar. Aev. 2:161, lines 37-40: "the lord of the harvest ... to send workers into his harvest [among the Avars], so that, when asked, he may say to them, just as his own protector and unique friend Christ the God said to his disciples: 'Go, behold I send you'". Compare this with *Vita Willibrordi*, p. 119, lines 15-16, and p. 121, lines 14-15, where these parables describe the saint's work, without reference to secular power.

[50] *Ep.* 111, MGH Epp. Kar. Aev. 2:162, lines 2-3: "his is the power and dispensation of Christ's vineyard, that is God's churches".

[51] For precedents in Gregory, see W. Fritze, "Universalis gentium confessio: Formeln, Träger und Wege universalmissionarischen Denkens im 7. Jahrhundert", *Frühmittelalterliche Studien* 3 (1969), 108-13; and R. A. Markus, "Gregory the Great's Europe", *Transactions of the Royal Historical Society*, 5th ser., 31 (1981), 21-36, reprinted in Markus, *From Augustine to Gregory the Great: History and Christianity in Late Antiquity* (London, 1983), no. 15, with original pagination.

among the nations.[52] Alcuin's concept of the *imperium christianum* emphasises each individual's *ministerium* according to his *ordo* or status in the social hierarchy of the *corpus Christi*. These ideas on the organisation of the *populus christianus* and the obligation of all orders, including laymen, to live according to a Christian rule had already appeared in the *Admonitio generalis* of 789 and continued to guide Carolingian reform.[53] This reform fostered the exaltation of Charlemagne's lordship over his subjects, since the king as *rector* claimed the power to regulate and correct his subjects' behaviour. Alcuin accepted the king's claims and, in fact, helped to formulate them. But Alcuin's letters on the Avar mission reveal his perception of a gap between the king's idealistic claims and the reality of Carolingian imperialism. Holding up an ideal image of a Christ-like king who is "lord of the harvest", Alcuin corrected Charlemagne, reminding him through allusions to New Testament parables that he was obliged as *rector* to serve the church's eschatological mission through the proper administration of his talent, wisdom. When all members of the *corpus Christi* administer their talents in peace and unanimity under his wise lordship, every baptised Christian can preach to fellow Christians and convert pagans. Together, the king and his *populus christianus* carry on the warfare of Christ's *imperium*, the apocalyptic struggle against pagan idolatry in the last age of world history. This period's conflicts will fade away when Christ comes again to judge all his servants on the administration of their talents. With this set of ideas, Alcuin was trying to show how, after so many military triumphs, Charlemagne could exercise his *imperium* wisely in Christ's kingdom.

Alcuin devised this concept of empire just as much from his desire to convert Charlemagne and his court to a deeper understanding of their Christian obligations as from his desire to convert the pagan Avars. As he invoked Gospel parables to promote a concept of a Christian empire based on service, Alcuin expressed

---

[52] Beumann, "Nomen Imperatoris", pp. 537-46; and J. Fried, "Der karolingische Herrschaftsverband", pp. 21-24.

[53] G. Brown, "Introduction: The Carolingian Renaissance", in *Carolingian Culture*, ed. McKitterick, pp. 1-51 (pp. 23-26); and Becher, *Eid und Herrschaft*, pp. 165-75.

his reservations about the court's triumphant imperialism and eagerness to profit from recent conquests.[54] Alcuin's constant references to immanent judgement attest to his ambivalence toward Charlemagne's success in extending his military and political power within his empire. Alcuin's admonitions were meant to recall Charlemagne and his magnates to pious regard for their service within God's plans for salvation history. At the same time, Alcuin recognised in his interpretation of the parable of the vineyard that Charlemagne, a new David, wielded enormous power over the church as the "lord of the harvest". Alcuin was willing to accept the exaltation of Charlemagne's davidic monarchy only if it was based on service to objective standards found in the Gospels' precepts on the office Christ gives the king.

[54] M. McCormick, *Eternal Victory: Triumphal Rulership in Late Antiquity, Byzantium and the Early Medieval West* (Cambridge, 1986), pp. 342-87.

The Formation of the Scandinavian Parish, with some Remarks Regarding the English Impact on the Process

Stefan Brink

In this paper, I shall discuss the organisation of the Church in Scandinavia, especially on the lowest (i.e. the parochial) level. To make the ecclesiastical organisation clear, I must, however, first outline the conversion and the introduction of the new Christian or, perhaps more accurately, continental cultural phenomena that reached Scandinavia during the revolutionary period that the Viking Age represents. I shall also discuss the obvious influences from England in this respect and touch upon the possibility of tracing the origin of or the impulse for the formation of the Scandinavian parish in the Anglo-Saxon or Danelaw area.[1]

---

[1] This paper is based in several respects on my PhD thesis: S. Brink, "Sockenbildning och sockennamn. Studier i äldre territoriell indelning i Norden. Parish-formation and parish-names. Studies in early territorial division in Scandinavia" (University of Uppsala, 1990), and also on my articles: S. Brink, "Sockenbildningen i Sverige", in *Kyrka och socken i medeltidens Sverige*, ed. O. Ferm, Studier till Det medeltida Sverige 5 (Stockholm, 1991), pp. 113-42; "Våra socknars ursprung och deras namn", *Kungl. Humanistiska Vetenskaps-Samfundet i Uppsala. Årsbok 1991-1992*, Annales Societatis Litterarum Humaniorum Regiae Upsaliensis (1992), 159-70; "Kristnande och kyrklig organisation i Jämtland", in *Jämtlands kristnande*, ed. S. Brink, Projektet

Outline of the Christianisation of Scandinavia

It seems plausible to think that a Christian cultural influence first penetrated Scandinavia during the latter half of the first millennium. It is a well-known fact that we lack the written sources that could shed some light for us on this penetration; one exception is, of course, the *Vita Ansgarii*, however problematic it may be as a historical source. We have more numerous accounts for the tenth and eleventh centuries, although by comparison with those for later historical periods they are very rare and difficult to interpret. The archaeological evidence is also problematic. We can dig up artefacts that can be linked to the Christian religion in different ways, but we cannot say with certainty whether these "Christian artefacts" bear witness to a Christian belief or merely indicate the impact of continental culture and hence have no further religious or metaphysical connotations.[2]

In my opinion, the driving force that gradually implemented Christianity in Scandinavian society did not come so much from itinerant missionaries or from the fact that Scandinavians visited Christian countries; instead, this decisive force was the well-known strategy of turning to the head of society, the king and the upper social strata. We are told of the existence of "bishops" and presumably well-educated clergy as advisers in close proximity to the king: well-known examples are Grímkell alongside King Óláfr the Holy in Norway and, of course, Archbishop Wulfstan of York alongside Knut the Great.[3] This co-operation is symptomatic of the early phase of Christianisation, and the symbiosis between the

Sveriges kristnande 4 (Uppsala, 1996), pp. 155-88; and "Tidig kyrklig organisation i Sverige – aktörerna i sockenbildningen", in *Sveriges kristnande*, ed. B. Nilsson, Projektet Sveriges kristnande 5 (Uppsala, 1996), pp. 269-90.

[2] For the archaeological evidence regarding Christianisation, see especially A.-S. Gräslund, "Arkeologin och kristnandet", in *Sveriges kristnande*, ed. Nilsson, pp. 19-44.

[3] See, for example, H. Koht, "De første norske biskoper", *Historisk tidsskrift* 5:5 (1924), 128-34, and J. A. Hellström, *Biskop och landskapssamhälle i tidig svensk medeltid*, Rättshistoriskt bibliotek 16 (Stockholm, 1971), pp. 19-22.

"State" and the Church is even more discernible when we turn to the initial organisation of the early Church.

The few sources we have to rely on all state that Sweden had a later conversion to Christianity than Denmark, Norway and Iceland. If this is correct, one must seek the cause of this retardation. An answer to this question which is at least stimulating, or to some provocative, is that in central Sweden there was a pagan stronghold, the sacral kingship of the Swedes, which, for some reason, was able to hold its own against the new religion for a few decades – perhaps as much as a century – longer than in Denmark and Norway.

In Denmark, the obvious point of departure for the discussion is King Harald's own words c. AD 980 on one of the Jelling rune-stones: "haraltr ias [...] tani karþi kristna" (fig. 1).[4] It is interesting that these words have a counterpart in another runic inscription on the Frösö rune-stone in the province of Jämtland in northern Sweden (fig. 2). The inscription on this stone states that "austmaþr kuþfastaʀ sun [...]lit kristna eatalant".[5] In this latter case, one interpretation is that this Austmaðr was some chief in the province, and another that he was the lawman of the *jämtamot*; the *thing* of the province. If the first interpretation is correct, we are faced with a kind of "forced" conversion that implies resistance and is characterised by vertical action, from top to bottom. If the second is the correct interpretation, we see obvious similarities with what happened in Iceland at the annual assembly, the Althing, c. AD 1000, when the Icelanders decided by general consent to convert to Christianity. This is a more horizontally-agreed decision, with this Austmaðr acting as mediator, a kind of *primus inter pares*.

In Norway, the two Olafs have long had a central position in the discussion regarding the conversion. King Óláfr Tryggvason managed in the decades around AD 1000 to unite "Norway". He had a very offensive or perhaps aggressive way of introducing the new religion into the country and beside him stood clerical advisers from

---

[4] "Harald made the Danes Christians", ed. L. Jacobsen and E. Moltke, *Danmarks runeindskrifter* (Copenhagen 1942), no. 42.

[5] "Austmaðr Guðfastarsun had Jämtland Christianised". See H. Williams, "Runjämtskan på Frösöstenen och Östmans bro", in *Jämtlands kristnande*, ed. Brink, pp. 45-63.

England. The other Óláfr, Haraldsson, later called "the Holy", continued in the footsteps of his predecessor. He also had an Anglo-Saxon "bishop" at his side as counsellor: the illustrious Grímkell. The sagas claim that these two, King Óláfr Haraldsson and Bishop Grímkell, laid the foundation of the Norwegian Church, especially at a famous *thing* on the island of Moster in AD 1024; an assembly probably for the whole country in the sense of "Norway", at which the Christian religion was proclaimed the only legal religion in Norway. It is, of course, extremely hazardous to rely on the Old Scandinavian sagas; however, in this case we can supplement the account with two more reliable sources. On the one hand, there are several statements and paragraphs in the old Gulating Law that testify to this *thing* at Moster; on the other, there is also a contemporary rune-stone at Kuli in Nordmøre that tells us that it was raised "tualf uintr hafþi kristin tumr uirit inuriki" (fig. 3).[6] A modern interpretation is that this alludes to the *thing* at Moster, the one that King Óláfr and Grímkell held.[7]

One could summarise this sketchy outline in a few key words. The first and perhaps the most important one is *symbiosis*, the symbiosis that we find between the Church and royal power in all the regions of northern Europe. It is obvious that the Church and central power went hand in hand in reshaping society in this period. The strategy of the Church was to win whole countries, political units or peoples (Latin *gentes*); hence, it preferred to aim at the top of society. This proved to be the fastest and easiest way of gaining a solid bridgehead in these regions; the target was the rulers and the political leaders.

---

[6] "After Christianity had been in Norway for twelve winters", ed. A. Liestøl, *Norges Indskrifter med de yngre runer* 4 (Oslo, 1957), no. 449.

[7] N. Hallan, "Kulisteinen og kristenrettsvedtaket på Mostertinget", *Du mitt Nordmøre* (1966), 21-28. See also J. R. Hagland, "Kuli-steinen – endå ein gong", *Heidersskrift til Nils Hallan på 65-årsdagen 13. desember 1991*, ed. G. Alhaug, K. Kruken and H. Salvesen (Oslo, 1991), pp. 157-65; and G. Steinsland and P. Meulengracht Sørensen, *Menneske og makter i vikingenes verden* (Oslo, 1994), p. 216. A traditional interpretation is that the rune-inscription alludes to a *thing* at Dragseid in c. 996: see Liestøl, *Norges indskrifter*, p. 287.

The men who struggled for power and land saw the advantages of the new religion for their political purposes and the help they could get from the well-organised Church. As distinguished from the old, pagan religion, the new, Christian one was fundamental for the formation of a state; it was a "state-supporting" religion. This was knowledge that was obvious after deep and frequent contacts with the continent.

Another key concept is the *thing* or assembly. Old Scandinavian society was a *thing* society. On different levels in this society, people assembled for *things*. In the cases in which a king, a lord or a great man did not force or, more gently, set an example to, the people in the conversion process, it is obvious that a decision taken jointly at a *thing* was another method of conversion.[8]

The Organisation of the Church and the Building of Churches

Peter Sawyer has written: "The early history of the Church in Scandinavia, especially in Sweden, is, and probably always will be, hidden by a dense growth of legend".[9] I fully agree with this but careful examination reveals some interesting information.

During the early missionary phase, "bishops" were sent to Scandinavia and, in the Hamburg-Bremen see, steps were taken to

[8] During the last decade or so, a new and modified view has been presented by several scholars regarding conversion to the Christian religion in Scandinavia and the organisation of the Church, in which the discussion has been set more firmly in a social context. This new angle can be found in surveys and syntheses by E. Nyborg, "Enkeltmæn og fællesskaber i organiseringen af det romanske sognkirkebyggeri", in *Streiflys over Danmarks bygningskultur. Festskrift til Harald Langberg*, ed. R. Egevang (Copenhagen, 1979), pp. 37-64; Brink, "Sockenbildning och sockennamn" and "Sockenbildningen i Sverige"; and D. Skre, *Gård og kirke, bygd og sogn. Organiseringsmodeller og organiseringsenheter i middelalderens kirkebygging i Sør-Gudbrandsdalen*, Riksantikvariens Rapporter 16 (Oslo, 1988), and "Kirken før sognet. Den tidligste kirkeordningen i Norge", in *Møtet mellom hedendom og kristendom i Norge*, ed. H.-E. Lidén (Oslo, 1995), pp. 170-233.

[9] P. H. Sawyer, *Kings and Vikings. Scandinavia and Europe AD 700-1100* (London and New York, 1982), p. 143.

divide the Nordic region into missionary areas, for which missionary bishops were consecrated. One can see that these proto-sees, or whatever they should be called, coincided with the ancient "folklands", an observation congruent with the statement above that the Church aimed at winning over whole political units and *gentes*. The well-known Florence List of c. 1120, in which early sees and *civitates* are mentioned – although some never became actual sees – is perhaps a programmatical document that shows the strategy of the Church for incorporating Scandinavia into the ecclesiastical world.[10] It is worth noting that the Church programmatically adapted its higher organisation to an already existing division in Scandinavia.[11]

The organisation of the Church in lower ranks of the hierarchy than the sees was to a large extent subordinate to the erection of churches. During this early phase, there were two actors in this process, the nobility and the kings. In this case, the nobility should be understood as consisting of prominent persons, chieftains, rich farmers and so on in settlement districts, rather than aristocrats in the continental sense of nobility, since large parts of Scandinavia never had a feudal-like nobility.

In the same way as on the continent and in England, the nobility, especially in the Viking Age and in medieval Denmark, erected small, private churches on their manors (fig. 4). Normally the first churches were small oratories built of wood, which were succeeded by stone churches, especially in the twelfth century. One must also reckon with the possibility of a co-operative of farmers jointly building a church in their village, as is known from the Danelaw.[12] These churches later on constituted the foundation for the formation of parishes in these areas.

The other actor in this early church-building process was the king, the central power. In this phase, the king, in symbiosis with the Church, erected churches on the royal estates. It may well be that at first wooden churches were built; however, in the twelfth century, the general practice was to erect huge, fortified, stone

[10] See C. F. Hallencreutz, "När Sverige blev europeiskt", *Kyrkohistorisk årsskrift 1992* (1992), 163-73 (p. 168).

[11] See Hellström, *Biskop och landskapssamhälle*, p. 102.

[12] See Nyborg, "Enkeltmæn og fællesskaber", p. 57.

churches in these places. I interpret these churches as not primarily designed for defence, for protection during unsettled times, but instead as manifestations of the central power and of the Church in the fairly autonomous provinces.[13]

This was obviously the situation, for example, in the provinces of Trøndelag in Norway and of Hälsingland in northern Sweden (fig. 5). In both these provinces, this kind of fortified stone church was erected during the latter part of the twelfth century on the important royal estates.

Parish Formation in Scandinavia

Although the organisation of the Church started as early as the eleventh century with consecrated bishops in more or less fixed sees, conversion was a slow process that took several centuries. The formation of parishes was, by contrast, probably somewhat more rapid. Owing to the lack of sources to illuminate this process, the formation of parishes in Scandinavia becomes very difficult to trace. The introduction of tithes during the twelfth century was obviously decisive for this ecclesiastical division. Where there were already-existing churches – private churches or churches on royal estates – parishes were formed around them. Hence, in Denmark, about 2,000 parishes seem to have been already in existence during the second half of the twelfth century. In Iceland, parishes (*þing*) were created around the already existing, private churches.

For Norway and Sweden, north of the province of Skåne, the process was more complex. However, a general feature here is that the Church clearly used the settlement district as a model for parishes to a great extent. In these cases, we may presume that the congregation of the settlement district, with or without pressure from outside, decided to erect a church. It is most likely that this decision was taken at a *thing*, and it is noteworthy that the churches in many cases were erected on the actual assembly places of the settlement districts.

---

[13] Brink, "Sockenbildning och sockennamn", p. 158.

Consequently, it is possible to make an important distinction when one is talking about the formation of parishes in Scandinavia. In the southern parts, the parishes were to a great extent formed around existing churches, which could be related to manors. Hence, if there was a dense population with many villages and manors, the parishes could be very small, though not too small. It had to be possible for the parish priest to live on the tithe collected in the parish, otherwise the church would end up as an annexe church or be abandoned, as was the case especially in the province of Västergötland.

From a theoretical point of view, the parishes may have developed in two ways (fig. 6). Firstly, the development may have been a slow process, in which a parish was organised around a kind of "mother-church"; this could be termed a vertical or hierarchical parish formation. From this parish, "daughter-churches" (annexes) were formed, which later on became independent parishes, perhaps with new "daughter-churches". This kind of development, with the existence of what can be termed "extended parishes", may very well have existed, but it is practically impossible to trace it in the source material. However, one can make more or less plausible re-constructions of such "extended parishes" which may have existed in an early phase in the organisation of the Church. This case resembles the minster parish, the early *parochia*, in Anglo-Saxon England.[14] Secondly, the parish formation may have been a more rapid process, during which in a short period of time several churches were built and parishes organised around them, a case which could be termed a horizontal or equilibrated parish formation. Most probably both cases existed in Scandinavia.

The first of these two forms of development was the general model for explaining the early church organisation in Norway used by most earlier scholars but also by contemporary scholars in the

[14] See, for example, J. Blair, "Introduction: From Minster to Parish Church", in *Minsters and Parish Churches. The Local Church in Transition 950-1200*, ed. J. Blair, Oxford University Committee for Archaeology Monograph 17 (Oxford, 1988), pp. 1-10.

field such as Knut Helle and Jørn Sandnes.[15] However, in a couple of new and important works, this vertical or hierarchical, parish-formation development has been (re-)emphasised for Scandinavia. Sigurd Rahmqvist has demonstrated that the province of Uppland in central Sweden obviously had some sort of "extended parish" during the twelfth century, preceding the "normal" parish, founded especially during the thirteenth century in this province.[16] Mats Anglert has discussed in the same way a similar development for parts of the province of Skåne in southern Sweden (medieval Denmark).[17] Dagfinn Skre has presented strong arguments for this "extended parish" model for Norway.[18] He argues that Norway had the same clerical structure as was found in early England, comprising several priests and clergymen attached to a minster, serving a large but not territorialised area. Skre thinks that he can trace this structure in parts of Norway as far as the late Middle Ages.[19] As I have argued before, this kind of "extended parish" may well have existed in provinces like Trøndelag in Norway and Hälsingland in Sweden, where we have a couple of large early churches preceding most of the ordinary thirteenth-century parish churches, around which there may have been some kind of early

[15] See for early references Brink, "Sockenbildning och sockennamn", pp. 101-09; for a "Stand der Forschung" of today, see K. Helle, "The Organisation of the Twelfth-Century Norwegian Church", in *St Magnus Cathedral and Orkney's Twelfth Century Renaissance*, ed. B. Crawford (Aberdeen, 1988), pp. 50-51, and the references in the works of J. Sandnes, in note 20 below.

[16] S. Rahmqvist, *Sätesgård och gods. De medeltida frälsegodsens framväxt mot bakgrund av Upplands bebyggelsehistoria*, Upplands fornminnesförenings tidskrift 53 (Uppsala, 1996), pp. 61-68.

[17] M. Anglert, "Den kyrkliga organisationen under äldre medeltid", in *By, huvudgård och kyrka. Studier i Ystadsområdets medeltid*, ed. H. Andersson and M. Anglert, Lund Studies in Medieval Archaeology 5 (Stockholm, 1989) pp. 236-39; and his *Kyrkor och herravälde. Från kristnande till sockenbildning i Skåne*, Lund Studies in Medieval Archaeology 16 (Lund, 1995), pp. 179-82.

[18] D. Skre, "Kirken før sognet. Den tidligste", and "Kirken før sognet", in *Kristendommen slår rot*, ed. A. Ågotnes, Onsdagskvelder i Brygges Museum 10 (Bergen, 1995), pp. 55-75.

[19] Skre, "Kirken før sognet. Den tidligste", pp. 188-203.

"extended parish".[20] The horizontal model, with a rapid formation of parishes, has been suggested for the island and province of Gotland, where we find many small parishes with churches obviously erected during the same, rather short period of time.[21]

This difference in the formation of parishes in Scandinavia is also discernible when looking at parish names. In the southern parts, nearly all the names go back to a farm or a hamlet name; this is clearly a consequence of the many private churches on manors and in villages. In northern Sweden and parts of Norway, we find instead parish names that go back to the names of old settlement districts (Swedish *bygder*). Thus, these names mirror the actual structure of the parish, where the provinces were divided into natural settlement districts. We may therefore deduce some kind of rule regarding the parish names in Scandinavia: "settlement names in the south, but settlement-district names in the north", and this rule probably also reflects the origin of the parishes to a great extent.

Anglo-Saxon Influence on the Scandinavian Conversion and the Organisation of the Church

The importance of Anglo-Saxon influence in Scandinavia during the Viking Age is obvious and well-established. This influence had many facets, some of which will be discussed here. The most striking aspect – and the one which still survives – is perhaps the new terminology that followed in the steps of the new religion. Some central words, such as *kyrka* "church", *kristendom* "Christianity", *ärkebiskop* "archbishop" and *munk* "monk" have

---

[20] See Brink, "Sockenbildning och sockennamn", pp. 116-22, 151-58; J. Sandnes, *Namdalens historie til år 1600* (Namsos, 1965), pp. 295-96; his "Fylkeskirkene i Trøndelag i middelalderen. En del notater og detaljmateriale", in *Årbok for Trøndelag* (Trondheim, 1969), 116-36; and his "Middelalderens Trøndelag. Den kirkelige organisasjon i landsdelen, fylkeskirker, sognekirker, klostre", in *Hikuin* 20 (1993), 105-12.

[21] See S.-O. Lindquist, "Sockenbildningen på Gotland. En korologisk studie", *Gotländskt arkiv 1981* (1981), 45-63.

Anglo-Saxon origins.[22] This of course means that the English Church must have had a great impact on the Christianisation of Scandinavia and on the early organisation of the Church in Scandinavia.

Another important aspect is the presence of English "bishops" and clergy in Scandinavia. These ecclesiastics were obviously highly-educated persons. They were men of great learning; they had knowledge of Church organisation and they also had a knowledge of and an insight into the culture and intellectual world of the continent. And the fact that they were sent to, or voluntarily went to, the barbarians in the north, reveals that they were also personally courageous and had an entrepreneurial skill which was very useful in their task of organising the Church in Scandinavia. Hence, the importance of these English bishops and missionaries in Scandinavia should be emphasised; their contribution must not be underestimated.

More general cultural contacts between England and Scandinavia must also, for obvious reasons, have been very extensive during the Viking Age and the Anglo-Saxon Church seems to have been dynamic and on the offensive.[23] A major influence on Scandinavia in this respect must have been exerted during the reign of Knut the Great, in which a key figure, such as Archbishop Wulfstan of York, must have had an important role.[24]

[22] See A. Taranger, *Den angelsaksiske kirkes indflydelse paa den norske* (Kristiania, 1890); E. Jørgensen, *Fremmed indflydelse under den danske kirkes tidligste udvikling* (Copenhagen, 1908); and C.-E. Thors, *Den kristna terminologien i fornsvenskan*, Studier i nordisk filologi 45 (Helsinki and Copenhagen, 1957).

[23] D. Whitelock, *The Beginnings of English Society* (Harmondsworth, 1974), pp. 187-88.

[24] For discussions of Wulfstan's role, see M. K. Lawson, *Cnut. The Danes in England in the Early Eleventh Century* (London and New York, 1993), pp. 117-210; A. R. Rumble, ed., *The Reign of Cnut: King of England, Denmark and Norway* (London, 1994); H. Loyn, *The Vikings in Britain* (Oxford and Cambridge, Mass., 1994), pp. 66, 79-80.

Vital in this connection – however biased – are, of course, the words of Adam of Bremen (book 2, chapter 49):[25]

> Hos duos episcopos solummodo in Iudlant fuisse comperimus, antequam Chnud regnum intraret. Solus ex nostris Odinkar transmarinas aliquando visitavit ecclesias, Esico domi sedit, persecutio ceteros tardavit. Archiepiscopus etiam alios viros doctissimos ordinavit in Norvegiam vel Suediam; alios vero in Anglia ordinatos pro amicita regum, cum satisfaceret, ad aedificandam dimisit ecclesiam.[26]

And further, in chapter 55, Adam writes:

> Victor Chnud ab Anglia rediens in ditione sua per multos annos regnum Daniae possedit et Angliae. Quo tempore episcopos ab Anglia multos adduxit in Daniam. De quibus Bernardum posuit in Sconiam, Gerbrandum in Seland, Reginbertum in Fune. Zelatus est hoc uoster archiepiscopus Unwan. Et dicitur Gerbrandum redeuntem ab Anglia cepisse, quem ab Elnodo Anglorum archiepiscopo cognovit esse ordinatum. Ille, quod necessitas persuasit, satisfaciens, fidelitatem Hammaburgensi cathdrae cum subiectione debitam spondens familiarissimus deinceps archiepiscopo effectus est. Per quem ille suos

---

[25] For Adam of Bremen see, for example, *Magistri Adam Bremensis Gesta Hammaburgensis ecclesiae pontificum*, ed. B. Schmeidler, MGH SRG, 3rd ed. (Hanover and Leipzig, 1917), or the Swedish translation in *Adam av Bremen. Historien om Hamburgstiftet och dess biskopar*, trans. E. Svenberg, Skrifter utg. av Samfundet Pro Fide et Christianismo 6 (Stockholm, 1984).

[26] "I have understood that only these two bishops [Poppo and Odinkar] were in Jutland, before Knut came to power. Odinkar was the only one of our bishops that on any occasion visited the churches on the other side of the sea. Esiko stayed at home, and persecution restrained the others. The archbishop [Unwan] also consecrated other well-educated men for Norway and Sweden. In addition, he sent men consecrated in England, as a tribute of friendship to the kings, to build up the Church, on the condition that they for the rest fulfilled their duties": Adam, *Gesta*, ed. Schmeidler, p. 110.

etiam legatos ad Chnud regem transmittens cum
muneribus congratulatus est ei de rebus bene
gestis in Anglia, sed corripiut eum de
presumptione episcoporum, quos transtulit ex
Anglia. Quod rex gratanter accipiens ita
postmodum coniunctus est archiepiscopo, ut ex
sententia eius omnia deinceps facere maluerit.
Haec nobis de avunculo suo rex Danorum innotuit
et de captione Gerbrandi non tacuit.[27]

With regard to Norway, Adam states (chapter 57):

Habuitque secum multos episcopos et presbyteros
ab Anglia [...]. Quorum clari doctrina et virtutibus
erant Sigafrid, Grimkil, Rudolf et Bernard. Hii
etiam iussu regis [ad] Suediam, Gothiam et omnes
insulas, quae trans Nortmanniam sunt.[28]

I do not think that it is going too far to state that the
foundation for the organisation of the early Church in Scandinavia
was to a great extent laid by representatives of the Anglo-Saxon
Church. During this vital period of the eleventh century,

---

[27] "When Knut returned to England after his victories, he had supremacy
over Denmark and England. During this time he brought many bishops from
England to Denmark. He placed Bernhard in Scania, Gerbrand on Zealand and
Reginbert on Fünen. This upset our archbishop Unwan. It is said that he also
captured Gerbrand, on his way from England, since he understood that this
Gerbrand had been consecrated by the English archbishop Ælnoth. Gerbrand
made an apology, as necessity demanded, and when he promised loyalty and
submission to the see in Hamburg, he became from then onwards a close friend
to the archbishop. Through his mediation Unwan sent an envoy to King Knut
and congratulated him on his successes in England but expressed his
dissatisfaction with the fact that he had high-handedly brought bishops from
England. The king received this criticism without objections and later became so
closely linked with the archbishop that he acted in accordance with his will in all
respects. This the king of the Danes has told me about his uncle, and he did not
conceal the capturing of Gerbrand": Adam, *Gesta*, ed. Schmeidler, pp. 115-16.

[28] "He [King Olaf] also had with him many bishops and clergymen from
England [...]. Amongst them were Sigfrid, Grimkel, Rudolf and Bernard, known
for their learning and powerful characters. On the king's command they also
visited Sweden, Götaland and all the islands beyond the Northland": Adam,
Gesta, ed. Schmeidler, pp. 117-18.

Scandinavia acquired its first episcopal sees, for example, c. 1020: Roskilde and Odense in Denmark, and Skara in Sweden; c. 1060: Viborg and Børglum in Denmark, Lund and Dalby in Skåne, Sigtuna in Sweden and Oslo in Norway; c. 1075: Bjorgvin and Nidaros in Norway (fig. 7). Furthermore, churches were erected, especially in southern Scandinavia, on a tremendous scale, as Adam states c. 1070: "Daniae ... et nunc plena ecclesiis. Sconia bis tantum habet in spacia quam Seland, hoc est CCCtas ecclesias, cum Seland dicatur habere dimidium, Funis terciam partem".[29] Hence, Denmark must have had c. 550 churches as early as c. 1070.

This applies to the organisation of the Church in the sense of establishing sees with consecrated bishops and the building of churches. The actual ecclesiastical organisation came, as noted above, with the introduction of tithing. But, for Scandinavia this belongs to the twelfth century. As hinted above, there may have been an intermediate period between the first Christian penetration in Scandinavia and the actual parish formation during the twelfth and thirteenth centuries; namely a stage in which there were some kinds of "mother churches" or non-territorialised, "extended parishes", probably during the eleventh and twelfth centuries. As argued by Helle, Sandnes, Ramqvist, Skre, Anglert and myself, these "extended parishes", which several of us have traced even if direct written evidence is missing, may have been the predecessors of the ordinary parishes. As Skre in particular has pointed out,[30] this pre-parochial structure, with several clergymen attached to an ecclesiastical "node" or "mother-church", most certainly had the English minster and *parochia* as models, and was implemented in Scandinavia by the bishops and clergy from England.[31]

---

[29] "Denmark ... is now full of churches. Skåne ... has 300 churches, while Zealand half that number, Fünen a third": Adam, *Gesta*, 4.7, ed. Schmeidler, pp. 234-35.

[30] Skre, "Kirken før sognet. Den tidligste", pp. 181-88.

[31] See Brink, "Sockenbildningen i Sverige".

The Origin of the Scandinavian Parish : Anglo-Saxon Influence in Scandinavia or Vice Versa?

A much-debated problem among scholars in Scandinavia is the institution of the parish (OScand. *sōkn*). The discussion runs along two principal lines, the first being that the term and the concept of "parish" are internal phenomena and the second that we have to reckon with a loan – of both term and concept or of one of the two – from outside.

It can be established that the OScand. term *sokn* has a long history in the Nordic languages. It is a Proto-Germanic verbal noun, **sōkini-*, **sōkni-*, derived from the Pr.-Germ. verb *sōkian* 'seeking, pursuit', and is found in most Germanic languages. It can be shown that in the old Scandinavian languages this word was one of the most central terms in legal language, with meanings like 'dispute', 'legal question', or 'request'. Hence, it has an older history than the ecclesiastical parish in Scandinavia. The question is, then, why did it become the technical term for an ecclesiastical parish?

A first hypothesis is that there existed a kind of pre-Christian parish, a prehistoric *sokn*. One scholar reckons that this was a district related to the territorial division in the old naval organisation called the *ledung*.[32] Another reckons that a *sokn* was a small, prehistoric, settlement district (Swedish *bygd*) that assembled to form a *thing*.[33] The first interpretation can probably be dismissed, though the second one is plausible and must be considered as a possibility. There are some compounds in Old Scandinavian, such as *þingsokn* "*thing*-assembly", that seem to give support to such an interpretation.

However, there are many indications that make it reasonable to assume external influence in this question. I have demonstrated

---

[32] G. Hafström, "Sockenindelningens ursprung", in *Historiska studier tillägnade Nils Ahnlund 23/8/1949* (Stockholm, 1949), pp. 51-67; and his "Från kultsocken till storkommun", *Från bygd till vildmark. Luleå stifts årsbok* 51 (1964), 29-50.

[33] T. Andersson, "Den medeltida sockenbildningen från språklig synpunkt", *Kungliga Vitterhets Historie och Antikvitets Akademiens årsskrift* (1988), 65-82.

above the extensive cultural exchange that must have taken place during the eleventh century between Scandinavia and England, especially the Danelaw. This makes it interesting to turn the spotlight onto England in dealing with this question.[34]

During the tenth century, there was a steady growth of manors in England. By degrees, the lords, bishops and others who owned these manors gained a kind of private jurisdiction over the manors granted by the king. This private jurisdiction was known by the alliterative expression *sacu et sócn*, the first term meaning "case", and the latter "seeking of a lord or a court". This expression is used as early as the tenth century, and it is also used in Middle English, in the form of *sake and soke*. Later on, it was possible to use only the word *sócn* "soke" for this private jurisdiction, for example, in c. 975 Archbishop Oswald of York said in a memorandum that his estate of Sherbourne had lost half its soke.[35] Thus, within a relatively short space of time we find references to not only a personal soke, but also a territorial soke, which is mentioned in documents at least from c. 1030.[36]

It is only to be expected, in view of all the private churches that were erected on the manors during this period, that very soon the congregation attending such a church would also be called a *soke*. And later on, as Addleshaw has pointed out, with the introduction of the tithe, this soke became a territorial unit, a parish district.[37]

The origin and historical background of the *sócn* institution and the related term *sokemen* are veiled in obscurity. The *sokes* and *sokemen* seem to have had a close connection with the Danelaw area. In this area, the *soke* was more of a free institution, while in

---

[34] For this discussion, see especially Brink, "Sockenbildningen i Sverige".

[35] F. Stenton, *Anglo-Saxon England*, 3rd ed. (Oxford, 1971), p. 496.

[36] See P. Vinogradoff, *English Society in the Eleventh Century. Essays in English Mediaeval History* (Oxford, 1908), pp. 128-30; F. E. Harmer, ed., *Anglo-Saxon Writs* (Manchester, 1952), pp. 74-76.

[37] G. W. O. Addleshaw, *The Beginnings of the Parochial System*, 3rd ed., St Anthony's Hall Publications 3 (York, 1970), and his *The Development of the Parochial System from Charlemagne (768-814) to Urban II (1088-1099)*, 2nd ed., St Anthony's Hall Publications 6 (York, 1970).

southern England a *soke* was closely linked with the manor. Hence the central question is whether the term – and maybe the concept – was brought to England by the Danes or whether it had an older, Anglo-Saxon origin.

It has long been disputed whether different words and concepts, especially in the Danelaw area, have a Nordic or an Anglo-Saxon origin, and this dispute has its roots in the question of how intense and extensive the Scandinavian cultural impact was. A complicating factor in this dispute is, of course, the close relationship between the languages and the societies of the Anglo-Saxons and the Scandinavian peoples, especially the Danes. A related problem is how many Scandinavians actually settled in England during the Viking Age. Earlier scholars believed that this immigration was massive and, to support this theory, Frank Stenton argued that the *sokemen* class – obviously closely related to the *soke* – consisted originally of Danish soldiers.[38] At the same time, Svend Aakjær stated that the English *sokeman* in the Danelaw and Kent was a counterpart of the royal, free farmer in Denmark.[39] In later research, R. H. C. Davis and Peter Sawyer have challenged this view.[40] Davis was able to demonstrate that the *sochemanni* of East Anglia must have had a history older than the Scandinavian

---

[38] F. Stenton, "Free Peasantry and the Northern Danelaw", *Bulletin de la Société Royale des Lettres de Lund 1925-26* (1926), p. 79; see also Vinogradoff, *English Society in the Eleventh Century* passim; F. W. Maitland, *Domesday Book and Beyond. Three Essays in the Early History of England* (Cambridge, 1907), pp. 131-41; S. Aakjær, "Om det olddanske herred og sogn", *Festskrift til Kristian Erslevden 28. decbr. 1927 fra danske historikere* (Copenhagen, 1927), pp. 1-30 (p. 18). Later advocates of this theory include H. R. Loyn, *Anglo-Saxon England and the Norman Conquest* (London, 1962), p. 55, and K. Cameron, *Scandinavian Settlement in the Territory of the Five Boroughs. The Place-name Evidence* (Nottingham, 1965), pp. 10-11.

[39] Aakjær, "Om det olddanske herred og sogn", p. 22.

[40] R. H. C. Davis, ed., *The Kalendar of Abbot Samson of Bury St. Edmunds*, Camden 3rd ser., vol. 84 (London, 1954), p. XXXII; and his "East Anglia and the Danelaw", *Transactions of the Royal Historical Society* 5th ser. 5 (1955), 23-39; P. H. Sawyer, "The Density of the Danish Settlement in England", *University of Birmingham Historical Journal* 4 (1957), 1-17; and his *The Age of the Vikings*, 2nd ed. (London, 1971).

invasion and Sawyer states that "Unfortunately there is no evidence for the association of sokemen and Danes" and he remarks on the oddity of the very few sokemen in Yorkshire.[41] Sawyer has also drawn attention to the fact that the Anglo-Saxon settlement structure at the time of the Scandinavian invasion depended very heavily on estates.[42] The Anglo-Saxon *hundred*, as H. Munro Chadwick and Helen Cam have demonstrated, also originated in a district or estate, although it was dependent on the king's *tūn* and administered by the king's reeve.[43] These Anglo-Saxon estates were called *shires*, *lathes* or *sokes*.[44] This is an indication that the term and concept of *soke* were not brought from Scandinavia by the Vikings, but instead originated in Anglo-Saxon society. Despite this, one cannot exclude the possibility of the case being the other way round.[45] The question of the Scandinavian impact is thus difficult to answer. One may end by citing H. C. Darby: "One can only conclude that the Scandinavian settlement may have been a much more complicated process than was at one time thought".[46]

As we have seen above, the word *sócn*, later *soke*, was used in England during the tenth and eleventh centuries for an assembly and quite soon also for an ecclesiastical, territorial district. In view of all the bishops and clergy who, especially during the eleventh century, went to Scandinavia and organised the Scandinavian Church, it seems plausible and natural to assume that they may have brought with them this new concept of *sócn* for a congregation attached to a church. Whether both the word *sócn* and the concept of the parish were transferred may however be questioned. In any case, the

[41] Sawyer, *Age of the Vikings*, p. 171.

[42] Sawyer, *Kings and Vikings*, p. 105.

[43] H. Munro Chadwick, *Studies in Anglo-Saxon Institutions* (Cambridge, 1905), pp. 239-41; H. Cam, "*Manerium cum hundredo*. The Hundred and the Hundredal Manor", *English Historical Review* 47 (1932), 353-55.

[44] Sawyer, *Kings and Vikings*, p. 105.

[45] For a modern "Stand der Forschung" regarding these problems, see A. K. G. Kristensen, "Danelaw Institutions and Danish Society in the Viking Age", *Mediaeval Scandinavia* 8 (1975), 27-85; and C. Hart, *The Danelaw* (London and Rio Grande, 1992), pp. 231-79.

[46] H. C. Darby, *Domesday England* (Cambridge and London, 1977), p. 62.

general and instant use of the OScand. term *sokn* for a parish, found all over Scandinavia, except Iceland, seems to support this interpretation. If this interpretation is correct, there are two possibilities regarding the origin of the word *sócn*: (*i*) that it is the Anglo-Saxon word *sócn* or (*ii*) that it is the Scandinavian word *sokn*, brought to England by the Vikings in the ninth century and then, most probably during the eleventh century, taken back to Scandinavia, but now with a new ecclesiastical meaning. A third possibility is that the Anglo-Saxon *soke* has a completely Scandinavian background, and that it was brought to England by the Vikings in the sense of some kind of jurisdictional district with an assembly-court and later on found especially in the Danelaw. This last hypothesis could thus support Thorsten Andersson's idea of the existence of a prehistoric, *thing*-settlement district in Scandinavia. Perhaps further research will throw some new light on this very obscure problem.

To sum up, during the second half of the first millennium, Christianity was successively introduced into Scandinavia, where two key elements on the process were the symbiosis between the Church and the uppermost stratum in Scandinavian society, and the *thing*, which was the social channel or arena in Late Iron Age society in Scandinavia. The first churches were built by kings on their estates or nobility on their farms. Settlement districts and *thing* congregations erected churches, perhaps at a later stage, for their own purposes. With the introduction of the tithe followed the parish formation, which in Scandinavia took place during the twelfth and thirteenth centuries. At an early stage, one may discern some kind of large "extended parishes" in several regions that later on must have been split up into smaller districts. The Anglo-Saxon impact on Scandinavia in this period is obvious. It is even possible that the parish, *sokn*, in Scandinavia was introduced from England, both as a word and as a concept. The implications of the evidence examined above show why this is such an interesting hypothesis, although the difficulty at present of arriving at any definitive conclusions suggests that there are opportunities for further detailed investigations.

Fig. 1 The larger of the two rune-stones at Jelling, Denmark. (Photo: National Museum, Copenhagen).

Fig. 2 The rune-stone on Frösön, Jämtland, Sweden. (Photo: Jämtlands Läns Museum, Östersund).

STEFAN BRINK

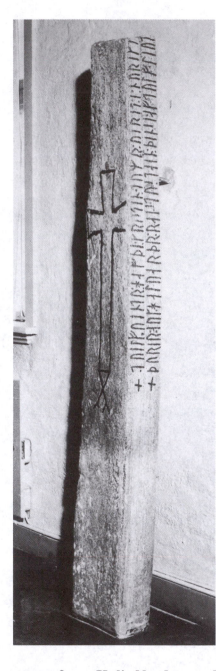

Fig. 3 The rune-stone from Kuli, Nordmøre, Norway. (Photo: Science Museum, Trondheim).

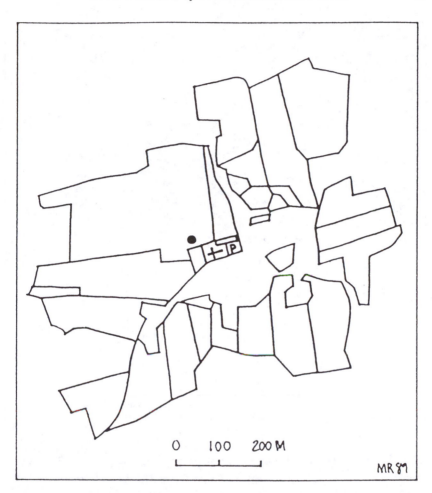

Fig. 4 A rare example of a church (+) erected on the site of a late Viking Age and medieval manor (•) at Bjäresjö in southern Skåne, Sweden. The (P) represents the parsonage. (Drawing: M. Riddersporre. From *By, huvudgård och kyrka*, ed. H. Andersson and M. Anglert, Lund Studies in Medieval Archaeology, 5 (Stockholm, 1989), p. 99).

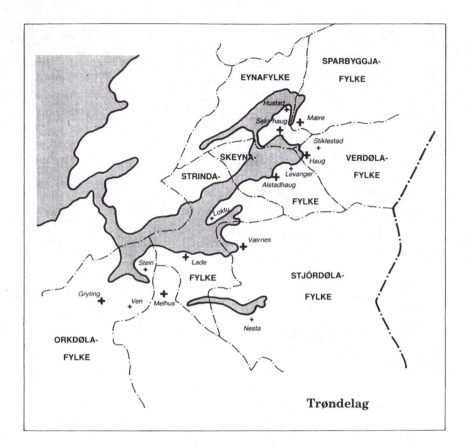

Fig. 5 The *fylke* districts in Trøndelag, Norway, and the *fylke* churches erected on early royal estates. (From Brink, "Sockenbildning och sockennamn", p. 117).

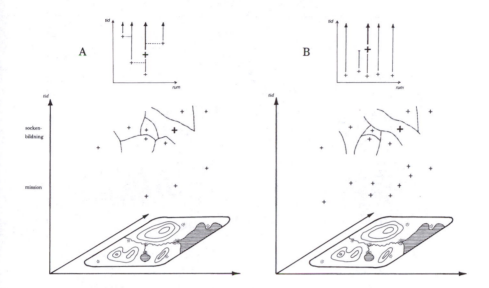

Fig. 6 Two possible developments regarding the formation of parishes: (A) a vertical or hierarchical process with a successive growth of parishes from a "mother-church" and (B) a horizontal or equilibrated process in which churches were built and parishes founded more or less simultaneously. (From Brink, "Sockenbildning och sockennamn, p. 119).

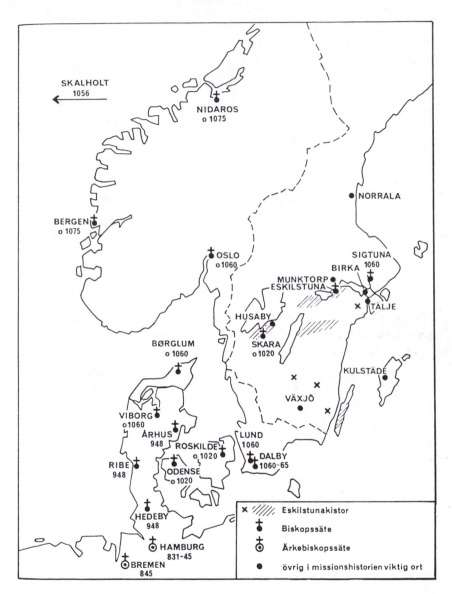

Fig. 7 Early episcopal sees (biskopssäte) and archiepiscopal sees (ärkebiskopssäte) in Scandinavia, with foundation years (From *Vikingatidens ABC*, ed. L. Thunmark-Nylén et al., Historia i fickformat, Statens historiska museum (Stockholm, 1981), p. 173).

Sense of Community and Civic Identity in the Italian Communes

Edward Coleman

On 29 May 1176, the combined forces of the first Lombard League met the army of Frederick I Barbarossa and his allies in battle at Legnano near Milan. The decisive victory won by the Lombards had considerable implications. Most obviously it caused the retreat of Barbarossa from Italy and the abandonment of his plans for re-establishing imperial control there. The peace treaty drawn up between the two sides at Constance in 1183 was, in effect, an imperial climb-down.

The consequences for the communes were, perhaps, of even greater significance. As Frederick Barbarossa had manifestly failed to make his writ run in Italy despite an armed struggle lasting just under two decades, the way was open for an important adjustment in the legal relationship between the emperor and the communes. The insistence on the constitutional illegality of the communes, which had been the basis of the programme laid out by imperialist lawyers at Roncaglia in 1158, was dropped. Concessions were made to all communes that had adhered to the Lombard League; a different approach from that of Frederick's predecessors who had preferred to

The author gratefully acknowledges the financial assistance of University College Dublin towards the preparation of this article.

negotiate separately with each city. In short, the communes *en bloc* obtained recognition as legitimate political institutions.[1]

The reasons why Barbarossa came so badly unstuck in Italy have often been debated. Certainly he met with practical difficulties, such as long lines of communication and Italy's malarial climate. He also had to contend with the perennial hostility of the papacy, the Roman population and the Norman kings of Sicily. Yet Frederick's lack of success in Lombardy, an area where he had a sound legal basis to exercise authority and where his predecessors back to Otto I had intervened actively, perhaps requires further explanation. In particular, one might reflect on the extent to which Frederick's arrival coincided with, and indeed stimulated, a maturing of civic consciousness amongst the communes, and consider the influence this may have had on the course of events.

It has been suggested that part of the reason for Frederick's failure was that most Italians had no historical memory of the Italian kingdom he sought to recreate and therefore saw no reason to give the emperor their loyalty. Rather, they viewed him as at best a temporary help in a local power struggle against a neighbour, for

---

[1] Sources: H. Appelt, ed., *Frederici Diplomata*, MGH Dip. reg. et imp. Ger. 10.1-5 (Hanover, 1975-90) (for Diet of Roncaglia 10.2:237-42, for Peace of Constance 10.4:848). See also C. Vignati, ed., *Storia Diplomatica della Lega Lombarda* (Milan, 1866). For Frederick I and the Lombard League see, amongst many works, P. Brezzi, "I comuni italiani e l'impero medievale", in *Nuove Questioni di Storia Medioevale* (Milan, 1964), pp. 177-207; and G. Fasoli, "Federico Barbarossa e le città lombarde" and "La Lega Lombarda – antecedenti, formazione, struttura", both in *Scritti di Storia Medievale*, ed. F. Bocchi, A. Carile and A. I. Pini (Bologna, 1974), pp. 229-55, 257-78 respectively. A number of conferences have been devoted to the theme, including *Popolo e Stato in Italia nell' età di Federico Barbarossa, Alessandria e la Lega Lombarda*, Congresso Storico Subalpino 33 (Turin, 1970); R. Manselli and J. Riedmann, eds, *Federico Barbarossa nel dibattito storiografico in Italia e Germania*, Annali dell' Istituto Storico italo-germanico in Trento 10 (Trento, 1982); *Studi sulla Pace di Costanza 1183*, Deputazione di storia patria per le province parmensi (Milan, 1984); *La Pace di Costanza (1183): un difficile equilibrio di poteri fra società italiana e impero*, Studi e testi di storia medievale 8 (Bologna, 1984); and *Federico i Barbarossa e l'Italia*, reviewed in *Quaderni Medievali* 30 (1990), pp. 251-58.

example, Cremona, Pavia, Como and others against Milan, or at worst as one of a long line of invaders of the peninsula, going back to the Goths and Vandals, who had brought nothing but trouble.[2] If there was indeed such indifference towards the Empire in Italy, Frederick's plans were ill-starred from the beginning. But the emperor himself was persuaded otherwise and he held fast to this belief through nearly two decades of costly and unproductive conflict.

Much of what Barbarossa knew (or thought he knew) about the Italian scene in the 1150s he probably owed to his uncle and biographer Bishop Otto of Freising (1111/15-1158). Otto of Freising enjoys a high reputation amongst modern historians: Italian medievalists in particular have long considered him to be something of a *cognoscente* of Italian affairs, and rightly so, for in his *Chronica de duabus civitatibus* (1149) and, especially, in his *Gesta Friderici* (1157) the learned bishop has interesting things to say about the social structure, customs and political life of the peninsula. He also explains why he believed Italy was so unwelcoming to Frederick.[3]

[2] C. Wickham, "Sense of the Past in Italian Communal Narratives", in *The Perception of the Past in Twelfth Century Europe*, ed. P. Magdalino (London, 1992), pp. 173-90 (pp. 182-84); reprinted (with further references) in Wickham, *Land and Power. Studies in Italian and European Social History 400-1200* (London, 1994), pp. 295-312.

[3] Otto of Freising, *Chronica sive Historia de duabus civitatibus*, ed. A. Hofmeister, MGH SRG (in us. schol.) 45 (Hanover and Leipzig, 1912). English translation in C. C. Mierow, *The Two Cities. A Chronicle of Universal History* (New York, 1928; repr. 1966). Otto of Freising and Rahewin, *Gesta Friderici I imperatoris*, edited with German translation by F. J. Schmale (Darmstadt and Berlin, 1965); also edited by B. de Simson, MGH SRG (in us. schol.) 46 (Hanover and Leipzig, 1912; repr. Hanover, 1978); translated by C. C. Mierow, *The Deeds of Frederick Barbarossa* (New York, 1953). For discussion see P. Brezzi, "Le fonti dei 'Gesta Friderici imperatori' di Ottone e Rahewino", *Bullettino dell' Istituto storico per medio evo* 75 (1963), 105-21, reprinted (with updated references) in Brezzi, *Paesaggi urbani e spirituali dell'uomo medioevale* (Naples, 1985), pp. 33-48; R. Bordone, *La società cittadina del Regno d'Italia. Formazione e sviluppo delle caratteristiche urbane nei secoli xi e xii* (Turin, 1987), pp. 9-18. On Hohenstaufen "court historiography" see T. Reuter, "Past, Present and No Future in the Twelfth-Century 'Regnum

According to Bishop Otto there were two principal reasons. The first was *absentia regis* – the absence of the king – a not unreasonable conclusion to reach from a German point of view, given that none of Frederick's twelfth-century predecessors had spent significant amounts of time in Italy; indeed, Conrad III did not cross the Alps at all in his fourteen-year reign (1138-52).

The second reason was the more-or-less permanent state of war that existed between neighbouring cities, particularly in the restricted geographical spaces that were the Arno and Po plains. The bishop devotes an entire chapter of his chronicle to a description of the conflicts that were ravaging Tuscany and the Veneto ("with fire and sword") in the 1140s.[4] For Otto the point was that these wars were disruptive of the general peace in the kingdom and would continue to be so unless the situation was taken in hand by the emperor in person. It is reasonable to believe this assessment influenced Frederick. At any rate, in a letter written by Frederick to Otto (reproduced in the preface to the *Gesta*) which summarises the state of the Empire in the year following his imperial coronation (1154), reference is made to the ills of the Italian kingdom occasioned by the absence of the emperors.[5]

Teutonicum'", in *Perception of the Past*, ed. Magdalino, pp. 15-36, and his references.

[4] Otto of Freising, *Chronica* 7:29: "His diebus propter absentiam regis Italiae urbibus in insolentiam decidentibus ... At Pisani et Lucenses propter nimiam viciniae oportunitatem indefesso furore bellantes ruinae suae omnes Tusciae vires implicuere ..." (and so on in the same vein). ("During these days, the cities of Italy waxed insolent on account of the king's absence ... The inhabitants of Pisa and Lucca, because of the great opportunities for fight afforded by their nearness to one another, waged war with unwearied frenzy, involving all the strength of Tuscany in their own ruin": Mierow, *Two Cities*, pp. 438-39).

[5] Compare Otto of Freising and Rahewin, *Gesta Friderici I imperatoris*, ed. Schmale, p. 2: "Post haec expeditionem Romam movimus et in valida manu Langobardium intravimus, haec quia propter longam absentiam imperatorem ad insolentiam declinaverat et suis confisa viribus aliquantum rebellare coeperat". ("After this we undertook the Roman expedition and entered Lombardy in force. Because this land, on account of the prolonged absence of the emperors, had become arrogant and conscious of its strength, had initiated rebellion": Mierow,

Otto of Freising therefore was clearly convinced (and may have persuaded his nephew) that unchecked armed conflict between neighbouring cities was something a ruler of Italy had to curtail in order to be effective. He tended, however, to stop short of investigating the causes of these wars. Only when discussing the Lombards' love of "liberty" (and by *libertas* he probably meant 'customs' rather than 'liberty', as the communes seem to have done when using the term) did the bishop come close to identifying the civic spirit and pride of each town as an important factor.[6]

Yet it is precisely this that comes across most strongly from contemporary Italian sources. For example, part of the entry in the annals of Milan for the year 1160, when Barbarossa was campaigning in Italy, reads as follows:

> Item eodem die Obertus archiepiscopus et Milo archiepresibyter et Galdinus diaconus et Alghisius cimilarcha suaserent populo, et ex parte Dei omnipotentis et beati Ambrosii praeceperent eis, ut confidentur ad bellum procederent, scientes, quos Dominus essent cum illis ... Celebrato itaque divino officio et confessione facta et poenitentia accepta, processerunt ad bellum cum carozeno, quod nocte fecerant.[7]

The key features here are common action in the face of a common threat; prominent involvement of the clergy from the archbishop downwards; inspiration from God (naturally), but also (and equally) from St. Ambrose, Milan's patron saint; elaborate

---

Deeds of Frederick Barbarossa, p. 18). The account continues with a description of military operations against Milan.

[6] Otto of Freising, *Gesta* 2:13 and also Rahewin, *Gesta* 3:45. For the notion of *libertas* in Italian texts see Bordone, *La società cittadina*, pp. 129-41.

[7] G. H. Pertz, ed., *Annales Mediolanensis 1154-1230*, MGH SS 18 (Hanover, 1843). "Archbishop Oberto and the arch priest Milo and the deacon Galdino and Alghiso, the treasurer, exhorted the people in the name of Almighty God and Blessed Ambrose and informed them that they should go to war confidently, knowing God was with them ... When they had celebrated the divine office, made confession and received penance they went forth to war with their *caroccio* which they had made during the night". Only one of the two versions of the annal has this final detail about the *caroccio*.

collective ritual and the use of civic symbols, in particular the *caroccio*, a kind of chariot used as a standard on the battlefield. We may reasonably characterise this *ensemble* as civic identity or *campanilismo*. Before examining this in more depth it might be useful to indicate briefly the relevant source materials.

The earliest extant texts that can be classified as civic literature (which is not to exclude the possibility that earlier works have not survived) are the so-called "praise poems" (*laudes*) written to celebrate the beauty and strength of the cities of Verona and Milan in the eighth century.[8] Relatively little similar material survives from the following two centuries (at least from the "Lombard" parts of northern and central Italy) but from the eleventh century onwards there is significant literary and historical output of relevance. For this period we have, firstly, a set of related poems that recount the naval campaigns of Pisa against the Saracens in the Mediterranean, whilst three major chronicles from Milan cover events associated with the Patarine movement and the Investitures Conflict.[9]

---

[8] G. B. Pighi, ed., *Versus de Verona, Versum de Mediolano civitate* (Bologna, 1960). For discussion see G. Fasoli, "La coscienza civica nelle 'Laudes civitatum'", in *La coscienza cittadina nei comuni italiani del duecento*, Convegno del Centro di studi sulla spiritualità medievale 11 (Todi, 1972), pp. 11-44; C. Frugoni, *Una lontana città. Sentimenti e immagini nel Medioevo* (Turin, 1983). English translation by W. McCuaig, *A Distant City: Images of Urban Experience in the Medieval World* (Oxford, 1991), pp. 54-64.

[9] "Il carme pisano sull impresa contro i Saraceni del 1087", in *Studi di filologia romanza offerti a S. Pellegrini*, ed. G. Scalia (Padua, 1971), pp. 565-627; C. Calisse, ed., *Liber Maiolichinus de gestis Pisanorum illustribus*, FSI 29 (Rome, 1904). For discussion of Pisan texts see C. B. Fisher, "The Pisan Clergy and the Awakening of Historical Interest in the Medieval Commune", *Studies in Medieval and Renaissance History* 3 (1966), 144-219. A. Cutola, ed., *Landulphi Senioris Mediolanensis Historiae libri quatuor*, RIS[2] IV.2 (Bologna, 1942); L. C. Bethmann and W. Wattenbach, eds, *Arnulfi, Gesta Archiepiscoporum Mediolanensium usque ad 1077*, MGH SS 8 (Hanover, 1848); for comment see O. Capitani, "Storiografia e riforma della chiesa in Italia (Arnolfo e Landolfo seniore di Milano)", in *La storiografia altomedievale*, Settimane di studio del Centro italiano di studi sull'alto medioevo 17 (Spoleto, 1970), pp. 557-629. C. Castiglioni, ed., *Landulphi Iuniores sive de Sancto Paulo, Historia Mediolanensis ab anno 1095 usque ad anno 1137*, RIS[2] V.3 (Bologna, 1934);

Communal chronicles begin to be written from the middle of the twelfth century. The classic works here concern the great maritime cities – the annals of Caffaro and his continuators for Genoa and the work of Bernardo Maragone for Pisa. The Milan annals, quoted above, and the earliest chronicles from a number of other cities, including Brescia, Cremona, Ferrara, Parma and Piacenza, also date from around this time.[10] So what do these sources, which become relatively abundant by the late twelfth century, have to tell us about civic identity? There is space here only to outline some of the essential features of the evidence they provide and to allude briefly to some points of methodology and interpretation in conclusion.

One of the basic building blocks in the construction of a sense of community and civic identity was the collective arrangements urban communities made for their protection and defence. This is

for comment see R. Rossini, "Note alla 'Historia Mediolanensis' di Landolfo Iuniore", in *Contributi dell'Istituto di Storia Medievale I: Raccolta in memoria di G. Soranzo* (Milan, 1968), pp. 411-80.

[10] L. T. Belgrano and C. Imperiale di Sant'Angelo, eds, *Annali genovesi di Caffaro e de' suoi continuatori*, 5 vols, FSI 11-14 bis (Rome, 1890-1929); on which see G. Arnaldi, "Cronache con documenti 'autentiche' e pubblica storiografia", in *Storici e Storiografia del Medioevo Italiano*, ed. G. Zanella (Bologna, 1984), pp. 117-37; R. D. Face, "Secular History in Twelfth-Century Italy: Caffaro of Genoa", *Journal of Medieval History* 6 (1980), 169-84, and Wickham, "Italian Communal Narratives". M. Lupo Gentile, ed., *Gli Annales Pisani di Bernardo Maragone*, RIS² VI.2 (Bologna, 1930-36): on which see E. Cristiani, "Aspetti di una coscienza cittadina nella storia pisana dei secoli xii e xiii", in *La coscienza cittadina*, pp. 347-55 and Fisher, "Pisan Clergy". Other twelfth-century city chronicles and annals are contained in MGH SS 18, ed. G. H. Pertz (Hanover, 1843), and 19, ed. G. H. Pertz (Hanover, 1846). An idea of the extent of the corpus of civic literature for the early and later medieval periods can be had from O. Capitani, "Motivi e momenti di storiografia medioevale italiana: secoli v-xiv", in *Nuove Questioni di Storia Medioevale*, pp. 729-800; G. Martini, "Lo spirito cittadino e le origini della storiografia comunale lombarda", *Nuova Rivistica Storica* 54 fasc. I-II (1970), 1-22; and Bordone, *La società cittadina*, pp. 18-26. It may be noted, in passing, that the genre is unparalleled in northern Europe: P. Classen, "*Res Gestae*, Universal History, Apocalypse", in *Renaissance and Renewal in the Twelfth Century*, ed. R. L. Benson and G. Constable (Oxford, 1982), pp. 387-421 (esp. pp. 393-98).

evident from the earlier texts: the concern with high walls and strong gates that runs through the early praise poems of Milan and Verona remains a constant theme of civic literature thereafter. It was a major preoccupation of communal writers such as Caffaro and Maragone in the twelfth century. Indeed, Caffaro tells us that Genoa's walls were hastily strengthened in just eight days when Barbarossa was threatening northern Italy in 1158.[11]

Walls were erected or reinforced to meet a perceived threat. If we take Magyar raiding in tenth century by way of example, it is not hard to find illustrations of a common defensive response in both documentary and narrative sources. In a celebrated diploma of 904, for example, King Berengar I granted the bishop of Bergamo and his fellow citizens (*concives*) the right to fortify their city against Magyar attack, whilst we learn from a prose description of the city of Modena – the *Mutinensis urbis descripto* – that in 910 the citizens barricaded themselves inside their cathedral with their bishop when the Magyars arrived.[12]

Fortunately for the Modenese the Magyars moved on to cause destruction elsewhere. The cathedral of Modena may actually have been fortified on this occasion, but above all the citizens took comfort in the knowledge that they were under the protection of S.

---

[11] *Versum de Mediolano civitate*, v. 3-5; *Versus de Verona*, lines 4-7. Belgrano and Imperiale di Sant'Angelo, eds, *Annali genovesi*, AD 1158: "Interim vero viri et mulieres qui Ianue erant, petras et arenam ad muram die vel nocte trahere non cessantes, tantum muri civitatis infra octo dies construxerunt". ("Meanwhile the men and women of Genoa constructed city walls in eight days by unceasingly dragging stones and sand to the wall day and night"). On the sources for the imagery of walls, gates, etc., in Italian civic literature see J. Le Goff, "L'immaginario urbano nell Italia medievale (secc. v-xv)", in *Storia d'Italia, Annali 5: Il Paesaggio*, ed. C. de Seta (Turin, 1982), pp. 5-43 (pp. 15-19).

[12] L. Schiaparelli, ed., *Diplomi di Berengario I*, FSI 35 (Rome, 1903), no. 47 (AD 904). L. A. Muratori, ed., *Mutinensis urbis descripto sive additamemtum ad vitam sancti Geminiani*, RIS[1] II.2 (Milan, 1726). For Magyar raids, see G. Fasoli, *Le incursioni ungare in Europa nel secolo x* (Florence, 1945), and more recently (in revisionist mode) A. A. Settia, "Gli Ungari in Italia e i mutamenti territoriali fra viii e x secolo", in *Magistra Barbaritas: i barbari in Italia* (Milan, 1984), pp. 185-218.

Gimignano, whose relics where interred there. This brings us to the second key factor of civic identity: civic cults and the role of the bishop.

That the cult of the patron saint was the spiritual focus of city life can be taken as read.[13] A prerequisite of the development of a civic cult was, of course, the possession of relics, and the mania for collecting (or if necessary stealing) them was strongly felt in Italy.[14] As relics were normally deposited in the city's cathedral the bishop assumed responsibility for the cult. The eighth-century praise poem of Verona, mentioned earlier, relates how Bishop Anno brought back relics of saints who had been martyred in the city but entombed elsewhere, implying that by doing so he also brought their protection and favour.[15] Some civic patron saints had themselves been bishops – St Ambrose of Milan is an obvious example, but S. Gimignano too had been one of the early bishops of Modena – and this also served to strengthen the link between bishop and civic cult from an early stage.[16]

---

[13] The literature is too large to begin to summarise. See in general, P. Brown, *The Cult of Saints: its Rise and Function in Latin Christianity* (London, 1981). For Italy, H. C. Peyer, *Stadt und Stadtpatron in mittelalterlichen Italien* (Zurich, 1955); A. M. Orselli, *L'idea del culto santo patrono cittadino nella letteratura latina cristiana* (Bologna, 1965). Examples of local studies: G. Rossetti, "Contributo allo studio dell' origine e della diffusione del culto dei santi in territorio milanese", in *Contributi dell' Istituto di Storia Medievale dell' Università Cattolica del Sacro Cuore: Raccolta di Studi in memoria di S. Mochi Onory* (Milan, 1972), pp. 573-607; P. Golinelli, *Indiscreta sanctitas. Studi sui rapporti tra culti, poteri e società nel pieno medioevo*, Istituto storico italiano per il medioevo, Studi storici 197, 198 (Rome, 1988).

[14] P. J. Geary, *Furta Sacra: Thefts of Relics in the Central Middle Ages* (Princeton, 1978) discusses a number of Italian examples.

[15] *Versus de Verona*, lines 67-84.

[16] For example, for Milan see A. Ambrosiani, "Gli arcivescovi di Milano e la nuova coscienza cittadina", in *L'Evoluzione delle città italiane nell' xi secolo*, ed. R. Bordone and J. Jarnut, Annali dell' Istituto storico italo-germanico in Trento 25 (Bologna, 1988), pp. 193-222; for Modena and other cities in Emilia-Romagna see P. Golinelli, "Istituzioni cittadini e culti episcopali in area matilidica avanti al sorgere dei comuni", in *Culto dei santi. Istituzioni e classi sociali in età pre-industriale*, ed. S. Boesch-Gajano and L. Sebastiani (L'Aquila, 1984), pp. 141-98.

Later, the devolution of extensive secular powers (taxation, justice, defence) to bishops in their cities by the Carolingian and Ottonian rulers of Italy allowed the idea of the bishop as ruler of the city on behalf of the saint to become embedded in civic consciousness. In the eleventh century, with commercial expansion and urban growth and the associated rise of territorial rivalries, for many bishops it proved to be a short step from taking responsibility for city defences to leading the city's army into battle against its enemies.[17]

It is not difficult to find examples of militarised bishops in eleventh- and twelfth-century sources. The exploits of Archbishop Daimbert of Pisa on the First Crusade are well known, and it was Archbishop Anselm of Milan who was largely responsible for organising the Lombard army that went East (to disaster) in 1101 in the wake of the Christian capture of Jerusalem.[18] The Crusade is to

---

[17] E. Dupré-Theseider, "Vescovi e città nell' Italia precomunale", in *Vescovi e diocesi in Italia nel medioevo (secc. ix-xiii)*, Italia Sacra 5 (Padua, 1964), pp. 55-109; G. Rossetti, "Origine sociale e formazione dei vescovi del 'Regnum Italiae' nei secoli xi e xii", in *Le istituzioni ecclesiastiche della 'societas christiana' dei secoli xi e xii*, Miscellanea del Centro di studi medioevali 8 (Milan, 1977), pp. 57-84; P. Racine, "Evêques et cité dans la royaume de 'Italia'", *Cahiers du civilisation médiévale* 27 1/2 (1984), 129-39; G. Tabacco, "La sintesi istituzionale di vescovo e città in Italia e il suo superamento nella 'res publica' comunale", in Tabacco, *Egemonie sociali e strutture del potere nel medioevo italiano* (Turin, 1979); translated into English by R. Brown Jensen as *The Struggle for Power in Medieval Italy: Structures of Political Rule* (Cambridge, 1989), Appendix.

[18] Lupo Gentile, ed., *Annales Pisani*, p. 89: "AD. mxcviiii populus pisanus iussu domini Pape Urbani II in navibus cxx ad liberandum Ierusalem de manibus paganorum profectus est. Quorum rector et ductor Daibertus Pisane urbis archiepiscopus extitit, qui postea Ierosolima factus Patriarcha remansit". ("AD 1099. On the orders of the lord pope, the inhabitants of Pisa set out in one hundred and twenty ships to free Jerusalem from the hands of the pagans. Their leader was Daimbert, Archbishop of Pisa, who later remained in Jerusalem, having been made Patriarch"); F. Cardini, "Profilo di un crociato. Daibert arcivescovo di Pisa", in Cardini, *Studi sulla storia e sull'idea di Crociata* (Rome, 1993), pp. 85-106. On the Milanese crusade: Castiglioni, ed., *Landulphi Iunioris ... Historia Mediolanensis*, part 3, chap. 4, p. 5; *Da Ariberto al Barbarossa 1002-1152*, Storia di Milano 3 (Milan, 1954), p. 255.

some extent extraneous to a discussion of civic identity, but it is significant nevertheless that the citizens looked to their bishops for military as well as spiritual leadership in these circumstances. Moreover, there is evidence too that bishops fulfilled this role in considerably less idealistic conflicts.

In early twelfth-century works such as Landulph Junior's *Historia Mediolanensis* or the *Liber Cumanus*, which describes the nine-year (1118-27) war between Milan and Como, we read frequently of bishops who urge their citizens to take up arms for their church and city against rival cities. Indeed Archbishop Aribert II of Milan (1018-45) is credited with being the first to use (in 1039) the *caroccio* on the battlefield.[19]

City defences, civic cults and warfare were therefore crucial elements in moulding a sense of community in the Lombard towns over several centuries. They are *leitmotifs* of civic literature, but not the only ones. We might equally well have considered the public manifestations of civic pride through festivals and ceremonies, the embellishment of prestige buildings, especially the cathedral and communal palace, or the interest of city dwellers in controlling their hinterland, the *contado*. However, to conclude it is important to look briefly at how interpretations are conditioned by the available evidence.

From the brief discussion of the sources above it will be apparent that their survival is uneven. Between the *laudes* of the eighth century and the prose works of the late eleventh and twelfth century, for example, there is virtually nothing. This gap in the evidence is not confined to civic literature. However, it is potentially significant in this context as it is generally acknowledged that the

---

[19] L. A. Muratori, ed., *Anonymus Novocomensis, Cumanus sive Poema de bello et excidio urbis Comensis (1118-27)*, RIS[1] V (Milan, 1724), v. 265; *Landulphi Iunioris ... Historia Mediolanensis*, chap. 68, p. 39; H. E. J. Cowdrey, "Archbishop Aribert of Milan", *History* 51 (1966), 1-15. The history of the *caroccio* is now amply covered in E. Voltmer, *Il Caroccio* (Turin, 1994) and H. Zug Tucci, "Il caroccio nella vita comunale italiana", *Quellen und Forschungen aus Italienischen Archiven und Bibliotheken* 65 (1985), 1-104; see also D. Webb, "Cities of God: the Italian Communes at War", in *The Church and War*, ed. W. J. Shiels, Studies in Church History 20 (Oxford, 1983), pp. 111-28.

civic pride evident in twelfth-century sources focuses firmly on the *civitas*, that is the city, rather than the commune. In fact, the beginnings of the commune as a political institution seem not to have been invested with great importance at the time.[20] Civic identity was therefore part of a continuing tradition rather than a new phenomenon, and it is a pity we have so little information about what people thought about such matters before the twelfth century.[21] As it is, we can only surmise from the evidence that the civic sentiments expressed in the Milan and Verona poems in the eighth century survived in some form or other to be revived in the twelfth century.

The late eleventh-/twelfth-century evidence presents its own problems, however. For example, whilst Otto of Freising and the other "German" authors who comment on Italy do so against the broad canvas constituted by the Empire, contemporary "Italian" texts are all highly localised. Landulph Senior, Arnulf and Landulph Junior may be the most interesting and informative sources for pre-communal Lombardy, but it cannot be denied that these authors are concerned almost exclusively with Milan. It is therefore risky to generalise too freely from their evidence given the exceptionally strong local patriotism characteristic of that city. Indeed, recent work suggests that Milan's social structure and political institutions (about which we are well informed both in these narratives and in documentary sources) were not necessarily replicated elsewhere.[22]

[20] This has been conclusively demonstrated in a number of studies, for example, O. Banti, "'Civitas' e 'comune' nelle fonti dei secoli xi e xii", in *Forme di potere e struttura sociale in Italia nel Medioevo*, ed. G. Rossetti (Bologna, 1977), pp. 217-32; G. Tabacco, "La sintesi istituzionale"; H. Keller, "Gli inizi del comune in Lombardia: limiti della documentazione e metodi di ricerca", in *L'evoluzione delle città*, pp. 45-70.

[21] A possible exception is late tenth-century Verona as described by Rather: *Ratheris Veronensis, Qualitas conjetura cujusdam*, PL 136, col. 542. Interestingly, according to Frugoni, *A Distant City*, p. 57, it appears that Rather may have possessed a manuscript of the *Versus de Verona*.

[22] F. Menant, "La société d'ordres en Lombardie", *Cahiers du civilisation médiévale* 26/3 (1983), 228-37; R. Bordone, "Tema cittadino e 'ritorno alla terra'", *Quaderni Storici* 52 (1983), 255-77.

In consequence we cannot assume that notions of civic identity formed as fast or in the same ways in other Lombard cities.

Beyond the risks of "Milanocentricity" there is a question of methodology connected to the authorship, audience and dissemination of these texts. Are we to think in terms of élites or of shared cultural values spanning distinct social groups? Does civic literature simply reflect urban society or actually shape it? In short, whose *campanilismo* are we dealing with?

At least there are few mysteries with regard to authorship. Late eleventh- and early twelfth-century works (all of the Milanese texts cited, for example) tended to be written by clerics; communal chronicles from c.1150 were written by laymen, usually civic office holders, notaries and the like. The civic literature of both the precommunal and communal period therefore reflects the worldview of élite, literate, ruling circles. It has been guessed that within these circles may have been groups who, in writing history (or, for that matter drawing up *brevia* or statutes) used different points of reference, symbols and touchstones.[23] This is intriguing and can hopefully be pursued further, but we remain here in the same *milieu*. The extent to which the rulers' view was shared, if at all, by the majority of the population, is of course more difficult to ascertain.

The *populus* normally appears in communal narratives *en bloc*, participating in public assemblies, internal city conflicts and war. Consequently those few texts which give it the role of protagonist rather than merely cipher for the manoeuvrings of bishops, consuls, families or parties are particularly worthy of attention. One such is the *Relatio translationis corporis sancti Geminiani*[24] which describes the consecration of a new shrine (in 1099) for S.

---

[23] Wickham, "Italian Communal Narratives", p. 180.

[24] G. Bertoni, ed., *Relatio translationis corporis sancti Geminiani*, RIS² VI.1 (Città di Castello, 1907). Modena had a strong tradition of civic identity, or at least a high survival of texts which express it. Apart from the *Relatio* and the *Mutinensis urbis descriptio* of 910 [see note 12 above], there is a poetic work, the *Canto delle scolte modenesi*, supposedly based on songs sung by sentries guarding the city's walls in the tenth century (A. Roncaglia, "Il 'Canto delle scolte modenesi'", *Cultura neolatina* 3 (1948), 5-46; Frugoni, *A Distant City* p. 67).

Gimignano, patron saint of Modena, whose protection had saved the city from the Magyars in the tenth century, as was noted earlier. The *Relatio* has relevance for a number of the issues we have touched on here, in particular the attention focused on the civic cult, but also (as the text informs us) the fact that not only the Modenese but the population of the surrounding region converged on the cathedral to be present at the ceremony. The *Relatio* is in some respects an exceptional work, but it is nevertheless notable that in it the *populus* is represented as a homogeneous group, "all for one and one for all" in its devotion to the cult of S. Gimignano, regardless of social background, wealth or place of residence. This may indeed be an accurate reflection. Nevertheless, one is bound to suspect that the generic nouns habitually used by communal authors to describe inhabitants of cities – *Mutinenses, Mediolanenses, Cremonenses*, etc. – tend to obscure social gradation, divergent interests and differing opinions.

In this respect documentary evidence can be helpful. The information documents provide about the gender, origins, social connections and material possessions of the individuals that made up the *populus* enables us to appreciate to some extent the variegated reality which lies behind the generalisations of the narrative sources. It is therefore appropriate that documents are the principal source material on which a number of analyses of the social fabric of Lombard towns has been based.[25]

Documentary sources can also inform on the question of civic identity. On occasions when the urban population was convoked to witness and approve some decision or action of common interest to the city, feelings of solidarity and group consciousness must have been particularly intense. In Cremona in 1118, for example, the *populus* gathered *ante ecclesiam maiorem* to endorse a military alliance with the locality of Soncino in the *contado*, designed to secure Cremona's frontier against her enemies, Crema and Milan.

---

[25] For an excellent example of a prosopographical study based on the rich documentary archives of Milan and other cities of western Lombardy see H. Keller, *Adelsherrschaft und Städtische Gesellschaft in Oberitalien (9-12 Jahrhundert)* (Tübingen, 1979). On the evaluation of narrative sources: Bordone, *La società cittadina*, pp. 21-22.

Another civic assembly was summoned there by trumpets and bells – *per tubam et campana* – in 1138.[26]

The repeated use of the same location for events of this kind, which were to become part of the political life of the communes, must have invested that public space with powerful civic symbolism. Here would be found the major public buildings: the communal palace and cathedral – Cremona's *Piazza Maggiore* is an excellent surviving example. Here too the symbols of *campanilismo*: the saint's cult, the *caroccio* (when not in use), the *campanile* itself.

The practice of holding public assemblies in the heart of the city was not an innovation of the communes: the earlier Lombard *conventus ante ecclesiam* is well attested. But the relationship between the organisation of urban space and notions of civic identity both during the communal period and before could bear further examination.[27] By the twelfth century (and perhaps earlier in some cities) the disposition, construction and demolition (one thinks, for example, of imperial *palatii*) of buildings in the civic centre had become matters of collective concern to the urban community. There is also evidence for an "archaeological" interest in the remains of the classical past within cities at this time, again interpreted in symbolic terms relevant to the present.[28]

[26] E. Falconi, ed., *Le Carte Cremonesi dei secoli viii-xii*, 4 vols (Cremona, 1979-89), vol. 2, no. 273 (AD 1118); L. Astegiano, ed., *Codex Diplomaticus Cremonae*, 2 vols (Turin, 1896-99), vol. 1, no. 108 (AD 1138): "in platea que est ante ecclesiam maiorem in publica contione collecta per tubam et campana".

[27] The many works of E. Guidoni on this theme, such as *Storia dell'urbanistica: Il Duecento* (Rome and Bari, 1989) and *Storia dell'urbanistica. Il Medioevo: secc. vi-xii* (Rome and Bari, 1991), whilst useful, are largely descriptive rather than analytical. P. Racine, "Naissance de la place publique en Italie", in *Fortifications, portes de villes, places publiques dans la monde méditerranéen*, ed. J. Heers, Cultures et civilisations médiévales 4 (Paris, 1985), and in general, J. C. Marie-Viguer, ed., *D'une ville à l'autre: structures matérielles et organisation de l'espace dans les villes européennes (xiii-xvi siècles)*, Collection de l'Ecôle française de Rome 122 (Rome, 1989) point the way for future work.

[28] C. La Rocca, "Using the Roman Past. Abandoned Towns and Local Power in Eleventh-Century Piemonte", *Early Medieval Europe* 5 (1996), 45-69.

Sentiments of civic identity are therefore increasingly evident in the city communes of northern Italy during the second half of the twelfth century, and as we have seen, these found expression in a variety of ways: in urban planning and architecture, in political life and on the field of battle, in the written word. The threat presented to communal "liberties" by Frederick Barbarossa clearly assisted this development in that, albeit briefly, it pushed rival factions within cities towards a common consensus, and united traditionally hostile cities in the Lombard League.

The years between the Diet of Roncaglia in 1158 and the Peace of Constance in 1183 were therefore crucial, but it is important to remember that civic identity was not created *ex nihilo* at this time. On the contrary, its deep historical roots are evident despite the lacuna in the early medieval documentary record. Even in the age of the communes, civic loyalties remained concentrated on the concept of the *civitas* whose predominantly religious symbols (the bishop, the cathedral, the patron saint) were not in the hands of one party or faction.

Equally, the triumph of the communes at the Peace of Constance does not represent an end point but, as it was closely followed by another period of *absentia regis* after the death of Frederick I in 1190, the beginning of a phase in which civic identity was further consolidated and developed. This was also the period in which the cities approached the zenith of their demographic and commercial expansion and this gave scope for more elaborate civic rituals, more ambitious building projects and more embellished civic literature; indeed, writers such as Bonvesin della Riva of Milan and Opicino de Canistris of Pavia represent the culmination of a tradition stretching back to the city *laudes* of the eighth century. The sense of civic identity expressed in these and similar texts remains a fundamental feature of the north Italian world view throughout the remainder of the medieval period.

Landscape and Power: The Frangipani Family and their Clients in the Twelfth-Century Roman Forum

Matthew Ellis

Family groups and family group rivalry defined the city of Rome both topographically and politically during the twelfth century. While the *Mirabilia* and the Investiture Controversy drew attention to the antique remains of the city, papal claims to the "Donation of Constantine" and imperial inheritance did not prevent papal dependence on aristocratic family support within Rome. Nowhere is this more apparent than in the relationship between the Frangipani family, based in the Forum area, and the twelfth-century papacy. The importance of family support to the reform papacy has been well documented, and the extent to which the city was under family control is illustrated by contemporary narrative accounts of pontificates such as that of Gelasius II (1118-1119).[1] The vivid

---

Unless otherwise indicated, all translations are the author's.

[1] P. Fedele, "Sull'origine dei Frangipane: a proposito di un recente lavoro", *ASRSP* 33 (1910), p. 495; D. Whitton, "Papal Policy in Rome, 1012-1124" (unpublished doctoral dissertation, University of Oxford, 1980), see particularly p. 285; S. A. Chodorow, "Ecclesiastical Politics and the Ending of the Investiture Contest: the Papal Election of 1119 and the Negotiations of Mouzon", *Speculum* 46 (1971), 613-40. Chodorow emphasises how aristocratic dependence on the part of the papacy dictated the pace of reconciliation in the Investiture Controversy (see particularly p. 634).

account in the *Liber pontificalis* of the interruption of Gelasius'
election, his subsequent kidnapping by the Frangipani and eventual
flight from Rome amply demonstrates the ability of rival families to
uphold or uproot a pontiff in the early part of the century. Similarly,
the family context for the Pierleoni anti-pope, Anacletus II, in the
schism of 1130 is central to an understanding of the division of
Rome and of the church until Anacletus' death in 1138.[2] The
topographical expression of this family rivalry was the creation of
fortified family houses, *casetorri*, and family quarters in Rome.[3]
The representation of this phenomenon is striking in both narrative
sources such as the *Liber pontificalis*, and in the wealth of
contemporary deeds and charters transcribed and published in the
Archivio della società romana di storia patria.[4] This paper will

---

[2] P. F. Palumbo, *Lo scisma del MCXXX, la vicenda romana, i precedenti
e le ripercussioni europee della lotta tra Anacleto e Innocenzo II* (Rome, 1942);
F. J. Schmale, *Studien zum Schisma des Jahres 1130* (Cologne, 1961); P. F.
Palumbo, "Nuovi studi (1942-1962) sullo scisma di Anacleto II", *Bullettino
dell'Istituto storico italiano per il medio evo e Archivio Muratoriano* 85 (1963),
71-103; M. Stroll, *The Jewish Pope: Ideology and Politics in the Papal Schism
of 1130* (Leiden, 1987). For the context of family competition as much as that of
the *novitii* versus *seniores*, see P. Brezzi, *Roma e l'impero medioevale 774-
1252*, Storia di Roma 10 (Bologna, 1947), p. 310; for the Pierleoni and
Anacletus, see P. Fedele, "La famiglie di Anacleto II e di Gelasio II", *ASRSP* 27
(1904), pp. 399-440.

[3] For the phenomenon of *casetorri* and the creation of family quarters see
L. Cassanelli, ed., *Le mura di Roma – l'architettura militare nella storia urbana*
(Rome, 1974). See particularly G. Delfini's essay "Le torri, elementi difensivi
isolati", pp. 71-75; E. De Ruggiero, *Il Foro Romano* (Rome, 1913), p. 108. For a
concordance of contemporary references and extant fortifications listed
according to *rioni* or districts, see A. Katermaa-Ottela, *Le casetorri in Roma*
(Helsinki, 1981).

[4] Edited by P. Fedele in "Carte del monastero dei Ss. Cosma e Damiano",
ASRSP 21 (1898), 459-534; *ASRSP* 22 (1899), 25-107, 383-447; and in P.
Fedele, "Tabularium S. Maria Nova", *ASRSP* 23 (1900), 171-237; *ASRSP* 24
(1901), 159-96; *ASRSP* 26 (1903), 21-141. P. Fedele, ed., "Tabularium S.
Praxedis", *ASRSP* 27 (1904), 27-78; *ASRSP* 28 (1905), 41-114. V. Federici, ed.,
"Regesto del monastero di S. Silvestro de Capite", *ASRSP* 22 (1899), 213-300,
489-538; *ASRSP* 23 (1900), 67-128. G. Ferri, ed., "Le carte dell'Archivio
Liberiano", *ASRSP* 27 (1904), 147-202, 441-59; *ASRSP* 28 (1905), 23-39;

focus on the single largest charter collection, that of S. Maria Nova, as an excellent source for references to the Frangipani family and the eastern Forum area. Cartulary evidence offers an insight into the practical exercise of family power through client families as well as through towers and fortified family residences. The peculiar importance of both the Frangipani family and the eastern Forum area to an understanding of Roman politics in the twelfth century will be demonstrated through a synthesis of narrative and charter evidence. Specifically, the role of the Mancini and Sassi/Sassoni families in the articulation of Frangipani influence will be examined with reference to family property accumulation and the interruption of the papal election of Gelasius II in 1118. Modern historians have conjured an enormous complex of Frangipani housing and fortification, stretching across the Forum and Palatine in the manner of a "Maginot Line".[5] This paper will demonstrate that the Frangipani holdings in the eastern Forum area were in fact fragmented, thereby emphasising how clientage and kinship links were vital to the Frangipani's powerbase in Rome.

The Frangipani family dominated the Forum area in this period. Following a gradual accumulation of agricultural land, *terra seminativa*, in the Sabina and outside the Porta Maggiore over the course of the tenth and eleventh centuries, the Frangipani are first recorded holding property within Rome in 1039 on freehold land by

---

ASRSP 30 (1907), 119-68. A. Monaci, ed., "Regesto di S. Alessio all'Aventino", *ASRSP* 27 (1904), 351-98; *ASRSP* 28 (1905), 151-200, 395-449. L. Schiaparelli, ed., "Carte antiche dell'Archivio Capitolare di S. Pietro in Vaticano", *ASRSP* 24 (1901), 393-496. B. Trifone, ed., "Carte del monastero di S. Paolo di Roma", *ASRSP* 31 (1908), 267-313; *ASRSP* 32 (1909), 29-106. Hereafter, charters from these editions are cited thus: [name] [document number], [year].

[5] For a recent example of this view of Frangipani landholdings, see M. Fagiolo, "Arche-tipologia degli orti Farnesian", in *Gli orti Farnesiani sul Palatino*, ed. V. Cazzato and G. Morganti, Ecole Française di Roma (Rome, 1990), p. 247: Fagiolo describes a "system of fortification developed by the Frangipani in the twelfth century, a kind of 'Maginot Line' which crossed the Palatine in its entirety between the two extremities of the Colosseum and the Velabrum" ("sistema fortificato allestito nel secolo XII dai Frangipane, una sorta di 'linea Maginot' che attraversava tutto il Palatino tra i due estremi del Colosseo e del Velabro").

the *domus nova*.[6] This place name would suggest initial Frangipani land holding near the Basilica of Maxentius at the eastern end of the Forum, which was commonly referred to as *basilica nova* in late antiquity. This property was still held by Leo Frangipane in 1042 and his son, John Sardo, and brother, Romanus, both appear later on this land when parts of the family vineyards in the Forum area were sold.[7] The development of Frangipani holdings within Rome reflects the growing importance of the family in papal affairs towards the end of the eleventh century. Along with the Pierleoni, the Frangipani were counted by Gregory VII as strong supporters: in 1076, Gregory described Cencius Frangipani and Alberic Pierleoni as "nostri familiares ... ab ipsa pene adolescentia in Romano palatio nobiscum enutriti".[8] The importance of the Frangipani to Gregory VII was mirrored by their relationship with Paschal II. When Paschal visited southern Italy in 1108, he left Rome in the charge of Leo Frangipani and Petrus Pierleoni.[9] As the family grew in importance, so the Frangipani presence in the Forum continued. In the cartulary of S. Maria Nova, the family frequently appear engaged in collective action in the matters of selling and leasing land, granting land to S. Maria Nova and witnessing documents. Between 1070 and 1199, the Frangipani appear in twenty five charters, mostly involved with land transactions within and without the city walls. The brothers Oddo and Cencius appear on seven occasions between 1139 and 1164, granting, leasing and holding land and property, and the eastern Forum location clauses for the families' grants and holdings are clear: between 1139 and 1191, the Frangipani appear residing on or granting Forum land on five occasions, "in regione Colosei in loco qui dicitur Calcararii", and "in regione Coloxei in contrada Arcus Septem Lucernum", that is,

---

[6] S. Maria Nova XI, 1039. For the eleventh-century property accumulation of the Frangipani, see Whitton, "Papal Policy", pp. 209-10.

[7] S. Maria Nova XIII, 1042; XV, 1052; XXIII, 1070.

[8] Gregory VII, *Registrum* 3:21, in *Das Registers Gregors VII*, ed. E. Caspar, MGH Epistolae selectae 2 (Berlin, 1923), p. 288; "our familiars, brought up in the Roman [i.e. Lateran] palace with us almost from adolescence".

[9] L. Duchesne, ed., *Le Liber pontificalis*, 2 vols (Paris, 1892), 2:299.

the Arch of Titus.[10] The Frangipani holdings on the other side of the Palatine slope are indicated by the record of the grant of the Septizonium, a monumental façade at the foot of the south-eastern Palatine, and of a tower near or on the triumphal arch ("que vocatur de arco") at the head of the Circus Maximus, to the family in 1145 in the charters of S. Gregorio in Clivo Scauri:

> Anno 1145, XVIII martii ... locamus et concedimus tibi domino Cinthio Frajapanis tuisque heredibus et successoribus in perpetuum, idest unam turrim, que vocatur de Arco ... positam Rome in capite Circli Maximi ... et locamus tibi Trullam unum in integrum, quod vocatur Septem solia ... positum Rome prope supradictam turrim et prope diaconiam sancte Lucie.[11]

This important grant accompanied the Frangipani's support of the new Cistercian pope, Eugenius III, who had been consecrated barely a month prior to the grant on 15 February. Frangipani support

---

[10] S. Maria Nova XLIX, 1139; LXVI, 1152; CIX, 1176; CXVIII, 1182; CXXV, 1191. Note that the location clause of S. Maria Nova CIX, 1176, "in regione Coloxei in contrada Arcus Septem Lucernum", is important for the understanding of location clauses because it implies that the "region" of the Colosseum was seen to extend to the arch of Titus.

[11] "1145, 18 March ... we lease and grant to you, Lord Cencius Frangipane and to your heirs and successors in perpetuity a tower called *Arco* ... located in Rome at the head of the Circus Maximus ... and we lease to you a *Trullum* [an antique structure] whole and entire, which is called *Septem solia* ... located in Rome near the abovementioned tower and near S. Lucia". Only preserved in fragments: G. B. Mittarelli, ed., *Annales Camaldulenses ordinis sancti Benedicti* (Venice, 1755-1773), vol. 3, app., col. 417, no. 271, 1145. Note that two years later, the Septizonium is described as being fortified: vol. 3, app., col. 440, no. 284, 1147 "castrum Septemsontium". The Septizonium still displayed evidence of this fortification in the form of later masonry filling its arcading in the fifteenth century: see the sketches of Martin van Heemscerck in C. Hülsen, *Forum und Palatin* (Munich, 1927), p. 62. The *turris de Arco* still exists in a much-restored form, and at one point was incorporated in the nineteenth-century *Osteria della Moletta* at the eastern end of the Circus Maximus: see F. Tomasetti, *Le torri medievali di Roma: Reproduzione anastatica del ms. III, 69 nella Biblioteca della Pontificia Academia di Archeologia* (Rome, 1990), pp. 36-37.

enabled the pope to move into Rome from Farfa, and was central to
the development of the first mutual recognition between Senate and
Pope in that same year. The continued activity of the Frangipani
family outside the Forum area was also important. Their landholding is demonstrated by Cencius Frangipane's sale of property
inherited from his father, John de Imperato, in the western IX region
of Rome in 1066.[12] In 1075, Romanus subscribed to a lease outside
the Porta Maggiore. In the twelfth century, whilst holding property
in the centre of the city, the Frangipani still engaged in the lease and
sale of agricultural land in Rome's hinterland, particularly outside
the Porta Latina and the Porta Appia to the south. Between 1120 and
1199, the family were involved in eleven such transactions.[13]

Nevertheless, the concentration of Frangipani fortifications in
the *rioni* of the Forum area is striking. Of the thirty-one towers in
the family's possession between the eleventh and thirteenth
centuries, fifteen are in Rione I Monti, and eleven in Rione XII
Ripa, framing the Forum area.[14] It is unclear, however, how
coherent the Frangipani holdings were in the eastern Forum area and
whether the family's influence could have been centred on these
holdings.

In spite of abundant evidence for the presence of the family in
the eastern Forum area, there is less direct Frangipani ownership
than might be anticipated. The family appears in the charters of S.
Maria Nova in only five charters leasing or granting Forum land.[15]
Moreover, the minor representation of the Frangipani as neighbours
to leased property is striking. The simple fact that the Frangipani
appeared on Forum property boundaries (as distinct from actually
purchasing, selling or leasing land) in the Forum area only twice in

---

[12] S. Pietro in Vaticano XXIII, 1066.

[13] S. Maria Nova XL, 1120; LXV, 1150; LXXII, 1155; XCV, 1166;
CXVI, 1181; CXVII, 1182; CXX, 1183; CXXIV, 1185; CLIV, c. 1196; CLXIV,
1199.

[14] Katermaa-Ottela, *Casetorri in Roma*, pp. 22-69; a listing of recorded
and extant towers according to *rioni*.

[15] S. Maria Nova XLIX, 1139; LXVI, 1152; CIX, 1176; CXVIII, 1182;
CXXV, 1191.

over fifty contemporary transactions in the Forum area suggests fragmented or even minor holdings.[16]

The cartulary evidence shows that contrary to the impression given in contemporary narrative sources, the Frangipani possessed only a limited territorial powerbase in the Forum/Palatine area. Should we therefore consider the twelfth-century "Frangipani Quarter" a chimaera? The narrative sources are consistent in locating the family in the eastern Forum/Palatine area, and the *Liber pontificalis* strongly suggests Frangipani control. The account of the 1118 election of Gelasius II, Calixtus II's consequent demolition order for three Frangipani towers in 1119/1120, and the repeated references to papal shelter being provided in the Palatine area under the auspices of the Frangipani, will all be addressed later in this paper. Yet the incidence of the family in those S. Maria Nova deeds regarding Forum property is surprisingly low. On what, then, did the family base their evident power in the Forum area?

A closer examination of the narrative sources reconciles this seeming contradiction of the influence exercised by the Frangipani in an area where their territorial possessions were apparently minor. The account of Pandulph in the *Liber pontificalis* regarding the Frangipani assault on S. Maria in Pallara during Gelasius' election in 1118 indicates the manner in which Frangipani power depended upon client and kinship ties as much as on fortifications. According to Pandulph in the *Liber pontificalis*, the conclave that elected Gelasius in 1118 followed the papal election decree of 1059 and excluded both aristocratic families and the Roman populace from their decision. The Frangipani, closely involved with the pontifical government of Paschal II (1099-1118), seem to have pursued a vendetta against the new candidate as a consequence of their exclusion from the electoral decision. The proclamation of Gelasius' election was held in the monastery of S. Maria in Pallara, located on the Palatine slope above the Forum. Pandulph noted that this area was very much within Frangipani influence when he wrote of the assembly being held "in monasterio quodam quod Palladium dicitur,

---

[16] S. Maria Nova LXVI, 1152; CIX, 1176.

infra domos Leonis et scelestis Cencii Fraiapane".[17] From this
Frangipani holding, according to Pandulph's account, Cencius
physically interrupted the election "more draconis immanissimi
sibilans" and "papam per gulam accepit, distraxit, pugnis
calcibusque percussit" before abducting him.[18]

Following Gelasius' incarceration in the Frangipani "turris
iniquitatis", it is important to note how the intercession of Cencius
Frangipane's uncle, Stephanus Normanni, secured Gelasius' release
and ostensibly reconciled the two parties. This Normanni-
Frangipani kinship link is further illustrated by the names of the
family towers subsequently demolished at the order of Calixtus II
upon his arrival in Rome in 1119: the tower of Cencius, the tower of
"Iniquity" (that is, the place of Gelasius' incarceration) and the
tower of "Domna Bona", mother of Cencius and sister of Stephanus
Normanni.[19]

The central role of the Forum area in the election of 1118
should not be viewed in isolation. The lower Palatine slope and the
eastern Forum/Palatine fortifications, more than the Lateran or S.
Pietro, acted as places of papal shelter under the protection of the
Frangipani and as arenas for family conflict. Following the sack of
Rome by Robert Guiscard in 1084, and the consequent rebuilding
and fortification of the city, the Frangipani are first recorded
extending shelter to Urban II in 1094.[20] The development of
Frangipani holdings both within and without the city walls

---

[17] "in the monastery which was called *Palladium*, beneath the houses of
Leo and the infamous Cencius Frangipane": J. M. March, ed., *Liber pontificalis
prout exstat in codice manuscripto Dertusensi. Textum genuinum complectens
hactenus ex parte ineditum Pandulphi* (Barcinone, 1925), pp. 166-67, 174-75.

[18] "in the manner of a hissing serpent" and "seizing the pope by the throat,
shook him and struck him with stones as well as with fists": March, ed., *Liber
pontificalis Dertus*, p. 167.

[19] March, ed., *Liber pontificalis Dertus*, pp. 194-95: "Hic pro pace
servanda turres Cencii, domne Bone et Iniquitatis dirui et reparari non ibidem
precepit".

[20] For the 1084 sack of Rome by Robert Guiscard, see Duchesne, ed.,
Liber pontificalis, 2:290, and also R. Lanciani, *The Destruction of Ancient Rome*
(London, 1899), p. 186. For the 1094 shelterin g of Urban II see Godfrey of
Vendôme, *Epistolae* 1:8, PL 157, p. 47.

discussed earlier led not only to the election débâcle of 1118, but crucially to the family's early involvement in the papal schism of 1130. Boso's *Vita Innocentii II* in the *Liber pontificalis* records the sheltering of Innocent and his supporters in the "domos Fragepanum" in 1130, buildings which were then subject to an unsuccessful Pierleoni assault. Boso's account is complemented by that of Ptolemy of Lucca, who with a differing chronology recorded how in 1133 "The said Innocent, seeing the party of Pierleoni stronger in the City retreated to the house of the Frangipani".[21] Following the death of Innocent in 1143, his successor Celestine II was sheltered in S. Maria in Pallara until he died there in March 1144. Indeed, during Celestine's brief pontificate, it is important to note that it was Cencius Frangipane, along with Cardinal Ottaviano, who went to Palermo to negotiate with Roger II.[22] The consistent use of the Palatine for papal shelter and election, rather than the Lateran or S. Pietro in Vaticano, is further illustrated by the choice of S. Cesareo, the small monastery on the upper Palatine, for the 1145 election conclave of Eugenius III, and by the Palatine shelter offered to Alexander III in the aftermath of the Roman defeat by Barbarossa at the Battle of Monte Porzio in 1167.[23]

Despite the evident importance of both the Palatine/Forum area and the fortifications of the Frangipani to the reform papacy,

---

[21] For the 1118 election of Gelasius II see Pandulph, "Vita Gelasii II", in *Liber pontificalis Dertus*, ed. March, pp. 166-67, 174-75. For the 1130/1133 refuge of Innocent II, and the Pierleoni assault on the Frangipani fortifications see Boso, "Vita Innocentii II", in *Liber pontificalis*, ed. Duchesne, 2:380; for 1133 dating see Ptolemy of Lucca, *Annales*, ed. B. Schmeidler, MGH SRG Nova ser., 8 (Berlin, 1930), p. 47.

[22] For the 1143 shelter of Celestine II in S. Maria in Pallara and his death there in March 1144 see Boso, "Vita Celestinii II", in *Liber pontificalis*, ed. Duchesne, 2:385. Note that whilst Celestine was "in Palladio", it was Cencius Frangipane who accompanied Cardinal Ottaviano to Palermo to renegotiate the treaty with Roger II: see Brezzi, *Roma e l'impero medioevale*, p. 320.

[23] For the 1145 conclave for the election of Eugenius III in S. Cesareo see Boso, "Vita Eugenii II", in *Liber pontificalis*, ed. Duchesne, 2:386; see also Fedele, "Una chiesa del Palatino 'S. Maria in Pallara'", *ASRSP* 26 (1903), p. 345 for the Palatine top location of this monastery. For the 1167 shelter of Alexander III, see Boso's "Vita", in *Liber pontificalis*, ed. Duchesne, 2:416.

the *Liber pontificalis'* account of the 1118 assault on S. Maria in Pallara makes clear the role not simply of fortifications but pre-eminently of manpower. The Frangipani were ultimately forced to concede in 1118 not only by the intercession of Cencius' uncle, Stephanus Normanni, but also through the arrival of a force drawn from all fourteen Roman districts or *rioni*. The identity of the supporters of the Frangipani in this incident, that is to say their clients, may be demonstrated through the use of cartulary evidence.

The charters of S. Maria Nova indicate a complex clientage link between the Frangipani, Mancini and Sassi/Sassoni families involving property held in the eastern Forum area and outside the walls, as well as through patterns of witnessing to deeds in S. Maria Nova and other contemporary cartularies. The interconnection of these kinship groups is best approached through an examination of their respective land holdings and mutual activity in land transactions.

The Mancini and Sassi/Sassoni are well represented as land holders in the eastern Forum area in the twelfth century. On the Palatine slope near S. Maria Nova and below S. Maria in Pallara, "in ascensu Palatii"/"in Palladie", the Mancini are represented as holding multiple properties between 1139 and 1190, and in a deed of 1160 are explicitly identified as holding property adjacent to the Sassi/Sassoni.[24] The Sassi/Sassoni are recorded separately in the same area in 1147 and 1160, the latter record placing them adjacent to the Mancini.[25] In the eastern Forum immediately below these Palatine slope holdings, in the last quarter of the century the Mancini and Sassi/Sassoni held property near the Arch of Titus, "in contrada Arcus Septem Lucernarum", an area central to the Frangipani family holdings.[26] Extending eastwards towards the artisans' quarter adjacent to the Colosseum, "in Caldararii", the Sassoni are recorded as holding a house in the area in 1152, and more particularly as leasing a *turris* in 1161. This mention of a

---

[24] S. Maria Nova XLVII, 1139; LXXXII, 1160 – next to Sassoni; CXXXIII, 1190.

[25] S. Maria Nova LXII, 1147; LXXXII, 1160.

[26] Mancini – S. Maria Nova CXIX, 1183; Sassoni – S. Maria Nova CIX, 1176.

Sassi/Sassoni tower is an important indication of the diversity of minor family fortification which is neglected in the narrative sources in favour of a more simplistic model of family quarters in Rome. This narrative perspective offers a misleadingly monolithic impression of the holdings of larger kinship groups such as the Frangipani.

That the Mancini and Sassi/Sassoni families were important enough to be significant clients of the Frangipani in the Palatine/Forum area is shown by their witnessing activities outside this area. In S. Maria Nova, the Sassi/Sassoni appear on twenty-two occasions between 1123 and 1198, predominantly in a witnessing capacity, complemented by their record of local holdings discussed above. The extent of the group's witnessing activities outside this area is shown by the frequency of their appearances, again overwhelmingly as witnesses, in contemporary cartularies. In the north of Rome, in S. Silvestro de Capite the family appear in nine deeds between 1133 and 1279, leasing on two occasions outside the city walls. In the north-east, in S. Praxedis there are ten family appearances between 1137 and 1269, seven of which involve land leased or sold to the Sassi/Sassoni outside the Porta Nomentana. In the Archivio Liberiano (the deeds of S. Maria Maggiore and others) the Sassi/Sassoni make nine appearances between 1130 and 1291, witnessing deeds on all but one occasion when "Iohannes Sassonis" was cited as a neighbour in a fragmentary deed lacking a location clause. To the south of Rome, in S. Paolo, the family witnessed two deeds between 1139 and 1259. To the south-west, in S. Alessio all'Aventino the family make three appearances as witnesses between 1153 and 1202, whilst to the west on the other side of the river in S. Pietro in Vaticano, there seem to be eight appearances of the Sassi/Sassoni as witnesses between 1053 and 1195, but it is hard to establish whether all these deeds involve members of the same kinship group. Similarly, although there are four appearances of the Sassi/Sassoni as witnesses in the cartulary of Ss. Cosma e Damiano in Trastevere between 1033 and 1078, the identification of a consistent kinship group is uncertain.

Whilst the Sassi/Sassoni are not recorded as possessing property in the region of all these churches and instead appear in the capacity of witnesses, the general impression of family activity in the matter of land lease and sale throughout Rome is striking. It is an impression reinforced by a similar study of the Mancini family's activity in the capacity of witness in the same cartularies outside the Forum area during the same period. Mancini witnessing activity is apparent in S. Maria Nova between 1104 and 1190, with a total of twenty-two appearances. In other cartularies, the Mancini appear with less frequency than the Sassi/Sassoni. To the north, in the deeds of S. Silvestro de Capite they make eleven appearances between 1125 and 1263, three involving family land lease both within and without the city walls. In the Archivio Liberiano, they make only two appearances as witnesses between 1252 and 1263. In S. Praxedis, the Mancini make five appearances between 1151 and 1244, four of which involve family land lease outside the Porta Nomentana. In Ss. Cosma e Damiano they appear in four deeds as witnesses between 1041 and 1097, but the clear identification of a consistent kinship group is uncertain in some cases.

This pattern of witnessing by both the Mancini and the Sassi/Sassoni maintained across multiple cartularies from the eleventh to the thirteenth century, coupled with the record of their holdings in the eastern Forum area, identifies them as important and unusually active Roman families. Moreover, they are connected with the Frangipani in many ways. All three families hold property in common locations, pre-eminently in the eastern Forum area as recorded in S. Maria Nova. Both the Mancini and Sassi/Sassoni hold multiple properties on the Palatine slope above S. Maria Nova and below S. Maria in Pallara, the area crucial to the outcome of Gelasius II's election in 1118.[27] Whilst the Mancini are recorded in

---

[27] In 1139 Petrus, son of Petrus, sold a house "in regione Sanctae Mariae Novae in ascensu Palatii" ("in the region of S. Maria Nova at the slope of the Palatine hill") where "a tertio latere tenet Gerardus frater meus" ("the third side is held by Gerardus my brother") and where the deed was witnessed by Sasso de Mancino (S. Maria Nova XLVII, 1139); in 1160 Iohannes leased "domum" ("a house") "in Palladie" where "a primo latere tenet Cinthius Sassonis macellarii" ("the first side is held by Cencius Sassoni, butcher") (S. Maria Nova LXXXII, 1160); an 1190 prenuptial agreement regarding property "in regione Palladie" recorded "a .I. latere tenent heredes Gerardi de Mancino" ("the first side is held by the heirs of Gerardus Mancini") (S. Maria Nova CXXXIII, 1190). Sassi/Sassoni: in 1147 the brothers Bulgamino, Gregorio, Cencio and Guidone

an 1183 lease near the Arch of Titus, the mention of the Sassi/Sassoni in the same area in 1176 also records the Frangipani as neighbours.[28] This specific mention of the Frangipani as neighbours is complemented by the similar appearance of the two kinship groups, the Sassi/Sassoni and Frangipani, "in Caldararii" by the Colosseum on neighbouring properties in 1152.[29] Such identification between the groups, holding property in the same Forum areas and, moreover, holding neighbouring properties in these places, is reinforced by the activities of the Mancini and Sassi/Sassoni as witnesses to land transactions involving the Frangipani in S. Maria Nova and other contemporary cartularies. The Mancini appear in this capacity between 1104 and 1137 in S. Maria Nova and in the Archivio Liberiano in a single thirteenth-century instance.[30] The witnessing behaviour of the Mancini with regard to Frangipani holdings, primarily outside the walls to the south of Rome, is mirrored by that of the Sassi/Sassoni. The family witnesses deeds involving the Frangipani between 1137 and 1166 in S. Maria Nova and later, between 1148 and 1291 in the Archivio

Sassonis leased "duas criptas" ("two vaults") from S. Maria Nova "sub muro videlicet Palladie" ("below the wall, namely that of Palladie") (S. Maria Nova LXII, 1147); in 1160 Cinthius appeared on the first side of a house leased by Iohannes Mancini "in Palladie" (S. Maria Nova LXXXIII, 1160).

[28] The 1183 lease of "domum ad Arcum Septem Lucerne" recorded Girardus on the first and second sides (S. Maria Nova CXIX, 1183). Sassi/Sassoni: in 1176 the heirs of Gregorius are recorded on the third side of a house "in contrada Arcus Septem Lucernarum" whilst the Frangipani are on the second side (S. Maria Nova CIX, 1176).

[29] In 1152 Sasso is recorded on the third side of a house leased "in Caldararii", with Cencius Frangipane on the second side (S. Maria Nova LXVI, 1152); in 1161 Iohannes is recorded "in regione Coloxei ubi dicitur Caldararii" ("in the region of the Colosseum which is called 'Caldararii'") as a neighbour to leased property "a primo latere est turris tua iuris venerabilis monasterii beati Pauli et tenet Iohannes Sassonis de Martino" ("the first side is the tower which is under the jurisdiction of the honoured monastery of the blessed Paul and is leased by Iohannes Sassoni de Martino") (S. Maria Nova LXXXIII, 1161).

[30] S. Maria Nova XXXIII, 1104; XLVI, 1137; LI, 1140; CIX, 1176; CXVIII, 1182. Archivio Liberiano LIX, 1263.

Liberiano.[31] Indeed, the will of Adelascia Frangipane, daughter of Cencius, disposing of property in the area of S. Maria Nova in 1137, was witnessed by members of both groups.[32]

It might be argued that neighbours would witness deeds as a matter of course, and that neighbours would regularly appear as witnesses to any transactions involving adjoining properties. In the case of the Forum there is clear evidence that this argument is not valid: neighbours do not appear in this way consistently. The incidence of the Mancini, Sassi/Sassoni and Frangipani together – in the deeds of S. Maria Nova and elsewhere – is distinctive and important. The Mancini and the Sassi/Sassoni are representative of the minor Roman families which remain anonymous in the narrative sources and yet occupy a vital position in the exercise of family power in twelfth-century Rome. Furthermore, evidence for the interconnection of the Mancini and Sassi/Sassoni themselves illustrates the independent extension of kinship and client links below the more prominent families.

The holding of neighbouring properties in the Forum area is reinforced by the evidence for mutual land holdings outside the Porta Nomentana to the north-east of Rome. The property accumulation of the Mancini outside the Porta Nomentana is consistent over the course of the twelfth century.[33] Still more interesting is the record of the Mancini and Sassi/Sassoni both holding land outside the Porta Nomentana and being neighbours in the "Aqua Tutia" area.[34]

---

[31] S. Maria Nova XLVI, 1137; LXXXVI, 1162; XCIV, 1166. Archivio Liberiano XVII, 1148; XXI, 1176; XCI, 1291.

[32] S. Maria Nova XLVI, 1137: "Girardus de Mancino, testis. Sasso macellarius, testis".

[33] S. Maria Nova XLVIII, 1139; LX, 1146; LXIII, 1147. S. Praxedis XXXV, 1174; XXXIX, 1183; XLII, 1189; LXVIII, 1244.

[34] S. Praxedis XIX, 1137; XXII, 1139; XXXIX, 1183; LIV, 1223; LV, 1223; LVI, 1224; LXVIII, 1244; LXXVII, 1269. On the Sassi/Sassoni outside the Porta Nomentana, see G. Tommassetti, "Della Campagna Romana", *ASRSP* 30 (1907), p. 364 with reference to an 1195 charter of S. Maria in Via Lata leasing property on the Via Nomentana: "una 'cripta mercatorum, quam tenet Iohannes Saxonis' de Alberto".

Indeed this evidence for the independent activities of the Mancini and Sassi/Sassoni might explain their continued prominence in Roman affairs after the decline of the Frangipani. In this respect, such property accumulation independent of the Frangipani at the same time as there was a client relationship is interesting, particularly when the stature of the Sassi/Sassoni in the fourteenth, fifteenth and sixteenth centuries is considered.[35]

Political topography is vital to an understanding of the behaviour of both the curia and the city of Rome in the twelfth century. The attention paid to family fortifications has distracted from the fundamental importance of client and kinship links. In this context, it is relevant to note that the current initiative pursued by the Ecole Française in Rome and the Università di Roma "La Sapienza" only addresses the *complessi familiari* of major kinship groups, such as the Orsini.[36] Smaller families such as the Mancini and the Sassi/Sassoni and the critical importance of lower-level client links are neglected in such studies. The role of Frangipani-Normanni kinship ties (reinforced by the marriage of Jacopa dei Normanni and Graziano Frangipane in the thirteenth century), and of Frangipani-Mancini-Sassoni client links, offers a way of understanding the family context of Rome which is denied by narrative sources such as the *Liber pontificalis*. Such ties illuminate the actions of a reform papacy often dependent upon family favour to remain within the city, a dependency particularly indicated by the events surrounding the election of Gelasius II in 1118.

It is in this respect that the importance of cartulary sources becomes evident, not simply as illustrations of family property and fortifications, but more interestingly, as records of the identity and the activities of the minor families which articulated the influence of larger, better-documented kinship groups, such as the Frangipani. Indeed, the evidence for independent property accumulation and

---

[35] For the longevity of the Sassi/Sassoni in Roman affairs see V. Federici, "Della casa di Fabio Sassi in Parione", *ASRSP* 20 (1897), 479-89.

[36] For the early products of this initiative see F. Bosman, "Una torre medievale a Via Monte della Farina: ricerche topografiche e analisi della struttura", *Archeologia Medievale* 17 (1990), 633-60.

fortification on the part of these minor families offers a particularly important perspective on the operation of clientage between major and minor families which has been overlooked in other contemporary sources. It is through the further study of families such as the Mancini and Sassi/Sassoni that the complicated urban context of the twelfth-century papacy may be better understood.

The Geuissae and Bede:
On the Innovativeness of Bede's Concept
of the *Gens*

Harald Kleinschmidt

Introduction

In the following paper, I propose to revisit the problem of the meaning of the word and the concept of the *gens*, and I shall do so by discussing Bede's report on one conspicuous case of the change of the name of a *gens*. I have selected this case because its significance as an indicator of the change in the concept of the *gens* during the seventh and eighth centuries does not seem to have been duly recognised. I shall proceed in three steps. First, I shall outline the general background of the conceptual change of the *gens* which I shall relate to the process of settlement after the end of the large-scale migrations. Second, I shall investigate the evidential value of certain genealogical sources for "ethnic" traditions and customs of name-giving. Third, I shall argue that what Bede reported as the change of the name of a *gens* was in fact a structural change of the *gens* and that Bede, like other early medieval authors, purposefully neglected structural changes of *gentes*. For the purposes of this paper, I shall take for granted the general premise implied in Ogburn's semiotic triangle that concepts as descriptive and analytical tools need to be kept separate from those phenomena of the world of tangible or quasi tangible realities from which they have been abstracted. Hence, I shall refer to the "structure" of a *gens* as something that is different from the concept of a *gens* and that consists of, first, the dominant traditions pertaining to and transmitted inside the *gens* and, second, of one of the following factors which members of the *gens* may have believed to have constituted their *gens*, namely descent,[1] a contract,[2] an office,[3] or cohabitation in an area of settlement.[4]

Concepts of the Gens

Students of classical and early medieval ethnography and historiography as well as of legal records have long recognised that the word *gens* and its Greek counterpart γένος were used and sometimes interutilised with the words *natio*, *genus* and *genealogia* as well as their Greek counterparts in frequent references to a

---

[1] A concise description of this factor is already to be found in Cassiodorus, *Expositio psalmorum I-LXX*, CCSL 97 (Turnhout, 1958), chap. 2.9, p. 46. Cf. A. Dove, *Studien zur Vorgeschichte des deutschen Volksnamens*, Sitzungsberichte der Heidelberger Akademie der Wissenschaften, Philos.-Hist. Kl. 1916, 8 (Heidelberg, 1916), pp. 34-35.

[2] In some recently published studies, it has been emphasised that contractual agreements founding *Gefolgschaften* may have been an important factor for establishing warbands which were referred to as *gentes* in some sources. See P. Geary, "Ethnic Identity and Situational Construct in the Early Middle Ages", *Mitteilungen der Anthropologischen Gesellschaft Wien* 113 (1983), 15-26 (pp. 22-25) on Gregory of Tours' references to the *gens Francorum*; H. Wolfram, *Die Goten*, 3rd ed. (Munich, 1990), pp. 105-06 on the *Gothorum gens*.

[3] Salvianus, *Libri qui supersunt*, ed. K. Halm, MGH Auctores antiquissimi 1.1 (Berlin, 1877; repr. Munich, 1978), chap. 5.15, p. 58. Cf. R. Wenskus, *Stammesbildung und Verfassung*, 2nd ed. (Cologne, Graz, Vienna, 1977), pp. 38-39, 319-20.

[4] See E. Ewig, "Volkstum und Volksbewusstsein im Frankenreich des 7. Jahrhunderts", in *Caratteri del secolo VII in occidente*, Settimane di studio del Centro italiano di studi sull' alto medioevo 5 (Spoleto, 1958), pp. 588-648, (pp. 626-28); reprinted in Ewig, *Spätantikes und fränkisches Gallien*, vol. 1, Beihefte zur Francia 3 (Munich, 1976), pp. 231-73.

considerable variety of types of groups which could range from small bands of men and women to specific representations of human character or even mankind as a whole.[5] Among these various usages, the frequent oscillation between the use of the word *gens* for the concept of a group constituted by and maintained through beliefs in common descent[6] (called "descent groups" in this paper) on the one side and, on the other, for the concept of an "ethnic" group with a distinct political tradition of its own is most interesting for the purposes of the present paper.[7] For example, under the

[5] Tacitus, *Germania*, ed. R. Much, 3rd edition revised by H. Jankuhn and W. Lange (Heidelberg, 1967), chap. 4. Isidore, *Etymologiarvm sive originvm libri XX*, ed. W. M. Lindsay (Oxford, 1911), chap. 9.2.1, 9.4.4-6, 15.2.1. Jordanes, "Getica", chap. 122, in *Iordanis Romana et Getica*, ed. T. Mommsen, MGH Auctores antiquissimi 5.1 (Berlin, 1882; repr. Munich, 1982), p. 89. Cf. S. Reynolds, "Medieval *origines gentium* and the Community of the Realm", *History* 68 (1983), 375-409 (p. 383).

[6] The distinction is necessary because it has been shown that sources contain records of beliefs in common descent which cannot be confirmed by other sources. See Wenskus, *Stammesbildung*, pp. 14-38. Cf. W. Pohl, "Tradition, Ethnogenese und literarische Gestaltung", in *Ethnogenese und Überlieferung*, ed. K. Brunner et al. (Vienna, 1994), pp. 9-26 (pp. 10-11); H. Wolfram, "Theogonie, Ethnogenese und ein kompromittierter Grossvater im Stammbaum Theoderichs des Grossen", in *Festschrift für Helmut Beumann*, ed. R. Wenskus et al. (Sigmaringen, 1977), pp. 80-97; Wolfram, "Einige Überlegungen zur gotischen Origo gentis", in *Studia linguistica Alexandro Vasilii filio Issaatschenko oblata*, ed. H. Birnbaum et al. (Lund, 1978), pp. 487-99; Wolfram, "Gothic History and Historical Ethnography", *Journal of Medieval History* 7 (1981), 309-19.

[7] The concept of ethnicity or gentilicity is contested and has been obfuscated by various connotations in European languages. Among German historians, for example, the concept of the *gens* has sometimes been equated with that of the tribe *(Stamm)* and it has been dissociated from the *Volk* as a concept for a different type of political organisation which, it has been asserted, emerged only later in the Middle Ages. See Pohl, "Tradition, Ethnogenese", pp. 10-15. By contrast, anthropologists and sociologists have applied the concept statically for believed, apparent or manifest indicators of the social cohesiveness and political acceptance of norms, values and rules within groups whose members have a consciousness of and accept traditions of common origins and

principate, talk about descent groups such as the *gens Iulia* or the *gens Claudia* was as frequent as there were descriptions of various "ethnic" *gentes* outside the Roman Empire, such as the "Germanorum gentes".[8] Likewise, in early medieval historiographies and law codes, we find notes about descent groups such as the "gens nobilis Ayglolfinga"[9] or the Bavarian "genealogiae"[10] as we come across references to "ethnic" groups such as the "gens Saxonum"[11] or the "gens Francorum".[12] It is not uncommon to assume that cases in which diverse meanings were attached to a word or group of words display the use of such words for the expression of a widely defined and changing concept.

With regard to the *gens*, the truth of this assumption can be supported by two considerations. The first is that, in contexts where specific reference is made to either a descent group or to an "ethnic"

---

common past experiences. See W. E. Mühlmann, "Ethnogonie und Ethnogenese", in *Studien zur Ethnogenese*, Abhandlungen der Rheinisch-Westfälischen Akademie der Wissenschaften 72 (Opladen, 1985), pp. 9-27; W. Rudolph, "Ethnos und Kultur", in *Ethnologie*, ed. H. Fischer (Berlin, 1983), pp. 47-67; A. D. Smith, *The Ethnic Origins of Nations* (Oxford, 1986); J. F. Stack, Jr, "Ethnicity and Transnational Relations", in *Ethnicity in a Transnational World*, ed. Stack (Westport, CT, 1981), pp. 3-42; G. de Vos and L. Rommanucci-Ross, eds, *Ethnic Identity. Cultural Continuities and Change*, 2nd ed. (Chicago, 1982). While I shall use the concept according to this definition, I shall put the word "ethnic" and its derivatives into quotation marks in order to express my reservations about the belief in the durability of "ethnic" features.

[8] Tacitus, *Germania*, chap. 44.

[9] Fredegar, *Chronicarum libri IV*, chap. 4.52, ed. B. Krusch, MGH SRM 2 (Berlin, 1888; repr. Hanover, 1984), p. 146.

[10] *Lex Baiwariorum*, art. 3.1, ed. E. von Schwind, MGH LNG 5.2 (Berlin, 1926), pp. 312-13. Cf. J. Jarnut, *Agilolfingerstudien* (Stuttgart, 1986), pp. 110-16.

[11] Bede, *Historia ecclesiastica gentis Anglorum*, 5.11, ed. B. Colgrave and R. A. B. Mynors (Oxford, 1969), p. 486.

[12] Gregory of Tours, *Historiarum libri X*, chapters 2.12, 5 prologue, 6.2, ed. B. Krusch and W. Levison, MGH SRM 1.1 (Hanover, 1951), pp. 61, 193, 266; *Liber historiae Francorum*, chap. 1, ed. B. Krusch, MGH SRM 2 (Berlin, 1888; repr. Hanover, 1984), p. 241; *Lex Salica 100 Titel-Text*, ed. K. A. Eckhardt (Weimar, 1953), prologue, pp. 82-83.

group, the word *gens* was avoided. One of these cases is the statement by Jordanes that the Balthi and the Amali were the ruling dynasties of the Visigoths and the Ostrogoths respectively.[13] In this phrase, which would have allowed Jordanes the use of the word *gens* for the purpose of denoting either type of group, the word was carefully avoided and replaced by the slightly odd *familia* for the dynasties. Since Jordanes had to keep separate the concepts of the descent groups and of the "ethnic" group, *familia* was preferred over *gens* precisely because *gens* would have been too vague to specify only one type of group. Moreover, the second consideration is that the word *gens* was interutilised with the word *natio* for the expression of a single concept, namely that of an "ethnic" group. However, individual authors could have their own preferences. For example, Jordanes reported that the Vividarii were known to have formed a *gens* from a number of *nationes*,[14] and this report allows the contention that, in this case, a *natio* was to be an "ethnic" group smaller than a *gens* and, perhaps, part of the latter. But Bede, on the other hand, could explain that the *gens Nordanhymbrorum* is that part of the *natio Anglorum* whose members lived in areas north of the Humber.[15] This means that a *gens* was an "ethnic" group smaller than a *natio* and evidently part of the latter. Such differences of usage can only have occurred if both authors employed various words for different aspects of the concept of *gens*.

In addition, it has already been noted that the concept of the *gens* as an "ethnic" group was in itself not static, but that, during the seventh and eighth centuries, the previous variety of meanings attached to the word *gens* and its *similia* was reduced and that the word *gens* became a technical term for a settled "ethnic" group under the control of a ruler over land and people.[16] Two principal

---

[13] Jordanes, "Getica", chap. 42, p. 64. This phrase, of course, epitomises the commonplace that *gentes* can receive their "ethnic" identity during migrations through successful fighting alongside the descent groups of their rulers. See above note 3.

[14] Jordanes, "Getica", chap. 96 (pp. 82-83).

[15] Bede, *Historia ecclesiastica*, 2.9, p. 162.

[16] Ewig, "Volkstum und Volksbewusstsein", p. 648; J. Fried, "Gens und regnum. Wahrnehmungs- und Deutungskategorien politischen Wandels im

observations can be adduced in support of the argument that the concept of the *gens* underwent a fundamental change during these centuries.

The first of these observations results from doubts about the reliability of claims that traditions constituting and preserving early medieval post-migration *gentes* were actual continuations from the period of migrations. Such doubts have been fuelled by recent archaeological and toponomastic research. It has been found that most of the migrating groups were small and, at least at the onset of their migrations, can hardly have comprised more than 200 or 300 members[17] and that their group structures underwent frequent changes in the course of the migrations.[18] Moreover, place-names of Germanic origin in Britain, Gaul and areas east of the Rhine where immigration occurred reveal a formidable variety of types of groups among which small bands of contractual groups *(Gefolgschaften)* or neighbourhood groups seem to have been prominent. It is difficult to imagine that these contractual groups were constituted by beliefs in political traditions of common origin and, consequently, it is difficult to regard such groups as "ethnic" in kind. However, it is true that early medieval authors retrospectively subsumed these

früheren Mittelalter", in *Sozialer Wandel im Mittelalter*, ed. J. Miethke and K. Schreiner (Sigmaringen, 1994), pp. 73-104, (pp. 79-80); H. Thomas, "Theodiscus – Diutiskus – Regnum Teutonicorum", *Rheinische Vierteljahres-blätter* 51 (1987), 287-302; Thomas, "Der Ursprung des Wortes Theodiscus", *Historische Zeitschrift* 247 (1988), 295-331.

[17] R. Hachmann, *Die Goten und Skandinavien*, Quellen und Forschungen zur Sprach- und Kulturgeschichte der germanischen Völker, new ser., 34 (Berlin, 1970), pp. 279-389; H. Wolfram, "Einleitung oder Überlegungen zur origo gentis", in *Typen der Ethnogenese unter besonderer Berücksichtigung der Bayern*, vol. 1, ed. H. Wolfram and W. Pohl, Österreichische Akademie der Wissenschaften, Philos.-Hist. Kl., Denkschriften 201 (Vienna, 1990), pp. 19-33. Wolfram, "'Origo et religio'. Ethnic Traditions and Literature in Early Medieval Texts", in *Early Medieval Europe* 3 (1994), 19-38 (pp. 26-27).

[18] See for example Wolfram, *Die Goten*, passim.

manifold groups under "ethnic" labels such as "Angli", "Saxones", "Franci", "Burgundiones", "Alamanni" or "Baiuvarii".[19]

Nevertheless, there are cases in which it can be shown that the retrospective superimposition of such "ethnic" labels upon hetero-geneous types of groups was based on the contention of an "ethnic" uniformity of the migrating groups, although such cannot be inferred from available contemporary sources of the Migration Age.[20] Hence when these migration processes were reconstructed by authors such as Jordanes in the sixth century or by Bede in the eighth century, such reconstructions must *prima facie* be read as the products of the time when their authors lived and not as genuine records of the Migration Age. In short, it would appear to be necessary to take into consideration processes of the "invention of tradition"[21] after the settlement of the migrants, which, however, does not necessarily exclude the possibility that records of existing traditions may have continued to be transmitted into the early Middle Ages.[22]

[19] See among others P. Amory, "The Meaning and Purpose of Ethnic Terminology in the Burgundian Laws", *Early Medieval Europe* 2 (1993), 1-28; Ewig "Volkstum und Volksbewusstsein", pp. 609-44; W. Jungandreas, *Die Gudrunsage in den Ober- und Niederlanden* (Göttingen, 1948), pp. 91-105, 189-200; H. Moisl, "Kingship and Orally Transmitted Stammestradition among the Lombards and Franks", in *Die Baiern und ihre Nachbarn*, ed. H. Wolfram and A. Schwarcz, vol. 1 (Vienna, 1985), pp. 111-19; R. Wenskus, *Sächsischer Stammesadel und fränkischer Reichsadel*, Abhandlungen der Akademie der Wissenschaften in Göttingen, Phil.-Hist. Kl., 3rd ser., 93 (Göttingen, 1976), pp. 112-14; I. Wood, "Ethnicity and Ethnogenesis of the Burgundians", in *Typen der Ethnogenese*, ed. Wolfram and Pohl, pp. 53-69; H. Wolfram, "The Shaping of the Early Medieval Kingdom", *Viator* 1 (1970), 1-21; Wolfram, "The Shaping of the Early Medieval Principality as a Type of Non-Royal Rulership", *Viator* 2 (1971), 1-33.

[20] See H. Kleinschmidt, "Schwaben im frühmittelalterlichen England", *Alemannisches Jahrbuch* (1993/94), 9-32, and "Nomen und gens", *Beiträge zur Namenforschung*, new ser., 31 (1996), 123-60.

[21] I have borrowed this phrase from E. J. Hobsbawm and T. O. Ranger, eds, *The Invention of Tradition* (Cambridge, 1983; repr. 1992).

[22] This has been emphasised again by Pohl, "Tradition, Ethnogenese", pp. 21-24.

The second observation emerges from doubts about the structural affinity between migrating and post-migration *gentes*. Such doubts have been informed by recent historical investigations into the post-migration settlement processes.[23] Some historians have argued that, again during the seventh and eighth centuries, traditional names came into use for newly established *gentes* which were considered to be subject to a ruler and whose "ethnicity" was neither defined in terms of descent nor rooted in traditions which were connectable with the migrations. Instead, these new *gentes* were defined in accordance with areas of settlement.[24] Evidently, the introduction of geographical and administrative criteria into the use of seemingly traditional and "ethnic" names indicates that the groups so termed were conceived of as groups of settlers and not as migrants. Hence the new "ethnic" names were given to groups under someone's rule, whereby rule was understood as control over land and people.[25] The formula *liute ioh lant* seems to have appeared first in the tenth century.[26]

These observations seem to support the conclusion that the early medieval "ethnic" terminology may be misleading because it

---

[23] Geary, "Ethnic Identity", p. 22, uses the misleading term "territorialisation" for these processes. The term is misleading because the transformation of areas of settlements into clearly demarcated territories under a central administration reflects changes which occurred during the high and late Middle Ages.

[24] The earliest reference to this change is in Dove, *Studien zur Vorgeschichte*, p. 94. See also Ewig, "Volkstum und Volksbewusstsein", pp. 626-28, and H. Kleinschmidt, "Bede and the Jutes", *Northwest European Language Evolution* 24 (1994), 21-46. In Bede's "ethnic" terminology, it is a striking feature that, for two out of three of the "ethnic" groups of immigrants, he chose names which related to geographical areas on the continent to which Bede ascribed the origin of these groups, namely the Angles and Saxons; and it is, perhaps, more than an odd coincidence that these two "ethnic" names are also names for areas.

[25] For the concept of control over land and people see W. Schlesinger, *Die Entstehung der Landesherrschaft*, 2nd ed. (Darmstadt, 1964; repr. 1983), pp. 12-15.

[26] Schlesinger, *Die Entstehung*, p. 14.

suggests the continuity of traditions and of group structures from the Migration Age into the early Middle Ages. This has long been recognised in cases where specific early medieval *gentes* were interconnected by contemporary authors with *gentes* of the Migration Age. For instance, Raban Maur's association of the Vikings with the Marcomanni[27] or the retrospective identification of the Franks with the Sugambri[28] have long been regarded as spurious. But it has been overlooked that such retrospective associations between successively existing separate *gentes* were compatible with the contemporary early medieval concept of the *gens* which was defined, in Raban Maur's words, as "multitudo ab uno principio orta sive ab alia natione secundum proprium collectionem distincta".[29] This definition implies that the *gentes* were conceived as political groups with features which were regarded as continuous and which could distinguish one *gens* from others; these features were identified by Regino of Prüm as descent, customs, language and law.[30] Such beliefs in the continuity of the *gentes* forced the author of the Carolingian *Passio Sigismundi* to explain the disappearance of the names of certain "ethnic" groups in Gaul with the false argument that the Burgundians had massacred the residential population in the areas coming under their control.[31] But it is far from evident that this particular concept of the *gens* already existed at the time of the Migration Age. Instead, for the period in question, we have to take into account the likelihood that "ethnic" names were not fixed and could be applied as auto- and heterostereotypes to different types of groups and groups with a changing structure.[32]

[27] Cf. Fried, "Gens und regnum", p. 79.

[28] Ewig, "Volkstum und Volksbewusstsein", p. 632.

[29] Raban Maur, *De universo*, chap. 16.2, PL 111, col. 437: "a sizeable group of people which sprang from one origin or is distinguishable from another group according to a number of features of its own".

[30] Regino of Prüm, "Chronicon", ed. F. Kurze, *Reginonis abbatis Prumiensis Chronicon cum continuatione Treverensi*, MGH SRG (in us. schol.) 50 (Berlin, 1890; repr. Hanover, 1989), praefatio, p. XX.

[31] Ewig, "Volkstum und Volksbewusstsein, p. 648.

[32] Wenskus, "Stammesbildung", pp. 59-65.

In sum, these two observations seem to confirm that a change in the concept of the *gens* as an "ethnic" group occurred after the end of the migrations. As a consequence of this change, the concept of the *gens* became narrowed down to that of an "ethnic" group which was understood as the group of settlers under the control of a ruler over land and people and in which traditions of migration were transformed into instruments for the legitimation of such rule. Hence, the word and the concept of the *gens* are problematic in two ways. The first is that the uniformity of the concept of the *gens* as an "ethnic" group of settlers under the control of a ruler over land and people was secondary and peculiar to post-migration early medieval sources. The second is that the word *gens* and its *similia* remained in use throughout late antiquity and the early Middle Ages not-withstanding the conceptual change which took place after the migrations had petered out.

These two problems also affected the use of Bede's "ethnic" terminology.[33] Specifically, they have obscured the meaning of a curious phrase in which Bede reported what he claimed to be a

---

[33] See among many: D. N. Dumville, "Kingship, Genealogies and Regnal Lists", in *Early Medieval Kingship*, ed. P. H. Sawyer and I. Wood (Leeds, 1977), pp. 72-104, reprinted in Dumville, *Histories and Pseudo-Histories of the Insular Middle Ages* (Aldershot, 1990), no. 15 with original pagination; H. Vollrath, "Die Landnahme der Angelsachsen nach dem Zeugnis der erzählenden Quellen", *Vorträge und Forschungen* 41 (1993), 317-37; C. P. Wormald, "Bede, the Bretwaldas and the Origins of the Gens Anglorum", in *Ideal and Reality in Frankish and Anglo-Saxon Society. Studies Presented to J. M. Wallace-Hadrill*, ed. C. P. Wormald, D. Bullough and R. Collins (Oxford, 1983), pp. 99-129 (p. 122); Wormald, "The Venerable Bede and the 'Church of the English'", in *The English Religious Tradition and the Genius of Anglicanism*, ed. G. Rowell (Wantage, 1992), pp. 13-32; Wormald, "Engla Lond. The Creation of an Allegiance", *Journal of Historical Sociology* 7 (1994), 1-24; B. A. E. Yorke, "The Jutes of Hampshire and Wight and the Origins of Wessex", in *The Origins of Anglo-Saxon Kingdoms*, ed. S. Bassett (Leicester, 1989), pp. 92-93, 96; Yorke, *Kings and Kingdoms of Early Anglo-Saxon England* (London, 1990), pp. 128-56.

change of the name of a *gens*.[34] He did so on the occasion of his description of the beginning of the Roman mission in Wessex. Dating the arrival of missionaries in Wessex to the reign of King Cynegisl, Bede wrote that the "gens Occidentalium Saxonum" under the rule of Cynegisl had "antiquitus" been called "Geuissae".[35] Bede's statement has remained problematic for two reasons: first, it has remained unclear which the temporal extension is that the word *antiquitus* may have been meant to express; second, Bede did not specify the manner in which he may have wished to see the two group names correlated. *Antiquitus* can be considered to imply either that the change from the name Geuissae to the name *Occidentales Saxones* had occurred a long time ago or that the name Geuissae had been an old one and had been abandoned only shortly before Bede's time of writing. Although present scholarship tends to accept the latter interpretation,[36] there remains the important task of investigating what can be discovered about the relative age of the name Geuissae which, despite Bede's contention to the contrary, does not bear obvious signs of great antiquity.[37] Moreover, the other

---

[34] That changes in the naming of *gentes* occurred c. 700 has long been recognised. See H. M. Chadwick, *The Origin of the English Nation* (Cambridge, 1924), p. 31; M. Förster, *Der Flussname Themse und seine Sippe* (Munich, 1941), p. 290; H. E. Walker, "Bede and the Gewissae", *English Historical Review* 12 (1956), 174-86; D. P. Kirby, "Problems of Early West Saxon History", *English Historical Review* 80 (1965), 10-29 (p. 12); W. Davies and H. Vierck, "The Contexts of Tribal Hidage", *Frühmittelalterliche Studien* 8 (1974), 223-93 (pp. 231-32, 240, 268, 283); cf. W. Goffart, "The Supposedly 'Frankish' Table of Nations", *Frühmittelalterliche Studien* 17 (1983), 98-130 (pp. 126-27).

[35] Bede, *Historia ecclesiastica*, 3.7, p. 232.

[36] Dumville, "Kingship, Genealogies" and Walker, "Bede and the Gewissae".

[37] It is not easy to connect the name with the continental evidence from the *Notitia dignitatum*, ed. O. Seeck (Berlin, 1876), p. 61. Cf. M. W. C. Hassall, "Britain in the Notitia", in *Aspects of the Notitia Dignitatum*, ed. R. Goodburn and P. Bartholomew (Oxford, 1976), pp. 103-17. Possible insular parallels are of questionable value: among the latter are the name *Wissa* in the Latin and Old English versions of Felix's Life of Saint Guthlac. See *Felix's Life of Saint Guthlac*, chap. 53, ed. B. Colgrave (Cambridge, 1956; repr. 1985), p. 168; *Das*

problem of the semasiological interconnection between the two group names has not actually been tackled, since most scholars have accepted Bede's supposition that the *gens* called the "Geuissae" and the "gens Occidentalium Saxonum" were, in fact, drawn on the same concept of the *gens* and, thus, had a compatible group structure. I shall therefore narrow down the problem of the conceptual relationship between the two *gentes* to a reconsideration of the age of the group name Geuissae and shall then argue that Bede's identification of the Geuissae with the "gens Occidentalium Saxonum" resulted from a retrospective, but untenable application of the early medieval concept of the *gens*.

The Genealogical Tradition of the Geuissae and the Dating of their Name in Relative Chronology

Assumptions about the age of the name Geuissae as about most early medieval groups with a tradition of their own can be derived from materials contained in genealogies. As Cassiodorus already noticed, the power of a ruling dynasty *(stirps regia)* as a descent group depended on the length of its genealogy.[38] As collections of "intentional data", royal genealogies reflect the self-esteem of those who transmit them and, consequently, can be used as sources for the claims of the rulers associated with them.[39] In the case of the

---

angelsächsische Prosaleben des hl. Guthlac, chap. 22, ed. P. Gonser (Heidelberg, 1909), p. 172. Cf. the place-name *Wixna* of the Tribal Hidage (Davies and Vierck, "Contexts of Tribal Hidage", pp. 231-32, 240). See also R. E. Zachrisson, *English Place-Names and River-Names Containing the Primitive Germanic Roots *vis, *vask* (Uppsala, 1926), pp. 14, 18-20.

[38] Cassiodorus, *Variarum libri XII*, book 11.1, ed. A. J. Fridh, CCSL 96 (Turnhout, 1973), p. 424.

[39] See on the evidential value of genealogies: L. Genicot, *Les généalogies*, Typologie des sources du moyen âge occidental 15 (Turnhout, 1975), pp. 14-24, 35-44; K. Hauck, "Carmina antiqua", *Zeitschrift für bayerische Landesgeschichte* 27 (1964), 1-33;. Hauck, "Lebensnormen und Kultmythen in germanischen Stammes- und Herrschergenealogien", *Saeculum* 6 (1955), 186-223; J. L. Nelson, "Reconstructing a Royal Family", in *People and Places in*

Geuissae, considerations of genealogical matters have usually taken their starting point from the elaborate genealogy preserved in the Old English annals for the year 855 and in later written records.[40]

Northern Europe 500-1600. Essays in Honour of Peter Hayes Sawyer, ed. I. Wood and N. Lund (Woodbridge, 1991), pp. 47-66; G. Scheibelreiter, "Zur Typologie und Kritik genealogischer Quellen", *Archivum* 37 (1992), 1-26; H. Taviani-Carozzi, "De l'histoire au mythe. La généalogie royale anglo-saxonne", *Cahiers de civilisation médiévale* 36 (1993), 355-70.

[40] See on the West-Saxon genealogical records: E. E. Barker, "The Anglo-Saxon Chronicle Used by Aethelweard", *Bulletin of the Institute of Historical Research* 40 (1967), 74-91 (p. 83); A. Bell, "The West Saxon Genealogy in Gaimar", *Philological Quarterly* 2 (1923), 173-86; A. Brandl, "Die Urstammtafel der Westsachsen und das Beowulfepos", *Archiv für das Studium der neueren Sprachen und Literaturen* 137 (1918), 6-24 (pp. 8, 21); Brandl, "Einige Tatsachen betreffend Scyld Scefing", in *A Grammatical Miscellany offered to Otto Jespersen*, ed. N. Bøgholm (Copenhagen and London, 1930), pp. 31-37 (p. 35); A. F. Cameron, "Saint Gildas and Scyld Scefing", *Neuphilologische Mitteilungen* 70 (1969), 240-46; D. N. Dumville, "The Anglian Collection of Royal Genealogies and Regnal Lists", *Anglo-Saxon England* 5 (1976), 23-50 (p. 34); Dumville, "The West Saxon Genealogical Regnal List", *Anglia* 104 (1986), 1-32 (p. 24); Dumville, "The West Saxon Genealogical Regnal List and the Chronology of Early Wessex", *Peritia* 4 (1986), 21-66 (pp. 60-61); R. D. Fulk, "An Eddic Analogue to the Scyld Scefing Story", *Review of English Studies* 40 (1989), 313-22; E. Hackenberg, "Die Stammtafeln der angelsächsischen Königreiche" (unpublished doctoral dissertation, University of Berlin, 1918), pp. 1-87; R. Henning, "Sceaf und die westsächsische Stammtafel", *Zeitschrift für deutsches Altertum und deutsche Literatur* 41 (1897), 156-69; T. D. Hill, "Scyld Scefing and the *stirps regia*", in *Magister Regis. Studies in Honor of Robert Earl Kaske*, ed. A. Groos (New York, 1986), pp. 37-47; A. Hönger, "Die Entwicklung der literarisichen Darstellung der Genealogie bei den germanischen Stämmen bis in die Karolingerzeit" (unpublished doctoral dissertation, University of Leipzig, 1912); J. M. Kemble, *Ueber die Stammtafel der Westsachsen* (Munich, 1836); Kirby "Problems of Early West Saxon History"; Kirby, *The Earliest English Kings* (London, 1991), p. 49; M. Lapidge, "'Beowulf', Aldhelm, the 'Liber Monstrorum' and Wessex", *Studi medievali*, 3rd ser., 23 (1982), 151-92 (pp. 184-88); A. L. Meaney, "Scyld Scefing and the Dating of Beowulf – Again", *Bulletin of the John Rylands University Library of Manchester* 71 (1989), 7-40

But this scholarly custom takes no account of the fact that the oldest genealogy related to the Geuissae stems from c. AD 700 and survives in a late eighth-century manuscript of apparently Anglian provenance, Cambridge, Corpus Christi College, MS 183, fol. 67.[41] The date of the genealogy contained in this manuscript can be gleaned from the fact that it is a pedigree beginning with Ine,[42] while ignoring all subsequent West-Saxon rulers. This pedigree receives its significance from the possibility that it is the only extant West-Saxon genealogical record that can be associated with Bede's lifetime and, consequently, can be investigated for evidence of the age of the name Geuissae. Such investigation can begin with a comparison between what the pedigree tells about Ine's ancestry and the contents of the Bernician pedigree of Ecgfrith preserved in the same manuscript.

It has frequently been observed that both pedigrees contain the names of Woden, Baeldaeg, Alusa/Aluca as well as the name of Brand, although the latter is monothematic in Ine's genealogy, whereas it appears twice in the dithematic names of Ingibrand and Waegbrand in Ecgfrith's pedigree. By contrast, the main difference between both records lies in the fact that the name Beornic in

(p. 32); H. Moisl, "Anglo-Saxon Royal Genealogies and Germanic Oral Tradition", *Journal of Medieval History* 7 (1981), 215-48 (pp. 234-35); E. Schröder, "Die nordhumbrische Königsgenealogie", *Nachrichten der Gesellschaft der Wissenschaften zu Göttingen*, Phil.-Hist. Kl. 4 (1938), 127-38; E. Sievers, "Sceaf in den nordischen Genealogien", *Beiträge zur Geschichte der deutschen Sprache und Literatur* 16 (1892), 361-63; K. Sisam, "Anglo-Saxon Royal Genealogies", *Proceedings of the British Academy* 39 (1953), 287-348 (pp. 291, 294-322); C. W. von Sydow, "Scyld Scefing", *Namn och bygd* 12 (1924), 63-95; Taviani-Carozzi "De l'histoire au mythe"; R. Wenskus, "Zum Problem der Ansippung", in his *Ausgewählte Aufsätze zum frühen und preussischen Mittelalter* (Sigmaringen, 1986), pp. 85-95 (pp. 92-93); G. H. Wheeler, "The Genealogy of the Early West Saxon Kings", *English Historical Review* 36 (1921), 161-71.

[41] Dumville, "Anglian Collection", pp. 32, 34a.

[42] There is no recent study of Ine, but see E. A. Freeman, "King Ine", *Proceedings of the Somersetshire Archaeological and Natural History Society* 18 (1872), 1-59; 20 (1874), 1-57.

Ecgfrith's pedigree was replaced by that of Giwis in Ine's, with the positions of the names of Giwis and Beornic in relation to that of Brand being interchanged.

There is little doubt that the parallelisms resulted from the transfer of genealogical traditions from the Beornice of Northumbria onto the Geuissae.[43] For the duplicity of the name pairs Beornic/ Beornice and Giwis/Geuissae fuels the suspicion that Giwis was not an old traditional name among the "Geuissae". This is so because in the Northumbrian case, the name pair is consistent with the political terminology current among the population under the rule of Northumbrian kings; by contrast, such consistency did not exist in the case of the Geuissae. Beornic is recognisable as a derivation from Beornice, the Old English name for the population in the territory of Bernicia which, in turn, is derived from a name of Celtic origin. Thus, although the ancestral name Beornic as contained in the Anglian version of Ida's pedigree can be discerned to be a retrospective genealogical construct and not an element of ancient tradition, it was nevertheless suitable as a construct, because it matched the name of the territory inhabited by the population groups over which the Beornice claimed to hold rights of rule. By contrast, no such consistency existed in the case of the Geuissae. There is no name of a territory with which the name Geuissae can directly or indirectly be linked, and in Bede's day, the name of the "gens Occidentalium Saxonum" was not connectable with an ancestral name listed in the West-Saxon genealogies; for, had such been the case, this ancestral name would have had to be Seax or a variant of this ancestral name, but not the actual Giwis. Moreover, the listing of Giwis in Ine's pedigree conflicts with the abundance of ninth-century and later genealogical records according to which Cerdic, but not Giwis, was the common ancestor of all branches of the West-Saxon *stirps regia*.[44] It therefore is legitimate to postulate

---

[43] For details, see H. Kleinschmidt, "The Geuissae, the West Saxons, the Angles and the English", *Northwest European Language Evolution* 30 (1997), 51-91. Contra Wenskus, "Zum Problem", who argued for a transfer of the genealogical material from Wessex to Northumbria.

[44] Hackenberg, "Die Stammtafeln"; J. M. Bately, ed., *MS A, The Anglo-Saxon Chronicle*, vol. 3 (Cambridge, 1986), *s. a.* 755, p. 37; *s. a.* 784, p. 39.

that the derivation of the ancestral name Giwis is even younger than
that of the ancestral name Beornic, so that the change of the
Northumbrian name pair Beornic/Beornice into Giwis/Geuissae
represents the partial adaptation of a Northumbrian name-giving
custom to different conditions of rule among the Geuissae, and not
vice versa. Thus, at the time of the compilation of Ine's pedigree,
the name pair Giwis/Geuissae can hardly be expected to have
contained generally accepted and widely understood ancient
traditions of the *gens* communicated among groups in Wessex. This
implies the necessity to dissociate the derivation of the ancestral
name Giwis from the wider continental background of Germanic
name-giving customs.

In terms of relative chronology, the following three name-
giving customs can be discerned:
1. the derivation of the name of a *gens* from an ancestral name
belonging to oral tradition of ultimately continental origin; this
custom reflects a practice according to which – at least intentionally
– a *stirps regia* becomes identified as the descent kin group
succeeding to a *heros eponymos*;[45]
2. the orally communicated insular derivation of an ancestral name
as the name of a fictive *heros eponymos*; this custom is derived from
the continental name-giving practice, but replaces the *stirps regia* as
a descent group by a group of population as the inhabitants of a
territory;[46]

---

[45] Insular cases: Wuffa/Wuffingas, Bede, *Historia ecclesiastica*, 2.15, p.
190; Oisc/Osicingas, Bede, 2.5, p. 150; Icel/ Iclingas, Felix, *Life of Saint
Guthlac*, Latin version, chap. 2, p. 74; Old English version, chap. 1, p. 104.
"Iclingas" appears only in the vernacular version.

[46] Insular case: Beornic/Beornice. For the group name, see Bede, *Historia
ecclesiastica*, 3.6, p. 230: "Derorum et Berniciorum prouinciae". And *The Old
English Version of Bede's Ecclesiastical History of the English People*, ed. T.
Miller, Early English Text Society os 95 (London, 1890; repr. 1959), book 3,
chap. 4, p. 166: "mægða Norðhymbra, Dere and Beornice". For the personal
name, see Dumville "Anglian Collection", p. 32.

3. the retrospective literary compilation of rulers' pedigrees on the basis of extant written sources by learned genealogists.[47]

Evidently, the name pair Giwis/Geuissae belongs to the second category, but it represents an imperfect adaptation, because it remains unclear what the structure of the group was for which the name of the *heros eponymos* was created; in other words, the making of the ancestral name Giwis reflects a traditional name-giving practice for a group about whose traditionality doubts can have existed already at the time of the name-giving. Therefore, the name pair Giwis/Geuissae belongs to a late traditional name-giving custom, different from the making of learned genealogy, but not containing ancient traditions of the *gens*. What remains to be done is the fixing of the second name-giving custom in terms of absolute chronology. This requires the clarification of the group structure of the Geuissae in view of their genealogical record.

The Changing Group Structure of the Geuissae and the Absolute Chronology of their Name Change

The changes in the sequence of names in Ecgfrith's and Ine's pedigrees support the assumption that the communication of the genealogies and the traditions contained in them was oral in kind, so that the genealogical constructs did not result from the work of a learned literate genealogist, for a literate genealogist is unlikely to have changed the sequence of names available to him in writing. This assumption can be confirmed by comparison with Ida's genealogy contained in the Parker manuscript of the Old English annals under the year 547. In this entry, Ida's ancestry is listed in the West-Saxon sequence "Brand – Baeldaeg – Woden", corresponding to that in the Parker Chronicle entry for 855, but differing from that in the Anglian tradition. Hence, the annalist responsible for the entry for 547 did not have at his disposal genuine

---

[47] Insular cases in the Anglian collection. See Dumville, "Anglian Collection"; cf. the genealogical entries in the Parker manuscript of the Old English annals *s. a.* 560, 597, 611, 648, 661, 674, 676, 685, 688, 718, 728, 784, 855: Bately, ed., *MS A*, pp. 23, 25, 26-27, 29, 30-32, 34, 35, 37-39, 45-46.

oral traditions from Northumbria, but simply copied the genealogical material contained in the entry for 855 or other ninth-century genealogical sources of West-Saxon provenance.[48] At that time, a learned literate genealogist could only feel justified in proceeding in this way under the condition that, in the ninth century, knowledge of the originally common stock of the genealogies from Wessex and Northumbria was still extant. In other words, the confusion of Ida's and Ine's genealogies in the ninth century was possible because, at that time, memories of a common ultimate ancestor of the ruling kin groups of both areas were still strong enough to enforce the view that what was valid for Ine was also true for Ida, and vice versa.

The change in the medium for the transmission of the genealogical traditions for Wessex and Northumbria in the course of the eighth century thus allows three conclusions, first, that the transfer of genealogical traditions from the *stirps regia* of Northumbria onto the Geuissae prior to the eighth century reflects the existence of actual kin relations among both groups; second, that this transfer must have occurred no later than during Ine's lifetime as well as that the then orally transferred genealogical traditions must have included the name of Woden as the ultimate ancestor; and, third, that, at the time of transfer, the name Giwis must have been considered important enough to stipulate the deletion of the name Beornic. The third conclusion constitutes the problem, because it implies that, at the time of the transfer of the traditions, the name Giwis must have represented the accepted common ancestor of all Geuissae, though not necessarily of the entire West-Saxon *stirps regia* and certainly not that of the "gens Occidentalium Saxonum".

The transfer of the genealogical traditions from Northumbria onto the Geuissae tells something about the shakiness of traditions about the *gens* among the Geuissae, among whom no ancient tradition of Wodanistic ancestry and of continental origins seems to have existed. Hence we are faced with the paradoxical evidence that, if the personal name Giwis had been created after the Northumbrian model of Beornic, this can only have occurred

---

[48] Bately, ed., *MS A, s. a.* 547, p. 22; *s. a.* 855, pp. 45-46.

relatively shortly before the group name Geuissae was dropped according to Bede. In consequence, we are left with the puzzle that one of the two following unlikely conclusions must be true: that it would have been difficult to abandon the group name Geuissae if the ancestral name Giwis was accepted as the genuine focus of a *gens* tradition, or that, conversely, the conservation of the ancestral name Giwis must have militated against the deletion of the group name Geuissae. The solution of the puzzle seems to be possible only under the condition that it can be shown, first, that the name pair Giwis/Geuissae was no longer considered as involving traditions about the *gens* at the time of the abolition of the group name, and, second, that Giwis was not an ancestral name claimed by the entire West-Saxon *stirps regia*, but only by an identifiable part of it. In sum, dating the change in the name pair Giwis/Geuissae requires the specification what kind of group the Geuissae were at what time.

Whether or not the name Geuissae was understood as the focal point of any kind of tradition about the *gens*, can be decided after a discussion of the meaning of the word *geuissae*. But the meaning of the word is difficult to clarify, mainly because it is far from obvious to which language group the word may originally have belonged. Were it to be considered to be of Celtic origin,[49] it would be arguable that the original meaning of its Celtic etymon was no longer understood by the end of the seventh century, so that then the name Geuissae could be abandoned. Yet the Celtic reading of the name is unlikely, because, as late as in the ninth century, Asser rather defiantly maintained that the Welsh still used the word "Geguuis" for the West-Saxon *stirps regia*.[50] Asser's insistence is remarkable in view of the fact that the Alfredian translations of

[49] A. Anscombe, "The Name Cerdic", *Y Cymmrodor* 29 (1919), 151-202 (pp. 160, 165, 188); A. Holder, *Alt-celtischer Sprachschatz* (Leipzig, 1891-96), vol. 1, p. 2017; M. Redin, "Studies in Uncompounded Personal Names in Old English" (unpublished doctoral dissertation, University of Uppsala, 1919), p. 30.

[50] Asser, *Life of King Alfred*, chap. 1, ed. W. H. Stevenson (Oxford, 1904; repr. 1959), p. 2. Later recordings of the name denote an area under the rule of King Alfred; see *Annales Cambriae*, *s. a.* 900, ed. J. W. ab Ithel (London, 1860; repr. 1965), p. 16; "Brut y Tywysogion" in *The Text of the Brut from the Red Book of Hergest*, ed. J. Rhys and J. G. Evans, vol. 2 (Oxford, 1890), p. 260.

Bede's *Historia ecclesiastica* carefully deleted the Geuissae from Bede's Latin text. Therefore it has to be surmised that the Welsh had not followed suit in the abolition of the group name Geuissae, a convention which is common in the use of foreign names, as shown by the parallel use of the Cymric variant of the name Saxons for the English. If the Welsh usage of the name Geuissae displays a convention related to alien names, it is difficult to believe that the word *geuissae* had its roots in a Celtic etymon. By contrast, it is likely that the word was recognisable as being of Germanic origin.

The Germanic reading of the name allows at least two different interpretations: the first going back to Karl Müllenhoff, who opted for a meaning equivalent to Latin *socii* or *foederati*;[51] the second going back to the eighteenth century, when the word *geuissae* was associated with the word *visi* as contained in the *gens* name Visigoths and traced back to the Common Germanic root **uesi* (good).[52] The first interpretation has gained ground since the discovery of fifth-century graves and settlements in the upper Thames valley which might have been occupied by mercenaries with a federate status granted by sub-Roman authorities.[53] In fact, however, yet further archaeological discoveries have rendered this interpretation less likely, precisely because of the increasing number of presumably early Germanic mercenary settlements in sub-Roman Britain. If there were a substantial number of mercenaries in sub-Roman Britain, a group name meaning "mercenaries" would have been incapable of conveying a group's specific identity, so that the

---

[51] K. Müllenhoff, *Beovulf* (Berlin, 1889), p. 63. Cf. C. N. L. Brooke, *The Saxon and Norman Kings* (London, 1963), p. 89; C. Oman, *England Before the Norman Conquest* (London, 1910), p. 228; W. H. Stevenson, "The Beginnings of Wessex", *English Historical Review* 14 (1899), 32-46 (p. 36).

[52] Goffart, "Supposedly 'Frankish' Table of Nations"; H. Rosenfeld, "Ost- und Westgoten", *Die Welt als Geschichte* 17 (1957), 245-58 (pp. 246-47); Stevenson, "Beginnings of Wessex". See also above note 37.

[53] Cf. T. M. Dickinson, *Cuddesdon and Dorchester-on-Thames* (Oxford, 1974); V. I. Evison, "Distribution Maps and England in the First Two Phases", in *Angles, Saxons and Jutes. Essays Presented to J. N. L. Myres*, ed. V. I. Evison (Oxford, 1981), pp. 126-67 (pp. 141-43); H. Hamerow, *Excavations at Mucking*, vol. 2 (London, 1993).

members of such a group would have been induced to employ additional differentiating names; but there is no evidence for such a search among the Geuissae. Thus the second interpretation can hardly be dismissed prima facie. Admittedly, the association of the Geuissae with a name containing Common Germanic *uesi* has encountered the serious objection that there is no reason to believe that the Geuissae can be associated with the Visigoths, for no traces whatsoever of Gothic tradition seem to survive among the Geuissae or any part of the West-Saxon aristocracy, although Gothic traditions appear to be extant elsewhere in the British Isles.[54] Nevertheless, the interpretation remains possible if it goes no further than suggesting that the group name Geuissae is the recorded first part of an originally dithematic group name the second part of which was lost before the time of the earliest written records.[55] This suggestion would lead to the view that, by the end of the seventh century, the group name Geuissae was no longer understood as the bearer of a recognisable tradition, formerly contained in its lost second part, and could then be dropped without additional loss of tradition. On the basis of this assumption, it is possible to date the abolition of the *gens*-name Geuissae to the reign of Ine and, further, to associate the derivation of the ancestral name Giwis with a condition under which the group name Geuissae had already lost its tradition-bearing second part. The conclusion then is that the derivation of the ancestral name Giwis and the abolition of the group name Geuissae were closely related in time and belong to the later seventh century.

This conclusion leads to the problem of the identification of a particular group in whose interest it may have been to abolish the group name Geuissae while creating and preserving the ancestral name Giwis. Put differently, the question is which group can be identified as benefiting from the claim that Giwis was their ancestor while dropping their tradition as the *gens Geuissae*. The

[54] I have argued for the possibility of interconnecting the so-called Jutish *stirps regia* in Kent with Gothic traditions; see my "Bede and the Jutes".

[55] Goffart, "Supposedly 'Frankish' Table of Nations", has suggested that a similar loss of tradition may account for the formation of the name Walagothi in replacement for previous Visigothi among the Franks c. 700.

identification of this group is not difficult once due attention is given to the fact that Giwis is first recorded in Ine's pedigree. Hence the claim that Giwis was the common ancestor of the West-Saxon *stirps regia* cannot be derived from any written source older than Ine's pedigree. Therefore, the evidence appearing from Ine's pedigree is unique and supports the assumption that positing Giwis as an ancestor followed the Bernician precedent and represented a partial claim which was not shared by all members of the West-Saxon *stirps regia*. Specifically, it was ignored by Ine's eighth-century successors who belonged to at least one different branch of the West-Saxon *stirps regia*. In short, it is possible that, during Ine's reign, the name pair Giwis/Geuissae was recognisable as standing in opposition to traditions shared by rival members of the West-Saxon *stirps regia* who could understand that the ancestral name Giwis was only contained in the intentional data claimed by that particular branch whose representative was then reigning as king.

The Ine branch of the West-Saxon *stirps regia* could benefit from the deletion of the group name Geuissae because this name no longer preserved an authoritative tradition of the *gens*. Instead, what was more important and useful for the Ine branch was the genealogical expression of its own partial claim for longer and more powerful traditions of origin than those of any other branch of the West-Saxon *stirps regia*. This condition was fulfilled with the Bernician affiliation through which descent from Wodan was conveyed upon the West-Saxon *stirps regia*. At the time of Ine's father Coenred, the Ine branch stood out among the rival branches of the West-Saxon *stirps regia* in its use of Northumbrian name material[56] and in its marriage affiliation with Northumbrian rulers, whence it is more probable that the descent from Wodan was

---

[56] See J. Gerchow, *Die Gedenküberlieferung der Angelsachsen* (Berlin and New York, 1988), pp. 307, 309-14, 316-20; H. Hahn, "Die Namen der bonifazischen Briefe", *Neues Archiv für ältere deutsche Geschichtskunde* 12 (1887), 111-27 (p. 124); A. Hruschka, *Zur angelsächsischen Namenforschung*, pt 2, Schulprogramm Prag, Staats-Oberrealschule (Prague, 1884), pp. 29-30; R. Müller, *Über die Namen des nordhumbrischen Liber Vitae* (Berlin, 1901), pp. 100, 126; Redin, "Studies in Uncompounded Personal Names", p. 123; Wenskus, "Zum Problem", pp. 93-94.

transferred onto the West-Saxon *stirps regia* towards the end of the seventh century than that the transfer occurred at its beginning.[57]

The Ine branch could also benefit from preserving the ancestral name Giwis as that of Cerdic's grandfather because Giwis could serve as the desired genealogical expression of an ancestry longer than that of Cerdic which the rival branches of the West-Saxon *stirps regia* seem to have adhered to. It would then appear to have been consistent from the point of view of the Ine branch to concoct the ancestral name Giwis in accordance with the Bernician model, even if the group name Geuissae was abandoned. This may have been so, because it could have been understood by Ine's late seventh-century contemporaries that what was claimed for the alleged descendants of Giwis was not a tradition binding the entire West-Saxon *stirps regia*. However, in consequence of the abolition of the group name Geuissae, it can no longer be clarified whether that name had originally been the property of the entire West-Saxon *stirps regia* or just that of the branch represented by Ine at the end of the seventh century.

Conclusion

That indeed the ancestral name Giwis may have been regarded as spurious by Ine's contemporaries is suggested by the fact that, against his practice in other cases, Bede did not explain the group name Geuissae as a derivative from the ancestral name Giwis.[58] Moreover, the evidence suffices to support the conclusion that Bede's equation of the Geuissae with the "gens Occidentalium Saxonum" represents a historically spurious identification of probably a part of the West-Saxon *stirps regia* with the group of population under the rule of that *stirps*. Instead, what Bede reported was a change in the self-esteem of the Ine group of the West-Saxon

[57] Contra Dumville, "Kingship, Genealogies", pp. 80-81, who prefers to connect the transfer with Oswald's presence at the ceremony of a West-Saxon baptism early in the seventh century.

[58] Bede, *Historia ecclesiastica*, 3.7, p. 232.

stirps regia.[59] From the vantage point of the Ine group, the entire *stirps regia* ceased to be regarded as a descent group all of whose members were equally eligible for succession to kingship and was narrowed down to a group of kin-related office-holders as rulers over land and people with an essentially patrilinear succession rule. The Ine group denied the applicability of the concept of *gens* to the West-Saxon *stirps regia* as a descent group and, instead, styled themselves as the rulers of the West Saxons as a *gens*. Through this redefinition of the concept of the *gens*, they paved the way for Bede who was then able to apply the same concept of the *gens* retrospectively, though erroneously, to the Geuissae. Hence, it is difficult to imagine that Bede could have been induced to manipulate the intentional data of the West-Saxon *stirps regia* on any other account than the vested interests of the Ine branch of that *stirps*.[60] Bede's closeness to the Ine group of the West-Saxon *stirps*

[59] See J. Campbell, *Bede's reges and principes*, Jarrow Lecture 1979 (Jarrow, 1979), now conveniently reprinted in *Bede and his World. The Jarrow Lectures 1958-1993*, ed. M. Lapidge (Aldershot, 1994).

[60] In his preface, *Historia ecclesiastica*, p. 4, Bede refers to Bishop Daniel of Winchester as a major source of information on Wessex. Daniel was well connected with the Ine group of the West-Saxon *stirps regia*, for Daniel's *subscriptiones* appear in several charters in the name of Ine. A Winchester literary tradition may be behind the use of the title "rex Gewisorum" in the *intitulatio* of a spurious Malmesbury charter in the name of Cuthred, dated AD 745, and signed by Daniel of Winchester in the year of his death. The title was subsequently reemployed in the *subscriptio* of a suspicious charter in the name of Cynewulf, dated AD 766, and it reappears in the *intitulatio* of the spurious excerpt of a charter in the name of Aethelwulf, dated AD 854. The title can only have been applied to the inhabitants of a territory (as in the cases of the three charters), if their authors retrospectively applied the name Geuissae in Bede's sense to the West-Saxons. See W. de Gray Birch, ed., *Cartularium Saxonicum*, vol. 1 (London, 1885; repr. 1964), vol. 2 (London, 1887; repr. 1964), nos 170, 200, 481; P. H. Sawyer, *Anglo-Saxon Charters* (London, 1968), nos 256, 262, 306. For comments see H. Edwards, *The Charters of the Early West Saxon Kingdom* (Oxford, 1988), pp. 116-19, 259-61; A. Scharer, "Die Intitulationes der angelsächsischen Könige im 7. und 8. Jahrhundert", in *Intitulatio*, vol. 3, ed. H. Wolfram and A. Scharer (Vienna, Cologne and Graz, 1988), pp. 9-73 (pp. 70-73).

regia can be confirmed by the exceptional praise which he awarded
to both Ine and his predecessor Caedwalla for their pilgrimages to
Rome where both died.[61] There is therefore no reason to doubt that
Bede accepted the unilateral claim by the Ine group of the West-
Saxon *stirps regia* that they and only they were the legitimate rulers
of the "gens Occidentalium Saxonum".

Bede's usage of the concept of the *gens* was thus entirely
congruent with the novel conceptualisation of the *gens* as a group of
settlers that was in the process of forming during the seventh and
eighth centuries. Like Raban Maur later, he "took into consideration
migrations, but not changes" of groups.[62] Therefore, Bede could
portray the rulers of the *gentes*, not as the leaders of changing bands
of migrants, but as the rulers over land and people. Although he
could not ignore changes in the territorial substrate of that rule, he
could still insist that the groups of migrants remained structurally
the same. Like other early medieval proponents of the "ethnic"
continuity hypothesis, Bede gave priority to descriptions of the
gentes as durable "ethnic" groups on at least two occasions. In the
first instance, he did so when he reflected on the Germanic
immigration to Britain. On this occasion, he limited the number of
migrating groups essentially to those two *gentes* which could be
conceptualised as groups of settlers within given areas in the
beginning of the eighth century; these two groups were the Angles
and the Saxons. Bede insisted that the immigrants who were to
occupy by far the largest part of Britain belonged to these two
gentes only.[63] Thus, in this instance, Bede insisted that the migrating
gentes were the same as the *gentes* of settlers in his own time. The
second instance occurred when Bede was confronted with the
claims by the Ine group of the West-Saxon *stirps regia*. On this
occasion, he responded by simply ignoring that a descent group of

---

[61] Bede, *Historia ecclesiastica*, 5.7, pp. 470, 472. Caedwalla and Ine
claimed descent from Cerdic through the same line of ancestors.

[62] Fried, "Gens und regnum", p. 79.

[63] I have argued elsewhere that the name of the *Iutae* may be spurious and
may have been concocted by Bede as a comprehensive name for groups which
could not be subsumed under the other two *gentes*. See Kleinschmidt, "Bede and
the Jutes".

rulers was different from a group of settlers in a given area. In both instances, Bede abandoned the conventional varieties of usages of the word *gens* and its *similia* as well as the wider concept of the *gens*. Instead, he gave priority to the novel uniform concept of the *gens* as no more than an "ethnic" group of settlers under the control of a ruler over land and people. In doing so, Bede opened up a widening horizon for the application of this concept of the *gens*, and made thinkable the inclusion into a larger and uniform *gens Anglorum* of all settled Germanic immigrants to Britain after they had been converted to Christianity.[64]

---

[64] See Wormald, "Engla Lond. The Creation of an Allegiance".

La Mutation Familiale:
A Suitable Case for Caution

Pauline Stafford

Change in the structure of the family has been a central plank of the alleged changes of the eleventh century. Though it has been defined primarily, but not exclusively, by French historians for France, it has had a wide impact on interpretations of the period from the ninth to twelfth centuries. Briefly stated, this change is said to have redefined kin structures, narrowing the kingroup, and favouring a restricted male line of direct descent. Specifically this entailed the affirmation of the primacy of male heirs, and of the privileges of the eldest son and the regrouping of the kin, rarely wider than the three-generation family, around the patrimonial land. This latter became its major source of wealth, to be conserved and passed on intact.[1] On the wider canvas the alleged changes involved a shift from cognatic kindreds – i.e. large horizontal groupings of maternal and

I am particularly grateful to Janet Nelson who read an earlier version of this paper and provided much generous and perceptive comment. Much of the research was made possible thanks to my holding of a British Academy Research Readership, 1994-96. This paper was written and delivered in 1995.

[1] For the clearest statements of this see G. Duby, "Lignage, noblesse et chevalerie au XIIe siècle dans le region mâconnaise: une revision", first published in *Annales: Economies, sociétés, civilisations* 27 (1972), 803-23, reprinted in Duby, *La Société Chevaleresque* (Paris, 1979 and 1988), pp. 83-116 and "Structures familiales dans le Moyen Age occidentale", reprinted in Duby, *Mâle Moyen Age* (Paris, 1988), pp. 129-38.

paternal kin – to a vertical agnatic structure, which stressed the direct line of descent from male to male.[2] The whole is described as a reinforcement of lineage, a change in family consciousness. It alleges contrasts between, for example, a tenth century of will and individualism and an eleventh century of family cohesion and solidarity.[3]

These changes have been linked to the changing structure of public power, particularly in Western Francia. The cognatic kindreds are associated in this historiography with the ninth century and the impact of strong royal power and its capacity for patronage; here advancement is sought through whatever relative is closest to the powerful, whether it be mother's or father's kin. The agnatic lineage regrouped around its patrilineal trunk is thus in part a response to the decline of that power and patronage; it is the grouping of the narrower family for protection in a more uncertain world, though it is not entirely clear why a wider cognatic group would not have been more effective in this particular kin function. The changes are an integral part of an alleged shift from a free-floating Reichsaristokratie, with Europe-wide links and horizons, to a deep-rooted provincial nobility.

These changes, it is claimed, had particular implications for women. They involved strategies of inheritance which restricted a widow's dower claims, particularly restricting her right of free disposal of dower to a lifetime usufruct;[4] the growth of the practice of joint property-holding by husband and wife with the husband

---

[2] See especially K. Schmid, "Zur Problematik von Familie, Sippe und Geschlecht, Haus und Dynastie beim mittelalterlichen Adel. Vortragen zum thema: Adel und Herrschaft im Mittelalter", *Zeitschrift für die Geschichte der Oberrheins* 105 (1957), 1-62, reprinted in his collected essays, *Gebetsgedenken und adliges Selbstverständnis im Mittelalter* (Sigmaringen, 1983), pp. 183-239.

[3] M. Aurell i Cardona, "Les avatars de la viduité princière: Ermessende (c. 975-1058), comtesse de Barcelona", in *Veuves et Veuvage dans le Haut Moyen Age*, ed. M. Parisse (Paris, 1993), pp. 201-32 (p. 219).

[4] See additionally on this R. Le Jan-Hennebicque, "Aux origines du douaire médiéval (VIᵉ-Xᵉ siècles)", in *Veuves et Veuvage*, ed. Parisse, pp. 107-22 and M. Aurell i Cardona, "La détérioration du statut de la femme aristocratique en Provence, Xᵉ-XIIIᵉ siècles", *Le Moyen Age* 91 (1985), 5-32.

administering the whole;[5] and a shift from dower to dowry, which involved the exclusion of daughters from inheritance claims.[6] All this was designed to protect the patrimony destined for male heirs. These alleged changes thus involve a deterioration of women's status, especially as landholders. They entail a view of tenth-century and earlier freedoms contrasted with eleventh-century restriction.

This great narrative of family history derives ultimately from the work of such scholars as Tellenbach, Schmid and Bloch. Although many have contributed to its formulation, this central narrative is associated especially with the name of Georges Duby and his seminal work on the Mâconnais.[7] It is certainly not my intention to attack this picture as a whole, or to suggest that it is entirely wrong. It has proved enormously stimulating,[8] and has advanced our knowledge of these critical centuries in many ways. But as a historian of women I want to raise some doubts and cautions, about the problems of generalisation in family history, about the documentary base of such generalisation, and especially about the interpretation of documents concerned with women's landholding from the ninth to eleventh centuries. The study of women's history may potentially act as a transforming and not merely an additional element in medieval studies; the release of that potential depends on an open-minded approach to some existing generalisations.

These alleged changes should first be put into perspective. Momentous as they are, if they occurred, they are not quite as momentous as they appear at first sight. They need not amount to a major mutation in kinship structure from a cognatic to a unilineal

---

[5] J. Verdon, "La femme et la vie familiale en France aux IXe-XIe siècles", *Travaux et mémoires de l'Université de Limoges, Coll. Histoire* 2 (Dec 1977), 63-83.

[6] D. Owen Hughes, "From Brideprice to Dowry in Mediterranean Europe", *Journal of Family History* 3 (1978), 262-96.

[7] For another statement of these changes see R. Fossier, *La terre et les hommes en Picardie*, 2 vols (Louvain, 1968), especially 2:534-46.

[8] Less so in England than elsewhere, though see J. Holt, "Feudal Society and the Family in Early Medieval England: I. The Revolution of 1066", *Transactions of the Royal Historical Society* 5th ser., 32 (1982), 193-212, especially pp. 199-201.

system.[9] As far as we can tell, most early medieval European kinship was more or less cognatic, i.e. kin was claimed for various purposes bilaterally through father's and mother's kin.[10] Such a system can be very complex. It can, and frequently does, have strong biases within it, for example patrilineal or patrilateral.[11] In other words cognatic kinship systems may favour male over female, father's kin over mother's kin. Strongly agnatic elements can exist within them for certain purposes, whilst cognatic principles may be used for others. Thus for example males may be favoured for inheritance, but a wider grouping be called on when recruiting support for feud or other expressions of solidarity.[12] Agnatic principles may be utilised when land is at issue, whereas bilateral kinship may be important for status.[13] Cognatic kinship structures

[9] In what follows I have largely ignored the current doubts of anthropologists about the problems and desirability of producing kinship models, on which see for example A. Kuper, "Lineage Theory: a Critical Retrospect", *Annual Review of Anthropology* 11 (1982), 71-95; M. Verdon, "Descent: an Operational View", *Man* new ser., 15 (1980), 129-50 and A. Shimizu "On the Notion of Kinship", *Man* new ser., 26 (1991), 377-402. Although I have used "cognatic/bilateral" and "agnatic" as handy shorthand for systems, I am aware of the danger of reifying such systems and of trying "to enclose societies within too rigid a series of classifications" and of "overschematic presentation of filiation systems", see M. Segalen, *Historical Anthropology of the Family* (Cambridge, 1986), p. 55.

[10] B. Philpott, *Kindred and Clan in the Middle Ages and After: A Study in the Sociology of the Teutonic Races* (Cambridge, 1913) long ago expressed her doubts about the old consensus that early Germanic kinship was unilineal; her insights have been followed up and strengthened by A. C. Murray, *Germanic Kinship Structure: Studies in Law and Society in Antiquity and the Early Middle Ages* (Toronto, 1983).

[11] See for example Murray, *Germanic Kinship Structure*; R. Fox, *Kinship and Marriage* (London, 1967); J. D. Freedman, "On the Concept of the Kindred", *Journal of the Royal Anthropological Institute* 91 (1961), 192-220; and cf. for example, M. Fortes, *Kinship and the Social Order* (London, 1969), p. 130.

[12] Murray, *Germanic Kinship Structure*, p. 36; Fox, *Kinship and Marriage*, p. 167.

[13] See T. M. Charles-Edwards, *Early Irish and Welsh Kinship* (Oxford, 1993), p. 87. This is perhaps the most sophisticated discussion of kinship in

can contain and express different family strategies, even different inheritance strategies. They can accommodate for instance the preference for male heirs and preference by age, coupled with dowry and postponed inheritance of daughters. Recognised features of the eleventh century and later are perfectly consistent, in fact it has even been suggested are "hallmarks" of, bilateral cognatic systems.[14] Sons, and daughters, are the immediate heirs of their mother; and daughters inherit alongside, though usually after brothers – in other words daughters count in the same category of kin as sons, they are postponed by sons, but not by all male heirs.[15]

So we already have a cognatic system capable of expressing agnatic bias before the tenth century, and features, even of inheritance, consistent with cognatic kinship claims survive even into the twelfth century. Many historians have recognised this coexistence.[16] Constance Bouchard, Karl Leyser, Stephen White and

early medieval societies, and chapter 1 on Ireland is of particular importance as an analysis of coexisting agnatic and bilateral principles of kinship.

[14] See Murray's general discussion of Frankish inheritance in *Germanic Kinship Structure* and p. 219 for such "hallmarks". Fox, *Kinship and Marriage*, p. 167 sees the essence of a kindred as the duties and claims of all cognates up to a certain degree; Glanvill's recognition in mid-twelfth-century England of the various degrees of kin who had claims in default of direct heirs recalls such a structure, see G. D. G. Hall, ed., *The Treatise on the Laws and Customs of the Realm of England commonly called Glanvill* (London, 1965; repr. Oxford, 1993), pp. 75 and 79.

[15] Duby provides examples of both practices from the late eleventh-century Mâconnais: for daughters inheriting instead of cousins and uncles see A. Bernard and A. Bruel, eds, *Recueil des chartes de l'abbaye de Cluny*, 6 vols (Paris, 1876-1903) [hereafter C], nos 3874, 3821, 3654 and discussion in G. Duby, *The Knight, the Lady and the Priest*, trans. B. Bray (London, 1984), p. 103; for the continued claims of daughters alongside their brothers see the case he discusses on p. 104, C 3744. J. Hudson, *Land, Law and Lordship in Anglo-Norman England* (Oxford, 1994), p. 111, notes a case from the 1160s in England which makes it clear that daughters were preferred to nephews in inheritance, though here from the father.

[16] K. Leyser, "The German Aristocracy from the Ninth to the Early Twelfth Century: a Historical and Cultural Sketch", *Past and Present* 41 (1968), 25-53, reprinted in his *Medieval Germany and its Neighbours* (London, 1982), pp. 161-89 (p. 170), criticises the Schmid approach to *Libri memoriales*. D.

Dominique Barthélemy, for example, have all warned that people mobilise different family links in different situations. "Rising men", from the ninth to twelfth century, in pursuit of their ambitions, may reach out to wider family groupings through marriage ties and contact with remote but powerful kin; but when such men seek to hand on the inheritance they have thus acquired, they turn to their own children, especially their sons; they retrench to a narrow patrilineal view of the family.[17] In ceremonies of remembrance and group solidarity, like securing prayers for the dead, people may recognise a wide group of kin; but a much narrower one for purposes of inheritance.

The corollary of all this is that we must be very clear that we are seeing enough certain and one-way change to have a social mutation in the eleventh century: that we are not merely witnessing the expression of agnatic bias by particular families in particular circumstances and contexts, nor just the revelation of agnatic bias more clearly in fuller documentation. We must not be confusing the revelation of elements which had long coexisted for real change over time.[18]

This growing wariness of many historians has been rooted in caution about the evidence we have; in awareness of the danger of confusing changes in the nature and scale of the evidence for social change. In particular the impact of new foundations and refoundations of monasteries has emerged as significant for the

---

Barthélemy, "Kinship", in *A History of Private Life vol. 2, Revelations of the Medieval World*, ed. G. Duby, trans. A. Goldhammer (Cambridge, Mass. and London, 1988), pp. 85-155 and S. D. White, *Custom, Kinship and Gifts to Saints: the Laudatio Parentum in Western France, 1050-1150* (Chapel Hill and London, 1988) have recently made similar points in relation to the *laudatio parentum*, that is the group of relatives who consented to or authorised grants of land. As Barthélemy, "Kinship", p. 92 puts it, "these ambiguous documents should not be confused with the customs associated with inheritance". White's book is an essential reassessment of the whole significance of *laudatio*.

[17] See C. Bouchard, "Family Structure and Family Consciousness among the Aristocracy in the Ninth to Eleventh Century", *Francia* 14 (1986), 639-58.

[18] See D. Barthélemy, *La Société dans le comté de Vendôme de l'an mil au XIVe siècle* (Paris, 1993), pp. 514, 545-46 and note the importance of the first section entitled "La Mutation Documentaire".

preservation of records and for the nature of the records produced. They and their records may account for much of what has been seen as an eleventh-century mutation. Duby himself worried whether the changes he saw were shifts in documentation;[19] those worries have grown as recent work has raised many questions about the record sources of these early centuries in general and of the tenth and eleventh centuries in particular. Apparently neutral, passive and transparent record sources have been revealed as partial, *ex parte* statements, often active participants in the very processes we might feel they are merely recording.[20] At the most straightforward level we must allow for changes in the quantity of evidence. The gaps in the pre-1000 evidence mean that we can often go no further than saying two people were kin; by the eleventh century it is much easier to sort out precise family relations. That change in the evidence can too easily look like a shift from an amorphous cognatic kin to a clearly defined agnatic one.[21] With increased quantity may come changes in the nature of evidence. Barthélemy has seen a "documentary mutation" in eleventh-century Vendôme, a new documentation which reveals the social context of grants and with it pre-existing family and other social structures; here both the increase in quantity and the change in nature of the documentation are clearly linked to stages in the foundation or refoundation of the

[19] See G. Duby, *The Knight, the Lady*, p. 93 and cf. Barthélemy, *Vendôme*, p. 514.

[20] Records of disputes, charters, even surveys like the English Domesday Book itself have come to be seen in a new light as a result. It is invidious to single out individuals in what has been a widespread phenomenon, but for discussion particularly relevant to this theme see for example White, *Custom, Kinship* on *laudatio parentum*; Nicholas Brooks' seminal work on Canterbury in the ninth century, *The Early History of the Church of Canterbury* (Leicester, 1984), pp. 175-206; the collection *The Settlement of Disputes in Early Medieval Europe*, ed. W. Davies and P. Fouracre (Cambridge, 1986); and Barthélemy, *Vendôme*. S. Reynolds, *Fiefs and Vassals* (Oxford, 1994) is a significant fruit of the sort of rethink it provokes. I have discussed the specific problems of using Domesday as a source for women in "Women in Domesday", *Medieval Women in Southern England*, ed. K. Bate and others, Reading Medieval Studies 15 (Reading, 1989), pp. 75-94.

[21] See Bouchard, "Family Structure", p. 649.

local abbeys of Marmoutier and La Trinité, Vendôme. At the most complex level, an active process of remembering, forgetting, reshaping the recorded memory of families may be involved. Patrick Geary has issued a powerful warning about contrasting French and German family consciousness c. 1000 AD. For "French" we should really read "monastic"; for "monastic", "reformed"; and for "reformed" "aspiring to autonomy".[22] The documents which such houses have left us do not provide so much a genealogy of families as of patrons, really of land given to monasteries. It is, moreover, a genealogy edited in the process of disputes, tailored to the claims of monastic houses, preserved by communities which survived. It is certainly no simple guide to the structure of families, or their views of themselves.

The detailed implications of these approaches for the alleged "family mutation" have already become clear in the question of consenting relatives, i.e. the so-called *laudatio parentum*, the record of the consents to a grant of land by a group of relatives. Duby saw the emergence of this consenting group of relatives in the charters as a sign of their grouping around the ancestral patrimony, even of the regrouping of a narrow family as a protection in time of general trouble. But these consents are far from simple maps of family structure. They may give a picture of kin who matter for some purpose, in this case claims on land. But only those whose claims matter at any one point in time; they are not a picture of all inheritance claims let alone practices. They provide at best a snapshot of a particular family at a particular point, of the power balance within the family at that point, for example who is adult and who a minor, which daughter is married and living away and which close. And that power balance will look different depending on when in the family lifecycle the picture is taken.[23]

---

[22] See P. Geary, *Phantoms of Remembrance* (Princeton, 1995), chapter 2.

[23] It may tell us some general things: for example that daughters have claims but little clout: "right with little force", whilst bastards have "force with less right". But those general points are themselves undermined by specific circumstances, such as whether a daughter is married or unmarried, where she is living, whether a bastard son has a powerful patron and so on: Barthélemy, *Vendôme*, pp. 536 and 539. Consents of brothers together may for example tell

And the snapshot is not a picture in the family album. Who is holding and pointing the camera is critically important. That was the ecclesiastical beneficiary; its role in deciding who was included and who excluded was critical. The pressure to record consents intensified, though it did not begin, in the ninth century[24] – and either in the ninth century, or earlier or later the pressure to record came from the receiving churches.[25] Beneficiaries continued to be the major determiners of the pattern of consents in, for example, twelfth-century England.[26] That pressure increased as such churches became "more numerous, richer and better organized",[27] which exactly describes the nature of the sort of communities central to Geary and Barthélemy's arguments. The recording of consents may reflect scribal practice and the influence of existing documentary models. Although St Gall and Fulda record consents in eighth-

us that brothers were living close together, but it will not tell us whether geographically remoter sisters' claims are extinguished, nor whether close residence is a new or long-standing phenomenon.

[24] There are eighth-century records of consents from St Gall, for example H. Wartmann, ed., *Urkundenbuch der Abtei Sanct Gallen*, vol. 1 (Zurich 1863, repr. Frankfurt, 1981), no. 49, AD 764, 4 brothers; no. 52, AD 769, 4 brothers and a father; no. 81, AD 776, Count Agilulf and a family group of brothers, sons and nephews etc. See also evidence from Fulda, though many charters here record wives' consents only, but see for example E. E. Stengel, ed., *Urkundenbuch des Klosters Fulda*, vol. 1 (Marburg, 1958), no. 89, AD 779, a sister; no. 82, AD 777, 2 sisters; no. 49, AD 754x68, a son etc. It is probable that many of the unidentified *signa* in these eighth-century charters are of relatives and this can be demonstrated from two gifts of Count Laidrat to Fulda, one witnessed by his sister Irminswind, no. 40, the other, no. 41, with the *signum* of a unidentified Irminswinde, almost certainly the same person.

[25] Reynolds, *Fiefs and Vassals*, p. 105 citing J. D. Laplanche, *La Réserve coutumière dans l'ancien droit français* (Paris, 1925), pp. 54-68. The provisions of the 818-19 capitulary acknowledged the right of free kin who had not been consulted about an alienation of land to take it back, thus providing an extra incentive to record such consents.

[26] J. Hudson, *Land, Law and Lordship*, p. 190. Here heirs' consents occur especially in the charters drafted by beneficiaries recording grants made by lesser nobles, with other critical factors being the concentration of the family's lands in the area and a close link between the family and the church.

[27] Reynolds, *Fiefs and Vassals*, pp. 148-49.

century charters, neither shows a sudden flowering. In both cases
scribes may be adhering to older formulae.[28] The documentary
archives of churches like Cluny have been critical sources for the
alleged family changes. In the case of family consents, their
appearance in such sources may tell us as much about the anxieties
of a church like Cluny, about their development over time, about the
political context in which such a church operated, about local scribal
practice, as about the families they seem to record. Clearly Cluny's
records will have some relationship to the family realities of the
time, but teasing this out will not be straightforward.

The impact of a church, especially the sort of rich well-
organised communities of Geary's, Barthélemy's and Reynolds'
arguments, potentially affects not only documentation but also
inheritance itself. It may not merely reveal an existing situation, but
possibly also change it, though not necessarily in a long-term,
irreversible way, and not in the same way for all the individuals and
families involved. Duby's seminal study of the Mâconnais was
based on an area experiencing such impact: the foundation and
growth of the great abbey of Cluny. Cluny was a Father Christmas
in reverse, gobbling up gifts in the tenth-century Mâconnais and in
Burgundy more widely. If giving is a vital context in which claims
on land are defined,[29] then Cluny's growth must have had an effect
on the local definition of land claims. The tenth-century Mâconnais
apparently shows a wider group of people claiming to give and
alienate land than the eleventh; is this a long-standing situation, or
the result of the arrival of Cluny itself? Cluny required the consent
of a group of possible claimants; surely that consent increased the
awareness in those claimants of their claims.[30] Members of families
entered Cluny, taking land with them; the claims of all brothers to

---

[28] And for what it is worth, given all these caveats, the consenting groups
of relatives in eighth-century charters from Fulda and St Gall are as restricted as
those in later tenth- and eleventh-century charters which are alleged to show the
narrowing family of the eleventh-century mutation.

[29] For a nuanced discussion of this see J. C. Holt, "Notions of Patrimony",
Transactions of the Royal Historical Society 5th ser., 32 (1983), 193-220.

[30] Compare the possibility that incest restrictions led to more family
awareness, see Duby, *The Knight, the Lady*, p. 173.

inherit and alienate land may not always have been as strong as when brothers entered Cluny and took their claims with them.

Cluny's foundation produced a wealth of documentation. The horizon of that documentation was the late ninth century, a generation or so before the foundation of the abbey. It is thus difficult to map inheritance or other structures before the abbey's arrival, or to tell whether any tenth- to eleventh-century changes are part of a recurring cycle or a once and for all momentous event. As various people gave or attempted to give to Cluny, its presence affected the whole climate of dispute and worries about inheritance in which inheritance practice is constantly defined and redefined.[31] In this sense it may be a factor for closer definition of inheritance customs, not merely revealing but also sharpening aspects of older practice – and maybe some aspects more than others.[32] Indeed it may be the tenth century which is odd, or more generally any period after the arrival of a land-hungry, highly organised, potentially autonomous and ultimately successful[33] great church in an area, and

[31] A comparable complex relationship between Cluny and the family structure and inheritance practices of local families at a rather later date is suggested by J. Wollasch, "Parenté noble et monachisme reformateur: observations sur les 'conversions' à la vie monastique aux XIe et XIIe siècles", *Revue Historique* 264 (1980), 3-24, where monastic conversions are seen as a way of retaining family land, continuing, via the child, administration of land given away.

[32] See B. H. Rosenwein, *To be the Neighbour of St Peter. The Social Meaning of Cluny's Property, 909-1049* (Ithaca, NY and London, 1989), for much thought on Cluny's arrival and impact, though not specifically concerned with the questions of family structure and women's landholding with which I am dealing.

[33] These qualifications are necessary since clearly donations to churches were a more or less constant feature of the early Middle Ages. Giving to any church is likely to have some impact on inheritance and other land-structures, as witness the probable changes after the arrival of Christianity in England and Germany for example – the latter well charted by K. Leyser in *Rule and Conflict in an Early Medieval Society, Ottonian Saxony* (London, 1979). But as Geary, *Phantoms of Remembrance*, has suggested concerning *memoria* and com-memoration of the dead, the nature of the church, and its relationship to lay donors and aspirations to and potential for autonomy may be critical. I am

the eleventh century which represents a return to more normal inheritance patterns.[34] Perhaps we should allow for an even more complex picture, one in which different individuals and families responded to Cluny or a similar church in different ways – ways which met the varied individual needs and desires of family inheritance.[35] Cluny and its documentation may thus reveal existing inheritance strategies, catalyse and affect them, and become a factor to be utilised in them.

And this impact would have extended to women – to the claims they could exercise, and to the definitions of those claims. In fact it may have extended in particular to women because of the peculiar position of their landholding. I would like to suggest that it may be women's landholding which shows particularly clearly the need to recognise the difficulties of interpreting the sources, the problems of generalising the results, and the danger in assuming any unilineal, once and for all change in inheritance.

It must be stressed at the outset that women had claims on land. They were real but debatable, especially likely to lead to problems where kinship contained a mix of cognatic and agnatic elements. Inheritance was governed by strong, and often

grateful to Matthew Innes whose questions prompted a clarification of my ideas on this issue.

[34] See C. Wickham, *The Mountain and the City, the Tuscan Appennines in the Early Middle Ages* (Oxford, 1988) for discussion of the arrival of churches and patterns of giving and the end of such patterns as the abbey becomes itself a new force in the area, see for example pp. 196, 214-15, 266-67; "alienations to the Church would normally stop before the social patterns that produced them were terminally undermined", p. 267. If the impact on families was varied, and interests within them differed between individuals, the recognition of that point in the case of family inheritance structures may have been difficult, and the cycles of giving not necessarily identical to those proposed by Wickham.

[35] The situation Barthélemy saw revealed in the Vendôme, a variety of claims on land which he termed "anarchie lignagère", *Vendôme*, pp. 533-34, might be compared. This situation again suggests the potential for the opening up of claims the arrival of a religious community might have.

contradictory norms.[36] Both the widow and the direct heir, for example, had strong claims on family land; claims arguable from the ninth to the twelfth century and probably beyond.[37] Those two norms are found in the earliest laws and formulae,[38] and they conflict. Dower is a prime example.[39] Normally male heirs postponed females; but dower postponed male heirs; and if a widow remarried it might be lost altogether to a second husband and his male heirs. The claims of widows and heirs were thus likely to cause dispute; the outcome of that dispute depends on individual family circumstances, external powers and support – all of which may change over the lifecycle of individuals.

Women's landholding is contested and contestable. It is over-represented in disputes;[40] disputes about women's land are, indeed,

---

[36] See, for example White, *Custom, Kinship*, pp. 70-78, on this whole issue of conflicting norms.

[37] Both are abundantly clear from the various "barbarian law codes"; I am not qualified to say whether they continue to be important after the early twelfth century, but recurring attempts to provide for widows as well as heirs through dower and later jointures might suggest that they were. On these see for example J. S. Loengard, "'Of the Gift of her Husband', English Dower and its Consequences in the Year 1200", in *Women of the Medieval World*, ed. J. Kirshner and S. Wemple (Oxford, 1985), pp. 215-55, on dower in the twelfth century and R. Archer, "Rich Old Ladies, the Problem of Late Medieval Dowagers", in *Property and Politics, Essays in Later Medieval English History*, ed. T. Pollard (Gloucester, 1984), pp. 15-35.

[38] Le Jan-Hennebicque, "Aux origines du douaire", pp. 115-17.

[39] Le Jan-Hennebicque makes the important point that it is the use of land as opposed to movables which enhances the problems surrounding dower, cf. J. Nelson, "The Wary Widow", in *Property and Power in the Early Middle Ages*, ed. W. Davies and P. Fouracre (Cambridge, 1995), pp. 82-113 (p. 86).

[40] See J. Nelson, "Commentary on the Papers of J. Verdon, S. F. Wemple and M. Parisse", in *Frauen in Spätantike und Frühmittelalter*, ed. W. Affeldt (Sigmaringen, 1990), pp. 325-32 (p. 331) and my comments on Domesday Book in "Women in Domesday". John Hudson not only notes the relationship of twelfth-century English consents to particular types of document, but also signals their link with certain types of transaction. A large proportion of women's grants record consent; see Hudson, *Land, Law and Lordship*, p. 197. See Nelson, "Wary Widow", for general discussion of the precariousness of widows' lands.

systemic to this type of kinship structure. And disputes provided an entree for outside forces into the realm of family, for kings, lords, powerful religious institutions. External forces thus become an element in the defence of claims, but also in their definition; their aid can determine what is a viable claim. And the more disputable the case the more the outcome is likely to reflect power relations, internal and external to the family concerned.[41] Women's land thus has a critical place in a nexus of individual family and external political circumstances. Its interpretation is particularly fraught and generalisation based on superficial interpretations of it particularly dangerous.

Any arguments about women's land must always be read in full context, and their interpretation very carefully weighed. Take for example the career of Ermessende of Barcelona, which has been seen as charting the move from tenth-century women's freedoms to eleventh-century lineage solidarity. A critical text for this is her recognition of the superior claims of her grandson in 1056; she renounces her claims on land and recognises his superior descent from father and grandfather and his blood lineage.[42] But this statement is in a document drawn up for the grandson. Moreover, it comes at the end of her long career, when her great moment of power is past. It is not surprising if in 1056 Ermessende's grandson's best argument is recognised; at other stages her best arguments for the dower rights of a widow might have been uppermost.[43] For whom was the document drawn up, at what point in the lifecycle of a woman, or of a marriage: these are critical

[41] As Hudson puts it "politics rather than custom" will determine such disputes, *Land, Law and Lordship*, pp. 114-15.

[42] "Ego predicta Ermessendis, quia scio, recognosco et confiteor quoniam predicte res fuerunt avi tui Raimundi predicti, et propinquitate paterna et aviala ac linea consanguineali ... magis debentur tibi ... eiusdem Raimundi nepoti quam mihi", quoted by Aurell i Cardona, "Les avatars", p. 219. "I the aforesaid Ermessende know, recognise and confess that the aforesaid things belonged to your grandfather the aforesaid Raimund and by paternal, grandpaternal and consanguineous descent ... belong rather to you ... grandson of Raimund than to me".

[43] We must, however, be equally wary about statements that women are heirs; they too may be strategic, and the strategy someone else's.

questions. Ermessende's career is arguably a revelation of the coexistence of the claims of widow and heir, and their shifting strength over an individual lifecycle, not of a shift from the tenth to eleventh centuries.

The 1056 document concerning Ermessende is a specific instance of the difficulty of interpretation, and the ensuing hazards of arguing from such interpretation to wider change. Cluny presents us with a whole class of documents which both generally and specifically are difficult to interpret. They are the famous series of forty-odd dower documents which survive almost uniquely in Cluny's archives.[44] They have been used to present two central arguments concerning women and the proof of family mutation: particularly the alleged shift from women's free disposal of dower in the tenth century to usufruct in the eleventh, but also the increasing use of marginal as opposed to central patrimonial land as dower. Both are seen as indications of the decline of women's status as landholders which is central to the alleged agnatic shifts of the turn of the millennium. Barthélemy has recently sounded a note of caution concerning this alleged shift from "femme libre" to the hedged and limited women of the late eleventh century, seeing it as

---

[44] See A. Lemaire, "Les origines de la communauté de biens entre époux dans le droit coutumier français", *Revue historique de droit français et étranger*, ser. 4, 7 (1928), 584-643 at pp. 585, 598 on the problems of dower documentation before the thirteenth century and p. 590 on "la belle et malheureusement unique serie de dotalicia de Cluny"; L. Morelle, "Mariage et diplomatique: autour de cinq chartes de douaire dans le Laonnois-Soissonais, 1163-81", *Bibliothèque de l'Ecole des Chartes*, 146 (1988), 225-84 (p. 225) calls the Cluny documents "a unique fact", "a precious exception"; cf. D. Barthélemy, *Vendôme*, p. 544 for the rare fact of their preservation. L. Musset, "Actes Inédits du XIe siècle, III, Les plus anciennes chartes Normandes de l'abbaye de Bourgueil", *Bulletin de la société des Antiquaires de Normandie* 54 (1959, for 1957-58), 15-54 (p. 35) stresses how far our view of the transition from full property to usufruct is dependent on the Cluny charters and claims that the series of dower documents for the Norman countesses are our only evidence of this type for NW France in the tenth and eleventh centuries. His use of them to set a pattern is another indication of how important these Cluny charters have been in the history of dower in France, even before their absorption into the argument about family mutation.

rather a function of the fuller, more narrative nature of the later documentation.[45] The Cluny-preserved dower charters may look at first sight more trustworthy; they remain more formulaic throughout. But their use calls for considerable caution.

The first problem is the pattern of these documents. They more or less dry up after 1008. They will not take us very far into the eleventh century.[46] The last five do all speak of usufruct; but in fact the series as a whole shows no simple shift from free disposal to usufruct, and shows signs of an increasing variety of formulation from the mid-tenth century onwards.[47] The Cluny documentation

---

[45] Barthélemy, *Vendôme*, pp. 546-52. The early charters are formulaic, the later narrative and circumstantial. Increasing problems surrounding the alienation of family lands, or rather the impact of increased giving on claims, counterclaims and dispute and thus on the charter record, presumably lie behind these changes. Barthélemy's point is important as far as the Vendôme is concerned, and perhaps other areas with similar documentary developments.

[46] After c. 1035 there seems to have been a general feeling, for whatever reason, that the abbey did not need to keep the various charters related to the history of land which it acquired. See Lemaire, "Les origines de la communauté de biens", p. 595 and cf. Duby, *The Knight, the Lady*, p. 99. This more or less coincides with a critical shift in Cluny's organisation of its *memoria*, viz. the making of the earliest cartularies at Cluny, on which see D. Iogna Prat, "La geste des origines dans la historiographie clunisienne des xie-xiie siècles", *Revue Bénédictine* 102 (1992), 135-91, and "La confection des cartulaires et l'historiographie à Cluny", in *Les Cartulaires*, ed. O. Guyotjeannin, L. Morelle and M. Parisse, Mémoires et documents de l'Ecole des Chartes 39 (Paris, 1993), pp. 27-44.

[47] The run of Cluny dotalicia documents ends 1005x1008, with only one later example, C 2875, which is after 1031; the impression of change in the eleventh century thus cannot be taken very far in the documents. All the last five specify usufruct, C 2618 (AD 1005), C 2628 and 2633 (AD 1006), C 2659 (AD 1008) and C 2875. There are two examples of formulae specifying usufruct from 939 AD (C 496) and 940 AD (C 516); all the others are post 975: C 1412 and C 1413, virtually identical and for the same couple, AD 975; C 857 wrongly dated in the Cluny charters to 953, really 989; C 1390, AD 974 and C 858, AD 989. A number, however are unclear on whether they give free disposal or not, see nos C 439, 705, 1161, 1242, 1331, 1415, 1427, 1777, all dated 935 onwards. The usufruct charters show a range of formulations allowing for different reversions and two of the latest alleged "libera potestas" documents, C 1425 (AD 976) and

could indicate an increasing, but always varied attempt to express and be precise about a range of marital bargains, rather than a simple one way decisive shift.

The second problem is the lack of full context for almost any of these documents. Dower is a product of a bargain struck by two families, involving an evaluation of the match on both sides, and consideration of what constitutes a "good dower".[48] The relative standing of the families, the age and standing of the two individuals within them, the value of different types of property, and its potential future value, all enter in. Is the bride an heiress; is the groom oldest or youngest son; where are the bride's family lands located in relation to potential dower; what is the likely value of an asset in twenty years time? Even once initially decided on, dower may then be added to or changed in the course of a marriage;[49] it is by no means clear that these dower documents were all made at the beginning of marriage. Changing relations between husband and wife can thus affect them. And finally dower is defended, secured or lost in the circumstances of each specific widowhood. Thus dower is agreed, amended, secured and lost in specific individual and political circumstances.

C 2265 (AD 995), combine the standard formulae of earlier more formulaic ones into a more complex formulation. The latter has an elaborate proem, an exceptionally long list of *signa*, nineteen instead of the more usual five or seven, including Count Otto William, his wife Countess Ermentrude and his son Guy. This was an important match of Uldric, the lord of Bâgé in Bresse.

[48] See Morelle, "Mariage et diplomatique", esp. pp. 242-46.

[49] It is worth perhaps pointing out here that we do not always know at what point the Cluny dower documents were drawn up. There is an apparently simple distinction between those addressed to "uxor" and those to "sponsa" to warn us that some were made after marriage; there is no simple correlation between these and the distinction between disposal or usufruct clauses. But the terminology may not be an entirely accurate guide to the stage in a match at which a particular document was drawn up; see for example C 2628 which appears to be a dower document from AD 1006 between a groom and sponsa, but in fact the couple had been acquiring lands together since 988 AD, see A. Lemaire, "Les origines de la communauté de biens", p. 615. The extent to which *sponsalicia* documents can be misleading about the arrangements between a couple at every stage of their married life is highlighted by Lemaire, pp. 612-14.

This is clearest at the top of society, but must have applied in varying ways at all levels. The politically important dowry of Richard II of Normandy's sister Mathilda was much disputed; so much so that Musset was led to wonder whether different conceptions of marital gifts existed in the eleventh century and were employed as each side saw their own advantage,[50] precisely the sort of conflicting and coexisting norms which I would argue continued to complicate women's landholding throughout the eleventh century. Gerberga, wife first of Gilbert of Lotharingia then of Louis IV, kept her dower of her first marriage into her second; the political clout of husband and family were critical.[51] She lost it to her first husband's nephew after Louis IV's death, but quickly recovered it with her brother Bruno's backing. In 965 she gave part of it to St Peter's Ghent, a sort of restoration of church lands she had been holding; and in 968 as death approached, she gave the abbey of Meerssen, also part of her dower, to St Remi, Rheims. Gerberga's case clarifies the disputability of dower, the importance of external political circumstances at every stage of its securing and defence, as well, incidentally, as the importance of church land in initial dower arrangements. Where this context is unavailable, and this is usually the case for most dower arrangements of lesser people in the early centuries, we are not therefore justified in assuming it was unimportant. Lack of detailed knowledge makes generalisation more not less dangerous. Which type of dower was chosen, whether, for example, dower was near the edges or centre of a patrimony, will reflect the context, of which the protection of patrimony is at best only one part.[52] That context may also affect the formulae chosen.

The interpretation of the formulae of the dower documents is a critical question. Many of the tenth-century ones appear to give "libera potestas", the right to give, sell or exchange. Such formulae are a basis for the idea of earlier freedoms lost in the eleventh-

[50] Musset, "Actes Inédits", p. 36.

[51] The case is discussed by Le Jan-Hennebicque, "Aux origines du douaire", p. 120, although I think it indicates wider issues than the room for manoeuvre of high born widows which is the context in which she cites it.

[52] Musset, "Actes Inedits", has made this very clear for the various dowers of the tenth- and early eleventh-century duchesses of Normandy.

century mutation. These formulae are in fact based on Merovingian and Carolingian *libelli dotis* formulae, which grew up against Roman ideas of full possession and rights to give, sell and exchange.[53] It is at least debatable how far such archaic formulae can be taken at face value when used in the tenth and eleventh century. Barthélemy has warned about interpreting such archaic formulae when used in tenth- and eleventh-century enfranchisement documents.[54] Gerd Althoff has recently shown that formulae identical to those found in the Cluny series also occur in dower grants to Ottonian queens. Here they certainly did not mean that these women had rights to give, sell or exchange.[55] Like the Cluny ones these Ottonian charters allegedly give free disposition. Yet in Germany by the tenth century that wording masked real restrictions, in fact precisely the reversions and usufruct which the other type of Cluny dower document imposes.[56]

If these already old formulae should not always be taken at face value when we find them in tenth-century dower documents, this raises a very real question as to how much freedom women ever had in disposing of dower at any date before the eleventh century. When they do so the circumstances are often special and disposal is

[53] See for example full discussion in C. Laurenson-Rosaz, "Douaire et *sponsalicium*", in *Veuves et Veuvage*, ed. Parisse, pp. 99-105 and Le Jan-Hennebicque, "Aux origines du douaire", esp. p. 116.

[54] Barthélemy, *Vendôme*, pp. 40-44.

[55] G. Althoff, "Probleme um die dos der Koniginnen im 10. und 11. Jahrhundert", in *Veuves et Veuvage*, ed. Parisse, pp. 123-33, and cf. M. Uhlirz, "Die rechtliche Stellung der Kaiserinwitwe Adelheid im deutschen und italischen Reich", *Zeitschrift der Savigny-Stiftung für Rechtsgeschichte*, Germanistische Abteilung 74 (1957), 85-97 whose ideas he has developed.

[56] See Althoff, "Probleme um die dos", p. 131. These were in his view mere formulae with no enduring legal reality: "a considerable gap yawned between norm and reality". He demonstrates that the lands in question constantly returned to the royal estates, and that women who did try to alienate, like Adelaide, came up against enormous difficulties. The restrictions on alienation similarly date back to earlier laws and formulae, see Le Jan-Hennebicque, "Aux origines du douaire", p. 117.

almost always to a church or a great lord.[57] The fact that women often alienate to churches raises issues about the impact of churches on women's property.[58] It takes us back to Cluny.

[57] Adelaide, whom Althoff discusses, is a very interesting case. Althoff points out that she tries to alienate her dower, with little success in Germany, and in Italy only succeeds by having charters drafted in her young grandson's name, i.e. she herself does not dispose. But in fact she has disposed of her dower – and the circumstances are of great interest. It is during the minority of her grandson, when her own power was relatively greater. Moreover the land was in Italy, and the dower of her first marriage, over which her second husband's family had less claim, and concerning which Italian local courts and pressure might be more sympathetic, especially since she was alienating it to Italian churches. The latter fact is a final point of note. Alienation of disputed land like this to churches is common. For disposal to churches see also the cases cited by Aurell i Cardona, "La détérioration", pp. 5-32, cases of free disposal which seem always to be to churches, for example that cited on p. 5, which is thus not a good comparison with the issue of wardship with which it is there contrasted. Compare the "Renaissance" of widows' and women's rights which she claims for the late twelfth century which again coincides with a spate of new foundations of churches, "La détérioration", pp. 19-22. From tenth- and eleventh-century Normandy see Musset, "Actes Inédits", pp. 27-36, where alienations by duchesses seem all to be to churches – Lieutgard gave land to a certain knight, but it finally passed to Chartres, and the question of whether the original gift entailed reversion must be open. It is interesting that Le Jan-Hennebicque sees the church which the ninth-century widow Erkanfride gave in her will as the only part of her dower of which she was free to dispose, "Aux origines du douaire", p. 118; on this see also Nelson, "Wary Widow", pp. 105-06.

[58] There is not room to discuss this here, though I would argue it is a major factor in the variety of apparent rights over property we find amongst early medieval women. Leyser, *Rule and Conflict*, section 2, The Women of the Saxon Aristocracy, has made clear the importance of the coming of Christianity to an area for the endowment of women via the foundation of nunneries. P. Wormald, *How do we know so much about Anglo-Saxon Deerhurst?* Deerhurst Lecture 1991 (Deerhurst, 1993) has discussed briefly but illuminatingly how such land, given to be earmarked for vulnerable members of families, did not thereby escape from family control, but might become associated with the women of the family. Ironically in this way church land may have come to partake of some of the vulnerability of women's lands, a point very relevant to the disappearance of so many nunneries, or rather their chequered history of

Cluny preserved many apparently private family documents which have elsewhere disappeared. This is certainly a sign of the assiduousness of Cluny's record-keeping. But it is also, I would suggest, a sign that whatever else was affecting local families in the tenth- and eleventh-century Mâconnais and Burgundy, Cluny was.[59] Cluny altered the political circumstances of tenth- and eleventh-century Burgundy and with them the context within which individual inheritance was thrashed out. We should be wary of arguing on the basis of the dower formulae or of any general ideas of established women's freedoms that tenth-century Mâconnias women had great liberty to dispose of land. Any that they had may be more a result of Cluny's short-term impact than of any long-standing situation.

It is arguable that the arrival of Cluny had an impact on women's dower and their disposal of it: encouraging and facilitating the gift of dower lands; allowing local widows, and/or their husbands, to defend their dower by giving reversion to Cluny; perhaps in some cases backing or facilitating pressure on a woman to alienate: "the right to give" might be a mixed blessing, and disposal of dower no simple sign of women's freedoms. Cluny's impact may actually have filled the old formulae with new meanings, at least for some women in some circumstances. Cluny may have strengthened some of them at the expense of male heirs. In which case attempts at greater precision, the more regular specification of usufruct or reversion which we find in tenth-century dower documents may mean several things: the individual bargains of individual families, but alternatively or additionally a reaction to

reformation and refoundation. This is ironic since it is surely the greater freedom of property enshrined in the notions churches held about land which helped widows dispose of their property to the church, and arguably complicated dower left in reversion to the church with those notions of freer disposal. J. Hudson's discussion, in *Land, Law and Lordship*, of twelfth-century property notions and the impact of church ideas on them is of great interest; such impact is unlikely to have been confined to the twelfth century. At the same time churches could be a threat as well as a protection to women's land. I hope to return to these questions in more detail at another time.

[59] Just as Canterbury was probably affecting many families in ninth-century Kent: see below n. 62.

these new freedoms some women had achieved.[60] But this would not be a once-and-for-all mutation of a long-standing situation, rather a reaction to a recent development which itself probably affected only some women.

The evidence on women's landholding before the twelfth century is not easy to fit into the narrative which the eleventh-century family mutation demands, that is a picture of early high status and privileges, followed by a decline in the eleventh century.[61] Rather the evidence until at least the early twelfth century points to varied situations of individual women, suggesting a range of possibilities depending on a variety of circumstances. If asked to hypothesise an alternative pattern, I would propose not so much a simple narrative of long-established patterns altered in the eleventh century, but rather a model of short term changes and cycles, with some recurring themes and variations. We can find, for example, some of the signs alleged to show lineage formation in other times and places than tenth- to eleventh-century Burgundy, for example in early ninth-century Kent.[62] As a hypothetical model of family change it would have to take into account, at least until the twelfth

[60] It is worth noting that the second half of the tenth century was the great age of Cluny's landed expansion (Rosenwein, *To be the Neighbour of St Peter*, p. 199): exchanges, some of them designed to consolidate Cluny lands, peak in the Cluny documents in the late tenth century (see Rosenwein, pp. 87 and 91), at about the same time as the first *pancartae* indicate a definition of Cluny's ideas on the structure of its estates (Rosenwein, p. 162). The chronology of changes in dower thus roughly corresponds to the stage at which Cluny might be expected to be shifting from being a factor in local family politics to a major and potentially threatening player; cf. Wickham, *Mountain and the City*, for emphasis on the importance of such a stage.

[61] I have discussed the historiography of this and problems with the whole way in which the argument has been cast in "Women and the Norman Conquest", *Transactions of the Royal Historical Society*, 6th ser., 4 (1993), 221-49.

[62] Here an aggressive policy of land-acquisition by Canterbury was having similar impact on local families to that of Cluny in tenth-century Burgundy. See Brooks, *Early History*, for discussion of this. F. Harmer, *Select English Historical Documents of the Ninth and Tenth Centuries* (Cambridge, 1914) nos 2, 10 and 7, deal with various forms of reversion including widows' usufruct.

century, if not after, the possible coexistence of different norms of inheritance, their revelation or emphasis in different circumstances. As long as these are norms or custom rather than the rules of professional law and lawyers they are likely to remain flexible, which would place likely change in the later twelfth rather than the eleventh century. But even rules and professional law do not change the desire of families for flexibility, witness the development of jointures and other testamentary practices to endow wives later in the English Middle Ages in a much more certainly patrilineal agnatic context.[63] This model would not defy generalisation, nor be unaffected by long-term changes. But it would have to accommodate the great variety of individual family circumstances, the lifecycles of individuals and families, the divisions of interest and aims among different individuals within families, and the ideological, economic and political contexts within which opportunities to achieve those aims open and close. Its rhythms would therefore allow for the intersection of individual and family lifecycle with these wider contexts where unilineal change may be identifiable, but its potential complexity would not be subordinated to them. It would encompass the complex interaction of individual, family and exogenous factors which is always at work, for cyclical as well as uni-directional shifts.

This hypothesis is a suggested way forward, not a conclusion of the cautions with which I have dealt here. Even if the proposed alternative model is unacceptable, those cautions have called for a greater awareness of kinship definitions, but overwhelmingly for a more careful and contextual reading of the documents. They have also signalled the particular worries of a historian of women concerning the reading of those sources. As women's history starts to contribute its perspective on the Middle Ages the eleventh-century family mutation should remain at most a hypothesis, and these critical centuries a stage for debate and open-mindedness.

---

[63] See Archer, "Rich Old Ladies" and A. Kettle, "'My Wife shall have it': Marriage and Property in the Wills and Testaments of Later Medieval England", in *Marriage and Property*, ed. E. M. Craik (Aberdeen, 1984), pp. 89-103.

Gender Without Sexuality: Hrotsvitha's Imagining of a Chaste Female Community

L. M. C. Weston

The Gandersheim which fostered the tenth-century canoness Hrotsvitha was, in Peter Dronke's apt description, "a small, independent principality ruled by women".[1] This female world had, however, numerous connections with the outside world of royal dynastic politics and imperial culture. Founded in 832 by Liudolf, great-grandfather of Emperor Otto I, the abbey drew its resident nuns and canonesses from among the daughters of the royal family. Significantly, when the canoness turned her hand to epic hexameters, she authored twin histories, one of her abbey's foundation, *Primordia coenobii Gandeshemensis*, and one of the imperial dynasty, *Gesta Ottonis*. In Hrotsvitha's time, under the rule of the Emperor's niece, the abbess Gerberga II, it maintained close relations with the imperial court, and especially with the Emperor's younger brother Bruno, an influential figure in the Ottonian cultural renaissance. Indeed, Dronke posits, his reputed fondness for the Roman authors may provide a larger context for Hrotsvitha's attempt to answer and transform Terence. Certainly the dedicatory letter to "scientia longe excellentius perfecti",[2] a group of patrons

---

[1] P. Dronke, *Women Writers of the Middle Ages* (New York, 1984), p. 55.

[2] *Hrotsvithae opera*, ed. H. Homeyer (Munich, 1970), p. 235; all subsequent citations are taken from this edition. Katharina Wilson translates the

perhaps including Bruno and others at the imperial court, positions Hrotsvitha's drama both inside and outside the cloister. That double positioning, however, is not free of contest or anxiety. Hrotsvitha's work in fact opposes as often as it unites secular and monastic discourses, and in so doing offers its cloistered audience, the women of Gandersheim, a powerful redefinition of female community.

Her Preface indeed strongly and immediately opposes her conventual discourse, her own "strong voice" ("clamor validus") to that of Terence. The Roman's many readers outside the cloister, she says,

> dum dulcedine sermonis delectantur, nefandarum notitia rerum maculantur. Unde ego, Clamor Validus Gandeshemensis, non recusavi illum imitari dictando, dum alii colunt legendo, quo eodem dictationis genere, quo turpia lascivarum incesta feminarum recitabantur, laudabilis sacrarum castimonia virginum iuxta mei facultatem ingenioli celebraretur.[3]

Having begun by opposing "gentilium vanitatem librorum utilitati sacrarum scripturarum",[4] her Preface constructs a Hrotsvitha undertaking a Christian rewriting of a pagan Terence, chaste as he is lascivious – and significantly, female as he is male. Though pagan, secular authors might become part of the grammar curriculum, their seductiveness still endangers their readers, she suggests, especially, in this case, women like Hrotsvitha. The very act of reading Terence, then, becomes as much a struggle as the martyrdoms she

---

phrase as "the most outstanding among learned men" in *The Plays of Hrotsvit of Gandersheim* (New York, 1989), p. 4; all subsequent translations are taken from Wilson.

[3] *Hrotsvithae opera*, p. 233; "as they delight in the sweetness of his style and diction, they are stained by learning of wicked things in his depiction. Therefore I, the strong voice of Gandersheim, have not refused to imitate him in writing whom others laud in reading, so that in the selfsame form of composition in which the shameless acts of lascivious women are phrased, the laudable chastity of sacred virgins may be praised within the limits of my little talent", Wilson, p. 3.

[4] *Hrotsvithae opera*, p. 233; "the uselessness of pagan guile to the usefulness of Sacred Scripture", Wilson, p. 3.

dramatises. It is thus doubly appropriate that "the victories of triumphant innocence" will be her subject, she announces, "praesertim cum feminea fragilitas vinceret et virilis robur confusioni subiaceret".[5]

To be female, it seems, is to be weak: again and again she humbly counterpoints her own intellectual weaknesses to the mastery of both Terence and the "most outstanding among learned men". Indeed, Terence – or better, perhaps, "Terence" – may well represent the voice of her contemporaries as much if not more than her classical model.[6] But again and again, as Dronke notes, her reputed weakness is ironically undercut as the "strong voice of Gandersheim" – "clamor validus" rendering in Latin the Germanic Hrotsvit – nevertheless answers the authority of Terence's text even as her chaste heroines answer back to interrogation and temptation. At issue is the definition of woman, of the feminine, and especially Terence's conflation of women and "lasciviousness", that is, the necessary involvement of women in the sexual economy underwriting kinship and rightful inheritance.[7] Such a conflation of gender and sexuality effectively eliminates the possibility of a single chaste woman, let alone a community of chaste women.

---

[5] *Hrotsvithae opera*, pp. 233-34; "especially when female weakness triumphs in conclusion and male strength succumbs in confusion", Wilson, p. 3.

[6] In this essay I discuss only "Terence" in so far as he is constructed in the text of the Preface as antagonist for an equally artificial "Hrotsvitha". Numerous studies, however, have debated the depth of Hrotsvitha's debt to the Roman dramatist. For brief discussions, see Wilson, pp. xii-xxviii and Dronke, pp. 72-74, as well as K. DeLuca, "Hrotsvit's 'Imitation' of Terence", *Classical Folia* 28 (1974), 89-102. Hrotsvitha's opposition to the Roman author may well owe some debt, of course, to Jerome's letters to Eustochium and Laeta, which voice a similar anxiety about reading secular texts.

[7] DeLuca defends Terence against Hrotsvitha's charges by noting how far from central women are in his dramas, and how rarely his prostitutes are literally lascivious, how often they in fact enable the progress, even the legitimate marriage and inheritance of his male characters. For more theoretical discussion of the conflation of sexuality and gender in the sexual economy of marriage and giving in marriage, see G. Rubin, "The Traffic in Women: Notes on the 'Political Economy' of Sex", in *Toward an Anthropology of Women*, ed. R. Reiter (New York, 1975), pp. 157-210.

Hrotsvitha's answer, like the repeated answer of her virginal heroines to secular authority, reshapes existing images of women and chastity, and so imagines and defines a chaste female community as its own particular place. As Howard McNaughton notes, her "discursive swivel" in representing strong, resistant women as the subjects of her drama is, at base, "contestatory, appropriative and transpositional".[8] To read her drama is to read and to participate in a specific negotiation of and response to secular and clerical definitions of "woman" constructed within hegemonic discourses of gender and sexuality.

If she is to counter teachings of "wicked things" Hrotsvitha must alter the mode as well as the content of Terence's drama. She must construct a reader as vigilant and resistant to the Terentian text as her heroines are to the discourse of their tempters. Terence pleases and even titillates his audience; he "stains" his readers, seducing and corrupting them. Hrotsvitha and her chaste audience can resist that temptation only by dismantling the relationships which inscribe sexuality and gender within the gaze, and within the act of reading.

Within the dramas this resistance is enacted in the interplay of multiple and contesting audiences and gazes. Thus Hrotsvitha's Preface and dedicatory letter invoke an audience, putatively male, outside the cloister, which looks, with the Terence she opposes, on women as weak and passive objects; in her plays such an audience finds itself doubled by an audience of interrogators voyeuristically looking on the struggles of her heroines. Hrotsvitha portrays their gaze as a violent, sexual and sexualising act. For her as for patristic authorities like Jerome their gaze defiles, but for Hrotsvitha it defiles the one who gazes, the subject not the object of that gaze. Consequently the lustful gaze of such an audience is repeatedly revealed as ironically futile: as often as it attempts to sexualise chaste women, so often it fails utterly. *Dulcitius* (*The Martyrdom of the Holy Virgins Agape, Chionia and Hirena*), the play which most explicitly enacts "the victories of triumphant innocence ... especially

---

[8] "Hrotsvitha and the Dramaturgy of Liminality", *Journal of the Australasian Universities Language and Literature Association* 80 (1993), 1-6 (p. 3).

when female weakness triumphs in conclusion and male strength succumbs in confusion"[9] plays out most exactly the ironic defeat of the sexualising gaze. Like Diocletian, Dulcitius and Sisinnius within the play, readers may look on and see "quam pulchrae, quam venustae, quam egregiae" the three sisters are, how desirable;[10] yet all attempts to render the virgins as sexualised spectacles to be traded among male spectators fail. When Dulcitius orders them "vestibus publice denudentur", and exposed to masculine mockery, "vestimenta virgineis corporibus inhaerent velut coria", and the lascivious gaze is defeated.[11] When Sisinnius orders Agape and Chionia to the pyre, their bodies remain equally intact: "ecce, animae egressae sunt corpora, et nulla laesionis repperiuntur vestigia, sed nec capilli, nec vestimenta ab igne sunt ambusta, quo minus corpora".[12] In neither case can the virgins be violated or defiled.

In fact, it is the pagan authorities who defile their own bodies. Their gaze turns back upon itself, and they themselves become a spectacle for the mockery of an audience of the chaste virgins. Seeking to assault the virgins, a deluded Dulcitius succeeds only in raping the crockery, as the three sisters view his foolishness from within the female domestic enclosure of the pantry:

> Hirena: Accedite, quaeso, per rimulas perspicite!
> Agapes: Quid est?
> Hirena: Ecce, iste stultus, mente alienatus, aestimat se nostris uti amplexibus.
> Agapes: Quid facit?

---

[9] Wilson, p. 3; for discussion see above and footnote 5.

[10] *Hrotsvithae opera*, p. 270; "how beautiful, how graceful, how admirable", Wilson, p. 40.

[11] *Hrotsvithae opera*, p. 273; "to be publicly stripped of all their clothes ... their garments stick to their virginal bodies like skin", Wilson, p. 43.

[12] *Hrotsvithae opera*, p. 274. "Behold their souls are no longer bound to their bodies, yet no traces of injury can be found; neither hair, nor their clothes are burnt by the fire, and their bodies are not at all harmed by the pyre", Wilson, p. 45.

Hirena: Nunc ollas molli fovet gremio, nunc
sartagines et caccabos amplectitur, mitia libans
oscula.
Chionia: Ridiculum.[13]

This scene imagines a second kind of audience, not a group of
lustful voyeurs but a chaste community of virgins, an audience
closely doubling, perhaps, a textual community within the abbey of
Gandersheim. It is an audience which, because it is not itself
lascivious, can look on lasciviousness without being stained. In
essence Hrotsvitha imagines a contrary mode of perception, a gaze
which establishes a subject without violent objectification.

Moreover, refusing to accept the gaze as defined and deployed
within the discourse she identifies with Terence, Hrotsvitha refuses
as well to correlate sexual desire with gender. Terence's gaze, she
suggests, presents women as the passive "natural" objects of lust
and paradoxically "naturally" lascivious and inherently sexual
because their beauty is the efficient cause of desire in others.
Hrotsvitha rejects this slippage of responsibility from the one who
desires to the one desired. As Katharina Wilson and Kathryn
Gravdal, among other readers, have argued, in Hrotsvitha's dramas
and legends both men and women are equally subjects and objects
of lustful desires and appetites, because desire – sexuality, lust – is a
matter associated with the individual human will.[14] The
objectification of the beloved does not displace guilt. In *Calimachus*
(*The Resurrection of Drusiana and Calimachus*), for instance,
Calimachus first announces his affection simply: "amo". The
emotion, the appetite, precedes any object. His friends must wring
the less relevant information out of him as a process of necessary

---

[13] *Hrotsvithae opera*, p. 271. "Come here, please, and look through the
crack! / What is going on? / Look, the fool, the madman base, he thinks he is
enjoying our embrace. / What is he doing? / Into his lap he pulls the utensils, he
embraces the pots and pans, giving them tender kisses. / Ridiculous", Wilson, p.
41.

[14] Wilson, pp. xii-xxv; K. Gravdal, *Ravishing Maidens: Writing Rape in
Medieval French Literature and Law* (Philadelphia, 1991), pp. 29-35; E. Petroff,
"Eloquence and Heroic Virginity in Hrotsvit's Verse Legends", in her *Body and
Soul: Essays on Medieval Women and Mysticism* (New York, 1994), pp. 83-96.

grammatical modification: first, the impersonal "rem pulchram, rem venustam", then the somewhat more specific "mulierem", and only finally the personal name, Drusiana.[15] The scene's separation of the chaste woman from Calimachus' love reinforces her guiltlessness. The play's anatomy of desire continues when he later courts the lady. What legal or natural claim has his love upon her, she asks him, "quod ius consanguinitas, quaeve legalis conditio institutionis compellit te ad mei amorem?" Her beauty, he responds, stating Terence's reasoning nicely. "Mea pulchritudo?" she answers, "Quid ad te?"[16] Indeed, her beauty is nothing to him but an excuse for enacting his own illicit lust. His desire, like the erroneous objectification of his so-called beloved, which will lead him to plan and attempt necrophiliac rape, is his own. The remarkable beauty of Drusiana, like that of the three virgins, is guiltless. Those who surrender to desire – male or female – are pagans, for in the discourse of her drama paganism like lust follows from a failure of perception and will. In Augustinian and Pauline terms, the conflict is that of flesh against spirit.[17]

That conflict is, however, enacted in bodies and within societies – and social bodies have gender. In Hrotsvitha's dramas the conflict is continually waged in or over the body of a woman. In her Preface, of course, the body in question is that of Hrotsvitha herself. Not infrequently, she tells us, the reading of Terence's lascivious spectacles "facit non raro verecundari gravique rubore perfundi, quod, huiusmodi specie dictationis cogente detestabilem inlicite amantium dementiam et male dulcia colloquia eorum, quae nec nostro auditui permittuntur accommodari, dictando mente tractavi et stili officio designavi".[18] Her scarlet flushed cheeks

---

[15] *Hrotsvithae opera*, p. 284. "I love ... something comely, something lovely ... a woman", Wilson, p. 52.

[16] *Hrotsvithae opera*, p. 285; "what bond of kinship, what legal relationship compels you to love me? ... My beauty? What is my beauty to you?", Wilson, p. 54.

[17] Wilson, pp. xii-xxv.

[18] *Hrotsvithae opera*, p. 233; "caused me to blush and brought to my cheeks a scarlet flush, because being forced by the conventions of this composition, I had to contemplate and give a rendition of that detestable

constitute a corporeal sign of the active struggle against temptation. It is, moreover, a specifically feminine sign – a sign also of her inscription into a social discourse which defines her as a woman.

Similarly, in her individual dramas it is important that her heroines are women: not for her Jerome's dictum that virginity fosters an escape from gender, that chaste women become effectively male. Rather Hrotsvitha's heroines remain women as defined within the class and sex/gender systems she would have known as a daughter of the Ottonian imperial family: a woman, especially an aristocratic woman, is a commodity to be exchanged among men, among kin-groups to sustain or establish political and social order. Marriage inscribes gender, as well as, of course, a compulsory heterosexuality defining and defined by a distinction between active subjects and passive objects of the marriage exchange (and the gaze), and reinforced and reinforcing the "natural" division into active and passive sexual roles, strong and weak – i.e. male and female. To such a neat construction the woman who resists marriage and chooses virginity constitutes an aberration, a potential social irritant if not an impossibility. Hrotsvitha's construction of a community of chaste women thus involves an anxious paradox, and her response to this cognitive dilemma is the ironic redefinition of marriage and consequently of femininity.

Marriages – literal and figural, physical and spiritual, coincident with and divorced from sexuality – define women as women in Hrotsvitha's plays. The chaste woman acts as an intermediary between this world and the next, sometimes literally converting a pagan man into a Christian, bringing him from the world of flesh into the world of the spirit. In *Gallicanus* (*The Conversion of General Gallicanus*), Constantia is immediately placed in the situation of many an aristocratic woman in Hrotsvitha's world, exchanged to establish an alliance between her father Constantinus and his powerful general Gallicanus, whose aid and loyalty are required for the good of the Empire. Constantinus sees the dilemma clearly, and his own agency in it: "hinc coartor nimium, quia, si, quod debet fieri paterno more, te in proposito

madness of unlawful lovers and of their evil flattery, which we are not permitted even to hear", Wilson, p. 3.

permansum ire consensero, haut leve damnum patiar in publica re; si autem, quod absit, renitor, aeternis cruciandus poenis subiacebo".[19] As father and Christian, he should honour his daughter's vow; as Emperor he must insist on her marriage. The miraculous solution to the dilemma – the happy ending – is to allow God, through Constantia, to work Gallicanus' conversion. So complete, indeed, is Gallicanus' conversion that when Constantinus offers him the prospect of the chaste spiritual marriage – "cum vinculum Christi amoris in unius nos societate coniungat religionis, decet, ut, quasi gener augustorum, honorifice nobiscum habites intra palatium" – he rejects it.[20] Gallicanus refuses, that is, even the possibility of temptation: "nulla magis est vitanda temptatio quam oculorum concupiscentia. ... Unde non expedit me frequentius virginem intueri, quam prae parentibus, prae vita, prae anima a me scis amari".[21] His fear is that he will be unable to control his "eyes' wanton desire".

The distinction between sexualising secular marriage, seemingly required by aristocratic descent and female gender, and chaste heavenly marriage is similarly at issue in *Dulcitius*. Diocletian's persecution elides Christianity with resistance to marriage as a social – and in his eyes a natural – obligation:

> parentelae claritas ingenuitatis vestrumque
> serenitas pulchritudinis exigit, vos nuptiali lege
> primis in palatio copulari, quod nostri iussio

---

[19] *Hrotsvithae opera*, p. 247; "now I am sorely pressed because if I allow that you persevere in your vow (which is what I should do as your father) then I will suffer great harm in public affairs. If, however, God forbid, I force you to marry, I will have to undergo eternal punishment", Wilson, p. 12.

[20] *Hrotsvithae opera*, p. 257; "since the tie of Christ's love unites us in the fellowship of one religion, it is proper that you, the Emperor's son-in-law so to say, live honourably in the palace with us", Wilson, p. 27. See D. Elliott, *Spiritual Marriage: Sexual Abstinence in Medieval Wedlock* (Princeton, 1993), for a more thorough discussion of the tradition of chaste marriage.

[21] *Hrotsvithae opera*, p. 257; "no temptation is to be shunned more, Sire, than the eyes' wanton desire .... Therefore I am afraid to behold frequently the very maid whom, as you know, I love above my parents, my life, my very soul and ease", Wilson, p. 27.

annuerit fieri, si Christum negare nostrisque diis
sacrificia velitis ferre.[22]

His words here neatly conflate kinship duties, the virgins' "free and
noble descent", and beauty. Both are tied, as within the Terentian
discourse of the gaze, with a sexualisation of gender.

Likewise, in *Sapientia*, too, the arrival of Fides, Spes, Karitas
and their mother Sapientia in Rome disturbs the peace and "natural"
order of the pagan state. As Antiochus advises the Emperor Hadrian,
"haec igitur femina ... hortatur nostrates, avitos ritus deserere et
christianae religioni se dedere, ... Nam nostrae coniuges fastidiendo
nos contempnunt adeo, ut dedignantur nobiscum comedere, quanto
minus dormire".[23] Sapientia's threat is quite openly sexual as well as
religious; conversion to Christianity leads Roman wives to reject
sexuality, and the social bonds which unite them with their pagan
husbands. It is, moreover, specifically as mother to the three martyrs
that Sapientia is opposed by Hadrian, who claims to speak "pro tua
tuique filiarum salute paterno sollicitor amore".[24] His fatherly care
wishes to force them to follow those "ancestral and ancient rites" of
the secular world, appropriate to those of "noble descent"; she seeks
their consent to a chaste espousal with a heavenly Bridegroom.

In juxtaposing these two marriages, all three plays enact the
contest of flesh and spirit over but not in the bodies of women. The
holy virgins are stable in their purity, their virginity impervious to
either rhetorical or physical assault. All three implicitly reinforce a
cloistered audience's conversion from secular to monastic life. In
two plays, however, Hrotsvitha stages the contest in the female
body: *Abraham* (*The Fall and Repentance of Mary*) and *Pafnutius*
(*The Conversion of Thais the Whore*). Interestingly, both invoke a

---

[22] *Hrotsvithae opera*, p.268; "the renown of your free and noble descent,
and the brightness of your beauty demand that you be married to one of the
foremost men of my court. This will be done according to our command if you
deny Christ and comply by bringing offerings to our gods", Wilson, p. 37.

[23] *Hrotsvithae opera*, p. 358; "This woman exhorts our citizens and
clients to abandon the ancestral and ancient rites and to convert to Christianity.
Our wives despise us so that they refuse to eat with us, or even more to sleep
with us", Wilson, p. 126.

[24] *Hrotsvithae opera*, p. 360; "concerned with fatherly care for you and
your daughters' welfare", Wilson, p. 128.

cenobitical setting: when the female body is the site of sexual temptation, that is, Hrotsvitha stages her drama within the world of the cloister and its constant opposition to that of the city. Having renounced the world as a child, for example, the dedicated virgin Mary is nevertheless subject to temptation: "per illicitum cuiusdam simulatoris affectum, qui, monachico adveniens habitu, simulata eam visitatione frequentabat, donec indocile iuvenilis ingenium pectoris ad sui amorem inflexit, adeo, ut per fenestram ad patrandum facinus exilivit".[25] Her temptation comes in the guise of education; the discourse of the deceiver – like that of Terence, perhaps – leads her to sin. Yet she is a desiring subject, not merely the passive object of desire, and her Fall is of her own volition – indeed, she literally jumps from the innocence of her cell. Moreover, the "awful deed" is not alone what stains the girl: "ubi ipsa infelix se corruptam sensit, pectus pulsavit, faciem manu laceravit, vestes scidit, capillos eruit, voces in altum eiulando dedit".[26] Her gestures – tearing her hair, rending her garments, lamenting and weeping – are the stock gestures of a seduced and abandoned victim, but equally those of an active penitent. Had she persevered in such great remorse, we are told, she would have been saved. Instead she despaired, and it is her desperation as much as lasciviousness and a love of worldly vanities which confirms her sin.

Thais also sins knowingly and desperately, fully cognisant (as she confides to the disguised Pafnutius) of Divine judgement. Her lust enables other worldly vices: she is guilty especially of luxury and greed, and after her conversion Thais' first action is to burn the wealth she had amassed from her lovers. Indeed, it is a desire for accustomed luxury which threatens to derail her penitence. Thais

[25] *Hrotsvithae opera*, p. 307; "through the forbidden passion of a certain deceiver who, disguised as a monk, often came to her under the pretence of instructive visits, until he ignited the undisciplined instincts of her youthful heart to burn in love for him, so much so that she jumped from her window to perform that awful deed", Wilson, p. 75.

[26] *Hrotsvithae opera*, p. 307; "when the wretched girl, so beguiled, found herself lapsed and defiled, she beat her breasts, lacerated her face and hands, tore her clothes amid sighs, pulled out her hair and raised her voice in lamentation to the skies", Wilson, pp. 75-76.

has an aristocratic woman's realistic concerns about her cell: "quid inoportunius quidve poterit esse incommodius, quam quod in uno eodemque loco diversa corporis necessaria supplere debebo. Nec dubium, quin ocius fiat inhabitabilis prae nimietate foetoris".[27] Unlike the virgin martyrs, whose deaths announce their eternal conversion and stability, both Thais and Mary can still be tempted. The secular world – its deceiving discourse as well as its wealth and comfort – remains an alluring and threatening possibility beyond the cloister.

It is the whole community within that cloister, accordingly, which must assist their salvation. Both Thais and Mary are redeemed through the actions of monks, Abraham and Pafnutius, who willingly absent themselves from their monasteries and risk temptation by disguising themselves as worldly lovers in order to win the prostitutes to abjure fornication. The parallels to Christ's Incarnation and redemption of sinful mankind, as well as to the Bridegroom in the Song of Songs, are, of course, evident. But their dramatic impersonation of an otherwise illicit worldliness also bears some similarity, perhaps, to Hrotsvitha's reading Terence and consequent impersonation of the "detestabilem inlicite amantium dementiam ... quae nec nostro auditui permittuntur accommodari", so as to redeem the text and the honour of chaste women.[28] There is an androgyny to Hrotsvitha's monks: in presenting themselves as lovers to effect conversions they enact mediations like Constantia's and Drusiana's, exchanging themselves between the worlds of the cloister and the city. Within the dramas they function as Brides as well as stand-ins for the Bridegroom.

Thais and Mary can become Brides of Christ the Bridegroom, but only once they renounce sexuality – and so ironically become real women. Mary is betrothed to Christ by her foster father

---

[27] *Hrotsvithae opera*, p. 343; "what could be more unsuitable, what could be more uncomfortable, than that I would have to perform all necessary functions of the body in the very same room? I am sure that it will soon be uninhabitable because of the stench", Wilson, p. 115.

[28] *Hrotsvithae opera*, p. 233; "the detestable madness of unlawful lovers ... which we [presumably the nuns and canonesses of monastic houses like Gandersheim] are not permitted even to hear", Wilson, p. 3.

Abraham, but she gives appropriate free consent to this espousal, having been taught that she should strive to imitate her Namesake and be as stable as that Stella Maris:

> circa quam videlicet fertur mundus et rotatur polus
> .... Nam, si incorrupta et virgo permanebis, angelis
> dei fies aequalis; quibis tandem stipata, gravi
> corporis onere abiecta, pertransies aera,
> supergradieris aethera, zodiacum percurres
> circulum, nec subsistendo temperabis gressum,
> donec amplexaris amplexibus filii virginis in
> lucifluo thalamo sui genitricis.[29]

Incorrupt, she will be the "equal of God's angels" – and surrounded by them. Her marriage to the Virgin's Son will be consummated within "the luminous wedding chamber of His mother". Her espousal initiates her, it seems, into a virginal community in this life and the next.

When Mary falls from this role, she consequently violates cosmic order and affects more than just her own soul's peace. Her transgression troubles the entire community, giving rise to Abraham's premonitory visions and his need to court her back to the cloister and to restore the order breached by her sins. Thais' crimes, too, breach some kind of universal peace and order, disturbing the musical harmony Pafnutius teaches his disciples and causing his profound grief. Her actions lead to the dissipation of family fortunes and honours, and to civic violence:

> nec solum nugaces vilitatem suae familiaris rei
> dissipant illam colendo, sed etiam praepotentes
> viri pretiosae varietatem suppellectilis pessum-
> dant, non absque sui damno hanc ditando ... Qui

---

[29] *Hrotsvithae opera*, pp. 305-06; "'the star of the sea,' round which the earth is borne and the poles both turn. For if you remain incorrupt and a virgin, you will become the equal of God's angels; surrounded by them, when you have cast off the burden of your body, you will traverse the sky, rising above the ether high, and journey through the circle of the zodiac, not slowing down or delaying your flight until you have reached great delight in the arms of the Virgin's son, and are embraced by Him in the luminous wedding chamber of His mother", Wilson, p. 73.

> amentes, dum caeco corde, quis illam adeat,
> contendunt, convicia congerunt .... Deinde, inito
> certamine, nunc ora naresque pugnis frangendo,
> nunc armis vicissim eiciendo, decurrentis illuvie
> sanguinis madefaciunt limina lupanaris.[30]

Originally a false Bride, who weaves not concord but discord
between men, having purified herself through private and public
renunciation Thais can become the true Bride of the Bridegroom.
This identity is appropriately endorsed in the vision of another
member of the community: "videbam in visione lectulum candidulis
palliolis in caelo magnifice stratum, cui quattuor splendidae virgines
praeerant et quasi custodiendo astabant".[31] Her salvation affects all
in the monastery; the image of the bridal chamber with four virginal
guards similarly implicates a whole community. Further, this vision
reconstructs Thais as the object not of the violently lustful gaze of
her lovers but of a chaste, communal gaze. The play's audience
finds itself mirrored by both the monk outside and the four maidens
within the vision. The absent body of Thais in the bed becomes the
focus of a spectacle which melds subjects and objects of the gaze –
and unites rather than violently dividing a community.

This emphasis on unity is present, moreover, throughout
Hrotsvitha's dramatic texts. Sue-Ellen Case has remarked on "the
contiguous dependency among parts of the world" within her
plays.[32] Michael Evenden has similarly observed the way the plays
"celebrate community, shared selfhood, 'the blessed company of
virgins'": within Hrotsvitha's drama "individuality interpenetrates"
and "everything is held in a delicate web of mutuality" so that "one

---

[30] *Hrotsvithae opera*, p. 335; "not only frivolous youths dissipate their
families' few possessions on her, but even respected men waste their costly
treasures by lavishing gifts on her. [Her lovers] are blind in their hearts; they
contend and quarrel and fight with each other. Then when the fight has started,
they fracture each other's faces and noses with their fists; they attack each other
with their weapons and drench the threshold of the brothel with their blood
gushing forth", Wilson, p. 103.

[31] *Hrotsvithae opera* , p. 346; "in my vision of heaven, I saw a bed with
white linen beautifully spread surrounded by four resplendent maidens who
stood as if guarding the bed", Wilson, p. 119.

[32] "Re-viewing Hrotsvit", *Theatre Journal* 35 (1983), 533-42 (p. 539).

senses with unusual keenness the shared sensitivities of a religious community".[33] Indeed, while the penitential cell which houses the struggle against sexual temptation may be lonely, its heavenly double, the celestial bedchamber promised Mary and Thais as well as the holy virgins of the other plays, is replete with almost an excessive number of Brides. In all the plays, one of the benefits of remaining a chaste Bride on this earth is membership in the choir of Brides in the next, union in a larger community of chaste women.

Constantia, for example, converts not only Gallicanus but also his two daughters, Attica and Artemia. Agape, Chionia and Hirena, as well as Fides, Spes and Karitas, suffer and support each other as a group; when Agape and Chionia are martyred, their suffering only strengthens their third sister, and when Hirena is ordered into the defilement of a brothel, she is miraculously transported instead to a mountain where she is joined, in imitation of Christ's transfiguration, by two splendid figures reminiscent of if not explicitly identical with her sisters. Fides, Spes and Karitas suffer for their mother, who is joined at her daughters' burial site by a chorus of Roman matrons (perhaps women she had previously converted) who echo her prayer for reunion, that "quamvis non possum canticum virginitatis dicere, te tamen cum illis merear aeternaliter laudare".[34] Elsewhere, of course, Hrotsvitha proposes what A. Daniel Frankforter terms "a rather curious theory of technical virginity" which sites virginity in the spirit not the flesh, and which can therefore admit the repentant Mary and Thais, and also Sapientia the widow and Drusiana the chaste wife, into the virginal choir.[35] Such "technical virginity", countering patristic opinion that virginity once lost – under whatever circumstances – is

<hr />

[33] "Inter-mediate Stages: Reconsidering the Body in 'Closet Drama'", in *Reading the Social Body*, ed. C. Burroughs and J. D. Ehrenrich (Iowa City, 1993), pp. 244-69 (p. 250).

[34] *Hrotsvithae opera* , p. 375; "even though I cannot join them in chanting the canticles of virginal maidens, yet may I be permitted to join them in the eternal praise", Wilson, p. 149.

[35] "Sexism and the Search for the Thematic Structure of the Plays of Hroswitha of Gandersheim", *International Journal of Women's Studies* 2 (1979), 221-32 (p. 227).

lost forever, in common with the multiple contiguity of the chaste female choir, again reconfigures "woman" not as a violateable object but instead as an almost excessively permeable subject linked with other subjects within a virginal whole.

Virtue, chastity, is thus not just an individual struggle, even in the cases of Mary and Thais, but a matter of concern to the whole community. Similarly, then, when Hrotsvitha undertakes her dialogue with Terence she does so not alone, but for and in the company of her sisters. When she destabilises hegemonic discourse on gender and sexuality, when she imagines herself an active subject, a chaste woman, she does this not in isolation, not as an anomaly, but as one "strong voice" within a Gandersheim imagining itself as a powerful community of chaste women.

II SAINTS

Pollution, Penance and Sanctity: Ekkehard's *Life* of Iso of St Gall

Mayke de Jong

I

In around 1050 the monk of St Gall who goes by the name of "Ekkehard IV" wrote a continuation to the chronicle of his monastery.[1] By then, he was already an elderly man, having spent almost his entire life in St Gall.[2] When he took up the *Casus sancti Galli* where Ratpert (d. 890) had left off, Ekkehard was already the monastery's archivist, so the writing of history came naturally to him. His approach to monastic history was very different from that of his predecessor. Whereas Ratpert had been primarily interested in St Gall's institutional rights and their defence by subsequent abbots, Ekkehard concentrated on the "fortunia et infortunia", the ups and

---

[1] H. F. Haefele, ed., *Ekkehardi IV Casus sancti Galli*, Ausgewählte Quellen zur deutschen Geschichte des Mittelalters 10 (Darmstadt, 1980), henceforth: Ekkehard, *Casus s. Galli*.

[2] Ekkehard's year of birth and death are not certain, but he had already entered St Gall by the year 1000, and lived long enough to refer in a gloss to the death of Pope Victor (1057). See H. F. Haefele, "Ekkehard IV von St Gallen", in *Die deutsche Literatur des Mittelalters. Verfasserlexikon*, vol. 2 (1980), pp. 455-65, with references to older literature.

downs of his community.[3] His lead players were not only abbots, but also a large cast of (in)famous monks. In the best tradition of St Gall story-telling – reminiscent of Notker Balbulus – he related their often unconventional adventures in the cloister and in the world outside. Most likely Ekkehard intended to continue the *Casus* up to his own time, but death (c. 1060) must have prevented him from doing so. His history starts in 870, suddenly breaking off in the middle of a description of Emperor Otto I visiting St Gall in 972. It is, therefore, the record of a glorious but distant past, which nonetheless was still very much alive in the mid-eleventh century.[4]

Iso (c. 830-871) was one of the many monks Ekkehard drew into the limelight.[5] He educated three of St Gall's heroes: Notker Balbulus (d. 912), Tuotilo (d. 913) and the historian and *magister* Ratpert mentioned above. The chapters devoted to this celebrated trio are preceded by a rather curious miniature *vita* of their teacher Iso. This saint-to-be was conceived on Easter Saturday, in other words, at a time when marital intercourse was strictly forbidden. Immediately realising the seriousness of their sin, Iso's parents undertook a spontaneous public penance. When his mother turned out to be pregnant, she dreamt of giving birth to a hedgehog; little boys pulled out the animal's prickles and scratched with them on the wall. The father then consulted a hermit, who explained the dream to him. His wife would give birth a son who would be consecrated to St Gall;

---

[3] H. F. Haefele, "Zum Aufbau der Casus sancti Galli Ekkehards IV", in *Typologia litterarum. Festschrift für Max Wehrli*, ed. S. Sonderegger, A. M. Haas and H. Burger (Zürich, 1969), pp. 155-66.

[4] Ekkehard, *Casus s. Galli*, Praeloquium, p. 16: "Moniti a loci nostri fratribus id opere precium putantibus, quaedam cenobii sanctorum Galli et Othmari cum infortuniis tradere fortunia, rem arduam aggressi sumus". ("Spurred on by the brethren of our community who thought it worth the trouble, we have taken upon ourselves the arduous task of recounting some of the fortunes of the monastery of St Gall and St Otmar, along with its misfortunes").

[5] J. Duft, "Iso", in *Neue deutsche Biographie*, ed. Bayerische Akademie von Wissenschaften, Historische Kommission, vol. 10 (Berlin, 1974), p. 198; Duft, "Iso monachus - doctor nominatissimus", in *Churrätisches und st. gallisches Mittelalter. Festschrift für Otto P. Clavadetscher*, ed. H. Maurer (Sigmaringen, 1984), pp. 146-55.

raised and trained in the monastery, the boy would become a teacher who would arm many of his pupils with quills (the hedgehog's prickles). And indeed, Iso was offered to St Gall in childhood, in due course becoming so famous a schoolmaster that his services were even demanded in Burgundy. He died in Moutier-Grandval as a famous teacher, an able doctor and a successful miracle-worker. Even after his death, he worked wonders for those flocking to his grave.[6]

Most of this brief *vita* is devoted to events prior to Iso's birth. The mother's visionary dream belongs to the typical repertoire of hagiography,[7] but the tale of Iso's conception and his parents' penance is exceptional. It takes up the longest of the three chapters devoted to Iso, and must therefore have been crucial to Ekkehard's explanation of Iso's future sanctity. Though adding nothing to Iso's factual biography, the little narrative yields interesting information about notions of sanctity and penance in mid-eleventh-century St Gall. After providing an integral translation of the story of the parents' penance, I will explore the context of Iso's sainthood.[8]

II

"Iso was the son of not only highborn, but also saintly parents. Abstaining unanimously from food and other delights, as usual, and castigating themselves for God, they slept separately one Lent, taking a bath on Easter Saturday. After a period of ashes and sackcloth they dressed festively for the civic procession; being notable people, they could afford to do so. After her bath, exhausted from her vigil, the woman had a rest in her bed, which was made up more prettily than normally because of the festive time of year. Accidentally her husband entered her chamber, tempted by the Tempter. He went up to

[6] Ekkehard, *Casus s. Galli*, chapters 30-32, pp. 70-76.

[7] L. Zoepf, *Das Heiligen-Leben im 10. Jahrhundert* (Leipzig and Berlin 1908), pp. 52-53.

[8] This article is a development of – but in many respects diverges from – an earlier publication in Dutch on this topic: M. de Jong, "De boetedoening van Iso's ouders. Kanttekeningen bij een verhaal uit Ekkehard's 'Casus sancti Galli'", in *Ad fontes. Opstellen aangeboden aan prof. dr. C. van de Kieft*, ed. C. M. Cappon et alii (Hilversum, 1984), pp. 111-37.

her and had intercourse with her, without any objection on her part. But after their shameful deed both of them lamented so loudly that the members of the household, rushing to the scene, had no need to ask what had happened, for the couple itself invoked God and made very clear what they had been up to. In tears they washed themselves again; they again donned the sackcloth they had worn for so many weeks. Sprinkled with ashes and barefoot they prostrated themselves to the local priest, in front of the entire community. This sensible man accepted their penance in a compassionate manner, and while the people prayed loudly to God on their behalf, he granted them indulgence; having raised them to their feet, he imposed as a punishment that they should stand, excluded from communion, on the threshold of the church that day and night. As soon as the Mass of that day was over, they went to the priest of the neighbouring village, who had a reputation for sanctity. In the same penitential habit they revealed their lapse to him and his flock, and they asked him tearfully for permission to have communion the next day. He chastised them sternly and strictly for their temerity; yet they returned home with his blessing, and passed the night fasting, waking and crying.

Easter Day dawned; early in the morning they stood in front of the church, and when prior to Mass the Cross was carried outside, they followed in the very rear of the procession. But during the Kyrie Eleison the priest led them into the church, with the consent of the entire community, and brought them to a place in the rear. They did not ask for the Eucharist, for this had displeased the aforesaid priest. But when Communion was over, the priest from the neighbouring village – or so it seemed – rushed into the church, as if he was still about to say Mass for his flock. He took them by the hand and led them up to the altar. He opened his pyx and gave the sobbing couple Communion; hastily, as if in a hurry to return to his own, he gave them his blessing and kiss of peace, ordered them to dress again in Easter clothes, and returned. Everyone was overjoyed that they had received Communion from such a holy man. The rest of the day they spent joyfully, handing out alms. Part of these they sent with gifts to this saintly priest, by means of a servant on horseback. But then it emerged that he had never left his flock that particular day, and that it had been one of God's angels who had done everything – as has been publicised afterwards at a synod. Both man and wife subsequently thanked God day and night, and insisted even more assiduously upon performing good works".[9]

III

Ekkehard's story about Iso's parents depicts ideal behaviour, but it also reveals a lot about eleventh-century penitential practice. The then current system of penance originated in the Carolingian age. It has been characterised as a "dichotomie pénitentielle": secret sins merited a secret penance, public ones had to be atoned for publicly.[10] Presumably, this penitential dichotomy arose from the attempt of reform-minded bishops to revive the traditional canonical penance of Late Antiquity. By then, the very successful "tariffed" penance introduced by the Irish and Anglo-Saxon monks, which could be repeated often and imposed by ordinary priests, had led to a proliferation of contradictory *libri paenitentiales*. From 813 onwards, the bishops reasserted their authority in penitential matters, demanding a "canonical" (i.e. public), penance for grave and notorious sins. This Carolingian reform yielded a compromise which was to be operative up to the twelfth century. *Paenitentia publica* became the successor of traditional canonical penance; its imposition remained an episcopal prerogative, directed primarily against notorious crimes upsetting public order, such as murder, sedition, robbery and flagrant offences against sexual morality. Conversely, if sins had not attracted notoriety, they could be atoned for by a secret

---

[9] Ekkehard, *Casus s. Galli*, chapter 30, pp. 70-72.

[10] This view is best summarised in B. Poschmann, *Die abendländische Kirchenbusse im frühen Mittelalter*, Bresslauer Studien zur historischen Theologie 16 (Breslau, 1930), pp. 35, 95-101; C. Vogel, *Les "Libri paenitentiales"*, Typologie des sources du moyen âge occidental 27 (Turnhout, 1978), pp. 39-43. The best survey of the problem, with references to older literature, is that by R. Kottje "Busspraxis und Bussritus", in *Segni e riti nella chiesa altomedievale occidentale*, 2 vols, Settimane di studio del Centro italiano di studi sull'alto medioevo 33 (Spoleto, 1987), 1:369-95. Kottje (p. 393) refers to Ekkehard's story about Iso as an example of "Mischformen zwischen *paenitentia privata* und publica".

confession to a priest, who would then decide upon a proper "secret" penance (*paenitentia occulta* or *secreta*).

As I have argued elsewhere, this image of the "Carolingian dichotomy" is problematic at best, for it was devised by modern historians, who in turn based themselves on ninth-century clerics frantically trying to classify a disorderly and much more diverse reality.[11] This is not to say that the opposition between secret and public sin was entirely theoretical. On the contrary, the notion of "scandal" demanding some kind of public *satisfactio* was a fundamental one in Carolingian society, but for this very reason the divide between public and occult penance was not so tidy as ecclesiastical legislation made it out to be. In theory, priests had to ferret out candidates for public penance, presenting them to the bishop who would then perform the proper ritual; in practice, however, sins which caused public offence could lead to more informal and improvised rituals of atonement. Ekkehard's story about Iso's parents is an interesting case in point.

No doubt Ekkehard was familiar with the official liturgy of public penance. He had been ordained a priest[12] and had lived for roughly a decade in the household of Archbishop Aribo of Mainz (1021-1031).[13] Between 950 and 960 the scriptorium of St Alban's in Mainz had produced the influential *Pontificale Romano-Germanicum*, which contains an elaborate *ordo* for public penance based on the models provided by Regino of Prüm and older sources.[14]

---

[11] M. de Jong, "What was Public about Public Penance? *Paenitentia publica* in the Carolingian World", in *La giustizia nell'alto medioevo (secoli IX-XI)*, Settimane di studio del Centro italiano di studi sull'alto medioevo 44 (Spoleto, 1997), pp. 863-905.

[12] See F. L. Baumann, ed., *Dioeceses Augustensis, Constantiensis, curiensis*, MGH Necrologia Germaniae 1 (Berlin, 1888; repr. 1983), p. 483 (October 21st), where Ekkehard is referred to as "magister, monachus et presbyter".

[13] For Ekkehard's own reference to his period in Mainz, see *Casus s. Galli* chap. 66, pp. 140-42. See also E. Dümmler, "Ekkehard IV von Sankt Gallen", *Zeitschrift für deutsches Alterthum* 14 (1869), 1-73 (pp. 4-6).

[14] *Le Pontifical romano-germanique du Xe siècle. Le texte* 2, ed. C. Vogel and R. Elze, Studi e testi 227 (Vatican City, 1963), 99, chapters 71-73 and 244-51, pp. 21, 59-67. On the importance of this compilation see C. Vogel, "Le

No doubt Ekkehard witnessed formal rituals of public penance in the cathedral of Mainz, with sinners being driven out through the so-called "Adam's Gate" in the northern wall, and penitents attending Mass from a suitable distance in the sackcloth which made them visible as members of the *ordo paenitentum*.[15] Apart from this, he may also have been familiar with another important penitential document from the Rhineland, containing elaborate prescriptions with regard to "secret" penance: the *Corrector sive Medicus* compiled in 1008-1012 by Burchard of Worms.[16]

Together these two texts incorporate a long and venerable history of penitential legislation, but they also reveal some new developments. In the domain of secret penance Burchard allowed a reconciliation immediately after confession, before proper penance had been performed; around the turn of the millennium this had become common practice.[17] Moreover, by this time Lent had become the season *par excellence* for both public and secret penance. Since late antiquity "canonical" penance had been imposed on what later

Pontifical romano-germanique du Xe siècle. Nature, date et importance du document", *Cahiers de civilisation médiévale* 6 (1963), 27-48. For Regino on public penance see Regino of Prüm, *De synodalibus causis*, ed. H. Wasserschleben (Leipzig, 1840), 1:295, p. 136.

[15] C. Vogel, "Les rites de la pénitence publique au Xe et XIe siècles", in *Mélanges R. Crozet*, ed. P. Gallais and Y.-J. Riou (Poitiers, 1966), pp. 137-44. On the subject of the penitent "audientes" being present in the back of the church, benefiting from blessings but excluded from Communion, see Isaac of Langres (d. 880), *Capitula de poenitentibus*, chap. 17, ed. R. Pokorny and M. Stratmann, MGH Capitula episcoporum 2 (Hanover, 1995), pp. 192-93 (= Benedictus Levita, *Capitularia spuria*, 1, chap. 136, ed. G. H. Pertz, MGH LL 2.2 (Hanover, 1837), p. 53).

[16] Burchard's *Corrector* is in fact book 19 of his *Decretum*. Its first 33 chapters have been edited as the *Poenitentiale ecclesiarum Germaniae* by H. J. Schmitz, in *Die Bussbücher und das kanonische Bussverfahren* 2 (Düsseldorf, 1898), pp. 409-63. I will primarily refer to this edition; for other chapters, not edited by Schmitz, I will use PL 140, cols 949-1018. On the *Corrector* and its manuscripts see now H. Hoffmann and R. Pokorny, *Das Dekret des Bischofs Burchards von Worms. Textstufen – Frühe Verbreitung – Vorlagen* (Munich, 1991), pp. 157-58.

[17] Burchard, *Corrector*, chap. 4, p. 410; cf. B. Poschmann, *Der Ablass im Licht der Bussgeschichte*, Theophaneia 4 (Bonn, 1948), pp. 23-25.

became known as Ash Wednesday, while Maundy Thursday was the preferred day for reconciliation. Carolingian public penance followed this pattern, but increasingly Lent became the favoured season for doing whatever penance one had incurred, be it public or secret. Understandably so, for Lent had long been a period of purification; Carolingian bishops like Theodulf of Orléans and Radulf of Bourges had already insisted that the faithful prepare themselves for Easter Communion by fasting and abstaining from sexual intercourse.[18] Lent thus became a season of penitential spring-cleaning, with people flocking to confession to prepare themselves for Easter. This, at least, was what one "old boy" from St Gall had in mind: Bishop Ulrich of Augsburg (d. 973) enjoined his clergy to call the faithful to confession on the "feria quarta ante quadragesimam", imposing penance "not according to what your heart tells you, but according to your book of penance".[19] Even those not undertaking a penance shared in the general fervour of atonement. By the tenth century Ash Wednesday had assumed its still familiar shape: the imposition of ashes originally reserved for public penitents was now extended to all the faithful. On the "dies cineris et cilicii, qui caput ieiunii dicitur" all those coming to church received the ashes from the priest, signifying the beginning of the penitential season.[20]

This convergence of the rites of public and secret penance during Lent provides the context for Ekkehard's story. Iso's exemplary parents had not only discharged their usual Lent obligations of fasting and abstaining from the marriage bed, but they had also voluntarily worn sackcloth and ashes, the traditional outward signs of public penance. Thus adorned, they had purified themselves

---

[18] Theodulf of Orléans, *Capitulare* 1, chapters 36-43, ed. P. Brommer, MGH Capitula episcoporum 1 (Hanover, 1984), pp. 133-40; Radulf of Bourges, *Capitula*, chap. 29, ed. Brommer, MGH Capitula episcoporum 1, p. 256.

[19] Ulrich of Augsburg, *Sermo synodalis*, PL 135, cols 1072-73; similar instructions in Regino, *De synodalibus causis*, 1, notitia chap. 59, p. 23; Burchard, *Corrector*, p. 408. See J. A. Jungmann, *Die lateinischen Bussriten in ihren geschichtlichen Entwicklung* (Innsbruck, 1932), pp. 172-75.

[20] Jungmann, *Die lateinischen Bussriten*, pp. 59-60. On eleventh-century hagiographical texts mentioning the voluntary "carena" of Lent penance, see L. Hertling, "Hagiographische Texte zur frühmittelalterliche Bussgeschichte", *Zeitschrift für katholische Theologie* 50 (1931), pp. 114, 119.

for the first major event of Easter celebrations, the festive procession prior to Mass on Easter Saturday. Alas, their inadvertent lapse rendered all their previous efforts useless; fasting during Lent was worth virtually nothing if it were polluted by the *opus coniugalis*.[21] The ritual clock was therefore relentlessly reversed, and the couple dejectedly went back to their sackcloth and ashes. But before doing so, they practically cried their shameful deed from the rooftops. This represents a crucial turn in the narrative, by which Ekkehard made it very clear that the couple's sin was of a public nature. The entire household, rushing to the scene, had no need to ask what was the matter, for man and wife loudly proclaimed their guilt. *Mutatis mutandis*, an equally public type of penance was in order.

The rest of the story is dominated by the blatant publicity of the culprits' atonement, with most of the ritual described deriving from the liturgy of *paenitentia publica*. Their public confession in front of the local priest and his assembled flock closely resembles Regino's instructions for "official" public penitents appearing in front of their bishop on Ash Wednesday: in sackcloth and barefoot they should publicly prostrate themselves, loudly proclaiming their guilt.[22] The penance imposed on Iso's parents, standing shamefully in front of the church whenever there was a service, also belonged to the stock repertoire of *paenitentia publica*. The Council of Worms (868) ordered the murderer of a priest to stand *ante foras basilicae* during Mass for five years, a decree incorporated by both Regino and Burchard.[23] And last but not least, as in more formal rituals the couple's reconciliation was witnessed by a crowd, signifying that sinners who had grievously offended the community were once more

---

[21] Theodulf of Orléans, *Capitulare* 1, chapters 40 and 43, ed. Brommer, pp. 138-40; Radulf of Bourges, *Capitula*, chap. 29, ed. Brommer, p. 256; Burchard of Worms, *Decretum* 13, chap. 14, col. 887; Ivo of Chartres, *Decretum* pars IV, PL 161, col. 274 (chap. 47).

[22] Regino, *De synodalibus causis*, 1, chap. 295, pp. 135-36.

[23] Council of Worms (868), chap. 26, in J. D. Mansi, ed., *Sacrorum conciliorum nova et amplissima collectio*, vol. 15 (Venice, 1770), col. 874; Regino, *De synodalibus causis*, 2, chap. 6, pp. 216-17; Burchard, *Decretum* 6, chap. 1, col. 763-65. More examples in Jungmann, *Die lateinischen Bussriten*, pp. 66-67.

accepted in its midst. All should witness this event and rejoice, as the *cives* did in the case of Iso's parents.

Yet in other respects Ekkehard's tale does not fit the pattern of an official public penance. To begin with, there was not a bishop in sight; the fate of Iso's parents and their penance was entirely in the hands of priests. At one level the story reads like a celebration of local priesthood, for the intervening angel deigned to take the shape of a saintly but ordinary parish priest. Furthermore, public penance had radiated far beyond its episcopal and solemn confines, inspiring spontaneous and improvised rituals. After 1150 yet another scholarly attempt at classification would label such rituals as a *paenitentia publica non sollemnis*, but they certainly flourished long before theologians acknowledged their existence.[24]

In Ekkehard's tale the entire penitential sequence, normally taking up at least an entire *quadragesima*, was compressed into less than two days. Man and wife had to stand "pro foribus ecclesiae eo die et nocte".[25] The expression "eo die et nocte" refers to the remainder of Easter Saturday and the subsequent "vigilia in nocte Paschae", when the people flocked to church at the break of dawn.[26] The couple's greatest worry was to be refused Easter Communion, so they attempted to speed up the process. Their attempt to gain premature forgiveness from a neighbouring saintly priest was condemned as "temerity", but the overall intensity of their penitential efforts saved the day. It was precisely the repeated and humiliating

---

[24] From the 1160s onwards a "tripartite" model of penance emerged: *paenitentia privata*, *paenitentia publica non sollemnis* and *paenitentia sollemnis*. This classification attempted to integrate the many "disorderly" types of public penance within a new system; the category of "solemn" public penance served to accommodate the traditional canonical penance. See M. C. Mansfield, *The Humiliation of Sinners. Public Penance in Thirteenth-Century France*, (Ithaca and London, 1995), pp. 21-34.

[25] "On the threshold of the church that day and night". On the use of the *limen* in rites of passage (including penance), see especially A. Van Gennep, *Les rites de passage. Etude systématique des rites* (Paris, 1909), pp. 13-15, 19-26. English translation: *The Rites of Passage*, trans. M. B. Vizedom and G. L. Caffee, (London, 1960).

[26] *Le Pontifical romano-germanique*, 2, 99, chap. 399, p. 112.

publicity of their atonement which merited them a miraculous reconciliation.

This part of the story contains a fascinating mixture of tradition and innovation. Public humiliation had always been an integral part of *paenitentia publica*, to the extent that the entire ritual was geared towards shaming the culprits. Public confession and prostration, loud lamentations, wearing penitential garb, standing at the threshold of the church – all this was done in front of a disapproving multitude demanding *satisfactio*. Sincere compliance with such rituals no doubt went some way towards the ultimate redemption of sinners, but the essence of Carolingian public penance was its coercive nature: it was a punishment imposed on those having scandalised their local community, the diocese, the realm, or even the entire *ecclesia*.[27] Humiliation and coercion remained intricately connected; the stronger the element of coercion, the greater the humiliation.

For all his use of traditional penitential imagery, Ekkehard departed from this pattern by emphasising the couple's repeated and entirely voluntary self-abasement. It was their spontaneous confession in front of various crowds which earned them first an "indulgence" from their local priest, and subsequently the much-desired Easter Communion. In this respect the story of Iso's parents is not so much in keeping with the tradition of public penance as with the Pseudo-Augustinian treatise *De vera et falsa paenitentia*. This mid-eleventh-century text, soon to become extremely popular, stresses the redeeming effect of the shame inherent in confession, elevating the act of self-revelation into a penance meriting absolution. The redeeming power of confession would be enhanced if the sinner confessed to as many people as possible, thus increasing his or her shame: "qui erubescit pro Christo, fit dignus misericordia".[28]

Ekkehard's treatment of penitential themes reveals how such apparently new developments evolved from older patterns, with the traditional context legitimating ritual innovation. In the course of the twelfth century spontaneous confession gained an unparalleled importance, best expressed in the literary theme of the pious knight

---

[27] De Jong, "What was Public about Public Penance?".

[28] Ps. Augustinus, *De vera et falsa poenitentia*, PL 40, col. 1122 (chap. 10).

redeeming himself by confessing his sins to anybody who would hear them – even to his horse if nobody else happened to be around.[29] Such tales could not have been told in the Carolingian era, but the humiliation which then became an integral part of a "proper" *paenitentia publica* did prepare the ritual ground for the "cult of shame" flourishing in the twelfth century. Ekkehard's narrative about a spontaneous public atonement highlights the link between these seemingly different conceptions of penance. The historian of St Gall derived his idiom and inspiration from a long tradition of official public penance, which could nonetheless serve as a framework for newly invented ritual, effortlessly accommodating new views on the relative importance of confession and penance. And not only the game had changed, but also the players. In the early stages of its ninth-century revival, *paenitentia publica* had primarily served the needs of the new Carolingian state, being primarily directed against royal enemies and even kings themselves.[30] When Ekkehard wrote his *Casus sancti Galli*, however, ordinary laymen and priests could take centre stage in local and improvised, but yet eminently public rituals.

IV

Why did the curious history of his parents help to explain Iso's sanctity? Clearly Ekkehard wished to portray the saint's parents as a model of piety, using the occasion to depict an exemplary instance of spontaneous penance. Yet the couple's extremely contrite behaviour is only part of the story. There was also the mother's vision during pregnancy which augured the birth of a future saint, and, more importantly, the time of Iso's conception. Although much of the story is one of persistent and ultimately successful purification, the parents'

---

[29] C. Vogel, *Le pêcheur et la pénitence au moyen âge* (Paris, 1969), pp. 32-33; J.-C. Payen, *Le motif du repentir dans la littérature française médiévale (des origines à 1230)* (Geneva, 1967).

[30] M. de Jong, "Power and Humility in Carolingian Society: the Public Penance of Louis the Pious", *Early Medieval Europe* 1 (1992), 29-52 and "What was Public about Public Penance?".

initial pollution remains at the centre of this hagiographical narrative. The starting point of Ekkehard's argument for Iso's sanctity is the fact that he was the issue of a dangerous transgression: he was conceived in sacred time, on Easter Saturday.

Such children could become either monsters or saints. From Gregory of Tours onwards, clerical authors had warned the faithful against sexual intercourse on a Sunday, in Lent, or on feast days: whoever broke this rule could expect to bring forth monstrous issue.[31] Ekkehard and his contemporaries remained firmly rooted in this long tradition. There is nothing sinful about marriage, said Bishop Thietmar of Merseburg (d. 1002), provided its legitimacy is affirmed by a strict purity on holy days. He underlined this view with a story of a woman who, having become pregnant on Innocents' day, gave birth "at an unusual time" to a crippled child.[32] Sins of this sort led to a state of impurity becoming manifest in the child: "Ex his autem procreari solent coeci, claudi, gibbi et lippi sive alii turpibus maculis aspersi".[33]

The idea of *pollutio* was central in Western medieval Christianity, especially in the earlier middle ages. Mary Douglas' classic, *Purity and Danger*, remains the best guide to this still largely

---

[31] On "sacred time" and sexual taboo, see J. L. Flandrin, *Un temps pour embrasser. Aux origines de la morale sexuelle occidentale (VIe-XIe siècle)* (Paris, 1983), pp. 8-40; P. J. Payer, *Sex and the Penitentials. The Development of a Sexual Code, 550-1150* (Toronto, 1984); M. de Jong, "To the Limits of Kinship: Anti-incest Legislation in the Early Medieval West (500-900)", in *From Sappho to De Sade. Moments in the History of Sexuality*, ed. J. Bremmer (London, 1989), pp. 36-59; and, especially, A. Demyttenaere, "The Cleric, Women and the Stain. Some Beliefs and Ritual Practices Concerning Women in the Early Middle Ages", in *Frauen im Spätantike und Frühmittelalter. Lebensbedingungen - Lebensnormen - Lebensformen*, ed. W. Affeldt (Sigmaringen, 1990), pp. 141-65.

[32] Thietmar of Merseburg, *Chronicon* 1, chapters 24-25, ed. W. Trillmich (Darmstadt, 1957), pp. 26-28; see also O. Menzel, ed., *Vita Litbirgae* chap. 33 (Leipzig, 1937), p. 37.

[33] Benedictus Levita, *Capitularia spuria*, 3, chap. 179, ed. G. H. Pertz, MGH LL 2.2 (Hanover, 1837), p. 113: "Such [unions] usually produced blind, crippled, hunchbacked and squinting children, and others afflicted with foul blemishes".

unexplored territory.[34] "Pollution" does not refer to detectable dirt, but rather to a state of moral impurity deriving from the violation of boundaries regarded as fundamental in a given society. These particularly involve the relationship between nature and culture, as well as that between humankind and the supernatural. "Taboo" is the seemingly natural abhorrence of crossing boundaries resulting from cultural classification; the fear of pollution serves to avoid a dangerous confusion of categories. A ritual cleansing after pollution is therefore not a hygienic gesture, but an attempt to recreate an order which has become disturbed. For this very reason Ekkehard had Iso's parents frantically washing themselves, once the danger to which they had exposed themselves had dawned upon them. Their subsequent penance was meant to restore their former state of purity, with Easter Sunday as a deadline. Yet pollution is not only dangerous, but it also has potentially sacred connotations. If handled carefully, in ritually controlled circumstances, the abnormal may become an extraordinary source of power. Both being "out of order" by transgressing cultural boundaries, impurity and sacredness represent two sides of the same coin.[35]

This seems to be the implicit meaning (or subtext) of Ekkehard's curious tale. Iso could have turned into a monstrous child – crippled, squinting, blind or a hunchback, in other words, one of society's outcasts. By their exemplary penance, however, his parents purified themselves sufficiently for their son to take the other route open to a child conceived in sacred time and therefore destined to remain abnormal: becoming a saint.

---

[34] M. Douglas, *Purity and Danger. An Analysis of the Concepts of Pollution and Taboo* (London, 1966). Her insights have inspired some early medievalists, notably A. Demyttenaere, "The Cleric, Women and the Stain" (see note 31 above) and R. Meens, "Pollution in the Early Middle Ages: the Case of Food Regulations in the Penitentials", *Early Medieval Europe* 4 (1995), 3-19.

[35] Douglas, *Purity and Danger*, pp. 159-79.

Saint Wilfrid:
Tribal Bishop, Civic Bishop or
Germanic Lord?

David Pelteret

When I was casting around for a topic with a northern English slant to pay tribute to Leeds for establishing the International Medieval Congress, I thought of that stormy petrel, Saint Wilfrid, and proceeded to ask myself a simple question: "How did Wilfrid interpret the rôle of a bishop?" An answer to this question I felt might help explain Wilfrid's misfortunes at the hands of both the secular and ecclesiastical authorities in the England of his day. Unfortunately, like many simple questions, it is not susceptible of a simple answer as I came to discover.

In order to gain some insight into what Wilfrid's perceptions may have been, we must first survey three other topics, themselves of vast dimension: kingship, monasticism and the episcopacy of the seventh century; because it is against the backdrop of these institutions that Wilfrid played out his adult life.

When Wilfrid was born in AD 634 Anglo-Saxon kingship may have been less than a century old. Though the *Anglo-Saxon Chronicle* and various king-lists may suggest an ancestry for kings going back at least to the fifth century,[1] it is far more reasonable to

---

[1] For the hazards of drawing historical conclusions from this material see D. N. Dumville, "Sub-Roman Britain: History and Legend", *History* new ser.,

consider kingship to be a phenomenon of the latter part of the sixth century. It is then that archaeologists start to see in the physical record the evidence of stratification based on wealth.[2] The institution took various forms within England. For instance, Northumbria was then divided into the two territories of Bernicia and Deira, with their centres respectively in Bamburgh and York. In the seventh century Bernicia and Deira sometimes had separate kings and at other times a sub-king of the one area was subordinate to an over-king based in the other region.[3]

In the seventh century we should regard Anglo-Saxon kingship as still taking institutional shape. Charismatic leaders could gain disproportionate power and in the process graft neighbouring peoples onto the tribe that they led. On their death, the newly formed polity could fall apart again.

The rewards of success, however, were enormous. We have only to ponder the finds from Sutton Hoo to see for ourselves what considerable riches were open to someone who became a king.[4] But to hold that position meant giving away much of that wealth: in lavish display, in gift-giving,[5] and – most important of all – in the bestowal of land and the rights inherent in that land. To continue

---

62 (1977), 173-92, reprinted in Dumville, *Histories and Pseudo-Histories of the Insular Middle Ages* (Aldershot, 1990), no. 1, with original pagination.

[2] For instance, the fifth-century site of Mucking betrays little evidence of material wealth; the early-seventh-century site at Sutton Hoo, on the other hand, reveals that considerable riches had by then been accumulated by a minority within Anglo-Saxon society who were clearly highly sensitive to issues of power. See further, C. Scull, "Before Sutton Hoo: Structures of Power and Society in Early East Anglia", in *The Age of Sutton Hoo: The Seventh Century in North-Western Europe*, ed. M. O. H. Carver (Woodbridge, 1992), pp. 3-23.

[3] For further details and a survey of recent scholarship see D. N. Dumville, "The Origins of Northumbria: Some Aspects of the British Background", in *The Origins of the Anglo-Saxon Kingdoms*, ed. S. Bassett, Studies in the Early History of Britain (London, 1989), pp. 213-22 and 284-86.

[4] *The Sutton Hoo Ship Burial*, ed. R. L. S. Bruce-Mitford, 3 volumes in 4 (London, 1975-83); *Age of Sutton Hoo*, ed. Carver.

[5] The classic study of this phenomenon is M. Mauss, *The Gift: Forms and Functions of Exchange in Archaic Societies*, trans. I. Cunnison (London, 1954; reprinted with corrections, 1969).

doing that required kingship to be predatory: the lands of neighbours were invaded to acquire their wealth in order to reward the king's supporters who had engaged in the fighting. Sutton Hoo is a graphic example of the instability of kingship. Even though the topography of the site reveals that those who were buried there well understood the significance of symbolic display, we cannot now be certain who was buried there and in spite of all the magnificence of the grave goods the East Anglian dynasty proved not to be of lasting significance. Bede and others record the fates of kings who were even less successful. With kinship being a binding force in society, many will have been kinsman of a king – and will have felt entitled to take over his mantle on his death. Kingship was still too young and unformed for any pattern of inheritance such as by an elder son to have become the norm. Close kinsmen might thus see the wealth acquired by their royal relative dissipated through the seizure of power by more distant kinsmen.

If being a king provided an uncertain career, how much more so must it have been for the early warriors who supported a king. Provided they survived the hazards of martial conflict, they might gain the satisfaction of a substantial superiority over a tract of land. But it was by precarious tenure.[6] The hope of establishing a family dynasty was not only contingent on producing sons who could perform (and survive) the same services their father had undertaken but also on the agility of members of the family in establishing a mutually supportive relationship with whoever became a deceased king's successor.

Monasteries, in common with kingship, were also relatively unformed institutions in the second half of the seventh century.[7] The influence of the eremitical form of monasticism must have been strong under the impact of the Celtic-speaking peoples of Ireland and the islands of western Scotland. Those living in such establishments were destined for an austere existence. But other

---

[6] E. John, *Land Tenure in Early England: A Discussion of Some Problems*, Studies in Early English History (Leicester, 1960), especially p. 51.

[7] For an introduction see S. Foot, "What was an Early Anglo-Saxon Monastery?", in *Monastic Studies: The Continuity of Tradition*, ed. J. Loades (Bangor, 1990), pp. 48-57.

models were possible. From Gaul, or perhaps from Spain, came the double monastery, where women and men lived in a single community, sometimes under the leadership of an abbess, as was the case at Whitby under Hild.[8] Benedict Biscop, the travelling companion of Wilfrid in his first trip abroad in 653, visited no less than seventeen monastic establishments and used a blend of their practices in the monastic houses he created at Monkwearmouth and Jarrow.[9] The monastic rule of the Italian monk, Benedict, which had so influenced Pope Gregory the Great, was only one of many competing models.[10] Much has been made of the supposed impact of the Benedictine Rule on early Northumbrian monasticism: Biscop himself has been claimed as a Benedictine, as has Bede.[11] Yet the only one for whom there is a clear assertion in the sources of following the ways of Benedict's Rule is Wilfrid.[12] In the light of Wilfrid's lifestyle (of which more anon), this may seem improbable. But the Rule did not exclude differences of wealth. What it stressed was a strongly communal and hierarchical life of persons of the same sex living together who owed total obedience to their leader,

[8] M. Bateson's study, "Origin and Early History of Double Monasteries", *Transactions of the Royal Historical Society* new ser., 13 (1899), 137-98, should now be supplemented by the more wide-ranging collection, *Doppelklöster und andere Formen der Symbiose männlicher und weiblicher Religiosen im Mittelalter*, ed. K. Elm and M. Parisse, Berliner historische Studien 18, Ordensstudien 8 (Berlin, 1992). See also J. Godfrey, "The Place of the Double Monastery in the Anglo-Saxon Minster System", in *Famulus Christi: Essays in Commemoration of the Thirteenth Centenary of the Birth of the Venerable Bede*, ed. G. Bonner (London, 1976), pp. 344-50.

[9] Bede, *Historia abbatum*, chap. 11, in Bede, *Historia ecclesiastica*, ed. C. Plummer, 2 vols (Oxford, 1896), 1:374-75 (text); *The Age of Bede*, trans. J. F. Webb, ed. with introduction and notes D. H. Farmer, revised ed. (Harmondsworth, 1983), p. 196 (translation).

[10] See M. Dunn, "Mastering Benedict: Monastic Rules and their Authors in the Early Medieval West", *English Historical Review* 105 (1990), 567-94.

[11] For a balanced assessment see P. Hunter Blair, *The World of Bede* (London, 1970), pp. 197-99.

[12] *The Life of Bishop Wilfrid by Eddius Stephanus*, chapters 14 and 47, ed. and trans. B. Colgrave (Cambridge, 1927), pp. 30 and 98. This edition will hereafter be cited as *Life of Bishop Wilfrid*.

the abbot.[13] Wilfrid's claim to have introduced Benedictinism into his monasteries, where it had not been practised before, needs to be given more credence.

In the uncertain world of the early English kingdoms monasticism must have been peculiarly attractive. Retirement to a monastery, at home or abroad in Rome, offered to a reigning king a graceful way of bowing out,[14] and for a royal kinsman it permitted withdrawal from the fray if he preferred a peaceful existence. It was also a natural place for royal women who by disposition or by circumstance were unlikely to find a spouse – or who wanted to escape one.[15]

With the emphasis that Anglo-Saxon historians tend to place on élites we often forget how uncertain existence must also have been for the peasantry: the kind of person whom the thegn Imma claimed to be when found still alive on the battlefield, the *ceorl* who was obliged to bring food for the warriors. Here evidence of Irish monasticism can provide us with some insights. It has always been a puzzle to me how early Northumbrian society could support no less than six hundred monks at Wearmouth and Jarrow.[16] Thomas Charles-Edwards, drawing on earlier work of Kathleen Hughes,[17] has pointed out that in Ireland a lay-tenant of a monastery could also

[13] Adalbert de Vogüé and Jean Neufville, eds and trans, *La Règle de Saint Benoît*, Sources Chrétiennes 181-87, 7 vols (Paris, 1971-77).

[14] For an introduction to these kings see S. J. Ridyard, "Monk-Kings and the Anglo-Saxon Hagiographic Tradition", *The Haskins Society Journal: Studies in Medieval History* 6, ed. R. B. Patterson (Woodbridge, 1995), pp. 15-27, with further literature there cited.

[15] P. Stafford, *Queens, Concubines and Dowagers: The King's Wife in the Early Middle Ages* (London, 1983), pp. 178-79.

[16] *Historia abbatum auctore anonymo*, chap. 33, in Bede, *Historia ecclesiastica*, ed. Plummer, 1:400 (text); D. Whitelock, ed. and trans., *English Historical Documents, Volume 1: c. 500-1042*, 2nd ed. (London, 1979), no. 155, p. 768 (translation).

[17] K. Hughes, *The Church in Early Irish Society* (London, 1966), pp. 136-37.

be called a monk or *manach*.[18] We do not have to imagine, therefore, six hundred monks chanting the offices of the day. Probably only a small proportion of that number devoted themselves primarily to worship and prayer. The vast majority would have been like the shy poetic cowherd with the British name, Cædmon.[19] Living on the monastic estate, they probably attended services on occasion, where they would have heard tell of Biblical stories in the Anglo-Saxon tongue, but their daily tasks would have been agrarian. Hild perceived Cædmon's talent and urged him to cast off his lay status, quite possibly because the number of true monks was small and people with ability were to be encouraged. Wilfrid is portrayed as being rather more forceful: he required that vows made to him be fulfilled by insisting that a seven-year-old British boy should enter the monastery at Ripon, much against his mother's wishes, even though she had earlier promised him to the church.[20] Perhaps the multiple churches to be found at places like Wilfrid's Hexham – where there is evidence of three[21] – were employed to cater for the diverse nature of the lay and ecclesiastical community of such a monastery.[22]

Finally, I turn to the episcopacy. In Ireland bishops in the sixth century had been attached especially to a people or tribe, the *tuath*.[23] With the expansion of monasticism, they often became subordinate

[18] T. Charles-Edwards, "The Pastoral Role of the Church in the Early Irish Laws", in *Pastoral Care Before the Parish*, ed. J. Blair and R. Sharpe, Studies in the Early History of Britain (Leicester, 1992), pp. 63-77 (p. 67).

[19] B. Colgrave and R. A. B. Mynors, eds and trans, *Bede's Ecclesiastical History of the English Church*, 4.24 (22), Oxford Medieval Texts, rev. ed. (Oxford, 1991), pp. 414-21 (text and translation). This edition will hereafter be cited as Bede, *Historia ecclesiastica*, ed. Colgrave and Mynors.

[20] *Life of Bishop Wilfrid*, chap. 18, pp. 38, 40.

[21] *Life of Bishop Wilfrid*, chap. 56, p. 122. See R. N. Bailey, "The Anglo-Saxon Church at Hexham", *Archaeologia Aeliana* 5th ser., 4 (1976), 47-67, especially pp. 66-67, for the possible identification of the hitherto unknown location of St Peter's Church at Hexham.

[22] Multiple churches were not unusual in England and on the Continent: this suggestion is not put forward as a universal explanation for the phenomenon.

[23] Hughes, *The Church in Early Irish Society*, p. 50.

to an abbot, though they retained what had been the traditional offices of baptising converts and ordaining priests, the latter being necessary for the proper performance of the mass.[24] In Gaul bishops were especially associated with the old Roman towns.[25] Frequently the descendants of established senatorial families,[26] they played a significant leadership rôle in local politics – sometimes at the cost of their lives. The number of bishoprics had led to the creation of metropolitans as early as the sixth century, though the latter status did not have much significance in Merovingian Gaul. Gregory of Tours was one such metropolitan.[27] In Italy bishops could influence international relations, especially through their participation in the annual papal synods in Rome.[28] The papal see itself preserved some of the great traditions of the late Roman empire such as the formulation of law and the adjudication of disputes, which were to be important factors in Wilfrid's life.

What is important to note here, therefore, is that the episcopacy in some measure was shaped by regional social institutions: the tribe, the monastery, the urban community, the practices of law and international diplomacy. We should not be surprised to find Wilfrid adopting the *mores* of his own society. What makes him so interesting (and, as I shall suggest, played a part in his misfortunes) was that he drew upon a variety of episcopal models in living out his episcopacy.

Wilfrid clearly came of a social background that made him acceptable to the ruling élite of his day since the wife of the Northumbrian over-king, Oswiu, took him under her wing while he was still a boy. His introduction to monasticism came at the age of fourteen when he entered Lindisfarne in order to look after an ailing

[24] Hughes, *The Church in Early Irish Society*, p. 126.

[25] For an introduction to the relationship between the administrative structure of Roman Gaul and the later episcopal geography of southern France see J. Harries, "Church and State in the *Notitia Galliarum*", *Journal of Roman Studies* 68 (1978), 26-43.

[26] R. W. Mathisen, *Roman Aristocrats in Barbarian Gaul: Strategies for Survival in an Age of Transition* (Austin, Texas, 1993), pp. 89-104 and 199-207.

[27] On metropolitans see *The History of the Franks by Gregory of Tours*, trans. with an introduction O. M. Dalton, 2 vols (Oxford, 1927), 1:268-69.

[28] P. Llewellyn, *Rome in the Dark Ages* (London, 1970), p. 129.

courtier who had retired there. In 653, he moved to Canterbury, where he was protected by the local king. His hopes of finding someone to accompany him to the papal see were successful when he met one of the giants of the early English church, Benedict Biscop. Together they set off for Rome, but Wilfrid tarried in Lyons while Benedict continued on his way.[29] Their subsequent history points to men of different temperaments: Benedict a scholar and inclined towards a monastic existence; Wilfrid, a doer, a lover of the cut-and-thrust of debate, an ambitious man. In Lyons Wilfrid had the chance to observe the life of a metropolitan bishop in an urban setting. He was not seduced into staying there; but it would have been strange if this experience did not leave him untouched at the impressionable age of nineteen. In Rome he would have seen the Lateran and, we may assume, many of the other large churches still standing in and around the city,[30] possibly guided by Boniface, archdeacon of Rome, who provided him with ecclesiastical instruction.[31] He may also have visited the catacombs, with their twisting corridors and dark underground vaults: the catacomb of Saints Marcellinus and Peter had recently been embellished during the pontificate of Honorius I, who had occupied the papal see at the

---

[29] *Life of Bishop Wilfrid*, chap. 3, p. 8.

[30] On the topography and architecture of medieval Rome see R. Krautheimer, *Rome: Profile of a City, 312-1308* (Princeton, 1980) and P. Hetherington, *Medieval Rome: A Portrait of the City and its Life* (London, 1994). See also T. F. X. Noble, "Rome in the Seventh Century", in *Archbishop Theodore: Commemorative Studies on his Life and Influence*, ed. M. Lapidge, Cambridge Studies in Anglo-Saxon England 11 (Cambridge, 1995), pp. 68-87, and the map of the churches and monasteries of seventh-century Rome in B. Bischoff and M. Lapidge, *Biblical Commentaries from the Canterbury School of Theodore and Hadrian*, Cambridge Studies in Anglo-Saxon England 10 (Cambridge, 1994), p. 568.

[31] *Life of Bishop Wilfrid*, chap. 5, p. 12, mentions that Wilfrid encountered Boniface in the course of his daily visits to the shrines of saints in Rome. The archdeacon evidently introduced him to canon law. It is not unreasonable to assume that Boniface acted as a personal guide as well as a spiritual mentor. On the archdeacon of Rome see Llewellyn, *Rome in the Dark Ages*, p. 117.

time of Wilfrid's birth.[32] He would have had the opportunity to encounter the complexities of theological debate: the monothelete controversy was causing agitation during the papacy of Martin, who was the incumbent of the papal throne (though under imperial arrest) at the time of Wilfrid's visit.[33] For a man of evidently forensic disposition, Wilfrid's trip would have afforded him an excellent opportunity to gain a grounding in canon law and theology, which he was to use to good effect at the Synod of Whitby in 664.

On his return to England he met Alcfrith, the son of Oswiu and the sub-king of Deira, through the good offices of the king of Wessex. He had thus already established a pattern of moving across tribal boundaries. Alcfrith gave him thirty hides of land and the monastery at Ripon.[34] Having become abbot, he was ordained to the priesthood by Agilbert, the Gallic-born bishop of Dorchester.[35] There could thus be no question about the validity of his orders.

This may well have been a concern for Wilfrid because the next year was to bring into contention at the Synod of Whitby the differences in liturgical practice between those who drew on the Irish tradition and those who looked to Rome.[36] As a consequence of the synod's decision the Northumbrian bishop, Colman, vacated his see. Precisely where his episcopal seat was is a matter of controversy in the sources: Stephen of Ripon[37] declares that Colman

---

[32] F. Mancinelli, *Catacombs and Basilicas: The Early Christians in Rome* (Florence, 1981), pp. 39-43.

[33] L. C. Rose, "Monothelitism", in *Dictionary of the Middle Ages*, ed. J. R. Strayer and others, 13 vols (New York, 1982-89), 8:479-80.

[34] *Life of Bishop Wilfrid*, chap. 8, p. 16.

[35] *Life of Bishop Wilfrid*, chap. 9, p. 18.

[36] There were also locally powerful political forces at play here which are explored by R. Abels in "The Council of Whitby: A Study in Early Anglo-Saxon Politics", *Journal of British Studies* 23 (1983-84), 1-25.

[37] He is often called Eddius (Stephanus) in the secondary literature. D. P. Kirby's study, "Bede, Eddius Stephanus and the 'Life of Wilfrid'", *English Historical Review* 98 (1983), 101-14, indicates that it is more accurate, however, to refer to the author of the *Uita Wilfridi* as Stephen.

was the metropolitan bishop of York.[38] His Irish background may have made the monastery of Lindisfarne more attractive to him; certainly his successor, Tuda, seems to have been based there.

We may fairly assume that Wilfrid's performance at Whitby led Alcfrith of Deira (whose territory included York) to select him as his bishop. Wilfrid, displaying a scrupulous concern for canonical rectitude, took himself off to Gaul to be consecrated by Agilbert, who by now had transferred to Paris.[39] The see at Canterbury was vacant and the canonical standing of bishops of England was doubtful.[40] Unfortunately for Wilfrid, in his absence Alcfrith rebelled against his father, Oswiu. Oswiu then arranged for Chad to be consecrated as bishop; a simoniac and two British bishops performed the consecration.[41]

After Theodore arrived in Britain as archbishop of Canterbury in 668, he reinstated Wilfrid as bishop.[42] Wilfrid hereafter was to steer his course in the channels set by the original Gregorian mission to England. The main intent of Gregory the Great in sending the mission is uncontroversial: to convert the English to Christianity and to establish a series of bishoprics under two metropolitans, in London and in York.[43] The man who sought to establish the see at York was Paulinus and Bede provides a graphic

[38] *Life of Bishop Wilfrid*, chap. 10, p. 20. There is no evidence that Colman ever received a *pallium*, the symbol of papal recognition of metropolitan status. I think that it is far more likely that this is a fiction on the part of Stephen designed retrospectively to support Wilfrid's later desire for that status. On the *pallium* see Bede, *Historia ecclesiastica*, ed. Plummer, 2:49-52, and Bede, *Historia ecclesiastica*, ed. Colgrave and Mynors, p. 104, note 2.

[39] *Life of Bishop Wilfrid*, chap. 12, p. 26.

[40] Stephen has Wilfrid claim that many of the bishops were Quartodecimans, which Colgrave points out in *Life of Bishop Wilfrid*, p. 159, is unjust. It is quite possible, however, that many of the bishops had not met all the requirements for canonical ordination as practised by the Gallic or Italian churches.

[41] *Life of Bishop Wilfrid*, chap. 14, p. 31; Bede, *Historia ecclesiastica*, ed. Colgrave and Mynors, p. 316, note 2.

[42] *Life of Bishop Wilfrid*, chap. 15, p. 32.

[43] Bede, *Historia ecclesiastica*, 1.29, ed. Colgrave and Mynors, pp. 104, 106.

illustration of his spending three weeks amongst a people in order to bring about their conversion. The vagaries of royal politics intervened and he had felt forced to vacate his see in 633. Nevertheless, Pope Honorius sent him a *pallium* in 634, thereby publicly declaring him to be of metropolitan status.[44] The desire to re-establish York as a metropolitan see may be regarded as the driving force behind many of Wilfrid's subsequent endeavours.

First, he had to have churches worthy of a bishop. He thoroughly restored Paulinus' old church at York. In Ripon he built a fine church whose crypt we can still see today, as we can the one at Hexham, constructed a few years after his episcopal accession.[45] Stephen of Ripon states that no other church north of the Alps equalled it in scale.[46] It was endowed in part by Æthelthryth, the wife of Oswiu's successor, Ecgfrith. Ecgfrith will reappear in this story. The crypt at Hexham was designed presumably to house a sacred relic in the area directly below the high altar. The staircases twist round in a way that differs from European crypts of the day; it has been suggested that the form of the crypt may have been inspired by the catacombs of Rome.[47] Wilfrid proceeded to acquire

[44] Bede, *Historia ecclesiastica*, 2.17, ed. Colgrave and Mynors, p. 194.

[45] On Ripon's crypt see R. A. Hall, "Observations in Ripon Cathedral Crypt, 1989", *Yorkshire Archaeological Journal* 65 (1993), 39-53, and on Hexham's see Bailey, "The Anglo-Saxon Church at Hexham" and R. N. Bailey and D. O'Sullivan with a contribution by D. J. Rackham, "Excavations over St Wilfrid's Crypt at Hexham, 1978", *Archaeologia Aeliana* 5th ser., 7 (1979), 145-57 and Plate XII, together with the further references these authors cite. On the crypts, which are structurally anomalous, see H. M. Taylor, "Corridor Crypts on the Continent and in England", *North Staffordshire Journal of Field Studies* 9 (1968), 17-52.

[46] *Life of Bishop Wilfrid*, chap. 22, p. 46. By implication Stephen is claiming that Wilfrid is of greater stature in this respect than the Merovingian bishops.

[47] R. Gem, "Towards an Iconography of Anglo-Saxon Architecture", *Journal of the Warburg and Courtauld Institutes* 46 (1983), p. 3, suggests that Wilfrid's crypts were influenced by the catacombs. See further E. O Carragáin, *The City of Rome and the World of Bede*, Jarrow Lecture 1994 (Jarrow, 1995), p. 51 note 27. The crypts are devoid of any wall-paintings: if they did indeed take their inspiration from the catacombs, they may well have originally been decorated, since Christians had commissioned wall-paintings to embellish the

yet further monasteries, and in them he established the Rule of St Benedict.[48]

I would suggest that Wilfrid's intent was not purely personal aggrandisement. Gregory, a monk who was enamoured of the Benedictine Rule, had intended that there not merely be a metropolitan based in York but that he should be assisted by twelve bishops.[49] They would have needed suitable churches and an appropriate endowment. Hexham and Ripon fitted into such a schema.

Additionally Wilfrid's mode of deportment as a bishop may have owed something to the examples he saw of episcopal behaviour in Gaul. Stephen tells us how he was lifted up and borne in state by twelve other bishops when Agilbert consecrated him.[50]

After Ecgfrith of Deira's accession as king of Northumbria, the king expanded his realm into Pictland in the north and Mercia in the south. Lindsey was regained. For a time Ecgfrith and Wilfrid seemed to get along but then the king turned against him. Wilfrid was deposed in 679 and Theodore, who had initially supported him on his arrival in England, proceeded to ordain three new bishops to Northumbria in his place.[51] Wilfrid decided to take his case to Rome.

Roman catacombs since about AD 200. Many of these survive to this day. How much more impressive they must have been 1200 years ago in Wilfrid's time. For an example of one rediscovered only in the 1950s see A. Ferrua, *The Unknown Catacomb: A Unique Discovery of Early Christian Art,* trans. B. Nardini (New Lanark, 1991); for the importance of the catacombs in the development of Christian iconography and for some useful plans see P. C. Finney, *The Invisible God: The Earliest Christians on Art* (New York, 1994), pp. 146-274.

[48] *Life of Bishop Wilfrid,* chap. 14, p. 30.

[49] Bede, *Historia ecclesiastica,* 1.29, ed. Colgrave and Mynors, p. 104.

[50] *Life of Bishop Wilfrid,* chap. 12, p. 26. Stephen no doubt expects us to make the connection between the twelve bishops elevating Wilfrid and the elevated status that Gregory intended the Bishop of York to hold over his twelve fellow bishops. The symbolism of the twelve is so obvious as not to need comment.

[51] *Life of Bishop Wilfrid,* chap. 24, p. 48.

His response to his deposition as portrayed by Stephen is interesting.[52] First, he is not depicted as opposing Theodore's actions inside England. He thus could not be accused of being a schismatic.[53] Second, on his way to Italy he went via Frisia, where he sought to convert the local inhabitants. His behaviour was entirely in keeping with a worthy successor of Gregory the Great and Paulinus.

We have some inkling of the proceedings from a now sadly deformed text from the medieval archives at Canterbury preserved in two manuscripts in the British Library, MS Cotton Vespasian B. xx, fols 227v-229v, and MS Harley 105, fols 218v-227v. Unfortunately Wilfrid's story got entangled in the disputes over precedence between Lanfranc and his successors and the archdiocese of York in the late eleventh and early twelfth centuries.[54] One of the two surviving manuscripts of Stephen of Ripon's *Life of Bishop Wilfrid* (now London, British Library, MS Cotton Vespasian D. vi) migrated to Canterbury. This manuscript now lacks two folios: one of them contained the chapter where Stephen refers to Wilfrid as a metropolitan.[55] So far I seem to be the only one who sees a link between Canterbury and the loss of these folios. Eadmer took on the task of writing a sanitised version of Wilfrid's life for Canterbury, presumably to replace Stephen's

---

[52] One has constantly to remember that one can only know Wilfrid through the portrayal of him by Stephen and by Bede: these portraits will frequently be shaped by literary considerations.

[53] H. Chadwick has suggested that Wilfrid may have called into question Theodore's orthodoxy when he was in Rome: see "Theodore of Tarsus and Monotheletism", in *Logos: Festschrift für Luise Abramowski*, ed. H. C. Brennecke, E. L. Grasmuck and C. Markschies, Beihefte zur Zeitschrift für die neutestamentliche Wissenschaft und die Kunde der alteren Kirche 67 (Berlin, 1993), pp. 534-44 (p. 544). Since Theodore appears to have been respected by the pope, this would not have been very astute tactics on Wilfrid's part, though he may have suggested there were some unorthodox elements within the English church, which may have prompted the despatch of John, the precentor of St Peter's, to England.

[54] R. W. Southern, "The Canterbury Forgeries", *English Historical Review* 73 (1958), 193-226.

[55] B. Colgrave in *Life of Bishop Wilfrid*, pp. xiii and 32, note 11.

version. I suggest that Canterbury must also have acquired a transcript of the papal proceedings held in Rome and produced a heavily doctored version, which has been preserved in the Vespasian B. xx and Harley 105 manuscripts. That a forger's hand has been at work cannot be doubted: Gregory the Great, for instance, is referred to as "Gregorius Primus" – yet Gregory II became pope only in 715.

The record of the Wilfrid's hearing in Rome has received the detailed attention of only two scholars so far: the great Wilhelm Levison, who published an edition of the text in 1912 (originally based on the seventeenth-century printed edition of Spelman), supplemented in 1930 by corrections based on the later discovery of the Cotton and Harley manuscripts,[56] and Marion Gibbs, who made the crucial link with the post-Conquest forgeries perpetrated at Canterbury in that see's quest to attain precedence over York.[57] Unfortunately she presented her case in an article of almost impenetrable opacity. Her central argument is that Wilfrid was seeking to attain metropolitan status but that Theodore had shifted ground because of changed political circumstances in England. A new figure had appeared on the horizon: in 674 Æthelred had ascended the throne of Mercia. He was hostile towards Canterbury, perhaps because Jaruman, his bishop, supported the Irish case. It was in Theodore's interests to form an alliance with Ecgfrith, who himself must have been concerned at Mercia's intentions. Wilfrid was the sacrificial lamb.

In its fundamentals I accept Gibbs' case. In the remainder of this paper I simply want to move the story on a little. I begin by turning to the text. So far as I can see, only two paragraphs can be said to be in their original form. The first can be verified from the

---

[56] W. Levison, "Die Akten der römischen Synode von 679", *Zeitschrift der Savigny-Stiftung für Rechtsgeschichte* 33, Kanonistische Abteilung 2 (1912), 249-82, and "Zu den Akten der römischen Synode von 679", *Zeitschrift der Savigny-Stiftung für Rechtsgeschichte* 50, Kanonistische Abteilung 19 (1930), 672-74, both repr. in *Aus rheinischer und fränkischer Frühzeit: Ausgewählte Aufsätze von Wilhelm Levison* (Düsseldorf, 1948), pp. 267-94.

[57] M. Gibbs, "The Decrees of Agatho and the Gregorian Plan for York", *Speculum* 48 (1973), 213-46.

records of a subsequent synod held in Rome in 680, which Wilfrid also attended and subscribed to.[58] Levison demonstrated this in his usual impeccably scholarly way.[59] The second is a paragraph that has hitherto merited no attention. Clause 7 declares that bishops should not use arms, should not possess minstrels or any musical instruments, nor should they permit entertainment and games in their presence. Their reading material should always concern matters of divine expression.[60] This may already strike a familiar

[58] R. Riedinger, ed., *Concilium Universale Constantinopolitanum Tertium. Concilii Actiones I-XI*, Acta Conciliorum Oecumenicorum 2.2.1 (Berlin, 1990), pp. 47-161. H. Chadwick in his review of this volume in *Journal of Ecclesiastical History* 42 (1991), 630-35, has rightly commended this as an admirable edition, but by printing the witnesses *seriatim* Riedinger masks the fact that the witness list must originally have been copied down in five columns, as R. L. Poole pointed out in "The Chronology of Bede's *Historia ecclesiastica* and the Councils of 679-680", *Journal of Theological Studies* 20 (1918), 24-40 (p. 35), reprinted in his *Studies in Chronology and History*, ed. A. Lane Poole (Oxford, 1934), pp. 50-51. Chadwick provides two thought-provoking studies of the background to this Council and Wilfrid's part in it in "Theodore of Tarsus and Monotheletism", in *Logos*, ed. Brennecke et al. (see above, n. 53), pp. 534-44, and "Theodore, the English Church and the Monothelete Controversy", in *Archbishop Theodore*, ed. Lapidge, pp. 88-95.

[59] Levison, "Die Akten", pp. 261-65 (reprinted in *Aus rheinischer und fränkischer Frühzeit*, pp. 276-79).

[60] "Statuimus etiam atque decernimus, ut episcopi uel quicunque ecclesiasticae ordinis religiosam uitam professi sunt, armis non utantur nec citharoedas habeant uel quaecunque symphonia nec quoscunque iocos uel ludos ante se permittant, quia omnia haec disciplina sanctae ecclesiae sacerdotes fideles suos habere non sinit, sed praecipit diuinis seruitiis et prouidentia pauperum [et] ecclesiasticis utilitatibus occupari, magisque diuinorum eloquiorum lectio ad aedificationem ecclesiarum semper legatur, quatenus cum nutrimentis corporeis pariter et animae audientium diuinis eloquiis nutriantur". ("We have also decided and declare that bishops or any who have professed the religious life of an ecclesiastical order should not wield arms nor have minstrels or any musical instruments nor should they permit any entertainment or games in their presence because all these things the discipline of the Sacred Church does not permit to its faithful priests, but it enjoins them to be engaged in divine services and the provision of the poor and matters of value to the Church; the reading of divine eloquence for the edification of the Church should always be chosen instead in order that the souls of the listeners should also be nourished

note with literary historians. This surely describes the entertainment typical of a royal court. I suggest that what we are witnessing in this paragraph is a sop being thrown by the papal curia to the presenter of Theodore's case. The curia could not possibly justify Wilfrid's uncanonical deposition, but they could not afford to humiliate the man who had been sent by the pope to Canterbury.[61] *Pace* D. H. Farmer, I do not believe that the papal curia was inadequately informed about English conditions.[62] Not merely did they have both the plaintiff, Wilfrid, and a representative of Theodore at the hearing but they were also able to consult Benedict Biscop, who was once more in Rome. His interests would have been to protect his monasteries and he is thus likely to have counselled a prudential course of action. And so the curia made a pious directive about appropriate episcopal behaviour in recognition of Theodore's case.

We have ample independent evidence of Wilfrid's personal and social behaviour, especially from Stephen of Ripon. When Dagobert II returned to Gaul, he was accompanied by an armed escort provided by Wilfrid.[63] When Wilfrid and his party were driven onto the shores of the pagan South Saxons, he was accompanied by an armed retinue who were adequately able to defend themselves.[64] Though Stephen claims Wilfrid was

---

equally with corporeal nourishment"). *Cithaerodas* (possibly a masculine 1st decl. noun, which is occasionally attested elsewhere) are, literally, players of the *cithara*, a musical instrument usually referred to as a "harp" or "lyre". The text is taken from Levison's 1912 edition as emended in 1930. I hope to return to this text and to Wilfrid's visit to Rome in 679-80 in a subsequent paper.

[61] A letter of Pope Agatho to the emperor Constantine IV, dated 27 March 680, shows that he was also held in high respect in Rome as a theologian. See further Bischoff and Lapidge, *Biblical Commentaries from the Canterbury School*, pp. 79-80, and J. Stevenson, *The 'Laterculus Malalianus' and the School of Archbishop Theodore*, Cambridge Studies in Anglo-Saxon England 14 (Cambridge 1995), pp. 34-35.

[62] D. H. Farmer, "Saint Wilfrid", in *Saint Wilfrid at Hexham*, ed. D. P. Kirby (Newcastle upon Tyne, 1974), p. 49: "Not for the first or the last time, however, Rome had reached a decision on limited information ...".

[63] *Life of Bishop Wilfrid*, chap. 28, p. 54.

[64] *Life of Bishop Wilfrid*, chap. 13, p. 26. The story, of course, has been shaped by hagiographic and biblical precedents. Thus Wilfrid promises the

abstemious, he did not shun feasts and leading men were prepared to entrust their sons to his care, secure in the knowledge that his training would not prevent them from becoming warriors if they so chose.[65] Stephen also proudly tells us of the splendour of Wilfrid's consecration of his church at Ripon and had earlier unselfconsciously told of his consecration in Gaul when he became a bishop.[66] Ecgfrith's wife had attacked Wilfrid for his lavish life-style.[67] Farmer in his very informative review of Wilfrid's life believes that he was inspired by Frankish Merovingian models in his behaviour.[68] I would rather suggest that Wilfrid decided to adopt the indigenous model of a secular king, with a band of young warriors, experienced counsellors, lavish entertainment and generous gift-giving. Certainly this is how Stephen seems to have viewed him in describing Wilfrid's last days. In the manner of an epic, Wilfrid had on an earlier occasion "omnem uitae suae conuersationem memorialiter ... enarrauit presbitero Tatberhto", who, significantly, was his kinsman and who thus had an interest in keeping his exploits alive.[69] Wilfrid then recited to him his oral will – and Stephen takes care to mention that his literary patron, Acca, had been bequeathed Wilfrid's monastery at Hexham. Stephen even

South Saxons a large sum of money to buy off his companions, the release of captives by the saint being a common topos in Merovingian saints' lives. The South Saxons were not so ignorant of Christianity as Stephen would have us believe: see S. Kelly, "The Bishopric of Selsey", in *Chichester Cathedral: An Historical Survey*, ed. M. Hobbs (Chichester, 1994), pp. 1 and 297.

[65] *Life of Bishop Wilfrid*, chap. 21, p. 44.

[66] Ian Wood underlines Wilfrid's strong debt to the Merovingian world in *The Merovingian Kingdoms 450-751* (London and New York, 1994), p. 315; see also his papers, "Ripon, Francia and the Frank's Casket in the Early Middle Ages", *Northern History* 26 (1990), 1-19 and "Northumbrians and Franks in the Age of Wilfrid", *Northern History* 31 (1995), 10-21.

[67] *Life of Bishop Wilfrid*, chap. 24, p. 48.

[68] Farmer, "Saint Wilfrid", in *Saint Wilfrid at Hexham*, ed. Kirby, p. 46-47.

[69] Wilfrid "narrated from memory the whole story of his life to the priest Tatberht": *Life of Bishop Wilfrid*, chap. 65, p. 140 (text); p. 141 (translation).

ascribes to Wilfrid a posthumous act of vengeance for the burning
of the monastery of Oundle in which he was buried.[70]

We can understand how Wilfrid thus could be regarded as
posing a threat to Ecgfrith. With lands extending beyond the bounds
of Northumbria and a mode of living that was regal in style, he
could be seen as thwarting Ecgfrith's expansionary pretensions.

Yet, from Wilfrid's point of view, he was simply pursuing an
end sanctioned by Gregory: the creation of a northern archdiocese.
Stephen of Ripon preserves a document that reveals Wilfrid's
intentions. In Wilfrid's second defence before a papal curia in 704, a
record of the Roman synod of 680 at which Wilfrid was present was
read out. *Inter alia*, he is alleged to have subscribed with words that
claimed "pro omni aquilonali parte Brittanniae et Hiberniae
insulisque quae ab Anglorum et Brittonum necnon Scottorum et
Pictorum gentibus colebantur, ueram et catholicam confessus fidem
et cum subscriptione sua corroborauit".[71] Records of this papal
synod are extant in both Latin and Greek versions. Wilfrid is named
as one of the participants, though not the geographical extent of his
claims.[72] Nevertheless, I think we can assume that for home
consumption Wilfrid had made it clear that this was his agenda. This
will explain why he, in effect, conceded before the curia the case for
splitting up his vast northern diocese. He had, with his building
efforts, been working with this eventual goal in mind but had never
received the *pallium* from Rome that would signify his metropolitan
status. By acceding to the demands for the division of his see

---

[70] *Life of Bishop Wilfrid*, chap. 67, p. 146.

[71] "He confessed the true and catholic faith for all the northern part of
Britain and Ireland and the islands, which are inhabited by the races of Angles
and Britons as well as Scots [i.e., Irish] and Picts": *Life of Bishop Wilfrid*, chap.
53, p. 114 (text); p. 115 (translation).

[72] In the Latin version he subscribes, in fact, as "Uilfridus humilis
episcopus sanctae ecclesiae Ebroicae insulae Brittaniae ..." ("Wilfrid, humble
bishop of the church of York of the island of Britain ..."): Riedinger, ed.,
Concilium Universale Constantinopolitanum Tertium (see above, n. 55), p. 149,
no. 49. The subscription in Greek (ibid., p. 148) is an almost literal equivalent
except that Wilfrid is described as "ελάχιστος" ("humilissimus").

provided the new bishops were from his diocese,[73] he, in fact, fortified his claims to metropolitan status and buttressed his position through having the new bishops receive papal approval. Again, I suggest his model was the Germanic lord: he could reward faithful supporters by the ecclesiastical equivalent of a land grant, namely, the bestowal of an episcopal see.

His claims to the adoption of the Benedictine Rule were in keeping with what he saw as the Gregorian vision for Britain; but we can well imagine that this would have brought him into conflict with those such as Hild of Whitby who lived in a dual monastery, something that was completely at variance with Benedictine precepts. Her support for Theodore against Wilfrid[74] thus becomes perfectly explicable. A more powerful Wilfrid posed a threat to the glorious variety of northern monasticism.

Unfortunately for Wilfrid the papacy in 680 could not deliver on its decision. Ecgfrith ignored the papal command to reinstate him. Wilfrid took himself off to Selsey, an area which, perhaps for geographical reasons, was beyond Canterbury's ambit at the time.[75] There he continued on the path established by Paulinus. Having been given a substantial endowment of land on the peninsula of Selsey, he proceeded to free two hundred and fifty slaves and baptise them, as a good bishop should.[76] We should not imagine that these people left the estate after being freed. It is far more likely that Wilfrid converted them into monastic tenants on the Irish model. Thereby he would have earned their gratitude, ensured the labour force necessary to maintain his new monastery and possibly even found some ecclesiastical recruits amongst the population.

This is not the place for a detailed discussion of the final quarter of a century or so of Wilfrid's life. He managed temporarily to regain his see of York in 686 and his monasteries of Hexham and

---

[73] On this issue see C. Cubitt, "Wilfrid's 'Usurping Bishops': Episcopal Elections in Anglo-Saxon England, c. 600-c. 800", *Northern History* 25 (1989), 18-38.

[74] *Life of Bishop Wilfrid*, chap. 54, p. 116.

[75] *Life of Bishop Wilfrid*, chap. 41, pp. 80-84; Bede, *Historia ecclesiastica*, 4.13, ed. Colgrave and Mynors, pp. 374, 376.

[76] Bede, *Historia ecclesiastica*, 4.13, ed. Colgrave and Mynors, p. 376.

Ripon. But Lindsey had been lost again to Mercia in 679 and the Picts had regained some of the north in 685, so his see was much reduced in territory, and new bishops were appointed to Lindisfarne in 687 and to Hexham in 688, thus reducing it yet further. Once more he fell foul of a king of Northumbria, this time Aldfrith, Ecgfrith's successor. He moved south to Mercia in about 692, now becoming bishop of Leicester. We can still see him acting as if he were a metropolitan by his consecrating a bishop for the Hwicce in the south-west Midlands and another for Frisia.[77]

His trials were not yet over. Stephen records a synod that was held at Austerfield, near Bawtry, in 702 or 703 under the aegis of Beorhtweald, Theodore's successor at Canterbury.[78] At the synod Wilfrid had the strong support of Æthelred, who was still king of Mercia. Again we may suspect Mercian hegemonic interests in Kent were at play. No less a factor, however, is likely to have been Beorhtweald's insecurity in his archiepiscopal position. Stephen has a story that Theodore was reconciled to Wilfrid before his death and that he was destined for Canterbury.[79] Quite possibly Kent and Northumbria opposed this. Nicholas Brooks has suggested that the archiepiscopal succession was disputed, which would explain why Beorhtweald was not consecrated by his English suffragans but took himself off to Lyons, where Wilfrid had ties, and then went on to Rome to receive the *pallium* from Pope Sergius I himself.[80] These were canny moves on Beorhtweald's part because Stephen suggests that Wilfrid had secured Sergius' support for the restoration of his northern see and monasteries. The conditions imposed on Wilfrid at the Synod of Austerfield were unacceptable to him and so he once more made an appeal to Rome.

[77] Farmer, "Saint Wilfrid", in *Saint Wilfrid at Hexham*, ed. Kirby, pp. 50-57.

[78] *Life of Bishop Wilfrid*, chap. 60, p. 132, and C. Cubitt, *Anglo-Saxon Church Councils c. 650-c. 850*, Studies in the Early History of Britain (London, 1995), especially pp. 50-52 and 302-03.

[79] *Life of Bishop Wilfrid*, chap. 43, p. 86.

[80] N. Brooks, *The Early History of the Church of Canterbury: Christ Church from 597 to 1066*, Studies in the Early History of Britain (Leicester, 1984), pp. 77-78.

Aldfrith of Northumbria died in December 704. Beorhtweald thereupon called a synod in 705 near the River Nidd.[81] John, who had been bishop of Hexham since 687, was transferred to York, and Wilfrid took his place, also regaining his monastery of Ripon. He was an old man now and, as so often happens, patterns of his youth were re-established. In his last days we can visualise him living as an abbot and bishop, closer to the Irish than the Gallic or Roman model. He still did not throw off the outlook of a Germanic lord, however. Like the dying Beowulf, who revelled in the wealth of the dragon hoard, he drew attention to his riches. "Nam non multo tempore ante beatae memoriae obitum Inripis cum duobus abbatibus et fratribus ualde fidelibus, omnes numero VIII, ad se inuitatis, gazofilacium aperire clauiculario praecepit et omne aurum et argentum cum lapidibus pretiosis in conspectu eorum deponere et in quattuor partes secundum suum iudicum dirimere iussit".[82] Right to the end the Christian bishop and Germanic lord were conjoined within him. Two parts were for gifts to churches and for the poor. A third reminds us of Wilfrid the politician: this portion was for the abbots of Ripon and Hexham "ut cum muneribus regum et episcoporum amicitiam perpetrare potuerint".[83] The final portion recalled his Germanic heritage: he declared that with this "Tertiam uero partem his, qui mecum longa exilia perpessi laborauerunt, et

[81] Cubitt, *Anglo-Saxon Church Councils*, especially pp. 88-91 and 290.

[82] "A short time before his ever-memorable and blessed death, he ordered his treasurer to open his treasury at Ripon in the presence of two abbots and some very faithful brethren, eight in number together, whom he had invited, and to put out in their sight all the gold, silver and precious stones; and he bade the treasurer divide it into four parts, according to his direction ...": *Life of Bishop Wilfrid*, chap. 63, p. 136 (text); p. 137 (translation). Presumably Stephen means us to think of Christ on his last evening with his eleven faithful disciples. Wilfrid's division of his estate into four undoubtedly was inspired by the *quadripartitum*, the traditional disposition of church revenues into four parts shared between the bishop, his clergy, the poor and widows, and church buildings.

[83] "to purchase the friendship of kings and bishops": *Life of Bishop Wilfrid*, chap. 63, p. 136 (text); p. 137 (translation).

quibus terras praediorum non dedi, secundum uniuscuiusque mensuram dispertite illis, ut habeant, unde se post me sustenent".[84]

---

[84] "you are to share among those who have laboured and suffered long exile with me and to whom I have given no lands and estates; distribute it according to the needs of each man so that they may have the means to maintain themselves after I have departed": *Life of Bishop Wilfrid*, chap. 63, p. 136 (text); p. 137 (translation).

Miracles and Horizontal Mobility in the
Early Middle Ages:
Some Methodological Reflections

Hedwig Röckelein

Horizontal mobility has so far been a subject of early medieval studies mostly with regard to the political and religious élites: the king, the aristocracy, the bishops and the abbots.[1] There can be no doubt that in the early medieval Frankish realms, mobility was a constitutive element of sovereignty and an instrument of asserting

---

[1] H. C. Peyer, "Das Reisekönigtum des Mittelalters", *Vierteljahrschrift für Sozial- und Wirtschaftsgeschichte* 51 (1964), 1-21; A. Gauert, "Zum Itinerar Karls des Großen", in *Karl der Große. Lebenswerk und Nachleben, vol. 1: Persönlichkeit und Geschichte*, ed. H. Beumann (Düsseldorf, 1965), pp. 307-21; E. Müller-Mertens, *Die Reichsstruktur im Spiegel der Herrschaftspraxis Ottos d.Gr.*, Forschungen zur mittelalterlichen Geschichte 25 (Berlin, 1980); C. Brühl, *Fodrum, Gistum, Servitium Regis. Studien zu den wirtschaftlichen Grundlaıgen des Königtums im Frankenreich und in den französischen Nachfolgestaaten Deutschland, Frankreich und Italien vom 6. bis zur Mitte des 14. Jahrhunderts*, 2 vols (Cologne and Vienna, 1981); *Die deutschen Königspfalzen. Repertorium der Pfalzen, Königshöfe und übrigen Aufenthaltsorte der Könige im deutschen Reich des Mittelalters*, Max-Planck-Institut für Geschichte (Göttingen, 1983-92), see on this project, T. Zotz, "Vorbemerkungen zum Repertorium der deutschen Königspfalzen", *Blätter für deutsche Landesgeschichte* 118 (1982), 177-203; J. W. Bernhardt, *Itinerant Kingship and Royal Monasteries in Early Medieval Germany c. 936-1075*, Cambridge Studies in Medieval Life and Thought 4th ser., 21 (Cambridge, 1993).

authority, both in times of peace and of war.[2] The horizontal mobility of those social groups beneath the aristocracy, however, has not yet aroused much interest in medieval studies; in general, the "dominated" social groups, the peasants in particular, are seen as not being mobile at all. It seems that the dichotomy of flexibility of the political élite on the one hand and inflexibility of the "dominated" groups on the other hand corresponds rather with an ideological conception of the nineteenth century than with the early medieval reality.[3] This view must certainly be revised as soon as one works with sources which have not yet been investigated with regard to horizontal mobility: manorial documents (carrying services etc.) and miracle accounts of the early Middle Ages.[4]

Among the miracle stories, the *miracula in vita* are less useful for an investigation of peasant mobility than are the *miracula post mortem*. The miracles which occurred in the saints' lifetimes tell us more about the saints' and missionaries' mobility than about the peasants' mobility. In contrast, those miracles occurring at the saint's tomb or during her or his translation, furnish us with information about the ordinary people, or at least about the sick among them.

My investigation is mainly, but not exclusively confined to miracle accounts in *vitae* and in translation and miracle collections from early medieval Saxony.[5] Since early medieval miracle accounts

---

[2] G. Althoff, "Vom Zwang zur Mobilität und ihren Problemen", in *Reisen und Reiseliteratur im Mittelalter und in der Frühen Neuzeit*, ed. X. von Ertzdorff and D. Neukirch (Amsterdam, 1992), pp. 91-111.

[3] See G. Jaritz and A. Müller, "Migrationsgeschichte. Zur Rekonzeptualisierung historiographischer Traditionen für neue sozialgeschichtliche Fragestellungen", in *Migration in der Feudalgesellschaft*, ed. G. Jaritz and A. Müller (Frankfurt and New York, 1988), pp. 9-20 (p. 12).

[4] See J.-P. Devroey, "Les services de transport à l'abbaye de Prüm au IXe siècle", *Revue du Nord* 61 (1979), 543-69, and J.-P. Devroey, "Un monastère dans l'économie d'échanges. Les services de transport à l'abbaye Saint-Germain-des-Prés au IXe siècle", *Annales: Economies, sociétés, civilisations* 39 (1984), 570-89.

[5] See my unpublished Habilitationsschrift, "Reliquientranslationen nach Sachsen im 9. Jahrhundert. Über Kommunikation, Mobilität und Öffentlichkeit im Frühmittelalter".

in contrast to those of the high and later middle ages provide no statistically relevant quantities, only a qualitative analysis seems possible. The qualitative analysis of early medieval miracle accounts, however, necessitates clarification of methodological questions and some theoretical reflections.

The Concept of Mobility

In medieval monasticism mobility was an ambivalent concept. The Irish missionaries followed the ideal of *peregrinatio*. Benedictine monasticism on the other hand assigned itself to *stabilitas loci*, *stabilitas mentis* and *constantia* and thought of mobility as something negative.

Outside the monastic context the term *mobilitas* is rarely used; we more often find *mobile, mobilia, mobilis* (used as an adjective to mean "movable" and as a noun to mean "movable property").[6] The term *mobilitas* can be found in formulas of pertinents of medieval charters concerning land transactions, that is, where mobile property is listed. Man and maid servants also belonged to the *mobiles res* or the *mobilitas* of the manor respectively. Thus, in the early medieval concept of property serfs count as mobile property.[7]

In modern scientific usage "horizontal mobility" signifies more than just "travelling": "Mobility is a much larger concept that includes, next to long-distance travel, all other forms of physical

---

[6] E. Brinckmeyer, *Glossarium diplomaticum latino-germanicum mediae et infimae aetatis e codicibus manuscriptis et libris impressis*, 2 vols (Hamburg, Gotha, 1855), 2:313; C. Du Cange, *Glossarium mediae et infimae latinitatis*, rev. by L. Favre, 7 vols (Paris, 1883-87), 5:431-32; J. F. Niermeyer, *Mediae latinitatis lexicon minus* (Leiden, 1976), p. 699.

[7] Du Cange, *Glossarium*, 5:432: "mobilitas de servis et ancillis dicitur, qui praedium rusticum excolunt" ("those male and female serfs who cultivate the rural estate are called chattel") (charter of AD 942); "inter res mobiles recensentur servi glebae adscripti" ("the serfs who are tied to the soil are to be numbered among the chattel") (AD 1353). Niermeyer, *Mediae latinitatis*, p. 699: "mansus indominicatus ... cum omni sua mobilitate, servis videlicet et ancillis" ("the manor with its demesne land, its chattel, its male and female serfs of course") (Urkundenbuch Cluny No. 523 I:508, AD 940/41).

movement within the social context".[8] Furthermore, "horizontal mobility" competes with the term "migration". Ludwig Schmugge understands by "mobility" a long-distance change of locality of individuals or groups who are at least temporarily removed from their previous situation and legal status. By "migration" he means the movements and the fluctuation of the population.[9]

In the miracle accounts horizontal mobility and migration cannot always be distinguished clearly. During the translation of St Liborius' relics from Le Mans to Paderborn in 836, in Bavaca (maybe Bavay, France, Dép. Nord) a woman was cured who had suffered from demonic persecution for fifteen years. The visit to the saint's bier, placed in the church, must be regarded as an act of horizontal mobility. After the woman had been healed, she took part in the transitional journey from Bavaca to Paderborn in Saxony. This is also an act of horizontal mobility. She then dedicated her life to God and the saint and decided to remain in Paderborn at the saint's tomb for the rest of her life.[10] Thereby, horizontal mobility becomes migration, i.e. a lasting change of the place of residence.

[8] G. Berings, "Transport and Communication in the Middle Ages", in *Kommunikation und Alltag im Spätmittelalter und Früher Neuzeit*, Österreichische Akademie der Wissenschaften, Philosophisch-historische Klasse 596 / Veröffentlichungen des Instituts für Realienkunde des Mittelalters und der frühen Neuzeit 15 (Vienna, 1992), p. 48.

[9] L. Schmugge, "Mobilität und Freiheit im Mittelalter", in *Die abendländische Freiheit vom 10. bis 14. Jahrhundert. Der Wirkungszusammenhang von Idee und Wirklichkeit im europäischen Vergleich*, ed. J. Fried, Vorträge und Forschungen 39 (Sigmaringen, 1991), p. 307.

[10] A. Cohausz, ed. and trans., *Translatio s. Liborii*, Avranches version, chap. 24; Paderborn version, chap. 28, Studien und Quellen zur Westfälischen Geschichte 6 (Paderborn, 1966), p. 101: "surrexit a daemonio liberata, ac divinitus inspirata promisit se in honore Dei [et] sancto Liborio servire per tempora vitae; propinquos et notos terramque contempsit, ad Saxoniam sanctum sequebatur Liborium". ("She got up, delivered from the demon and, divinely inspired, she promised to perform Saint Liborius' worship for the rest of her life; she disregarded her kin, her acquaintances and her native country, and followed Saint Liborius to Saxony").

Space: a Geographical, Social and Symbolic Concept

There are several circumstances defining horizontal mobility: time, space, the body of the mobile person (in the case of miracles the body of the sick person and the body of the pilgrim). Mobility is, in addition, based on lines of communication. The exchange of information on routes, destinations, means of travel, resting places etc. has to be ensured. Of these factors I would like to discuss some aspects of "space".

Space is neither an abstract nor an exclusively geographical variable, it is not identical with area or territory. Space is a historical, cultural, and therefore an artificial construction which is formed and transformed by people in social interaction.[11]

In the wonder-working of saints in the Middle Ages various spaces and symbolic spheres are of importance: the sphere of the Church and religion, the sphere of power, the sphere of faith and magic, and the sphere of healing. The question is: which criteria constitute the sphere of influence of a saint? Is religious propaganda the criterion, or is it the sphere of influence of a bishop, of a monastery, or the king or the lord's demesne, or the saint's particular healing ability? Or can the sphere of influence of a saint not be determined from particular factors at all?

In the miracles attributed to St Willehad, in Bremen for example, which were written down by his successor, Archbishop Ansgar, in the years 860 to 865, the places of residence of the healed pilgrims are widespread. There are sick persons who live directly at the place of worship, and there are others who have to cover a distance of up to eighty to a hundred kilometres in a direct line one way, for example, those who came from Eastern Frisia, the Ems-district at the lower course of the Ems (c. 100 km),[12] or those

[11] See E. Leach, *Culture and Communication. The Logic by which Symbols are Connected. An Introduction to the Use of Structuralist Analysis in Social Anthropology* (Cambridge, 1976), pp. 33-36: "The symbolic ordering of a man-made world: boundaries of social space and time".

[12] Anskar, *Virtutes et miracula s. Willehadi*, chap. 3, AASS Nov. vol. 3, ed. C. de Smedt et al. (Brussels, 1910), p. 848.

from the northern part of Wigmodia (80 km),[13] or those from Baldrikeswich in the Osterburgo-district on the middle course of the river Weser (100 km).[14] But why did the sick people decide to go to Bremen and not to another place of worship closer to their places of residence? And how did they find their way to Bremen?

Theoretically various meaningful relationships between the places of residence and the place of worship Bremen are conceivable: the distance between the two places with respect to the accessibility of the place of worship (topography, hydrography); the relationship of the saint's sphere of influence to the administrative boundaries (district borders); the relationship between the sphere of influence and ecclesiastical units (the borders of a bishopric); the relationship with the missionary activities of the wonder-working Willehad.

Projecting the pilgrims' places of origin onto maps, the following observations can be made: the pilgrims' places of origin are mostly situated within the diocese of Bremen in the ninth century (fig. 1). Only very few pilgrims come from different bishoprics. The close connection between the pilgrims and Bremen is easy to explain by Willehad's and Ansgar's activities. Willehad, the wonder-working saint, was the first missionary in the region of Bremen and the first bishop of Bremen. Ansgar, the author of the "miracula Willehadi", had already Christianised the region of Rüstringen in 826 when he accompanied the Danish king Harald Klak who was forced to flee the Danish kingdom and acquired a fief in Rüstringen from Louis the Pious.[15] After 845, Ansgar became bishop of Bremen.[16] His supervision and preaching caused him to travel around his diocese on a regular basis.[17] In spite of Willehad's and Ansgar's dominant position in the diocese of Bremen

---

[13] Anskar, *Virtutes et miracula*, chap. 21, AASS Nov. 3:850B.

[14] Anskar, *Virtutes et miracula*, chap. 8, AASS Nov. 3:848E-849A.

[15] Rimbert, *Vita Anskarii*, ed. G. Waitz, MGH SRG (in us. schol.) 55 (Hanover, 1884), pp. 5-79. See chapters 7-8, pp. 26-31.

[16] Rimbert, *Vita Anskarii*, chap. 22, p. 47.

[17] Rimbert gives an account of Ansgar's preaching activities in the Ostergau district in Frisia in the *Vita Anskarii*, chap. 37. One of Ansgar's sermons is edited as *Homilia 8 in evangel.*, PL 76:1104.

competing cults and places of worship were established within the diocese of Bremen, for example, St Alexander's place of worship at Wildeshausen,[18] as well as in neighbouring bishoprics, namely Verden and Minden.[19] Furthermore Willehad's sphere of influence extended towards the cult of St Vitus in Corvey, situated in the diocese of Paderborn. In the *Miracula s. Willehadi* one person who was healed in Bremen came from the Osterburg-district on the middle course of the river Weser.[20] In the *Translatio s. Viti* the *matrona* Hogard came from Loinga, a district between the river Weser and Aller; the female pilgrims to Corvey, Autburg and Thiatburg lived in Arkenberg near Liebenau, situated upon the river Weser.[21]

Space as a Variable of Time

The distances covered by the pilgrims between their places of residence and the place of worship have repeatedly been statistically interpreted in an attempt to map the sphere of influence of a place of worship.[22] And the pilgrims' dispensability could then be assessed.

[18] Anskar, *Virtutes et miracula*, chap. 11, AASS Nov. 3:849D, and chap. 12, AASS Nov. 3:849E (competition between Alexander and Willehad). For this, not only the miracles of Willehad, but also those of Alexander have to be taken into consideration, see B. Krusch, ed., *Translatio s. Alexandri*, chap. 7, in *Nachrichten der Gesellschaft der Wissenschaften zu Göttingen*, Philosophisch-historische Klasse (Berlin, 1933) pp. 431-32: a young boy coming from Wigmodia, north of Bremen, has been healed by Alexander at Wildeshausen.

[19] Eitze (Anskar, *Virtutes et miracula*, chap. 17, AASS Nov. 3:850A), and Wilsted (chap. 9, AASS Nov. 3:849A-B) are situated in the bishopric of Verden, Büchten (chap. 26, AASS Nov. 3:580E) and Baldrikeswich (chap. 8, AASS Nov. 3:848E-849A) in the bishopric of Minden.

[20] Anskar, *Virtutes et miracula*, chap. 8, AASS Nov. 3:848E-849A.

[21] I. Schmale-Ott, ed., *Translatio s. Viti*, chap. [32], Veröffentlichung der Historischen Kommission für Westfalen 41, Fontes minores 1 (Münster, 1979), p. 66.

[22] D. Gonthier and C. Le Bas, "Analyse socio-économique de quelques recueils de miracles dans la Normandie du XIe au XIIIe siècle", *Annales de Normandie* 24 (1974), 3-36; P.-A. Sigal, *L'homme et le miracle dans la France médiévale (XIe-XIIe siècle)* (Paris, 1985), chapter "D'où venaient les

Two cartographical techniques have been used: the first technique, the linear method, connects the place of worship with the place of residence by a direct line;[23] the second technique gives the distance in a circled radius.[24] The first method notes only spatial distance, whereas the second combines space and time, in taking into consideration that early medieval people did not calculate their journeys in kilometres or miles, but in units of time (in units of one day). The standard distance covered on foot or by a load-carrying vehicle per day is assumed to be twenty-five to thirty kilometres.[25] According to Sigal's calculations, a pilgrim of the early and high Middle Ages is thus able to reach a place of worship that is located at a distance of fifteen kilometres from his place of residence and walk back home in one day. To get to a place of worship situated at a distance of circa thirty kilometres, he or she needs two days (and

miraculés?", pp. 196-210; J. Paul, "Le rayonnement géographique du pèlerinage au tombeau de Louis d'Anjou", in *Le pèlerinage*, Cahiers de Fanjeaux 15 (Toulouse, 1980), pp. 137-58; L. Schmugge, "Die Pilger", in *Unterwegssein im Spätmittelalter*, ed. P. Moraw, Zeitschrift für Historische Forschung, Beiheft 1 (Berlin, 1985), pp. 17-48; R. C. Finucane, "Pilgrimage in Daily Life: Aspects of Medieval Communication Reflected in the Newly-established Cult of Thomas Cantilupe (d. 1282), its Dissemination and Effects upon Outlying Herefordshire Villagers", in *Wallfahrt und Alltag im Mittelalter und Früher Neuzeit*, Veröffentlichungen des Instituts für Realienkunde 14 (Vienna, 1992), pp. 165-217; B. Schuh, *Jenseitigkeit in diesseitigen Formen. Sozial- und mentalitätsgeschichtliche Aspekte spätmittelalterlicher Mirakelberichte*, Schriftenreihe des Instituts für Geschichte, Darstellungen 3 (Graz, 1989), pp. 90-97.

[23] Applied by J.-C. Poulin in *L'idéal de sainteté dans l'Aquitaine carolingienne d'après les sources hagiographiques (750-950)*, Travaux du laboratoire d'histoire religieuse de l'Université Laval 1 (Québec, 1975), p. 6, map A: "Lieux d'origine des miraculés", and p. 8, map B: "Lieux d'origine des miraculés de Saint-Philibert".

[24] Applied by Gonthier and Le Bas, "Analyse socio-économique", map after p. 10 and passim.

[25] D. Denecke, "Straße und Weg im Mittelalter als Lebensraum und Vermittler zwischen entfernten Orten", in *Mensch und Umwelt im Mittelalter*, ed. B. Herrmann (Frankfurt am Main, 1989), p. 215. See also the table, p. 217, which takes account of seasonal variation in the daily output.

so on).[26] Sigal consequently draws circles of fifteen, thirty and sixty kilometres around the places of worship; by this means, he is able to demonstrate how many days the pilgrims were absent from their home and their work.

The circle method is – like the linear method – based on direct lines and does not consider the actual road conditions on the ground. If we are realistic and take into consideration the obstacles and individual circumstances influencing the journey, we find a substantial reduction in the average distance covered daily. The average distance varies depending on whether the pilgrim travels by land or by ship, and on whether he or she travels in summer or winter.[27] The assumed distance covered daily by sick people (and only such people are mentioned in the miracle accounts) has to be considerably reduced. Most of the pilgrims suffered from physical disabilities, such as blindness, lameness or mutilation, which would have slowed down the speed of travelling substantially.

An example from thirteenth-century England may illustrate the huge problems faced by the peasant population.[28] As soon as several unfavourable circumstances occurred, the covering of even short distances became extraordinarily difficult. A son, who wanted to bring his crippled mother to St Thomas Cantilupe in Hereford,

---

[26] Sigal, *L'homme*, pp. 196-210: Distances to French places of worship (Rocamadour, Saint-Gilles-du-Gard and four more, regional places of worship), which were covered by pilgrims in the high Middle Ages:

Radius	Pilgrims
< 15 km	35%
< 30 km	24%
< 60 km	17%
> 60 km	24%

[27] Finucane, "Pilgrimage", p. 196, finds that the number of pilgrims to Hereford increases in the summer months (April-September). 72% of the pilgrims come at this time of the year; during the other months the pilgrimages do not stop completely, but substantially decrease in number. This observation corresponds with the results of B. P. Hindle, "Seasonal Variations in Travel in Medieval England", *Journal of Transport History* new ser., 4/3 (1978), 170-78. On the other hand, marshy grounds are faster and more easily travelled across in winter, when the ground is frozen, than in summer.

[28] Finucane, "Pilgrimage", pp. 174-75.

situated at a distance of five kilometres from their home, needed two months to prepare the journey. First of all, the work in the fields had to be done. Then a horse had to be organised and the money for the accommodation in the hospital had to be raised. Furthermore, the mother's state of health was not always stable enough for them to set out on that short journey.

These factors which strongly influence the average daily distance covered by a traveller are not considered in the linear or in the radial cartographical techniques. Therefore, these techniques do not offer a reliable basis to draw further conclusions. As an alternative that takes into account the time actually spent on travelling by the pilgrims, I suggest adapting the "cartes de voisinage" used by the Guide Michelin series. Here, the distance between places is not measured in kilometres but in time distances. This results in slightly strange patterns, but they give a realistic impression of the distance covered and the time consumed thereby.

In the early medieval miracle stories, the journey's course is seldom described, so only hypotheses of the general transport history can be put forward: the pre-condition of travelling is knowledge of long-distance highways, navigable waterways, bridges, fords and the general topography. Yet the behaviour of the travelling pilgrims does not always accord with to our expectations. We would, for example, expect the pilgrims to prefer going to Bremen by ship rather than by land.[29] The *Miracula s. Willehadi*, however, disappoint this expectation thoroughly: Ansgar does not say anything about pilgrims coming to Bremen by ship. This can only be concluded indirectly from the fact that many of the pilgrims travelling to St Willehad lived in settlements situated on the river Weser.[30] In contrast, the pilgrims described in the miracles of

---

[29] According to Rimbert's *Vita Anskarii*, the missionary and his fellow-travellers actually went by ship on most of their journeys.

[30] On this, see H. Schmidt, "Die Bremer Kirche und der Unterweserraum im frühen und hohen Mittelalter", in *Stadt - Kirche - Reich. Neue Forschungen zur Geschichte des Mittelalters anläßlich der 1200. Wiederkehr der ersten urkundlichen Erwähnung Bremens*, Schriften der Wittheit zu Bremen, new ser., 9 (Bremen, 1983), p. 10. That the pilgrim from the Frisian "Nordwidu" actually travelled to Bremen by sea and via the mouth of the river Weser, is rather

Einhard's *Translatio ss. Petri et Marcellini*, whom we would expect to go by land, proceeded to go to Seligenstadt by ship, travelling on the rivers Rhein and Main.[31] In addition, it is Einhard who quite often records embarkation miracles, although one would not necessarily expect them in this region.

Mobility and Economy

In scientific research on early medieval society one common opinion is that people not belonging to the élite, in particular the poor, were almost immobile. But from interpreting the miracle accounts a contrary conclusion can be drawn: in early medieval society poor people, disabled by illness, were not immobile at all, but condemned to mobility or migration. There are two grounds forcing mobility upon poor and/or sick people: the hope to be cured through a visit to a shrine, and the possibility of earning one's living by begging. Ansgar tells the story of a poor, blind man from Bremen.[32] The man wandered about with his stepdaughter, who was also blind, in order to earn their living and in the hope of being cured. Both of them were healed, partly by Alexander of Wildeshausen and partly by Willehad of Bremen. According to the *Translatio s. Alexandri*,[33] Alexander of Wildeshausen was also visited by a man from Deventer who had been deaf and dumb and blind from birth. He led the life of a beggar near the monastery of Deventer, where he asked for alms. In the village of Aulnay-aux-Planches (France, Dép. Marne) there lived a man who had been lame in the knees for 20 years.[34] This man earned his living as a beggar travelling from place to place on his donkey. He was healed

---

doubtful, since he first visited Wildeshausen (situated on the river Hunte), and afterwards came to Bremen.

[31] Einhard, *Translatio ss. Marcellini et Petri*, book 4, chap. 17, ed. G. Waitz and W. Wattenbach, MGH SS 15, 2 vols (Hanover, 1887), 1:263: a sick woman from Cologne travelling by a merchant's ship to Seligenstadt.

[32] Anskar, *Virtutes et miracula*, chap. 11, AASS Nov. 3:849D.

[33] Krusch, ed., *Translatio s. Alexandri*, chap. 8, p. 432.

[34] Schmale-Ott, ed., *Translatio s. Viti*, chap. (XII), p. 54.

during the translation of St Vitus' relics from St Denis to Corvey in 836.

The miracle narratives indicate that poor people could not afford a doctor. Richer people or those of a higher social status turned first to a doctor and only if his attempts to cure them failed did they ask a saint for help.[35] Poor people, the large majority of the population, had, in contrast, no other choice than to address the saints and hope for a miracle. Since the miraculous healer expected offerings for his cure, and fares and accommodation had to be paid, pilgrimage was not an inexpensive affair. But in comparison to doctors, miraculous healers were cheaper, all the more in Saxony, where the saints demanded almost exclusively prayers of gratitude instead of expensive offerings.

Illness often made people unfit for work. Then, abandoned by their families as extra unproductive mouths to feed, disabled people were transformed into beggars. Churches, monasteries and pious laymen and laywomen were enjoined to ease poverty by giving alms.[36] Since the donation of alms formed a significant part of Christian virtue, the sick and those unfit for work could count on being supported. Pious and saintly men and women like Ansgar,[37] Rimbert,[38] Catla[39] and the Countess Gisla[40] regularly distributed coins among the poor.

---

[35] Krusch, ed., *Translatio s. Alexandri*, chap. 14, p. 435.

[36] See E. Boshof, "Untersuchungen zur Armenfürsorge im fränkischen Reich des 9. Jahrhunderts", *Archiv für Kulturgeschichte* 58 (1976), 265-339; J. Wollasch, "Konventsstärke und Armensorge in mittelalterlichen Klöstern", *Saeculum* 39 (1988), 184-99.

[37] Rimbert, *Vita Anskarii*, chap. 35, pp. 68-69.

[38] G. Waitz, ed., *Vita Rimberti*, chap. 14, MGH SRG (in us. schol.) 55 (Hanover, 1884), p. 92.

[39] Rimbert, *Vita Anskarii*, chap. 20, pp. 44-46.

[40] O. Menzel, ed., *Vita Liutbirgae*, chap. 2, MGH Deutsches Mittelalter 3 (Leipzig, 1937), p. 11.

From Horizontal to Vertical Mobility – from Profane to Sacred Status

In medieval studies, the high Middle Ages are seen as a time of awakening of western society. A higher degree of horizontal mobility is accompanied by an increasing social, i.e. vertical mobility.[41] Is the link between horizontal and social mobility actually limited to the high and later Middle Ages? Or were these phenomena already related to each other in the early Middle Ages? The miracle narratives at least suggest such a connection.

Ansgar tells us of a female serf who worked in the gynaeceum of the Saxon Count Hermann and who had lost her voice. Out of pity and for the sake of his salvation, Count Hermann freed the dumb woman and permitted her to return to her parents' house. Having found her voice again in the cathedral of Bremen, she returned to her home. Her parents and relatives were delighted at her restored freedom and good health.[42] In this case, the restoration of personal freedom (enabling the maidservant to go on a pilgrimage to Bremen) is the precondition for horizontal mobility. Without the permission of her master, the maidservant was not allowed to leave her place of work. For the Saxon peasantry personal freedom (*libertas*), horizontal mobility, and good health (*sanitas*) ranked among the most desirable of possessions.

The woman from Bavaca, whom we encountered earlier, did not change her social status through horizontal mobility, but left the profane sphere and entered into the sacred space. She had followed St Liborius to Paderborn after her cure.[43] Out of gratitude she had consecrated her life to God and the saint, she joined the *religiosi*, the devotees. She spent her life in the service of St Liborius, and

[41] For example O. G. Oexle, "Das Bild der Moderne vom Mittelalter und die moderne Mittelalterforschung", *Frühmittelalterliche Studien* 24 (1990), 1-22 (p. 5); K. Bosl, *Die Grundlagen der modernen Gesellschaft im Mittelalter*, vol. 1, Monographien zur Geschichte des Mittelalters 4/1 (Stuttgart, 1972), p. 162.

[42] Ansgar, *Virtutes et miracula*, chap. 28, AASS Nov. 3:851B.

[43] Cohausz, ed., *Translatio s. Liborii*, Paderborn version, chap. 28, pp. 99, 101.

came under the legal protection of the Church, similar to the *cerocensuales*.[44]

Female Mobility

Although quantitative analyses of high and late medieval miracle accounts have demonstrated that women formed a minority among the pilgrims,[45] miracle narratives of the early Middle Ages nevertheless are amongst those rare texts which inform us to a great extent of the activities of women, that is of women who do not belong to the aristocracy or the royal family. From hagiography in a broader sense we get to know most about women who wandered from place to place. The woman from Bavaca who was healed by St Liborius and as a result decided to follow the saint to Paderborn to spend her life there is an example of a woman who travels over a long distance and thereby changes from the profane to the sacred sphere. A change in social status in the context of a miraculous healing is to be found in the case of the maidservant freed by Count Hermann. I will now mention a few more examples of voluntary and forced mobility and migration of women.

In the middle of the ninth century, Ansgar, the missionary of Sweden, met in Birka a wealthy and pious woman called Frideburg.[46] She had been among the first to be converted to Christianity, and in spite of the vacancy of the priest's incumbency in Birka, which lasted seven years, she remained loyal to the Christian faith. Before she died, she instructed her daughter Catla to

---

[44] *Cerocensuales* were freed and commended to the church under the obligation to pray for the soul of their former manor, see M. Borgolte, "Freigelassene im Dienst der Memoria. Kulttradition und Kultwandel zwischen Antike und Mittelalter", *Frühmittelalterliche Studien* 17 (1983), 234-50.

[45] Varying from one place of worship to another, 30-50% of the pilgrims were women, see D. Gonthier, and C. Le Bas, "Analyse socio-économique de quelques recueils de miracles dans la Normandie du XIe au XIIIe siècle", in *Annales de Normandie* 24 (1974), 3-36; B. Schuh, *"Jenseitigkeit in diesseitigen Formen". Sozial- und mentalitätsgeschichtliche Aspekte spätmittelalterlicher Mirakelberichte*, Schriftenreihe des Instituts für Geschichte, Darstellungen 3 (Graz, 1989), p. 47.

[46] Rimbert, *Vita Anskarii*, chap. 20, pp. 44-46.

sell all their property and distribute the proceeds among the poor of Birka. With the remaining money Catla was to travel to Dorestad in order to support churches, priests, clerics and the poor in that place. After Frideburg's death, the daughter carried out the mother's plans. Having arrived in Dorestad, Catla went to pious women who visited the sacred places with her. At each place they explained to her what to give as a donation. When Catla came into the hospice and put aside her empty purse, she later found it miraculously replenished. Catla and her mother belonged to the merchants' class of Birka, who maintained regular trade relations with the *emporii* of the North and the Baltic Sea and who specialised in luxury goods.[47] The name of Frideburg suggests that she was a native Frisian who moved to Sweden as a merchant later on.[48] In her lifetime, Frideburg had presumably taken her daughter Catla along with her on her journeys. Therefore, setting out on this long voyage was not a problem for Catla. It was only in Dorestad that she looked for the company of other women, who made her familiar with the customs and habits of the place.

That mobility could be threatening and dangerous for women is illustrated by another example in which mobility again changes into migration. In the *Translatio s. Alexandri*[49] a woman called Femburg, who was born in Frisia, had to flee her home, perhaps because of the Norman invasion. She found shelter in the house of a woman near Wildeshausen. This woman, however, took advantage of Femburg's defencelessness and decided to sell her into slavery. Femburg got to know of this plan in time, and found refuge and the protection of a powerful man. Shortly afterwards, she fell seriously ill; even those women skilled in medicine were unable to effect a cure. It was only St Alexander in Wildeshausen who released her from her convulsions.

If we want to investigate the horizontal mobility and migration of the lower classes of early medieval society, the mobility of

[47] Cf. S. Lebecq, *Marchands et navigateurs frisons du haut Moyen Age*, 2 vols (Lille, 1983).

[48] D. Jellema, "Frisian Trade in the Dark Ages", *Speculum* 30 (1955) 15-36 (p. 28).

[49] Krusch, ed., *Translatio s. Alexandri*, chap. 13, pp. 434-35.

peasants, of poor and sick women and men, we first have to give up some ideological conceptions, for example, the idea of a two-part society in reference to social and horizontal mobility. Secondly we have to invent techniques to visualise the relation of time and space which are adequate to the space-oriented perception of medieval people. Thirdly we have to connect the results that we gain from the research on hagiographical evidence, particularly the miracle narratives, on the manorial system, particularly the carrying services, and on general aspects of trade, transport and communication in history.

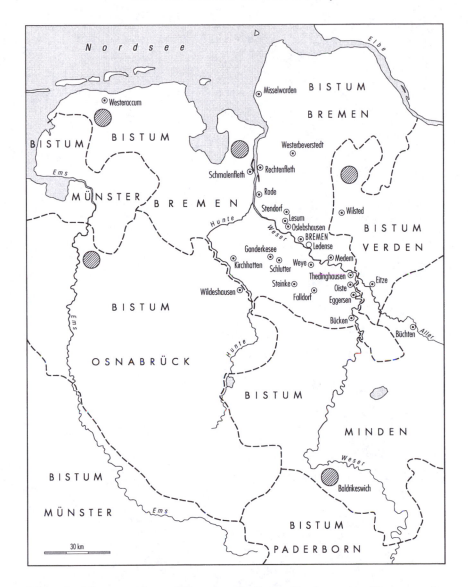

Fig. 1 Places of residence of the pilgrims to Bremen in correlation to the Saxon dioceses. Design: H. Röckelein.

III POWER

La *pietas* comme principe de gouvernement d'après le *Poème sur Louis le Pieux* d'Ermold le Noir

Philippe Depreux

Le règne de Louis le Pieux bénéficie d'un regain d'intérêt de la part des médiévistes,[1] ce qui conduit ces derniers à examiner avec plus de soin les sources relatives à cet empereur, au nombre desquelles compte le poème qu'Ermold le Noir, en exil à Strasbourg, adressa vers 826/828 à Louis le Pieux pour lui demander sa grâce.[2] Ermold entendait chanter les hauts faits de Louis: "Caesaris armigeri conor

---

[1] Cf. P. Godman et R. Collins, éds, *Charlemagne's Heir. New Perspectives on the Reign of Louis the Pious* (Oxford, 1990); P. Depreux, "Louis le Pieux reconsidéré? A propos des travaux récents consacrés à 'l'héritier de Charlemagne' et à son règne", *Francia* 21 (1994), 181-212.

[2] Ermold le Noir, *Poème sur Louis le Pieux et épîtres au roi Pépin*, éd. et trad. E. Faral, 2e éd. (Paris, 1964). Dans les grandes lignes, les quatre livres du poème se décomposent de la sorte: 1 = le gouvernement en Aquitaine; 2 = l'accession à l'Empire et les premières mesures prises par Louis; 3 = la politique de Louis à l'égard des Bretons; 4 = la politique de Louis à l'égard des Danois. Analyse détaillée du prologue et du livre 1 par P. Godman, "Louis 'the Pious' and his poets", *Frühmittelalterliche Studien* 19 (1985), 239-89 (pp. 259-65); présentation d'ensemble dans Godman, *Poets and Emperors. Frankish Politics and Carolingian Poetry* (Oxford, 1987), p. 111-30.

describere gesta, / Quae recitat merito mundus amore pio".[3] La plainte n'en est pas moins au coeur de son oeuvre, car Ermold n'eut pas recours à l'héxamètre dactylique, ainsi que le commande le genre épique, mais au distique élégiaque.[4] Il est vraisemblable qu'il faille voir ici une référence à Ovide,[5] qui composa dans ce style métrique ses *Epistolae ex Ponto*: elles étaient, elles aussi, l'oeuvre d'un poète en exil.[6]

Le poème d'Ermold le Noir a longtemps été méprisé par les historiens. Cependant, certains travaux indépendants les uns des autres, et dont l'*Elegiacum carmen* ne formait parfois pas l'objet d'étude principal, ont récemment contribué à la réhabilitation de cette source en montrant que, sur tel ou tel point de détail, le témoignage d'Ermold n'était pas erroné.[7] Ainsi, à l'occasion, on cite

---

[3] Ermold, *Poème* 1.40-41, p. 6: "J'entreprends la description des exploits de César en armes, que l'univers proclame en raison d'une juste et pieuse prédilection".

[4] D'où le titre *In honorem Hludowici christianissimi Caesaris Augusti Ermoldi Nigelli exulis Elegiacum Carmen* du manuscrit viennois n° 614 (Xe siècle).

[5] Godman, "Louis the Pious", p. 254, établit explicitement la filiation en ce qui concerne les Epîtres au roi Pépin; R. J. Hexter, *Ovid and Medieval Schooling. Studies in Medieval School Commentaries on Ovid's 'Ars Amatoria', 'Epistulae ex Ponto' and 'Epistulae Heroidum'* (München, 1986), p. 90, mentionne également l'*Elegiacum carmen*.

[6] Sur les oeuvres qu'Ovide composa pendant son exil, voir les études de H. Rahn, W. Marg et E. J. Kenney, rééditées par M. von Albrecht et E. Zinn, *Ovid* (Darmstadt, 1968), pp. 476-535.

[7] Présentation de ces travaux dans P. Depreux, "Poètes et historiens au temps de l'empereur Louis le Pieux", *Le Moyen Age* 99 (1993), 311-32, aux pp. 315-16. Cette tendance historiographique est néanmoins trop récente pour avoir pu influencer de manière sensible deux travaux datant des années soixante où l'on se serait attendu à ce que l'oeuvre d'Ermold le Noir fût prise en compte: H.-H. Anton, *Fürstenspiegel und Herrscherethos in der Karolingerzeit* (Bonn, 1968), pp. 190-98 (bien qu'il ne sous-estime pas l'intérêt de l'*Elegiacum carmen*, l'auteur concentre son analyse sur la seconde Epître au roi Pépin); H. Siemens, *Beiträge zum literarischen Bild Kaiser Ludwigs des Frommen in der Karolingerzeit* (Freiburg im Breisgau, 1966) – l'auteur, qui avoue avoir procédé à un choix parmi les sources, fait mention de l'*Elegiacum carmen* à propos de la "littérature panégyrique" (p. 6, note 3), mais ne s'explique pas sur les raisons de

l'interprétation du poète à tel ou tel propos.[8] Or l'analyse détaillée de l'*Elegiacum carmen* peut conduire l'historien – et pas seulement l'historien de la littérature – à cerner plus précisément la crédibilité d'Ermold.[9] Pour peu que l'on tente une analyse thématique, l'importance de ce poème devient évidente.[10] Néanmoins une analyse conséquente fait toujours défaut. C'est pourquoi il convient de s'interroger en premier lieu sur le portrait de Louis qu'offre Ermold. Certes, il s'agit à certains égards d'une présentation idéale,[11] mais ce trait ne contribue aucunement au discrédit de la source. Au contraire, puisqu'il rappelait aussi en acrostiche que c'est l'action de Louis qu'il voulait dépeindre,[12] Ermold ne craignait pas de présenter ce portrait à l'empereur – pour obtenir sa grâce: il faut se rendre à l'évidence que Louis pouvait ou, pour le moins, devait souhaiter se reconnaître dans cette description de l'empereur chrétien. On en trouve une autre illustration dans le *De laudibus sanctae crucis* de Raban Maur: Louis le Pieux y est représenté non en majesté, mais comme *miles Christi*.[13] Ce n'est aucunement l'effet du hasard, mais la mise en image d'un programme de gouvernement. Par conséquent, il semble qu'il faille non seulement s'abstenir de

son désintérêt pour cette oeuvre. En revanche, H. Kuhn, *Das literarische Porträt Ludwigs des Frommen* (Biel, 1930), p. 24, avait retenu le témoignage d'Ermold.

[8] Par exemple H. Löwe, "Von Theoderich dem Großen zu Karl dem Großen. Das Werden des Abendlandes im Geschichtsbild des frühen Mittelalters", *Deutsches Archiv* 9 (1951/52), 353-401 (pp. 386-87).

[9] Voir A. Ebenbauer, *Carmen historicum*, Untersuchungen zur historischen Dichtung im karolingischen Europa, tome 1 (Wien, 1978), pp. 101-49.

[10] Ebenbauer, *Carmen historicum*, pp. 135-37. On constate, par exemple, que la construction du livre 1 tend à prouver l'excellence de Louis (p. 105), dont le nom annonçait qu'il serait "puissant par les armes et pieux" (Ermold, *Poème* 1.78-79, p. 10), comme Ermold tente de l'expliquer par l'étymologie de *Hludowicus* (Ermold, *Poème*, 1.80-85, p. 10).

[11] Voir Kuhn, *Porträt*, p. 29.

[12] Ermold, *Poème*, Dédicace, pp. 2-4: "Ermoldus cecinit Hludoici Caesaris arma". ("Ermold chanta les combats de l'empereur Louis"). A ce propos, voir Ebenbauer, *Carmen historicum*, p. 102.

[13] Voir E. Sears, "Louis the Pious as *Miles Christi*. The Dedicatory Image in Hrabanus Maurus' *De laudibus sanctae crucis*", dans *Charlemagne's Heir*, éd. Godman et Collins, pp. 605-28.

dénigrer l'oeuvre d'Ermold le Noir, mais aussi analyser l'*Elegiacum carmen* selon sa nature propre:[14] c'est-à-dire comme une source de première importance quant à l'histoire des mentalités, en l'occurrence quant à l'idée que certains lettrés carolingiens se faisaient du gouvernement exercé par un empereur idéal, par un empereur chrétien. C'est dans cette nouvelle perspective qu'il convient de relire l'*Elegiacum carmen*. A cet égard, nous concentrerons ici notre attention sur un thème dont le poète semble faire l'un des principaux mobiles de la politique du successeur de Charlemagne: sa piété.

Louis "le Pieux"

Au fil de la description, la notion de piété – cette vertu première de la tradition romaine[15] – revient sans cesse: le substantif *pietas* et l'adjectif *pius* rythment l'*Elegiacum carmen* comme un leitmotiv.[16] Leur emploi est si fréquent qu'il peut sembler routinier, voire fade: ainsi, Judith est réputée pieuse ("pia pulcherrima conjunx") lorsqu'elle monte à cheval alors que les *proceres* l'entourent, en l'honneur du pieux roi.[17] Mais que penser lorsque l'épithète devient nom, lorsque Louis n'est plus désigné autrement que par la seule expression de "pieux"? C'est ainsi qu'Ermold décrit son entrée au palais d'Ingelheim, après le baptême de Harold et des Danois: "Inde pius moderando gradum pervenit in aedes, / Quo sibi Caesareo more parantur opes".[18] Or, même au coeur du combat, Louis demeure le *rex pius*.[19] En fait, l'épithète de "pieux" accolée au nom du fils de

[14] Voir Godman, "Louis the Pious", p. 259.
[15] Voir J. Liegle, "Pietas", *Zeitschrift für Numismatik* 42 (1932), 59-100, rééd. dans H. Oppermann, *Römische Wertbegriffe* (Darmstadt, 1974), pp. 229-73 (p. 229).
[16] Les termes *pietas* et *pius* sont employés environ 130 fois par Ermold, ce qui signifie que l'on trouve en moyenne une occurrence tous les vingt vers.
[17] Ermold, *Poème*, 4.2378-81, p. 182.
[18] Ermold, *Poème*, 4.2352-53, p. 180: "De là, conduisant (le cortège), le pieux gravit les marches menant au palais où des choses somptueuses lui sont préparées selon l'usage impérial".
[19] Ermold, *Poème*, 1.550-51, p. 44.

Charlemagne et visant depuis au moins le Xe siècle à le différencier des autres homonymes de Clovis prend directement son origine dans la titulature impériale.[20] Les diplômes de Louis le Pieux sont d'ailleurs datés des années de règne du "très pieux Auguste". Bien évidemment, l'on ne doit pas comprendre "pieux" au sens de "bigot", mais comme l'épithète désignant "celui qui craint Dieu"[21] – on peut également retenir ici l'acception antique, comme l'on parle du "pieux" Énée.[22] Le champ sémantique du mot *pietas* est en effet fort large: ce terme désigne le "sentiment qui fait reconnaître et accomplir tous les devoirs envers les dieux, les parents, la patrie, etc.", voire la "bienveillance"[23] – d'où l'ancien surnom de Louis "le Débonnaire".

Il serait fastidieux de commenter en détail chaque description des moeurs de Louis le Pieux – ou plutôt: des qualités à ce point propres à justifier son titre royal ou impérial qu'elles apparaissent comme inhérentes à son rang, comme l'est précisément l'épithète *pius*. Ermold décrit en Louis un prince "armé" (*armiger*) – et par conséquent: victorieux, comme le traduit E. Faral – "pacifique et pieux": c'est au nom d'un tel empereur que Witchaire salua le roi breton Morman.[24] Victorieux, pacifique et pieux – telles sont entre

---

[20] Voir R. Schieffer, "Ludwig 'der Fromme'. Zur Entstehung eines karolingischen Herrscherbeinamens", *Frühmittelalterliche Studien* 16 (1982), 58-73.

[21] La manière dont Michael Eytzinger (c. 1530-1598) traduit l'épithète *pius* est tout à fait significative. Dans ses *Thesauri principum hac aetate in Europa viventium paralipomena* (Köln, 1592), il parle de *Ludovicus cognomento pius* (p. 34); mais dans son *Iconographia regum Francorum* (Köln, 1587), il présente Louis comme "der Gotsfurchtig" (p. 25).

[22] Ebenbauer, *Carmen historicum*, p. 147, en doute. Il est cependant à noter que l'on peut éventuellement discerner une analogie établie par Ermold entre Enée et Louis: de même qu'Enée fut vainqueur du roi Turnus, de même Louis viendrait à bout de l'opposition du roi Murman (cf. Ermold, *Poème*, 3.1394-1403, p. 108).

[23] F. Gaffiot, *Dictionnaire Latin-Français* (Paris, 1934), p. 1179; cf. également Liegle, "Pietas", p. 243.

[24] Ermold, *Poème* 3.1360-61, p. 106. C'est également en tant que César *pacificusque pius* (Ermold, *Poème*, 3.1313, p. 102) que Louis exigeait sa soumission.

autres les épithètes propres à qualifier un empereur tel que Constantin ou Charlemagne.[25] C'est donc en s'inscrivant dans une prestigieuse tradition que Louis, agissant "solitae pietatis amore",[26] voulait rappeler le Breton rebelle à la raison, pour éviter le conflit armé. En recherchant la paix, l'empereur accomplissait une oeuvre pie.

Le respect des traditions

La piété de Louis était si légendaire que certains bruits couraient à son propos. Ainsi, le patriarche Paulin d'Aquilée[27] aurait prédit que le fils cadet de Charlemagne succéderait à ce dernier[28] car il s'agissait, à la différence de ses frères, d'un *vir sacer*,[29] d'un saint homme faisant preuve d'une dévotion sincère.[30] C'est donc au titre de sa *pietas* que Louis eut vocation à régner.[31] Plus loin, Ermold affirme que Louis rayonne par ses bijoux et ses vêtements, mais plus encore par sa piété.[32] D'ailleurs, il prétend que son héros l'emporte sur tous les autres princes par son amour de Dieu.[33] Ne s'agit-il cependant pas d'un *topos*? Le Gascon Loup Sanche est, lui aussi, réputé supérieur à ses ancêtres par la foi.[34]

[25] Cf. H. Wolfram, "Lateinische Herrschertitel im neunten und zehnten Jahrhundert", dans "Intitulatio II", *Lateinische Herrscher- und Fürstentitel im neunten und zehnten Jahrhundert* par Wolfram (Wien, Köln, Graz, 1973), pp. 19-178 (p. 53).

[26] Ermold, *Poème* 3.1562, p. 120.

[27] Selon une autre tradition, cette prophétie serait le fait d'Alcuin. Si tant est qu'elle eût réellement lieu, cette dernière est plus vraisemblable, voir Depreux, "Poètes et historiens", p. 315, note 16.

[28] Ermold, *Poème* 1.632-33, p. 50.

[29] Ermold, *Poème* 1.623, p. 50.

[30] Ermold, *Poème* 1.618-21, pp. 48-50.

[31] Voir Godman, *Poets and Emperors*, p. 116. On observe également cela dans les propos d'Eginhard en 813: Louis s'avérait digne de recevoir l'héritage impérial "par sa vaillance, par son intelligence et par sa foi" – "armis, ingenioque fide" (Ermold, *Poème* 2.697, p. 54).

[32] Ermold, *Poème* 2.866-67, p. 68.

[33] Ermold, *Poème* 1.36-37, p. 6.

[34] Ermold, *Poème* 1.167, p. 18.

Quoi qu'il en soit, un être pieux respecte les traditions: le respect des coutumes est en effet le gage d'une action juste. Le souci d'agir en accord avec la tradition de ses ancêtres sous-tend la politique de Louis. Ceci est d'autant plus important que le début du règne de cet empereur fut marqué par la volonté de procéder à une *Renovatio regni Francorum*.[35] Or cette "rénovation," pour être parfaite, devait s'avérer un retour à la pureté de la tradition. Quelques exemples illustrent ce souci. Les relations entre Louis le Pieux et l'évêque de Rome furent marquées d'événements majeurs pour l'histoire de la Papauté et de l'Empire: en 816 à Reims, le pape sacra Louis empereur;[36] en 817 fut conclu un pacte assurant définitivement l'unité du *Patrimonium sancti Petri*, complété par la *Constitutio romana* de 824 précisant les droits et devoirs de chacun.[37] A cet égard, Louis est censé, à l'occasion de son couronnement et de son sacre à Reims, avoir souligné sa volonté de mener une politique conforme aux traditions carolingiennes: "Ut mea progenies Petri servavit honorem, / Sic ego servabo, praesul, amore Dei".[38] En ce qui concerne l'administration de l'Empire, Louis se plie également à la tradition, par exemple lorsqu'il procède à la convocation des assemblées: en ordonnant aux *duces* préposés aux régions frontalières de venir à son plaid, Louis procède *more ...*

---

[35] Telle était la devise de la bulle de Louis le Pieux, voir l'appendice "Die Metallbullen der Karolinger", dans *Die zeitgenössischen Bildnisse Karls des Grossen* par P. E. Schramm (Leipzig, 1928), pp. 60-61. Sur le commencement du règne impérial de Louis le Pieux, voir J. Semmler, *"Renovatio Regni Francorum*. Die Herrschaft Ludwigs des Frommen im Frankenreich, 814-829/830", dans *Charlemagne's Heir*, éd. Godman et Collins, pp. 125-46.

[36] Voir P. Depreux, "Saint Remi et la royauté carolingienne", *Revue Historique* 285 (1991), 235-60, (pp. 236-41); Depreux, "Zur Echtheit einer Urkunde Kaiser Ludwigs des Frommen für die Reimser Kirche (BM² 801)", *Deutsches Archiv* 48 (1992), 1-16.

[37] On trouvera la bibliographie concernant ces questions dans P. Depreux, "Empereur, Empereur associé et Pape au temps de Louis le Pieux", *Revue belge de philologie et d'histoire* 70 (1992), 893-906.

[38] Ermold, *Poème* 2.1038-39, p. 80: "De même que ma famille préserva l'honneur de Pierre, de même, moi, je (le) préserverai, ô prélat, pour l'amour de Dieu".

prisco, selon un usage antique.[39] De même, dans le rapport qu'ils firent à Louis le Pieux en 819, les *missi* auxquels il avait confié l'inspection des monastères sont censés avoir loué l'action de l'empereur en soulignant comment ce dernier faisait observer l'enseignement des Anciens:[40] Louis, dans l'exercice de sa charge, se montre lui-même un exemple, qui s'inscrit dans la tradition des *priores*.

Le respect dû aux ancêtres s'applique évidemment au premier chef au propre père de Louis. Ainsi, au début de son règne, le nouvel empereur fit preuve de sa piété filiale en prenant certaines mesures pour le salut de l'âme de Charlemagne.[41] Louis multiplia les aumônes, d'où le commentaire d'Ermold: "O felix Carolus, sobolem qui liquit in orbe, / Qui satagit, caeli quo pater intret iter".[42] Mais le respect pour les défunts dont Louis fait montre ne s'applique pas qu'à son seul père. Au contraire, même un rebelle y a droit – tel Morman. Alors que le roi breton avait été tué lors de la campagne militaire engagée pour le soumettre, "Caesar at ipse pius telluri more cadaver / Inponi miserans pro pietate jubet".[43] De même, les Francs tués au combat sont inhumés "more pio".[44] Par ailleurs, Louis n'est pas un roi inhospitalier. Il accueille à sa table son fils Lothaire et son filleul Harold: ceux-ci prennent place "rege jubente pio".[45] Auparavant, Louis avait richement doté le prince au sortir du baptême.[46] Ainsi, nous observons que les implications diverses de la *pietas* antique trouvent leur écho dans le comportement de Louis. Néanmoins, c'est en tant que prince

[39] Ibid., 3.1258-59, p. 98.

[40] Ibid., 3.1790-91, p. 136: "Munia vestra docent quicquid docuere priores, / Et facis assidue haec recolere ipse tuis". ("Votre autorité enseigne la règle d'autrefois et la fait pratiquer avec exactitude": trad. Faral, p. 137).

[41] Ibid., 2.808-23, p. 64.

[42] Ibid., 2.818-19, p. 64: "Oh! le bienheureux Charles, qui a laissé sur la terre un rejeton se démenant afin que, par lui, son père accède au chemin du ciel!".

[43] Ibid., 3.1738-39, p. 132: "le pieux César, compatissant en raison de sa piété, ordonne de mettre la dépouille en terre selon la coutume".

[44] Ibid., 3.1740-41, p. 132: "selon la pieuse coutume".

[45] Ibid., 4.2426-27, p. 184: "sur l'ordre du pieux roi".

[46] Ibid., 4.2254-65, p. 172.

essentiellement chrétien qu'il entendait agir: ceci n'était pas sans conséquences. Voyons comment, d'après le poète, il assuma ses responsabilités.

Bonté, justice et ordo

A plusieurs reprises, Ermold chante les louanges de l'empereur. Ainsi, Harold est réputé avoir reconnu combien Louis était "insignis, patiens, fortisque piusque, / armiger et clemens".[47] Mainte fois, le poète souligne la bonté de l'empereur: il est *bonus*[48] et, même, *almus*.[49] D'ailleurs, Thégan le dit lent à la colère et prompt à la compassion.[50] Or face au pape, qui fonde son pouvoir sur son grade ecclésiastique, Louis tire sa force de sa bienveillance, de sa *bonitas*.[51] Le pape est d'ailleurs censé avoir affirmé à Reims que l'empereur s'avérait tout à la fois un père et un homme de Dieu nourrissant et défendant les siens.[52] A cet égard, la *pietas* semble avoir été le mobile du gouvernement ludovicien. Ermold l'affirme à propos des *missi* que Louis le Pieux avait, au début de son règne, dépêchés par tout l'Empire "inquirere et investigare, si alicui aliqua iniustitia perpetrata fuisset":[53] ils avaient pour mission de régir les peuples par la piété.[54] Dans ce dessein, il convenait de faire régner l'ordre.

---

[47] Ibid., 4.2458-59, p. 186: "insigne, patient, fort et pieux, clément les armes à la main".

[48] Ibid., 2.700, p. 54.

[49] Ibid., 3.1354, p. 104.

[50] Thégan, *Gesta Hludowici imperatoris*, chap. 19, éd. E. Tremp, MGH SRG (in us. schol.) 64 (Hannover, 1995), p. 202.

[51] Ermold, *Poème* 2.869, p. 68: "Ille gradu pollens, hic bonitate vigens". ("Tirant leur force celui-ci de son rang, celui-là de sa vertu": trad. Faral, p. 69).

[52] Ermold, *Poème* 2.1069, p. 84: "Et pater et sacer est, altor et arma suis". ("Plein de bonté et de religion, il est le tuteur et le salut des siens": trad. Faral, p. 85).

[53] Thégan, *Gesta* 13, p. 192: "pour enquêter et rechercher si quelque injustice avait été commise envers quelqu'un".

[54] Ermold, *Poème* 2.1158-59, p. 90: "Nam mihi mente sedet, dederim quod nuper in orbem / Legatos, populos qui pietate regant". ("Je ne perds pas de

L'on sait l'importance de la notion d'*ordo* pour la société du haut Moyen-Age.[55] Elle est soulignée à plusieurs reprises dans le poème d'Ermold le Noir. Déjà en Aquitaine, Louis redonna vie aux *regna* placés sous son autorité en définissant un *ordo*: c'est ainsi qu'il pouvait régir son peuple par le moyen de sa piété.[56] L'expression *ordine composito*, qu'Ermold utilise à cette occasion, signifie que Louis veilla à ce que chacun fût établi à sa place, comme le prouve son emploi dans la description du cortège à Ingelheim.[57] Ainsi, en 814, Louis accueillit ses nouveaux sujets *cum pietatis ope*, chacun selon son *ordo*.[58] Par conséquent, un bon gouvernement suppose que chacun joue pleinement son rôle au rang et à la place qui lui sont impartis. Ceci vaut pour l'Aquitaine – l'un des envoyés de Charlemagne vanta d'ailleurs auprès du vieil empereur l'*ordinatio* de ce royaume.[59] Ceci vaut également pour l'Empire. Ermold affirme en effet qu'une fois au pouvoir, Louis ordonn(a) l'Empire (qui lui avait été) confié.[60]

L'*ordinatio* de l'Empire dont parle le poète comporte au moins deux aspects. Il s'agit tout d'abord du souci manifesté par Louis d'admonester ses sujets à observer les obligations que, par l'autorité divine, l'*ordinatio* à laquelle ont procédé les hommes leur confère et

---

vue que précédemment j'ai envoyé mes agents par toute la terre pour gouverner les peuples selon la juste loi": trad. Faral, p. 90).

[55] Voir G. Brown, "Introduction: the Carolingian Renaissance", dans *Carolingian Culture: Emulation and Innovation*, éd. R. McKitterick (Cambridge, 1994), pp. 1-51 (pp. 24-28).

[56] Ermold, *Poème* 1.90-91, p. 10: "Ordine composito recreavit subdita regna, / Lege regens populum cum pietatis ope". ("Par une sage administration, il rend la vie à son royaume, gouvernant son peuple selon la rigueur de la loi, mais aussi avec le conseil de son indulgence": trad. Faral, p. 11).

[57] Ermold, *Poème* 4.2312, p. 176.

[58] Ermold, *Poème* 2.788-89, p. 62: "Conveniunt tandem, recipit quos rex pius omnes / Ordine quemque suo cum pietatis ope". ("Ils le joignent enfin et le pieux roi les accueille tous, chacun selon son rang, avec bonté": trad. Faral, p. 63).

[59] Astronome, *Vita Hludowici imperatoris* 19, éd. E. Tremp, MGH SRG (in us. schol.) 64 (Hannover, 1995), p. 340.

[60] Ermold, *Poème* 2.847, p. 66: "Commissum imperium ordinat, armat, alit". ("Il met en ordre, fortifie, vivifie ses Etats": trad. Faral, p. 67).

selon laquelle ils ont, chacun "à sa place et selon son rang", une "part" au "ministère" impérial.[61] Mais il s'agit aussi – les deux éléments sont liés – de protéger, voire de rétablir le droit.[62] C'est à ce titre que l'on peut comprendre pourquoi Béra, en 820, fit appel non pas à la "bonté" de Louis le Pieux, comme le traduit E. Faral, mais à son "amour de la piété" pour lui demander la permission de se disculper par un duel avec son accusateur.[63] L'*amor pietatis*, c'est en quelque sorte le respect de l'équité. A cet égard, il est important de souligner que l'expression *commissum imperium ordinat* d'Ermold est en fait la conclusion de sa description de l'envoi de

[61] *Admonitio ad omnes regni ordines* 3, dans *Capitula episcoporum* 1, éd. Brommer, n° 150, p. 303: "Sed quamquam summa huius ministerii in nostra persona consistere videatur, tamen et divina auctoritate et humana ordinatione ita per partes divisum esse cognoscitur, ut unusquisque vestrum in suo loco et ordine partem nostri ministerii habere cognoscatur". ("Mais quoiqu'il apparaisse que la somme de ce ministère réside en notre personne, cependant, et par l'*auctoritas* divine, et, par une *ordinatio* humaine, il [ce ministère] est reconnu être divisé par parties, en sorte que chacun de vous en sa place et en son ordre, soit reconnu avoir une partie de notre ministère": trad. Guillot, p. 466). Voir O. Guillot, "Une *ordinatio* méconnue. Le capitulaire de 823-825", dans *Charlemagne's Heir*, éd. Godman et Collins, pp. 455-86. Sur la datation de ce capitulaire, voir Depreux, "Empereur, Empereur associé", p. 903, note 80.

[62] Voir par exemple le *legationis capitulum* datant probablement du début de 826 (*Capitula episcoporum* 1, éd. Brommer, n° 152, pp. 309-10): "Volumus, ut missi nostri, quos ad hoc constitutos habemus, ut curam et sollicitudinem habeant, quatinus unusquisque qui rector a nobis populi nostri constitutus est in suo ordine officium sibi commissum iuste ac Deo placite ad honorem nostrum ac populi nostri utilitatem administret, in hunc modum cognoscendi diligentiam adhibeant, si ea quae in capitulari nostro, quod eis anno praeterito dedimus, continentur, secundum voluntatem Dei ac iussionem nostram fiant adimpleta". ("Nous voulons que nos *missi* – que nous avons constitués pour qu'ils veillent avec sollicitude à ce que chaque *rector* de notre peuple constitué par nous s'occupe, en son ordre, de l'office qui lui a été confié justement et d'une façon qui plaise à Dieu, pour notre honneur et pour le profit de notre peuple – s'enquièrent de cette façon avec zèle de l'exécution, selon la volonté de Dieu et notre ordre, de ce qui se trouve dans notre capitulaire, que nous leur donnâmes l'année dernière").

[63] Ermold, *Poème* 3.1816-17, p. 138: "Caesar, pietatis amore / Deprecor, ut ...". ("César, je fais appel à ta bonté pour qu[e] ...": trad. Faral, p. 139).

missi chargés par Louis le Pieux de restaurer la justice en rétablissant chacun dans ses droits[64] et de confirmer ces mesures par des chartes portant son seing,[65] ce que Thégan atteste également.[66]

La valeur du conseil

Certes, c'est au roi qu'appartient en dernier lieu la décision,[67] mais le rôle de ses conseillers n'est pourtant pas négligeable – surtout chez Louis le Pieux. Thégan lui avait reproché de leur accorder trop de crédit.[68] Quant à Ermold, il présente les faits sous un jour de prime abord inattendu, mais qui s'avère particulièrement propre à expliquer la position de Louis. L'action se situe lors qu'il n'était encore que roi d'Aquitaine, pendant le plaid où l'on décida la campagne contre Barcelone. Alors qu'il fallait prendre une décision concernant la prochaine campagne et l'itinéraire qu'emprunteraient les armées, le roi se tourna vers les *proceres* pour recevoir leur avis. Il le fit pour une raison bien simple: contrairement à lui-même, ils avaient une connaissance concrète de la situation sur le terrain. Les propos que le poète met dans la bouche du roi sont explicites: "Vobis nota satis res haec, incognita nobis: / Dicite consilium, quo peragamus iter".[69] D'où l'affirmation de la nécessité de consulter les "élus du peuple" (il faut entendre: ceux que la Providence a choisis en les portant au "faîte du royaume") pour prendre, sur leurs conseils, les décisions nécessaires.[70]

---

[64] Ermold, *Poème* 2.824-35, pp. 64-66.

[65] Ermold, *Poème* 2.836-37, p. 66.

[66] Thégan, *Gesta* 13, pp. 192-94.

[67] Ermold, *Poème* 1.168, p. 18: "Rex, censura tibi, nobis parere necesse est". ("Roi, à toi de disposer, à nous d'obéir": trad. Faral, p. 19).

[68] Thégan, *Gesta* 20, p. 204.

[69] Ermold, *Poème* 1.162-63, p. 16: "Vous connaissez bien la situation; elle nous est (en revanche) inconnue: prononcez votre conseil. Quel chemin devons-nous emprunter?".

[70] Ermold, *Poème* 1.147-49, p. 16: "... vocat / Scilicet electos populi, seu culmina regni, / Quorum consiliis res peragenda manet". ("[Il] tient l'assemblée habituelle des grands du royaume, dont les avis doivent inspirer ses actes": trad. Faral, p. 17).

Si l'on en croit Ermold, Louis le Pieux aurait pu se targuer de nombreuses qualités. Le poète met dans la bouche du comte Guillaume l'éloge suivant:[71] Louis est la "lumière des Francs" (*lux Francorum*); il est tout à la fois leur roi et leur père (*rex et pater*), leur défense et leur honneur (*arma decusque*). Bref, il possède *virtus* et *sapientia*, celui que le comte de Toulouse désigne comme "rector magne". Le terme mérite attention.[72] Certes, on a pu proposer de reconnaître dans certains traits du gouvernement de Louis le Pieux une influence de la règle bénédictine,[73] mais on ne peut pas pour autant assimiler le gouvernement de l'Empire à celui d'un grand monastère. Par conséquent, c'est non pas l'allusion à la fonction d'un *rector* monastique, mais l'étymologie de ce terme qui importe ici. Guillaume appelle Louis *rector* parce qu'en prenant conseil auprès des Francs, le *rex* entend parvenir à la décision lui permettant de gouverner *recte*, c'est-à-dire justement.[74] On a ici une nouvelle preuve de l'actualité de l'étymologie proposée par Isidore de Séville et dont les Pères du concile de Paris, en 829, soulignèrent les implications.[75] Or c'est en raison de sa *pietas* que Louis est appelé à écouter les conseils de Guillaume, à tenir compte de ses *vota*.[76] Il ne

---

[71] Ermold, *Poème* 1.174-77, p. 18.

[72] Ermold, *Poème* 1.176, p. 18: "grand *rector*". Voir également l'éloge de Louis le Pieux que prononce Harold (Ermold, *Poème* 4.2456-57, p. 186): "Caesar opime, Dei cultor, rectorque tuorum, / Quos tibi cunctipotens contulit, alme Deus ...".

[73] Voir T. F. X. Noble, "The Monastic Ideal as a Model for Empire: The Case of Louis the Pious", *Revue Bénédictine* 86 (1976), 235-50.

[74] Ainsi, c'est en tant que *rector regni Francorum* que Charlemagne publia l'*Admonitio generalis* (*Capitula episcoporum* 1, éd. Brommer, n° 22, p. 53). Sous Louis le Pieux, les hauts fonctionnaires sont également désignés comme *rectores*, voir supra note 62.

[75] *Episcoporum ad Hludowicum imperatorem relatio* 56, dans *Capitula episcoporum* 2, éd. R. Pokorny et M. Stratmann, MGH Capitula episcoporum 2 (Hannover, 1995), n° 196, pp. 46-51: "rex a recte agendo vocatur". ("Le roi tire son som du fait d'agir droitement"). Sur le *nomen regis*, Anton, *Fürstenspiegel*, pp. 384-404.

[76] Ermold, *Poème* 1.178-79, p. 18: "Rex, age, consiliis, si dignor, consule nostris / Atque meis votis, rex, pietate fave". ("Eh bien! roi, daigne écouter mon conseil! Roi, accueille mon voeu": trad. Faral, p. 19).

s'agit point là d'un appel à la faiblesse, mais le rappel à la notion toute romaine de lien[77] que suppose la *pietas*; autrement dit, Ermold affirme par le bais de Guillaume que Louis, outre la politesse avec laquelle la chose est formulée, est tenu de gouverner en prenant conseil auprès des Grands – c'est le gage du caratère juste des mesures prises par le *rex*. L'on observe alors la pertinence de l'analyse selon laquelle, sous Charlemagne et Louis le Pieux, le recours au *consensus fidelium* faisait désormais partie des traditions institutionnelles en tant que "concept complémentaire" de l'idéal du roi chrétien.[78] Le discours du comte de Toulouse, bien que construit par le poète, me semble par conséquent d'un intérêt capital pour la compréhension de la *pietas* en tant qu'éthique de gouvernement.

La vertu d'humilité

Il a été fait allusion plus haut à la prophétie de Paulin d'Aquilée. A voir défiler les fils de Charlemagne devant l'homme de Dieu, à voir celui-ci désigner le dernier seul capable de recevoir de Dieu l'*ordinatio* comme roi sur les Francs,[79] comment ne pas penser au choix de David par Samuel, pour recevoir l'onction (Samuel 16.1-13)? Il est vraisemblable que cette comparaison était assez répandue à la cour du temps de Louis, car Thégan fait expressément référence au sacre de David lorsqu'il présente le jeune roi des Aquitains. Mais, plus largement, c'est à une apologie des cadets que se livre le chorévêque de Trèves.[80] "Ultimus ecce venit Hludowicus".[81] Il est normal qu'il entre en dernier dans l'église, puisqu'il est le plus

---

[77] La "Bindung" dont parle Liegle, "Pietas", p. 243.

[78] Voir J. Hannig, *Consensus fidelium: Frühfeudale Interpretationen des Verhältnisses von Königtum und Adel am Beispiel des Frankenreiches* (Stuttgart, 1982), p. 199.

[79] Ermold, *Poème* 1.632-33, p. 50: "Si Deus e vestro Francorum semine regem / Ordinat, iste tuis sedibus aptus erit". ("Si Dieu, lui dit-il, veut donner aux Francs un roi de ta famille, c'est Louis qui saura tenir ta place": trad. Faral, p. 51).

[80] Thégan, *Gesta* 3, p. 178.

[81] Ermold, *Poème* 1.618, p. 48: "Venant le dernier, voici Louis ...": trad. Faral, p. 49.

jeune. En cette habitude, trente ans durant, à être le dernier réside vraisemblablement la complaisance avec laquelle Louis, une fois empereur, fait référence à sa *mediocritas*.[82]

La reconnaissance que d'autres sont plus que lui au fait de certains problèmes et une propension à l'humilité indéniable permettent de comprendre l'aveu que Louis est censé avoir prononcé en 816 à Reims: "Non meritis, ut credo, meis, sed patris honorem / Hunc miserans Christus cessit habere mihi. / Ergo precor fidos et te, praeclare sacerdos, / Ut mihi consilii rite feratis opem".[83] Louis ne dépréciait aucunement le rôle du pape[84] – au contraire (car l'importance que l'empereur accordait au *consilium*, s'il liait les conseillers à sa politique,[85] l'obligeait également à leur égard).

L'honor *impérial*

Cette déclaration de Louis le Pieux à Reims est du plus haut intérêt, notamment par la manière dont l'héritage qu'il reçoit est désigné: il s'agit non d'une *dignitas* certes insigne, mais d'un *honor*,[86] c'est-à-

---

[82] *Admonitio ad omnes regni ordines* 2, dans *Capitula episcoporum* 1, éd. P. Brommer, MGH Capitula episcoporum 1 (Hannover, 1984), p. 303: "Sed quoniam complacuit divinae providentiae nostram mediocritatem ad hoc constituere, ut sanctae suae ecclesiae et regni huius curam gereremus ...". ("Mais puisqu'il a plu à la divine Providence d'établir notre médiocrité pour que nous prenions soin de sa sainte Eglise et de ce *regnum* ...": trad. Guillot, p. 464).

[83] Ermold, *Poème* 2.946-49, p. 74: "Ce n'est, à ce qu'il me semble, pas en raison de mes mérites – tout au contraire! – que le Christ, par pitié, m'a accordé d'obtenir cet *honor* paternel. C'est pourquoi, (vous, mes) fidèles et toi, illustre prêtre (il s'agit du pape), je vous prie de m'assister de votre conseil".

[84] Voir en revanche J. Fried, "Ludwig der Fromme, das Papsttum und die fränkische Kirche", dans *Charlemagne's Heir*, éd. Godman et Collins, pp. 231-73 (pp. 250-52). Contra: Depreux, "Empereur, Empereur associé", p. 897.

[85] Les participants au conseil étaient en effet engagés par les décisions prises collégialement. On observe ce phénomène à l'état le plus pur dans le *pactum*, voir l'article "Pactus, pactum" dû à E. Kaufmann, *Handwörterbuch zur deutschen Rechtsgeschichte* 3 (Berlin, 1984), cols 1403-05.

[86] Voir également Ermold, *Poème* 1.156-59, p. 16: "Magnanimi proceres, meritis pro munere digni, / Limina quos patriae praeposuit Carolus, / Ob hoc Cunctipotens apicem concessit honoris / Nobis, ut populo rite feramus opem".

dire d'une charge publique qui ne diffère qu'en intensité, mais pas en nature, de celle d'un comte par exemple (ce que Louis affirme avec vigueur dans l'*Admonitio ad omnes regni ordines*); il s'agit par conséquent d'une charge révocable.[87] Or cette collaboration que Louis attend de tous, cette participation aux décisions par le *consilium* sont le gage d'un bon gouvernement: celui où règne la justice. En effet, le discours se poursuit avec le rappel des principes selon lesquels Louis, avec l'aide de chacun, veut gouverner: "Dives agat legem, pauper teneatur eadem, / Nec personarum sit locus atque modus".[88] "Corrigimus pravos, donamus munere justos, / Et facimus populum jura paterna sequi. Tum Deus excelsus nobis populoque sequaci / Praestabit miserans regna beata poli / Atque in praesenti nostrum servabit honorem: Infestos hostes hinc procul ire facit".[89] Point n'est besoin d'entrer ici dans la querelle relative à l'existence de la notion d'Etat aux temps carolingiens.[90] L'essentiel est ailleurs: de même qu'un Nithard avait pleinement conscience des exigences d'une véritable *respublica*,[91] Ermold montre dans cet extrait de l'*Elegiacum carmen* l'actualité du souci, pour l'empereur, de veiller

("Seigneurs magnanimes, dont les services méritent notre reconnaissance et que Charles a placés aux frontières de la patrie, le Tout-Puissant nous a établis au faîte des honneurs avec mission de protéger le peuple": trad. Faral, p. 17).

[87] Cela ne fut pas sans conséquences dramatiques. Voir M. de Jong, "Power and Humility in Carolingian Society: the Public Penance of Louis the Pious", *Early Medieval Europe* 1 (1992), 29-52.

[88] Ermold, *Poème* 2.958-59, p. 76: "Que le riche fasse le procès dans les formes, que le pauvre observe la loi; qu'il n'y ait pas d'égard pour la position et la qualité des personnes".

[89] Ermold, *Poème* 2.964-69, p. 76: "Corrigeons les mauvais, récompensons les justes, et veillons à ce que le peuple observe les lois ancestrales. Alors, le Dieu Très-Haut, dans sa miséricorde, nous donnera ainsi qu'au peuple qui nous obéit la béatitude du royaume céleste, et pour le présent, il conservera notre *honor*: il en éloignera les ennemis (qui lui sont) hostiles".

[90] Le sujet a fait couler beaucoup d'encre. On peut trouver une présentation synthétique de la question dans l'article de H. Keller, "Zum Charakter der 'Staatlichkeit' zwischen karolingischer Reichsreform und hochmittelalterlichem Herrschaftsausbau", *Frühmittelalterliche Studien* 23 (1989), 248-64.

[91] Voir P. Depreux, "Nithard et la *res publica*: un regard critique sur le règne de Louis le Pieux", *Médiévales* 22-23 (1992), 149-61.

au "bien commun" de son peuple – relevât-il pour partie de l'au-delà (l'on ne doit pas oublier que la lecture favorite de Charlemagne était la *Cité de Dieu*).[92]

Roi et prêtre

Evoquer le gouvernement de Louis "le Pieux" sans rappeler la réforme des monastères qu'il a encouragée serait inconcevable – c'est d'ailleurs l'un des aspects les mieux connus de son règne.[93] Ermold fait mention de certaines mesures. Il évoque la politique de Louis en Aquitaine, quand "rex pius interea, Christi succensus amore, / Dat pia christicolis moenia digna satis. / Namque ferunt multas monachorum rite catervas / Instituisse Deo sub ditione sua".[94] Et le poète de citer le cas de Conques.[95] En honorant l'Eglise, Louis ne se plie pas seulement à l'ordre intimé par son père,[96] mais il se montre reconnaissant envers une institution à laquelle ses ancêtres devaient leur promotion: grâce à l'Eglise, leur *nomen* fut exalté *in astra*.[97] Et, somme toute, si Louis le Pieux, qui

---

[92] Eginhard, *Vie de Charlemagne* 24, éd. L. Halphen (Paris, 1938), p. 72. A ce propos, voir T. Mayer, "Staatsauffassung in der Karolingerzeit", dans *Das Königtum. Seine geistigen und rechtlichen Grundlagen*, Vorträge und Forschungen 3 (Lindau et Konstanz, 1956), pp. 169-83 (p. 171).

[93] Présentation d'ensemble de cette réforme par J. Semmler, "Benedictus II: una regula - una consuetudo", dans *Benedictine Culture, 750-1050*, éd. W. Lourdaux et D. Verhelst (Leuven, 1983), pp. 1-49; sur la situation en Aquitaine, voir Semmler, "Benediktinische Reform und kaiserliches Privileg. Zur Frage des intitutionellen Zusammenschlusses der Klöster um Benedikt von Aniane", dans *Institutionen und Geschichte. Theoretische Aspekte und mittelalterliche Befunde*, éd. G. Melville (Köln, Weimar, Wien, 1992), pp. 259-93 (pp. 262-74).

[94] Ermold, *Poème* 1.224-27, p. 22: "Le pieux roi, embrasé par l'amour du Christ, donne en nombre suffisant des demeures appropriées aux chrétiens. En effet, on rapporte que, sous sa protection, de nombreux bataillons de moines se constituèrent pour Dieu".

[95] Ibid., 1.229-301, pp. 22-26.

[96] Ibid., 2.733, p. 58.

[97] Ibid., 2.1156-57, p. 90.

régit avec piété les clercs et son peuple,[98] restaure les églises,[99] ordonne que l'on épargne les églises lors des campagnes militaires[100] et veille à augmenter l'honneur de l'Eglise,[101] c'est pour que l'on puisse mener – au premier chef, ceci concerne les moines – une *pia vita*.[102]

En effet, plus que la réalité de la réforme, plus que la mise par écrit des engagements de Louis vis-à-vis de saint Pierre,[103] c'est la force du sentiment religieux qu'Ermold dépeint chez Louis qui retient l'attention. Deux traits sont à ce propos significatifs. Tout d'abord, lorsqu'il relate, concernant la fondation de Conques, l'entretien entre l'ermite Dadon et Louis, Ermold affirme qu'ils tenaient un même discours, étant l'un et l'autre égaux par leur religion.[104] D'ailleurs, l'Astronome était d'avis qu'eu égard à sa politique religieuse, Louis méritait non seulement le nom de *rex*, mais également celui de *sacerdos*.[105] Or il est une autre assertion d'Ermold tout aussi intéressante. Lorsqu'il évoque la fondation du monastère d'Inden près d'Aix-la-Chapelle, où selon ses dires Louis entendait pouvoir de temps à autre se reposer et s'adonner aux exercices spirituels,[106] Ermold affirme que "Benoît était le père de cet établissement, et Louis y est tout à la fois empereur et abbé".[107] L'on pourrait admettre que Louis exerçait à Inden les droits

---

[98] Ibid., 2.751, p. 58: "Clerum seu populum cum pietate regens". ("Traitant avec bonté clercs et laïques": trad. Faral, p. 519).

[99] Ibid., 1.88-89, p. 10.

[100] Ibid., 3.1592-93, p. 122.

[101] Ibid., 3.1756-57, pp. 132-34.

[102] Ibid., 2.1183, p. 92.

[103] Ibid., 2.1040-53, p. 82.

[104] Ibid., 1.296-97, p. 26: "Namque diem totum parili sermone trahebant / Rex famulusque Dei, relligione pares". ("Pendant des journées entières, le roi et le serviteur de Dieu s'entretiennent en égaux, avec une égale piété": trad. Faral, p. 27).

[105] Astronome, *Vita* 19, p. 334.

[106] Ermold, *Poème* 2.1218-19, p. 94. Nous savons par ailleurs que l'empereur était assidu à la prière, voir Thégan, *Gesta* 19, p. 202.

[107] Ermold, *Poème* 2.1248-49, p. 96. Je supprime la virgule placée entre "Caesar" et "et abba": "Namque idem Benedictus erat pater illius aedis, / Et Hludowicus adest Caesar et abba simul".

appartenant, selon l'*Eigenkirchenrecht*, au fondateur d'une église ou d'un monastère:[108] il est en effet attesté que l'ordre de fonder Inden fut donné par Louis, qui dota de ses biens le nouveau monastère.[109] Néanmoins, nous pouvons aller plus avant dans l'analyse et prendre Ermold au mot: s'il n'y a pas lieu de contester à Benoît le titre d'abbé d'Inden,[110] on se doit de noter qu'à la mort de Benoît d'Aniane (cinq à sept ans avant qu'Ermold ne compose son poème), Louis le Pieux prétendit exercer lui-même les fonctions abbatiales[111] – Benoît eut néanmoins un successeur en la personne de Wicard.[112]

La foi conquérante

La foi est un mobile important de la politique de Louis le Pieux. C'est mû par l'amour de Dieu que l'empereur veut entreprendre l'évangélisation des Danois[113] et Harold le reconnaît publique-

---

[108] A ce propos, voir W. Hartmann, "Der rechtliche Zustand der Kirchen auf dem Lande: die Eigenkirche in der fränkischen Gesetzgebung des 7. bis 9. Jahrhunderts", dans *Cristianizzazione ed organizzazione ecclesiastica delle campagne nell'alto medioevo: espansione e resistenze*, Settimane di studio del Centro italiano di studi sull'alto medioevo 28 (Spoleto, 1982), 1:397-441.

[109] Ardon, *Vita Benedicti abbatis Anianensis et Indensis* 35, éd. G. Waitz et W. Wattenbach, MGH SS 15.1 (Hannover, 1887), p. 215.

[110] Il est attesté comme tel dans le diplôme BM² 734(710).

[111] Ardon, *Vita* 42, p. 219: "et post eius discessum actenus abbatem se monasterii illius palam esse profitetur". ("Et depuis son décès jusqu'à présent, il se déclare publiquement l'abbé de son monastère"). Par ailleurs, dans une liste des frères de Saint-Denis destinée à la communauté de Saint-Remi de Reims, l'empereur est mentionné comme le premier des moines: M. Félibien, *Histoire de l'abbaye royale de Saint-Denys en France* (Paris, 1706), Recueil de pièces, n° 77, p. 58. Plus tard, Charles le Chauve retint pour lui-même l'abbatiat de Saint-Denis, voir *Annales de Saint-Bertin*, a. 867, éd. F. Grat et alii (Paris, 1964), pp. 134-35.

[112] Voir E. Stengel, "Die Immunitätsurkunde Ludwigs des Frommen für Kloster Inden (Cornelimünster)", *Neues Archiv* 29 (1904), 375-93 (p. 382); N. Kühn, *Die Reichsabtei Kornelimünster im Mittelalter. Geschichtliche Entwicklung, Verfassung, Konvent, Besitz*, Veröffentlichungen des Stadtarchivs Aachen 3 (Aachen, 1982), p. 26.

[113] Ermold, *Poème* 4.1900-03, p. 144.

ment.[114] Or le poète prétend que Louis agit au nom de Dieu[115] et qu'à ce titre, il entend moins s'emparer de nouveaux royaumes que faire oeuvre de conversion. C'est pourquoi il recommande à l'archevêque de Reims envoyé en mission chez Harold[116] de le rassurer sur ses intentions: "Non sua regna mihi cedant, hoc consulo, credat, / Sed quo plasma Dei lucrificare queam".[117] L'on pourrait taxer cette présentation de propagande; force est alors de constater qu'elle s'avère conséquente. En effet, en 818, l'important pour Louis le Pieux, c'était que Morman, qui avait reçu le baptême[118] mais s'était écarté ainsi que son peuple des pratiques chrétiennes,[119] rejoignît le "troupeau des adorateurs du Christ". A cette condition, l'empereur se dit prêt à renoncer à son projet de campagne militaire.[120]

Ce rôle primordial de la foi est affirmé par Ermold, puisqu'il prétend que sous Louis le Pieux, "gentibus et cunctis pax erat aucta fide".[121] L'on retrouve également ce trait dans le discours tenu par Louis pendant le plaid où le siège de Barcelone fut décidé. Si les Sarrasins acceptaient de se convertir, la campagne militaire n'aurait plus d'objet.[122] De même, les propos que Witchaire, le légat de Louis le Pieux, tint au roi Morman nous permettent de cerner quels motifs les Francs pouvaient alléguer vis-à-vis de leurs voisins pour exiger la soumission de ces dernier: l'excellence de leur roi fondait leurs prétentions. "Me tibi transmisit Hludowicus Caesar in orbe, /

[114] Ermold, *Poème* 4.2470-71, p. 188.
[115] Ermold, *Poème* 4.2514-19, p. 190.
[116] Voir P. Depreux, "La dévotion à saint Remi de Reims aux IXe et Xe siècles", *Cahiers de civilisation médiévale* 35 (1992), 111-29 (pp. 126-28).
[117] Ermold, *Poème* 4.1984-85, p. 150: "Qu'il ne croie pas – j'en atteste – que (je veuille) que ses royaumes me reviennent, mais qu'ainsi je sois en état de gagner (à la foi) une créature de Dieu".
[118] Ibid., 3.1322, p. 102.
[119] Ibid., 3.1298-99, p. 102.
[120] Ibid., 3.1572-77, p. 120.
[121] Ibid., 3.1255, p. 98: "par la foi, la paix fut élargie à tous les peuples".
[122] Ibid., 1.324-27, p. 30.

Gloria Francorum, christicolumque decus, / Pace fideque prior, nulli quoque Marte secundus, / Dogmate praecipuus et pietatis ope".[123]

L'oeuvre de la piété

L'expression *pietatis ops*, que nous avous déjà rencontrée plus haut,[124] est fort difficile à traduire. Ermold peut avoir voulu souligner à la fois le moyen de gouvernement qu'est l'exercice de la *pietas* et l'abondance de celle-ci. Le poète a eu recours à cette expression en une autre occasion, qui permet d'en cerner le sens: lors de l'entrevue de Reims, Louis le Pieux est censé avoir défini les devoirs du pape. Reprenant le fameux "pais mes brebis" de l'Evangile (Jean 21.15-18), Ermold ajoute qu'à l'instar de Pierre, le pape et l'empereur[125] doivent paître les brebis du Seigneur *cum pietatis ope*,[126] qu'E. Faral traduit par "avec amour". Or le poète explicite la portée de ce devoir. Louis est censé avoir continué son discours de la sorte: "Ergo, sacer, plebem nostri est curare subactam, / Nobis quam Dominus pascere constituit; / Tu sacer antestis; ego rex sum christicolarum: Servemus populum dogmate, lege, fide".[127] Paître les brebis du Seigneur *cum pietatis ope* signifie par conséquent veiller *dogmate, lege, fide* au salut et à l'unité du peuple qu'elles forment. Il s'agit donc de veiller à maintenir les liens "religieux" et "séculiers" qui les lient entre eux (le dogme et la loi) et à Dieu (la foi). Cela est possible "par le moyen de la piété": la

---

[123] Ibid., 3.1370-73, p. 106: "C'est Louis, César sur le monde, qui m'a envoyé à toi. Il est la gloire des Francs, l'honneur des chrétiens. Premier par la paix (qu'il étend) et par (sa) foi, aucunement le second par les armes, il prime par (son) orthodoxie et par le pouvoir de sa piété".

[124] Voir supra note 56.

[125] Ce texte est fondamental car il y appert que l'empereur avait un rôle pastoral, d'où les admonitions du roi aux évêques dont le plus célèbre exemple est l'*Admonitio generalis* de Charlemagne (789).

[126] Ermold, *Poème* 2.1027, p. 80.

[127] Ermold, *Poème* 2.1028-31, p. 80: "Donc, ô saint, il nous appartient de soigner la foule des sujets dont le Seigneur nous institua les pasteurs. Tu (es) le saint prélat, moi, je suis le roi des chrétiens: maintenons intact le peuple par la doctrine, par la loi, par la foi".

pietas apparaît donc bien comme ce mélange de respect et de souci de cohésion qui préside à la vie politique et sociale.

Louis et les Francs

A lire Ermold, on s'aperçoit que son témoignage concorde avec ce que l'on sait par ailleurs des desseins politiques de Louis le Pieux – c'est ce que j'espère avoir pour partie montré ici. Son règne s'inscrit dans le contexte d'une christianisation plus affirmée du concept de royauté, ayant pour conséquence un souci plus vif de respecter la justice, alors que la *patientia* et la *pietas* du roi sont exaltées;[128] c'est en prenant conseil que le roi juste gouverne désormais.[129] Or le prince du haut Moyen-Age qui s'efforça le plus de mettre cet idéal en pratique ne jouit pas du prestige que devrait lui valoir cette entreprise. Si l'on prend Charlemagne comme référence, force est de constater qu'aucun courtisan ne célébra avec le luxe de détails qui fait l'intérêt de l'*Elegiacum carmen* l'excellence de son gouvernement: faut-il y voir une injustice de la part des contemporains du père de Louis? Il se peut également qu'on puisse en tirer des conséquences plus crues sur la grandeur de Charles.[130]

Néanmoins, il convient de ne pas oublier que l'empereur – ou le roi – n'est pas seul: il guide un peuple dont il est solidaire. Ainsi, dans l'oeuvre d'Ermold le Noir, le rôle des Francs n'est aucunement passé sous silence: par exemple, lorsqu'il envoie Witchaire auprès du roi Morman, Louis recommande à son légat de conjurer le Breton de demander la paix aux Francs[131] – et non à l'empereur. La soumission à ce dernier lui vaudra de la part des Francs une paix

---

[128] Voir E. Ewig, "Zum christlichen Königsgedanken im Frühmittelalter", dans *Das Königtum*, pp. 7-73, rééd. dans *Spätantikes und fränkisches Gallien*, éd. H. Atsma, Beihefte der Francia 3 (Sigmaringen, 1976), 1:3-71 (pp. 13-39).

[129] Voir Hannig, *Consensus fidelium*, pp. 209-10.

[130] Il n'est pour autant pas nécessaire de chercher à y lire une trace de la "décomposition" dénoncée par F.-L. Ganshof dans son article sur "La fin du règne de Charlemagne: une décomposition", *Zeitschrift für schweizerische Geschichte* 28 (1948), 433-52.

[131] Ermold, *Poème* 3.1339, p. 104: "Francos pace rogando petat". ("Il faut qu'il demande la paix aux Francs": trad. Faral, p. 105).

perpétuelle[132] car c'est eux qu'il menace.[133] De même, en devenant le vassal de Louis le Pieux, Harold soumet ses territoires à la domination des "pieux" Francs: "Caesar at ipse manus manibus suscepit honestis; / Junguntur Francis Danica regna piis".[134] Il faut à ce propos souligner qu'Ermold utilise le verbe *jungere*, qui met en exergue l'idée d'union. Ermold se montre conséquent: un peu plus loin, le poète loue l'empereur de ce qu'il a réussi là où ses prédécesseurs, qui avaient recours aux armes, échouèrent.[135] Louis associe (*sociare*) des royaumes aux siens car le profit de cette action revient en théorie non à l'empereur, mais à Dieu.[136] Nous avons vu les Francs qualifiés de "pieux". Il sont également victorieux. Ce n'est pas en premier lieu en raison de leur bravoure, mais parce qu'ils son animés par la foi. Tel est ce qu'affirme Witchaire au roi Morman: "Gens est Francorum nulli virtute secunda, / Vincit amore Dei exsuperatque fide".[137] Ici intervient encore une union profonde entre le prince et son peuple, car c'est grâce à la vertu de l'empereur que la "pieuse *Francia*" est tant récompensée: "Francia plaude, decet; Hludowico fer, pia, grates, / Cujus virtute munera tanta capis".[138]

Il semblerait par conséquent que les Francs partagent la piété de leur chef, à la clémence de qui Ermold s'en remettait. Il composa son poème à une époque encore heureuse, que de graves querelles n'allaient pas tarder à troubler. Ermold était confiant parce que

---

[132] Ibid., 3.1382-87, pp. 106-08.

[133] Ibid., 3.1376-77, p. 106.

[134] Ibid., 4.2486-87, p. 188: "Et César lui-même reçut les mains (de Harold) en ses mains honnêtes; les royaumes danois sont liés aux pieux Francs".

[135] Ibid., 4.2516-19, p. 190.

[136] Ibid., 4.2514-15, p. 190: "Haec, Hludowice, Deo das tu quoque lucra potenti, / Et socias regnis inclita regna tuis". ("Voilà comment, Louis, tu assures des conquêtes à Dieu le tout-puissant et comment tu annexes des royaumes fameux": trad. Faral, p. 191).

[137] Ibid., 3.1406-07, p. 108: "La race des Francs n'est inférieure (à quiconque) en aucune de (ses) qualités, elle vainc en raison de (son) amour de Dieu et surpasse (les autres) par (sa) foi".

[138] Ibid., 4.2526-27, p. 192: "France, applaudis, (comme) il convient; pieuse, témoigne de la reconnaissance envers Louis, par la vertu de qui tu reçois tant de faveurs".

Louis recevait plus volontiers un *votum* que des *munera*;[139] autrement dit, il préférait aux présents une offrande engageant son sujet dans une démarche plus profonde et personnelle. A cet égard, les idéaux qui marquèrent le début du règne impérial de Louis le Pieux peuvent sembler n'avoir été qu'un leurre – pour tous les acteurs du drame.

---

[139] Ibid., 1.46-47, p. 6: "Sed me cunctantem refovet clementia regis, / Qui potius votum munera quam recipit". ("Mais, dans mon hésitation, je m'enhardis à considérer la clémence du roi, qui accueille les intentions plutôt que les présents": trad. Faral, p. 7).

Why Should Bishops be Involved in Marital Affairs?
Hincmar of Rheims on the Divorce of King Lothar II (855-869)

Karl Heidecker

On 25 January 860 Archbishop Hincmar of Rheims (845-882) received two important visitors: his colleague Hincmar of Laon, who happened to be his nephew, and Bishop Adventius of Metz (858-875). They had come to discuss a most delicate matter. Hincmar apparently did not respond very well, for he was feeling ill. We know that he was chronically troubled by gout and bowel problems.[1] A short note sent to Adventius the day after their meeting reveals that Hincmar did not feel entirely happy about his initial reaction. Obviously he was wary of any involvement in the explosive matter Adventius had brought to his attention: the marital troubles of King Lothar II (855-869), king of the northern part of the Middle Kingdom, later known after him as Lotharingia.

The marriage of King Lothar II and Queen Theutberga was falling apart, which created a big scandal. Even the women were chatting about it when they were weaving. There were awful rumours about Queen Theutberga. It was said that she had been polluted by

---

[1] J. Devisse, *Hincmar Archevêque de Reims (845-882)*, 3 vols (Geneva, 1976), 2:1104-05; H. Schrörs, *Hinkmar, Erzbischof von Reims. Sein Leben und seine Schriften* (Freiburg im Breisgau, 1884), pp. 470-71.

incestuous intercourse with her brother Hubert, which, to make matters worse, had been performed in a sodomitical fashion. Afterwards, people said, Theutberga attempted to conceal this shameful deed by an abortion. At least some of this had been revealed at a small meeting of four Lotharingian bishops and two abbots at Aachen on 9 January 860. It was made public to those present by Gunthar, Archbishop of Cologne, to whom Theutberga had confessed. In fact the rumours were not new; they had been going around for quite a while. Three years earlier, Theutberga had been accused of this in front of a court of noble laymen, but she had succeeded in purging herself through an ordeal by proxy. This time, however, she had confessed the awful things that had happened before the assembled bishops, abbots and laymen. The bishops and abbots thereupon had separated Lothar and Theutberga, and sent the latter off to a monastery to do penance. Subsequently, a second, bigger, meeting was called to deal with this thorny and complicated matter. Obviously a decision supported by the authority of more people was in order. For this reason bishops from several other Carolingian kingdoms were invited, including Hincmar of Rheims. The task of persuading Hincmar to participate in this enlarged synod fell to Adventius of Metz; this was the purpose of the visit mentioned above. Yet Hincmar did not attend this second synod, also held at Aachen (in mid-February 860), which confirmed the decisions of its predecessor. For a moment it looked as if Hincmar would stay out of the affair, but soon he would be taking centre stage.

King Lothar's divorce was an extremely complicated matter, which affected many different people for a variety of reasons.[2] It was of course a highly political affair, involving a king, Lothar, his kinsmen, i.e. the other kings and some nobles, a queen, Theutberga, her powerful kinsmen and allies. There was also another woman, Waldrada, a friend of Lothar's since his youth. Most likely Waldrada had already provided Lothar with offspring, and he was trying to

[2] For a detailed description of the marital affair of King Lothar II and of Hincmar's involvement in it, I refer to my thesis: "Kerk, huwelijk en politieke macht. De zaak Lotharius II (855-869)" ("Church, Marriage and Political Power. The Case of Lothar II (855-869)") (unpublished PhD thesis, University of Amsterdam, 1997).

make her his new queen. The actions of the participants in this affair were determined by diverse motives, such as ties of kinship, personal loyalty, friendship, fidelity to their lord, or simply the expectation of personal gain.

But here I want to focus on a special group of actors, who played an increasingly central role: the bishops. They were the ones to take the lead, pronouncing judgement on the marriage of a king. The case was all the more curious since there had been an earlier and unequivocal judgement; after due consultation with the bishops, Theutberga had been cleared by an ordeal conducted before a court of laymen. But now, three years later, an episcopal decision was revising this judgement. Where did these bishops derive the authority to have the final say in lay marital affairs? How did they dare to decide upon a king's marriage? Who was competent to judge in marital affairs, a clerical or lay court? Which laws were to be followed, secular ones or their canonical counterparts? These are the central questions I will now address.

I will concentrate on one bishop in particular: Hincmar of Rheims. One month after Adventius' visit he became irrevocably mixed up in the scandal surrounding Lothar, having received a request from some Lotharingian bishops and laymen who were apparently dissatisfied with the decisions reached at the Aachen synods. Towards the end of February 860 they sent Hincmar a list of questions. Was it true that Hincmar was in accord with the decisions of the earlier synods? Clearly, rumours kept spreading, which was as efficient a way as any to exert political influence. But most of the questions dealt with Lothar's divorce itself. How should his case be decided, and what should be the verdict? At this point, Hincmar could no longer stay aloof; as quickly as possible he replied with a lengthy treatise collecting whatever authoritative texts (the Bible, canon law collections, the Fathers, and also some secular laws) he could gather. This work is known as *De divortio Lotharii regis et Theutbergae reginae.*[3]

---

[3] I have used the edition of *De divortio* in the Monumenta Germaniae Historica by L. Böhringer. A substantial part of what I am saying is based on this excellent edition, which provides many new insights into Hincmar's method: Hinkmar von Reims, *De divortio Lotharii regis et Theutbergae reginae*,

So who was to decide in marital affairs? Hincmar approached this matter in two ways. First, he explained the relation between secular and ecclesiastical laws in marital cases, outlining the respective roles of secular and ecclesiastical judges. Secondly, he argued for the necessity of episcopal involvement by stressing the bishop's liturgical function.

At first sight it looks as if Hincmar deemed a lay court competent to judge in marital affairs. Laymen should pronounce judgement; if the accused was found guilty, the bishops should do no more than prescribe a fitting penance.[4] But this in fact is merely an idealised description. Of course, if everything functions smoothly, without conflict between lay and ecclesiastical courts, there is no problem whatsoever. But what if the secular court arrives at decisions displeasing to the bishop? Of course, Hincmar insists, secular law should be obeyed, but it must conform to Christianity.[5] This was not the case, for example, with secular law permitting a husband to kill a wife found guilty of adultery. A husband should not kill his wife, even when she is found guilty of adultery. There are laws taking precedence over secular legislation, namely divine and apostolic laws. By this expression Hincmar clearly refers to Christian rules as expressed in Scripture, the writings of the Fathers and conciliar decisions. Hincmar expresses his view entirely in legal terms. God is presented as the judge at the judgement of Doomsday. And Hincmar writes, "se in die iudicii nec Romanis nec Salicis nec Gundobadis, sed divinis et apostolicis legibus iudicandos".[6]

At the Day of Judgement the bishops are answerable to God for the souls of the members of the flocks committed to their care, meaning that they must judge the behaviour of the faithful and correct their sins. The bishops are judges of souls ("iudices animarum").[7] In

ed. L. Böhringer, MGH Concilia 4 supplementum 1 (Hanover, 1992); hereafter: *Div.*

[4] *Div.*, pp. 123-24, 139-42.

[5] *Div.*, pp. 137-38, 141, 145-46, 176.

[6] *Div.*, p. 145: "at the Day of Judgement, they will not be judged according to the laws of the Franks, Burgundians or Romans, but according to divine and apostolic laws".

[7] *Div.*, p. 171.

imposing penance after judging the sinners, they cleanse them of their sins.[8] By doing so, they determine the actions of the penitents, especially if the penance is public. They can suspend normal social life, notably where marital relations are concerned: penitents were to remain chaste for the duration of their penance.

Hincmar's second argument in defence of episcopal involvement in marital cases is the liturgical function of the priest. Marriage was instituted by God in Paradise through the benediction given to Adam and his wife. This benediction is continually reiterated by the vicars of Christ and successors of the apostles, the bishops. As the bishop has joined the couple in marriage by benediction, the marriage cannot be dissolved without episcopal consent.[9]

These general rules are applied to the case of Lothar. But the marriage of Lothar was not just any case. It involved a king, a person whose function made him a judge himself, someone with an authority deriving from God. It was a king's duty to correct the behaviour of his subjects, for whom he was answerable to God on Judgement day. A king's function strongly resembled that of a bishop. The anointing of kings was modelled on the episcopal ordination rite.[10] There were many opportunities for a clash of episcopal and royal competencies. Could a bishop indeed judge a king? And if so, for what reasons and how?

Despite these similarities, there were, however, differences between bishops and kings. Hincmar points them out emphatically, basing his argument on a clearly perceived hierarchy of responsibilities. The bishop's authority takes precedence, for his responsibility is greater: he is accountable for the souls of his flock, including the king's soul. Hincmar quotes well-known passages from Pope Gelasius' letter to the Emperor Anastasius, and from

---

[8] *Div.*, pp. 197-203, 250-51.

[9] *Div.*, pp. 136-40, 236.

[10] *Div.*, pp. 110, 188-89. Y. Congar, *L'ecclésiologie du haut moyen-age* (Paris, 1968), pp. 292-303; K. F. Morrison, *The Two Kingdoms. Ecclesiology in Carolingian Political Thought* (Princeton, 1964), pp. 26-34; J. Nelson, "Kingship, Law and Liturgy in the Thought of Hincmar of Rheims", *English Historical Review* 92 (1977), 241-79.

Ambrosius' letter to the Emperor Theodosius.[11] By virtue of his pastoral responsibility a bishop has the right to impose penance, even upon a king. Hincmar stresses this point repeatedly and quotes biblical examples for this, such as that of the prophets Samuel and Nathan and the kings Saul and David. Interestingly enough he also quotes the penance of Louis the Pious. It is a bishop's duty to judge and correct sins, even the sins of a king.[12] Or should we say, especially the sins of a king? Royal behaviour provides an example to the people; conversely, royal misbehaviour may lead others to misbehave as well. Moreover, if the king is contaminated by sin, this contamination will spread to his subjects. For this reason, Hincmar states, kings should correct themselves. A king who acts accordingly is a good king, standing above the law. However, if he fails to do so, he is subject to the law and must therefore be corrected to avoid further contamination of the realm.[13]

How should a king be judged? Hincmar had a strong preference for reserving important cases to general councils, which in his view carried the greatest authority. In his quotations he refers to them as the best sources of law. The biblical quotation referring to the apostles ("whenever two or three of you are together in my name I am amidst them": Matthew 18.20) is extended to general episcopal councils.[14] Hence Lothar's case should be judged by a general council, attended by bishops of all the Carolingian kingdoms. The matter involved the whole of the Frankish realm, still considered by Hincmar as a unity, "hoc autem regnum de multorum manibus in manu parentum nostrorum regum deo gratias fuerat adunatum".[15] This unity had never been destroyed by subsequent regnal partitions. There remained "unum regnum, una Christi columba, videlicet

---

[11] *Div.*, pp. 111, 247-50, 253-56, 259.

[12] *Div.*, pp. 201-03, 226, 247-49. See M. de Jong, "Power and Humility in Carolingian Society: the Public Penance of Louis the Pious", *Early Medieval Europe* 1 (1992), 29-52.

[13] *Div.*, pp. 246-61.

[14] *Div.*, pp. 239-40. For this line of reasoning, see Congar, *L'ecclésiologie*, pp. 133-35, 170-71.

[15] *Div.*, p. 187: "This kingdom had been united by God's will from the hands of many in the hand of the ancestors of our kings".

sancta ecclesia, unius Christianitatis lege, regni unius et unius ecclesie, quamquam per plures regni principes et ecclesiarum presules gubernacula moderentur".[16] Within this unity, at once Empire and Church, general episcopal councils were invested with supreme authority. Such a council should therefore judge Lothar's case, precisely because the marriage of a king and a queen was at stake: if this case were not resolved in the right way, the salvation of all the souls in the Holy Church would be at risk.[17] Hincmar's proposal that in Lothar's case the general council should consult the Bishop of Rome is based on the theological argument of Rome being the mother of all Churches.[18] But at this point he also raises a practical issue: while addressing the pope, his fellow bishops should avoid offending their king. Here Hincmar touches upon the heart of the matter: the thorny problem of competencies, responsibilities and power on a practical level. For it is one thing to claim politically far-reaching responsibility and competence for the bishops, but quite another to force them to neglect competing loyalties, which must have been equally important. Bishops were required to be loyal to their lord, their "senior", their king, by whom they had been appointed, and whose kingdom they should protect.[19] Hincmar's initial refusal to be drawn into the case is exemplary of a more general episcopal reluctance to act as judges of their lord, the king. For this reason Hincmar tried to avoid open hostility towards Lothar. But once involved, he left no doubt as to who has the highest authority. It belonged to the bishops, provided they were assembled in a general council.

Let me try to put the matter in a wider perspective. In the Carolingian period reformers, mainly clerics, but some laymen as

---

[16] *Div.*, p. 236: "one Empire and one Church, one dove of Christ, i.e. the Holy Church, under the law of one Christianity, of one realm and one Church, even if several princes of the realm and leaders of the Churches direct the government". Also *Div.*, p. 187.

[17] *Div.*, pp. 107-08, 124, 130, 236-42. Hincmar does not use the word "imperium" but "regnum", but he clearly refers to the Carolingian empire as a whole.

[18] *Div.*, pp. 107, 132.

[19] *Div.*, p. 132.

well, made a concerted effort to organise society along Christian lines. I am tempted to view Hincmar as the final representative of this reform movement; he harvested the crop of more than a century of Carolingian reform. But in the last years of his life, Hincmar's world, governed by the ideal of an organised Christian society, collapsed before his eyes into the chaos and destruction of the Viking attacks. His frustration becomes evident from his eye-witness account in the *Annals of Saint-Bertin*.[20]

One of the objectives of the Carolingian reform had been the creation of a corpus of authoritative texts, uniform and practical in their use and easy to reproduce.[21] Hence a standard liturgy was developed, on the basis of a Roman text, the late eighth-century *Sacramentarium Gregorio-Hadrianum*, which contains a marital benediction. Then there was a collection of canon law, the *Collectio Dionysio-Hadriana*, also received from Rome in the same period. Both texts were often copied and widely disseminated. Furthermore, reform-minded bishops tried to create an authoritative penitential.[22] Around 820 the aforementioned canon law collection, chrono-logically and geographically organised, was used to create a thematic collection of canon law: the *Collectio Dacheriana*, a text which also drew upon another collection, the *Collectio Hispana*. This eminently practical collection was organised according to subject-matter, making life easy for those wishing to look up all the relevant canons on a certain subject – marriage, for example. Hincmar made intensive use of the *Collectio Dacheriana*. None of these collections of canon law prescribes an obligatory marital benediction, however, and the same holds true for the Frankish royal capitularies and the councils up to the mid-ninth century. What we do find there is legislation

[20] *Annales Bertiniani*, a° 881-882, ed. F. Grat, J. Vieillard and S. Clémencet, with introduction and notes by L. Levillain, Ouvrages publiés par la Société de l'Histoire de France (Paris, 1964), pp. 243-51. *The Annals of St.-Bertin*, trans. J. Nelson (Manchester, 1991), pp. 222-26.

[21] For a description and analysis of the following, see Heidecker, "Kerk, huwelijk en politieke macht", pp. 16-40.

[22] C. Vogel, *Le pécheur et la pénitence au moyen âge* (Paris, 1969), pp. 15-27, 39-47. R. Kottje, "Einheit und Vielfalt des kirchlichen Lebens in der Karolingerzeit", *Zeitschrift für Kirchengeschichte* 76 (1965), 323-42.

about forbidden relationships: marriages between relatives, with the wives or fiancées of others, with religious women, abducted women, divorced women or with unfree partners.[23] In all but one of these cases marriages are defined by contrasting them with a negative. No constituting element is named, in the sense of an action without which a marriage would not be legal. We might say that, according to these explicit rules, a legal marriage is a marriage which is not illegal. That which is not sinful and forbidden is allowed. Something, however, changes in the middle of the ninth century. There was clearly a tendency to turn the priestly benediction of marriages into an obligation, notably in the Pseudo-Isidorian collections.[24] These added an obligatory priestly benediction to a whole series of equally binding secular customs; together, these comprised a legal marriage. The finest example is the decretal ascribed to the first-century pope Evarist, allegedly the first to make the benediction obligatory.[25] As far as we know, Hincmar was the first to use this decretal of Pseudo-Evarist, thus according a key-function to the priest in marital affairs. Conversely, there would be no divorce without priestly consent and Hincmar here equals priestly and episcopal consent.[26]

This far-reaching claim for episcopal judgement of important cases is consistent with other developments in this period. In a series of councils convened in 858-60 and dominated by Hincmar, the idea of the unity of the whole Carolingian Empire and Church was clearly expressed; it was a unity for which the bishops gathered in a general council should assume supreme responsibility.[27]

[23] The last prohibition, marriage with an unfree partner, is rather different from the others and I will not discuss it here.

[24] K. Ritzer, *Formen, Riten und religiöses Brauchtum der Eheschliessung in den Christlichen Kirchen des Ersten Jahrtausends*, 2nd ed., rev. (Münster, 1981), pp. 268-81.

[25] Pseudo-Evarist is contradicting himself, however. For discussion of this, see Heidecker, "Kerk, huwelijk en politieke macht", pp. 36-39.

[26] *Div.*, pp. 136-40, 229-30, 236.

[27] Quierzy (858) in *Die Konzilien der karolingischen Teilreiche (843-859)*, ed. W. Hartmann, MGH Concilia 3 (Hanover, 1984), pp. 408-27, especially pp. 424-27; Metz (859) aimed at judging King Louis the German for his sins, *Die Konzilien*, ed. Hartmann, pp. 438-44, especially pp. 438, 442, chap. 9, and p. 444, the answer of Louis the German to the legates of this council;

What did others have to say about this issue? This much is clear: Hincmar's *De divortio* was a controversial text, which provoked much discussion. Some of Lothar's supporters countered that meddling in the king's marital affairs was none of Hincmar's business, for "iste princeps rex est et nullorum legibus vel iudiciis subiacet nisi solius dei, qui eum in regno, quod suus pater illi dimisit, regem constituit. [...] Et quod facit et qualis est in regimine, divino fit nutu".[28] Hincmar angrily refuted this opinion in a supplement to *De divortio* written in the autumn of 860: "Haec vox non est catholici christiani, sed nimium blasphemi et spiritu diabolico pleni".[29]

As for appropriate and legal marriage rites, Adventius of Metz found himself in disagreement with Hincmar. A few years later, in 863, Adventius contended that Lothar had been joined legally, "in fide Dei", with Waldrada, the companion of his youth, long before he married Theutberga. In other words, Waldrada was to be considered his lawful wife. Their betrothal had been legally binding, for they had been joined together publicly, in front of witnesses, bishops and great noblemen, with the bridal gift (*dos*) having been stipulated. At the time, they merely had been too young actually to fulfil their marital obligations. The person joining them together had been young Lothar's father, the emperor Lothar I, "the most Christian emperor", which in itself guaranteed a valid marriage.[30] In Adventius' view, the

Savonnières (859) in *Die Konzilien*, ed. Hartmann, pp. 458-88, especially pp. 458-59, chap. 2 and the *libellus proclamationis* of Charles the Bald, p. 464, chap. 3; Tusey (860), in *Sacrorum conciliorum nova et amplissima collectio*, ed. J. D. Mansi, vol. 15 (Venice, 1770), cols 558-71.

[28] *Div.*, p. 246: "this prince is a king and not subject to any law or judgement except to God, who has appointed him king in the kingdom left to him by his father ... And whatever the king does, and however his rule, it is according to divine will".

[29] *Div.*, p. 247: "This is not the voice of a true Christian believer, but rather of a blasphemer, full of the devil's spirit".

[30] Adventius' description is preserved as a fragment of a text edited in *Epistolae ad divortium Lotharii II. regis pertinentes*, ed. E. Dümmler, MGH Epistolae 6, Epp. Kar. Aev. 4 (Berlin, 1925), pp. 215-17. This fragment is only known to us in a copy of the end of the sixteenth century. The scribe begins this text with the words: "I have left out the much too lengthy introduction about the

bishops' role in marriage proceedings was reduced to that of mere witnesses. The pivotal person had been Lothar I, as father and as emperor. This amounts to an almost entirely secular ritual, a betrothal (*desponsatio*) conceived of as the most important moment cementing the alliance. The truly Christian element in the conclusion of the marital union is the "most Christian emperor", who joins the two youngsters "in fide Dei".

Hincmar had a clear conception of the competence of a bishop to judge in marital cases, even if a king was involved. His point of departure was hierarchical responsibility: episcopal authority prevails, for bishops are answerable to God for the souls of their flocks – the king's soul not excluded. Whenever sins are committed, they can and must intervene. By imposing a fitting penance a bishop should correct the behaviour of his sinners. If the latter refuse to obey, the bishop can use his power of excommunication. Secondly, the priest has a liturgical monopoly. Given the fact that God instituted marriage, a priestly benediction is indispensable; and since no layman can undo a priestly benediction, no marriage is to be dissolved without priestly consent. To argue his case, Hincmar made maximum use of the intellectual and practical arsenal of texts systematised in the course of the Carolingian reform. His thoughts should not, however, be taken as representative of all clerical thought. There were others who did not accept Hincmar's view that priests held the keys to a legal and valid marriage.

kings' and the priests' authority". This leaves one wondering what Adventius wrote on that subject.

Ut in omnibus honorificetur Deus:
The *Corsnæd* Ordeal in
Anglo-Saxon England

Sarah Larratt Keefer

Until the Fourth Lateran Council of 1215 forbade participation of the clergy in the judicial ordeal process, guilt or innocence was determined by oath-taking or by the proof-testing of one of a number of ordeals, and the trials were presided over by the Church. The legal and liturgical documents of Anglo-Saxon England record four types:[1] *wætre* or *aqua fervens* (boiling water); *hatan isene* or

I am greatly indebted to two scholars for their encouragement and assistance: T. C. Graham, of the Parker Library, Corpus Christi College, Cambridge, and The Medieval Institute, Western Michigan University, for his generosity in providing me with xeroxes of the *corsnæd* ordeal contained in Corpus books, and for making me a transcription of John Joscelyn's copy of the *corsnæd* prayers, and D. R. Howlett of the Medieval Latin Dictionary, Oxford, for his advice and guidance in the translation of the *corsnæd* liturgy from Cambridge, Corpus Christi College, MS 391. My thanks are also due to the many members of ANSAXNET who shared their expertise and ideas with me for this project.

[1] W. Stubbs states: "neither trial by combat nor ordeal by the *corsnæd*, hot water, hot iron, or otherwise, was in common use except in cases where the accused had forfeited his credit by some previous crime, or was unable to produce compurgators": "The Anglo-Saxon Constitution", in *Lectures on Early English History*, ed. A. Hassall (London, 1906), pp. 1-17 (p. 15). This is misleading on two counts: because of the clear indication of the crimes for

iudicium ad ferrum ferventum (hot iron); *aqua gelida* (cold water); and *corsnæd*. This latter has been associated with *exorcismus panis hordeacei et casei ad probationem veri*, ordeal by barley bread and cheese, and is the most commonly found of the pre-Conquest ordeals, apparently reserved for the clergy. But, far from being an example of church privilege, this ordeal seems to have had within itself the possibility of proving at times extremely unpleasant: a close examination of its liturgy shows that the manifestations of guilt, as set out in the prayers themselves, could result from the ingestion of bread or cheese made from unpasteurised milk or poorly-dried barley, coupled with psychological suggestion at work on a susceptible imagination.

Our understanding of ordeals used in Anglo-Saxon England comes from two quite unrelated sources, the laws and the liturgy. The laws of the period show us when – and, to a lesser degree, how – ordeals were to be undertaken. They were a necessary next stage, not of "trial" but of "proof", after the preliminary test of oath-taking: if accused of criminal activity, a respectable individual could take an oath, providing at the same time three witnesses to support him by strengthening his oath-taking with theirs,[2] not unlike the character witness of today, in order to assert his innocence. The statute known as Wihtred 22 from the ninth century states "ðissa ealra aþ sie unlegnæ", "the oath of all these shall be incontrovertible".[3] If a man could provide no oath-takers, or were of disreputable character, or were accused of a more serious offence,

which each ordeal was prescribed, see note 10, below, and because no ready evidence exists to indicate that trial by combat was ever used in England before the Norman Conquest. See R. C. Van Caenegem, *The Birth of the English Common Law* (Cambridge, 1973), pp. 64-66; and Sir F. Pollock and F. W. Maitland, *The History of English Law Before the Time of Edward I*, 2 vols (Cambridge, 1968), 1:50-51; but also see T. Plucknett, *A Concise History of the Common Law*, 5th ed. (London, 1956), p. 116.

[2] See Pollock and Maitland, *History of English Law*, 1:39.

[3] Wihtred 19-22, and especially 21, in F. L. Attenborough, *The Laws of the Earliest English Kings* (Cambridge, 1922; repr. London, 1968), pp. 28-29.

he would proceed to proof of innocence or guilt by ordeal,[4] and provision for this procedure is set out in the Canons of Edgar[5] and in the Laws of Æthelred and Canute.[6]

Proof by simple, or at times the so-called "triple" ordeal[7] was also required when the case stood between English and Welsh disputants[8] and, later, between English and French.[9] It was the immediate sentence for treason, witchcraft, coining, arson, rape, murder or breaking into a church.[10] But while this may resemble secular judicial process, it is important to be aware that ecclesiastical authority was at all times present, determining where and when an ordeal might be held. No ordeal was permitted on church festivals, Sundays, during fasts or the two major penitential and subsequent festal periods of the year, namely Advent Sunday through Advent and Christmas to the Octave of the Circumcision (Jan. 8), and Septuagesima Sunday through Lent and Easter to a fortnight after Easter Sunday.[11] Ordeals could only be held in a royal borough, in the bishop's see or at his palace,[12] and the statute 2 Æthelred 23 states that all accused persons about to undergo

---

[4] See A. J. Robertson, *The Laws of the Kings of England from Edmund to Henry the First* (Cambridge, 1925) for 1 Æthelred 1.1, which was later confirmed in Wm 1 14.2, pp. 52-53 and 260-61.

[5] See Robertson, *Laws*, for Edgar 9, pp. 18-19.

[6] 1 Æthelred 1.4, and 2 Canute 30.1-3, in Robertson, *Laws*, pp. 52-53 and 188-91.

[7] See Pollock and Maitland, *History of English Law*, 1:39 and 52. See also 1 Edgar 9 and 2 Canute 30.3a, in Robertson, *Laws*, pp. 18-19 and 188-89.

[8] See Sir W. Holdsworth, *A History of English Law* (London, 1909; repr. 1966), 2:109.

[9] Pollock and Maitland, *History of English Law*, 1:39, and confirmed in Wm 1 2.1-3, in Robertson, *Laws*, pp. 232-33.

[10] 2 Æthelred 4-6.1 and 6.2 and 14.1, in Attenborough, *Earliest English Kings*, pp. 130-35; see also pp. 171 and 188-89.

[11] 5 Æthelred 18, 6 Æthelred 25 and 1 Canute 17, in Robertson, *Laws*, pp. 84-85, 98-99 and 166-67; also Edward and Guthrum 9, in Attenborough, *Earliest English Kings*, pp. 106-07.

[12] 3 Æthelred 6.1, in Robertson, *Laws*, pp 66-67; see also p. 320.

ordeal had to fast and attend mass for three days beforehand to prepare themselves as best they could.[13]

How were Anglo-Saxon ordeals conducted? As we have seen, they are described in the laws as consisting primarily of four kinds: boiling water, hot iron, cold water and *corsnæd*. At each of these tests, an *exorcista*, who was an ordained member of the clergy, would be called upon to purify and consecrate the necessary elements, and the bishop would then preside over the test itself. For the ordeal called *wætre* or *aqua fervens*, a stone was suspended in a vessel of boiling water, wrist-deep for a simple ordeal, elbow-deep for a triple ordeal, and the accused had to lift it out with one hand.[14] For the ordeal called *hatan isene*, or *iudicium ad ferrum ferventum*, an iron ball was heated in front of witnesses, and then had to be carried by the accused a pre-measured distance: for a simple ordeal, a one-pound ball was carried three feet; for a triple ordeal, a three-pound ball was carried nine feet. In each case, the hand of the accused would be bound up for three days, and then unwrapped. If it had become infected, this was proof of his guilt.[15] Cold water is not referred to as frequently as the boiling water or iron in the laws but it seems clearly enough described in 2 Æthelstan 23.1 to indicate its use in at least the early tenth century.[16] In addition to this, the rubrics "aqua tum gelida tum fervens" in the *Samson Pontifical*,[17] "Exorcismus aquae ad iudicium Dei demonstrandum" standing apart from the item "Adjuratio ferri uel aquae feruentis ad iudicium" in

---

[13] 2 Æthelstan 23.2, in Attenborough, *Earliest English Kings*, pp. 138-39; see also p. 188.

[14] See Ine 37, in Attenborough, *Earliest English Kings*, pp. 170-71. See also K. Thomas, *Religion and the Decline of Magic* (New York, 1971), p. 218; and Plucknett, *Common Law*, p. 114.

[15] See H. Goitein, *Primitive Ordeal and Modern Law* (London, 1923; repr. 1980), p. 60; see also Attenborough, *Earliest English Kings*, p. 15; and Plucknett, *Common Law*, p. 114.

[16] 2 Æthelstan 23.1, in Attenborough, *Earliest English Kings*, pp. 138-39.

[17] Cambridge, Corpus Christi College, MS 146, page 301. Described in M. R. James, *A Descriptive Catalogue of Manuscripts in the Library of Corpus Christi College, Cambridge*, 2 vols (Cambridge, 1902-12), 2:334, item 20.

the *Corpus-Canterbury Pontifical*,[18] and "Exorcismus aquae ad iudicium dei demonstrandum", clearly distinct from the hot iron and hot water ordeals in *The Red Book of Darley*,[19] all suggest the use of cold water through the early eleventh century and until at least 1061. The accused had his hands tied below his knees and was lowered into a pit of water which had previously been exorcised and consecrated.[20] If he sank to a prescribed depth of one and a half ells, or between twenty-seven and thirty-six inches,[21] he was innocent: the purified water had "received" him. If he failed to sink, the water had "rejected" his sin and he was deemed guilty.

Historians who study the Anglo-Saxon law-codes generally do not entirely agree with one another on their understanding of the ordeal process and the accused persons for whom each ordeal was intended. However, over the last and most interesting ordeal, the legal historians not only disagree but indeed at times seem to guess wildly as to what in fact it consisted of. This is the ordeal known as *corsnæd*, etymologically interpretable as "chosen morsel" or perhaps, more accurately "morsel FOR choice", suggesting that the effect of the morsel itself chooses innocence or guilt in the

[18] Cambridge, Corpus Christi College, MS 44, pages 365-66 and 369-79. Described in James, *Descriptive Catalogue*, 1:90, and M. O. Budny, *Insular, Anglo-Saxon and Early Anglo-Norman Manuscript Art at Corpus Christi College, Cambridge: An Illustrated Catalogue* (forthcoming from Medieval Institute Publications, Kalamazoo).

[19] Cambridge, Corpus Christi College, MS 422, page 319. I am grateful to T. C. Graham for permission to use his detailed description of this book, ultimately intended for volume 2 of *Anglo-Saxon Manuscripts in Microfiche Facsimile*, "Corpus MSS I" (forthcoming in Medieval and Renaissance Texts and Studies, Binghamton).

[20] See Goitein, *Primitive Ordeal*, pp. 55-57; Attenborough, *Earliest English Kings*, p. 209; and Plucknett, *Common Law*, p. 114.

[21] *An Anglo-Saxon Dictionary*, ed. J. Bosworth (London, 1898), *Supplement*, ed. T. Northcote Toller (London, 1921), repr. with revised and enlarged *Addenda*, ed. A. Campbell (London, 1973), pp. 247-48: "Eln: an ELL ... eighteen inches ... the ell in A. Sax. was sometimes about 24 inches, or 2 feet".

accused.[22] The term *corsnæd* occurs only six times in the Old
English lexicon, and in each case it is a legal term. Two of the laws
are from the Canons of Edgar,[23] two are from 8 Æthelred 22 and 24
in the late tenth century,[24] and two are from the early eleventh
century, 1 Canute 5.2a and 1 Canute 5.2c.[25] These six laws create
two sets of almost identical triads. Thus, 8 Æthelred 22, the first of
the Canons of Edgar statutes, and 1 Canute 5.2a: "Gif man
freondleas weofodþen mid tihtlan belecge, þe aðfultum næbbe, ga to
corsnæde 7 þar þonne æt gefare þæt þæt God wille, buton he on
husle ladian mode"; "If an accusation is brought against a minister
of the altar who has no friends and no one to support his oath, he
shall go to the ordeal of *corsnæd* and shall experience there what is
the will of God, unless he is allowed to clear himself by Holy
Communion".[26] And thus the second of Edgar's Canon statutes, 8
Æthelred 24 and 1 Canute 5.2c, with "And gif he sy mægleas, ladige
mid geferan oððe fæste to corsnæde 7 þaræt gefare þæt þæt God
ræde"; "and if he have no kin, he shall clear himself with the help of
his fellow-ecclesiastics, or fast in preparation for *corsnæd*, and
experience there what God shall decree".[27]

 Legal historians have tried to understand what *corsnæd* was
referring to. Plucknett's classical study of legal history tells us "still
another variety of ordeal was that of the cursed morsel which was
used only for the trial of clergy. This consisted of making the
accused swallow a piece of food in which was concealed a feather
or such like; if he was successful, he was innocent but if he choked,
he was guilty".[28] Careful consideration of all the evidence shows
this to be wide of the mark on several counts, as we shall see.
Robertson is closer: her translation of the law, omitted above,

[22] "Legal; trial morsel; piece of bread and cheese to be swallowed in trial
by ordeal; cf. OFris *korbita*", in *Dictionary of Old English: C*, ed. A. Amos, A.
di Paolo Healey et al. (Toronto, 1988), p. 788.
 [23] R. Fowler, ed., *Wulfstan's Canons of Edgar*, Early English Text
Society os 266 (London, 1972), sections 68h and 68i, p. 19.
 [24] 8 Æthelred 22 and 24, in Robertson, *Laws*, pp. 124-25.
 [25] 1 Canute 5.2a and 5.2c, in Robertson, *Laws*, pp. 160-61.
 [26] Robertson, *Laws*, p. 124.
 [27] Robertson, *Laws*, p. 124.
 [28] Plucknett, *Common Law*, p. 114.

renders *corsnæd* as "consecrated bread", although in her notes she expands the ordeal elements such that the accused must "clear himself by eating without apparent difficulty a certain quantity (generally one ounce) of bread or cheese".[29] Robertson suggests that the bread or cheese was later replaced by the sacrament, and that this ordeal, though she does not say in which form, was used by the Frisians and Franks.[30] Certainly the two triads of statutes, above, draw a distinction between *corsnæd* and the Holy Sacrament, such that the accused go to *corsnæd* "buton he on husle ladian mode", "unless he is allowed to clear himself with Holy Communion", so it seems practical to rule the term *corsnæd* as referring to the consecrated Host, out of our equations. A. K. R. Kiralfy says "the priest adjured the morsel of bread (*corsnæd*) to choke the swearer of a false oath".[31] Alan Harding reaffirms its restriction to the clergy and echoes Kiralfy and Plucknett by suggesting that it is choking on the morsel that indicates guilt.[32] And F. L. Attenborough has this to say: "trial by *corsnæd* in which the accused had to swallow a morsel of barley bread or cheese (sometimes but not always consecrated) is most frequently mentioned in the laws in connection with ecclesiastics, though it was not confined to them".[33] Even Fowler is inaccurate: "a method of ordeal sometimes administered when the accused was an ecclesiastic: a morsel of consecrated bread or cheese was given to the accused when he swore his innocence; if it stuck in his throat he was deemed guilty".[34]

The laws in which the term *corsnæd* is used uniformly refer to the accused for whom it is intended as *weofodþen*, an "altar-servant", loosely, a priest. Unlike the more widely-used *mæssepreost*, this again is a term that, like *corsnæd*, appears almost entirely within a legal context. It is found in the two sets of laws we

---

[29] Robertson, *Laws*, p. 340.

[30] Robertson, *Laws*, pp. 340-41.

[31] A. K. R. Kiralfy, *Potter's Historical Introduction to English Law and its Institutions*, 4th ed. (London, 1958), p. 353.

[32] A. Harding, *A Social History of English Law* (Gloucester, Mass., 1973), p. 24.

[33] Attenborough, *Earliest English Kings*, p. 187.

[34] Fowler, *Canons of Edgar*, p. 42.

have seen, in the Institutes of Polity,[35] in 8 Æthelred 18, 22 and 28 where it refers to "priesthood",[36] and in 2 Canute 39 where it stands in contrast with the term *preost* and thus must indicate a specificity of pastoral office,[37] and, perversely, it appears in 2 Canute 41, a law which is almost identical to an earlier law of Æthelred, except that where the Canute statute reads *weofodþen*, Æthelred reads *mæssepreost*.[38] It is also to be found in the legal canon called *Norðhumbra preosta lagum*[39] and in the homily *Larspel*.[40] It would therefore seem to be a variation on *mæssepreost* with perhaps a more particular, legalistic semantic register. And thus *corsnæd*, as set out in the laws of Edgar, Æthelred and Canute, is for *weofodþegnas* only: there seem to be no exceptions to that rule. This rigorous linkage of *corsnæd* with *weofodþen* apparently rejects Attenborough's insistence that the ordeal "was not confined to ecclesiastics".[41] Such an idea may have been influenced by the view that it was an impromptu trial by *corsnæd*, concerning responsibility for the death of Edward the Confessor's brother Alfred, which brought about Earl Godwin's sudden demise: the nineteenth-century legal ordeal expert Henry Lea is, however, a voice of doubt: "No great effort of scepticism is requisite to suggest that Edward ... may have made away with Godwin by poison, and then circulated the

---

[35] K. Jost, ed., *Die "Institutes of Polity, Civil and Ecclesiastical". Ein Werk Erzbischof Wulfstans von York*, Schweizer anglistische Arbeiten 47 (Bern, 1959), section 2.1.1: 148, 157, 161, 164, 209; and section 2.1.2: 42 and 104.

[36] 8 Æthelred 18, 22 and 28, in Robertson, *Laws*, pp. 122-25.

[37] 1 Canute 5.2a and 2 Canute 39, in Robertson, *Laws*, pp. 160-61 and 196-97.

[38] 2 Canute 41, in Robertson, *Laws*, pp. 196-97.

[39] "Norðhumbra preosta lagum", in *Die Gesetze der Angelsachsen*, ed. F. Liebermann (Halle, 1903; repr. Aalen, 1960), pp. 380-85.

[40] A. S. Napier, ed., *Wulfstan. Sammlung der ihm zugeschriebenen Homilien nebst Untersuchungen über Ihre Echtheit*, Sammlung englischer Denkmäler 4 (Berlin, 1883; repr. with bibliographical supplement by K. Ostheeren, Dublin and Zurich, 1967): Hom. 50 *Larspel*, pp. 246-50, line 142. This homily is not specified for a particular feast in either the Temporale or Sanctorale.

[41] Attenborough, *Earliest English Kings*, p. 187.

story related by the annalist to a credulous generation".[42] So, if the legal documents of the period indicate this ordeal called *corsnæd* is linked only to the priesthood, are we seeing here an example of church privilege? Boiling water or hot iron for the laity, but something considerably less onerous for the clergy?

How may we define the legal term *corsnæd*? As a piece of food with a feather in it? While *cor* clearly refers to choice, *snæd* is a morsel, piece, slice but not clearly confined to food. There is no contextual restriction within the laws to indicate that *corsnæd* must refer to something edible, but the laws themselves have little to say about the exact nature of this ordeal itself. However, when we turn back from law to liturgy, we find the missing pieces of the puzzle.

Ordeal liturgies, made up of prayers of purification together with the adjurations levelled at the accused in the various *ordines iudicii dei* are to be found in eight liturgical books that come from pre-Conquest England. They appear in six pontificals: the late-tenth /early-eleventh-century *Anderson Pontifical* (London, British Library, MS Additional 57337) and its closely-related contemporary, the *Sherborne Pontifical* (Paris, Bibliothèque nationale, MS 943); the early-eleventh-century *Lanalet Pontifical*[43] (Rouen, Bibliothèque municipale, MS 368) which resembles both *Anderson* and *Sherborne* as well, and the *Samson Pontifical* (Cambridge, Corpus Christi College, MS 146); the mid-eleventh-century sections of the fragmentary pontifical in London, British Library, MS Cotton Vitellius A.vii, and its contemporary, the *Corpus-Canterbury Pontifical* (Cambridge, Corpus Christi College, MS 44). Ordeal liturgies are also preserved in the *Red Book of Darley* (Cambridge, Corpus Christi College, MS 422 II) which contains a problematic mid-eleventh-century sacramentary with additional material, and also in a book that can only be correctly described as a compendium or "commonplace book". This is the

---

[42] H. C. Lea, *Superstition and Force: Essays on the Wager of Law, the Wager of Battle, the Ordeal, Torture* (Philadelphia, 1892), p. 265, note 2.

[43] G. H. Doble, ed., *Pontificale Lanaletense*, Henry Bradshaw Society 74 (London, 1937).

Portiforium of St Wulfstan[44] (Cambridge, Corpus Christi College, MS 391), from the later part of the eleventh century, and the most important of the English liturgical witnesses for this study.

No ordeal called by the vernacular legal term *corsnæd* is found in the liturgical books, but we do find the rubric "Incipit exorcismus panis hordeaceii et casei ad probationem veri", barley bread and cheese, used for discerning the truth, and generally to be found after the boiling water or iron exorcisms. This ordeal, modified in only one instance to use barley bread and salt (the Vitellius A.vii fragment), appears in various forms in all eight of the English manuscripts that contain ordeal exorcisms, and also in the eleventh-century Roman-German-type *Cracow Pontifical*[45] (Cracow, Jagellionian Library, MS 2057), suggesting a widespread use throughout early medieval Europe. This latter contains prayers that differ from the most complete liturgy, found in Corpus 391: while we cannot assume that these were used in England, we should nevertheless consider all the evidence associated with the ordeal by bread and cheese, to best understand the way in which it actually operated.

In some manuscripts the rubric reads "panis vel caseus", in others "panis et caseus". In the case of this ordeal, the opinion of Anglo-Saxon liturgical experts[46] is that *vel*, when used liturgically, resembles the modern and/or, but strongly suggests that both elements were consecrated. Indeed, in all cases, both the bread and the cheese are included in the prayers of exorcism and adjuration, and the preparatory rubric from Corpus 391, below, indicates the administration of the elements together. It is therefore probably incorrect to assume "a certain quantity of bread or cheese" or to generalise it to "a morsel of bread" alone.

---

[44] A. Hughes, ed., *The Portiforium of St Wulfstan*, 2 vols, Henry Bradshaw Society 89-90 (London, 1958-60).

[45] Z. Obertynski, ed., *The Cracow Pontifical*, Henry Bradshaw Society 100 (Manchester, 1967-71).

[46] I am grateful to R. W. Pfaff for his advice in this matter. In the Cracow Pontifical we find a rubric indicating division and distribution of both elements, see Obertynski, ed., *Cracow Pontifical*, p. 91.

Thus we have an equation to be made between the legal ordeal term *corsnæd* and the liturgical material dealing with the exorcism and adjurations of barley bread and cheese. Plucknett's fanciful "piece of food in which was concealed a feather" finds no place in this equation, nor does his description of it as "the cursed morsel": given the role of the *exorcista* in purifying and consecrating the elements for the ordeal in every instance, we can reject both the notion of "cursed" here, and at the same time Attenborough's attestations that the morsel is sometimes but not always consecrated.

Ordeal by iron, or water, hot or cold, seems physiologically-based, while at first glance the efficacy of the *corsnæd* ordeal appears rooted in the psychology of the guilty conscience.[47] Although we have no historical account of the performance of such a service, ordeal by bread and cheese was evidently a very successful process, as witnessed by its prevalence within liturgical books, and the scribal corrections from singular to plural forms within many of the manuscripts[48] suggest multiple ordeals held at the same time. It is certainly true that the psychological manipulation of the language of the ordeal liturgy would have had its greatest impact on a mind conditioned by training in the scriptural, liturgical and theological resonances that are present in the prayers of the *corsnæd* service.[49] But it is not so likely that this

---

[47] See Plucknett, *Common Law*, p. 114; Lea, *Superstition and Force*, p. 264; Thomas, *Religion and the Decline of Magic*, p. 219; and R. V. Colman, "Reason and Unreason in Early Medieval Law", *The Journal of Interdisciplinary Law* 4.1 (1973), 571-91, (p. 588); but see also R. Bartlett, *Trial by Fire and Water: The Medieval Judicial Ordeal* (Oxford, 1986), pp. 160-61 who rejects ordeal by *corsnæd* as a test with any psychological significance.

[48] These are evident in the text of the liturgy from Cambridge, Corpus Christi College, MS 391, pp. 571-76. and used here in the Appendix, although it should be noted that the changes are inconsistent at best. While it is not an insular witness, the Cracow Pontifical preserves a rubric and prayer (Obertynski, ed., *Cracow Pontifical*, pp. 91-92) for a multiple administration of *corsnæd*.

[49] As I have noted elsewhere ("Did God Speak Old English?: the Enigma of the Vernacular in Certain Synactic Texts", paper read at 31st International Congress on Medieval Studies at Kalamazoo, Western Michigan University, 1996, and in "The Use of the Vernacular in the Anglo-Saxon Synactic Canon" [working title], article in progress), the fact that the *corsnæd* adjuration, which is

is an indicator of clergy privilege: the physiological effect of this ordeal would have been unpleasant at the least, as we shall see, and the psychological influence of the adjuration would only have intensified that unpleasantness.

How did trial by *corsnæd* actually work? Lea calls it an ordeal that "addressed itself powerfully to the conscience and the imagination of the accused, whose callous fortitude no doubt often gave way under the trial".[50] There is, however, another side to this ordeal that has not been explored hitherto. Food safety and food preparation are considerations that modern scholars take for granted, and they rarely appear as a factor in historical study. It is significant that in every single case of the *corsnæd* ordeal, the bread is specified as *panis hordeacei*, barley bread, most probably because of the barley loaves used in the Feeding of the Five Thousand (John 6.9-13). However there would be a very great difference between barley that was dried and prepared in the hot Mediterranean, and barley produced in medieval England. Ann Hagen suggests that Anglo-Saxon drying kilns, often interpreted as malting floors, may have had both functions "as they were not particularly efficient at drying grain".[51] Wheat was therefore preferred over barley, oat or rye as the grain from which to make bread.[52] The eating of barley bread was apparently considered an act of ascetic piety:[53] Ælfric's Life of St Basil has the Emperor scoff, "Horse mete is bere", "barley is horse fodder".[54] Elsewhere we read, punningly, that "bere is swiðe earfoðe to gearcigenne, and þeahhwæðere fet ðone mann,

---

intended for the clergy only, is invariably found in Latin while other ordeal adjurations for the laity frequently appear in Old English, may shed light on the question of Latin literacy among the clergy in the last century of Anglo-Saxon England.

[50] Lea, *Superstition and Force*, p. 296.

[51] A. Hagen, *A Handbook of Anglo-Saxon Food: Processing and Consumption* (Wiltshire, 1992), p. 3.

[52] Hagen, *Anglo-Saxon Food*, p. 9.

[53] W. T. Mellows, *The Peterborough Chronicle of Hugh Candidus* (Peterborough, 1980), p. 37.

[54] W. W. Skeat, ed., *Ælfric's Lives of Saints* Early English Text Society os 76, 82, 94, 114 (London, 1881-1900; repr. in 2 vols, 1966), "St Basil", 1:50-90 (p. 62, line 216).

þonne he gearo bið", "barley is very onerous to prepare, and yet it can feed a man if he is prepared for it".[55] Even modern barley flour is high in protein, soluble gum, glutens and mucilage, low in starch and devoid of sugar; thus leavening is minimal and the soluble gum content has a drying effect in the mouth. But one must also take into consideration that early medieval grains had not yet undergone the selection process required for greater productivity to meet the needs of an increasing population, and thus would have been smaller and still higher in protein.[56] Flour from medieval barley would have produced a heavy, grainy, in all probability sticky commodity that was unrefined to the taste and exceedingly difficult to chew. Equally unrefined and bland would have been the unsalted fresh cheese commonly eaten by Anglo-Saxons.[57] Therefore, from a food-safety point of view, both the bread and cheese prescribed for this ordeal were prepared under primitive conditions and, when presented for forcible ingestion in the stressful circumstances of the test, would have been unpalatable to a very considerable degree. Their preparation might also have left them as carriers of food toxins of at least two sorts, and, as such, would have added an element of real risk to the undertaking of this ordeal.[58]

[55] B. Thorpe, ed., *The Homilies of the Anglo-Saxon Church. The First Part containing the Sermones Catholici, or Homilies of Ælfric*, 2 vols (London, 1844-46), vol. 1, Hom. 12, p. 188, line 4.

[56] See also Hagen, *Anglo-Saxon Food*, concerning corncockle: "As Anglo-Saxon grain size was smaller than that of modern cereal varieties, this difficulty would have been exacerbated", p. 112.

[57] Hagen, *Anglo-Saxon Food*, p. 23.

[58] For a discussion of the pharmacology of symptoms due specifically to salmonellosis from inadequate milk and cheese preparation, see Hagen, *Anglo-Saxon Food*, pp. 17-18, and J. M. Jones, *Food Safety* (Minnesota, 1992), pp. 114-15. For a discussion of aflatoxins in medieval grains and barley, see J. Renfrew, *Food and Cooking in Prehistoric Britain* (London, 1985), p. 27; and J. G. Heathcote and J. R. Hibbert, *Aflatoxins: Chemical and Biological Aspects* (New York, 1978), p. 18. The symptoms resulting from the mycotoxin that causes alimentary toxic aleukia (A.T.A.) as it is found in barley are discussed by P. M. Scott, H. L. Trenholm and M. D. Sutton, eds., *Mycotoxins: A Canadian Perspective* (Ottawa, 1985), pp. 55-58; J. E. Smith and M. O. Moss, *Mycotoxins: Formation, Analysis and Significance* (New York, 1985), passim; and Jones,

What then did this ordeal look like, and what can be learned of Anglo-Saxon England from a closer study of it? When reconstructed from all contemporary sources, the *corsnæd* ordeal liturgy consisted in England of at least ten different, and in places, lengthy prayers. The primary source here, presented and translated in the Appendix, is the service on pages 571-76 of Cambridge, Corpus Christi College, MS 391,[59] but variants are supplied in the notes from the *Cracow Pontifical* to clarify the procedure.[60] The service is as

Food Safety, p. 142. Finally, while this is an extreme case, A.T.A. is caused by the trichothecene mycotoxin known as T-2; this can develop from a broad range of fungi including Fusarium which is prevalent in barley, and does produce symptoms of "mouth and throat inflammation, gastroenteritis and vomiting" (Jones, *Food Safety*, p. 142) which are reminiscent of the "visceribus angustari eiusque guttur conclude" in the first *corsnæd* prayer, the telling phrase "ut panem vel caseum istum non possis manducare nisi inflato ore cum spuma & gemitu & dolore & lacrimis" in the final adjuration, and the equation, fundamental to the ordeal process, "si est culpabilis evomat illud, ut in omnibus honorificetur deus". See also note 60, below, for the Cracow Pontifical's variation, "sed sputumato ore et sputo sanguine mixto faucibus constrictis convictus appareat", yet another related symptom of mycotoxicity.

[59] And with corrections against the manuscript itself to Hughes' edition, *Portiforium of St. Wulfstan*, 1:169-72, in which a number of editorial errors have occurred.

[60] A comparison between the *corsnæd* service in Corpus 391 and that in the Cracow Pontifical is instructive. The Corpus 391 service consists of eight prayers, a statement placed between the seventh and eighth, and an adjuration. The liturgy is much more complex in the Cracow Pontifical: a full mass precedes the actual ordeal and the instructions are explicit and revealing, as we find in note 72, below. Corpus 391's prayer 1 is missing, and Cracow's first prayer is a substantial variant on Corpus 391's prayer 2 and begins with its second sentence (*Deus angelorum*): of importance to this study is the inclusion of phrasing such as "coram omnibus panis et caesi istius partem datam transglutire non possit, sed sputumato ore et sputo sanguine mixto faucibus constrictis convictus appareat", "before everyone he may not be able to swallow the piece of this bread and cheese given [to him], but let him be revealed as guilty through a salivating mouth and saliva mixed with blood and constricted jaws". Its second prayer is an exorcism of the bread and cheese itself, missing in Corpus 391; thereafter, beginning with a variant of the Trisagion it proceeds as in Corpus 391 to the end of *Suggero tibi* whereupon we find rubric instructions for group administration of the ordeal and two more prayers, *Admoneo frates*

follows, with Appendix reference numbers preceding each item: there is the beginning of the ordeal (i), five prayers (ii-vi), an exorcism (vii), another prayer (viii), the sentence affirming the ordeal (ix) and the adjuration to the accused (x).

I.i	*Incipit Exorcismus*
I.ii	*Conservator & creator humani generis*
I.iii	*Domine ihesu criste qui regnas*
I.iv	*Deus, cuius scientia senariam*
I.v	*Omnipotens sempiterne deus cuius sunt iusta*
I.vi	*Deus qui liberasti moysen*
I.vii	*Exorcizo te maledicta*
I.viii	*Suggero tibi maledicta*
I.ix	*Postea dicatur*
I.x	*Adjuratio: Coniuro te homo*

Many of the prayers are phrased inherently negatively, presenting the case for guilt rather than innocence, and the accused is reminded of God's all-seeing and all-knowing nature. In the fourth prayer of the sequence, we hear a clear echo of the Trisagion, with the Greek words transliterated here in Roman orthography: "omnipotens sempiterne deus, cuius sunt iusta iudica incommutabilia, agyos, agyos, agyos, sancte pater". The late-eleventh-century manuscript Oxford, Bodleian Library, MS Bodley 120 preserves a more traditional Trisagion in a Good Friday liturgy that contains the Reproaches from the Cross, and this liturgical quotation in the ordeal would hold within itself the resonance of Christ's sacrifice on behalf of sinful humanity. The prayer following this lists those Old and New Testament figures whom God has liberated from their

and *Adiuro te inmanissime draco,* that are again excluded from Corpus 391. Like the service in Corpus 391, the ordeal liturgy in Cracow ends with the *Coniuro te homo,* but it is interesting to note that in Corpus 391 only one prayer is said while the accused actually has the *corsnæd* in his mouth, while in Cracow there are three. The Latin text is of necessity semi-diplomatic in order to show the occasional changes made by the scribe from singular to plural, for multiple ordeals; I have also retained the Corpus 391 scribe's cancelled words, and his ampersand, capitalisation and spelling in order to be as accurate as possible.

trials; of these persons, one, the paralytic, is identified not by a name but by his infirmity, and this too may have some bearing on the relationship between physiological symptoms and "guilt" that forms the basis for judgement in all ordeal procedures. An exorcism, although of the Devil and not of the elements of bread and cheese, follows the prayer sequence in much the same tone, recalling theological, scriptural and related liturgical tropes that would have a significant effect on a guilty cleric's imagination, and exhorting God to close the throat of the accused so that he may not devour the bread and cheese.

Thus psychological stress would set the tone for the ordeal: an accused (and especially an accused who had a guilty conscience) had to listen to phrases like "faux ei claudatur", "may his jaw be closed", or "guttum eius stranguletur", "may his throat be constricted", while awaiting the administration of sticky bread together with tasteless cheese. To make immediate matters worse, a clinical symptom of nervousness is the drying up of saliva. The accused would have had the utmost difficult in masticating and swallowing bread and cheese of this unpalatability, and they would have remained unhappily in his mouth as the final prayer (or, as in the *Cracow Pontifical*, prayers) of adjuration were recited. And if the ordeal elements were in any way infected with toxins through faulty preparation, physiology would have taken over in the form of a pharmacological reaction and this, coupled with the gagging suggestions contained in the prayers, would surely have had its effect. Small wonder, then, if the accused choked on such a noxious combination: "et si est culpabilis euomat illud, ut in omnibus honorificetur deus", "and if he is guilty, let him vomit it up, that God may be honoured in all things".

After ("postea dicatur") the statement, "Hic panis uel hic caseus sit uobis ad probationem hodie ad discernendum uerum dei iudicium, amen", "this bread or this cheese be to you a test today for the discernment of the true judgement of God, Amen", we read the last prayer, the *adjuratio*. The description of guilt that it contains could plausibly be the result of unpalatable or even tainted bread or cheese and their effects on an overwrought imagination, to produce the inevitable gag reflex. The option of innocence, at the end of the *adjuratio*, stands in Corpus 391 not as part of the main text but as a note added in the margin, possibly for use in this direct address, only when some doubt existed as to the guilt of the accused. At any rate, it appears sequentially only after the imagination has been jolted and threatened and terrorised with elements that sound like the ancestors of Bible-belt fire and brimstone sermons.

As we have already noted, the prescribed amount of bread for the ordeal on p. 571 of Corpus 391 is "apensio unius sit uncie", which historians have commonly interpreted as an ounce.[61] It is, more correctly, a "one-twelfth" measure, in this case of a loaf apparently large enough to have the Pater Noster, and a brief list of stolen items and suspects inscribed upon it.[62] This is a substantial enough quantity of bread seriously to impede rapid mastication or ingestion under any circumstances, let alone those in which the accused is under great stress and duress, in a condition of fasting, and the unwilling audience for the awe-inspiring import of the prayers of the service itself. So, far from being an example of clergy privilege, ordeal by bread and cheese must have been a highly stressful process whose results might well have been determined by the relative quality of the ordeal elements together with the relative suggestiveness of the accused's imagination.

Matthew Parker's secretary John Joscelyn made a transcription from a now-lost order of service for this ordeal, which is preserved in London, British Library, MS Cotton Vitellius D.vii, on folio 16r. Although fire-damaged, it is still mostly legible. The text begins towards the end of the first prayer and runs until just into the third; thus the Trisagion, the scriptural references, and the adjuration are not included. The *Samson Pontifical* itself preserves no more than this; only the *Portiforium of St Wulfstan*, and the continental *Cracow Pontifical* contain what appears to be a more complete liturgy of ordeal by *corsnæd*. We have not yet found an answer as to why Joscelyn would want this piece of arcane jurisprudence from the pre-Conquest period. Was it just a curiosity, or did it have something to do with Parker's plan of establishing the credibility of the Church of England on the foundation of the Anglo-Saxon Church? Perhaps he regarded ordeal by barley bread and cheese as

---

[61] See Robertson, *Laws*, p. 340.
[62] See note 72, below.

an example of a more humanitarian past; without the legal component identifying it for *weofodþegnas* alone, its widespread inclusion in liturgical manuscripts would have it seem perhaps the "default" form of ordeal testing in Anglo-Saxon England, over and above that of hot water, hot iron or cold water. Joscelyn might therefore have seen the ordeal as indicative of a ecclesiastically-oriented judicial system that was compassionate towards its accused, and truly trusting in God's mercy.

APPENDIX

Taken from Cambridge, Corpus Christi College, MS 391 together with addenda and corrigenda from Cracow, Jagellionian Library, MS 2057.

I.i

INCIPIT EXORCISMUS PANIS ORDEACEI ET CASEI QUORUM APENSIO UNIUS SIT UNCIE Primitus faciat sacerdos ut supra diximur cum letania et omnes qui cum eo sunt ieiuni persistant donec consecratio panis et casei perficiatur & simul in os punatur et simul comedatur et si est culpabilis euomat illud. ut in omnibus honorificetur deus.

Here begins the exorcism of barley bread and cheese, the measure of which should be of one ounce. First, let the priest do as we said above with the litany and all those who are with him should remain fasting until the consecration of bread and cheese is completed, and let it be placed into the mouth together and let it be eaten together, and if he is guilty let him vomit it out that God may be honoured in all things.

I.ii

Oremus. Conseruator[63] & creator humani generis. dator gratiae spiritualis. largitor aeterne salutis. tu emitte spiritum tuum super hanc creaturam panis uel casei cum tremore & timore magnitudinis

eos

tuae brachii tui aduersos eum qui cum superbia & contumacia ac

uenerunt uolunt

zelo iniquo uenit & uult subuertere iustitiam. & conculcare

eos   eorum   a

iudicium. Fac eum domine in uisceribus angustari eiusque guttur conclude ut panem uel caseum istum in tuo nomine sanctificatum

---

[63] The rubrics and initial capitals of these prayers are variously coloured in red, green, purple or blue, intensifying the formality of the presentation.

int hi   erunt   erunt
deuorare non possit Hic qui iniuste iurauit ac negauit illud furtum.

                                                                   eis
uel homicidium. aut adulterium siue maleficium quod ab eo
inquiritur. & ius iurandum pro nichilo habuit & nomen tuum

                                        bant
nominauit. et quod rectum non fuerat perpetrabat, ubi

              ....

                                     is
rectum non erat, te quesumus ut non ei permittas illud abscondere.
quia iustus es domine. & rectum iudicium tuum, qui custodis
ueritatem in seculum faciens iudicium iniuriam patientibus; &
custodis pupillum & uiduam suscipis & uias malignorum
exterminabis. Ideo ostende nobis domine misericordiam tuam. ut
humiles ac mansueti & recti propter ueritatem gaudeant superbi uero
& iniqui & cupidi contristentur & humilientur. usque dum
confiteantur magno & sancto nomini tuo, & cognoscant ceteri quia
tibi nomen dominus & tu solus altissimus super omnem terram &
serui tui in te glorientur & laudent nomen tuum in secula. Amen.

Preserver and creator of mankind, giver of spiritual grace, bestower of eternal salvation, send out your spirit on this creature of bread or cheese, with fear and terror of your might of your arm against him/those who come(s) with pride and obstinacy and also wicked zeal, and wish(es) to subvert justice and abuse judgement. Lord, cause him/them cramping in the guts, choke his/their throat, that he/they may not devour this bread and/or cheese sanctified in your name. He/they who has/have sworn unjustly and denied that theft or murder or adultery or evildoing [witchcraft] for which he/they is being investigated, and has considered a sworn oath as naught, and [has named your name][64] and perpetrated that which was not righteous, where there was no righteousness, we ask you that you not permit him/them to hide it because you are just, O Lord, and righteous judgement is yours, who keep the truth forever, making judgement for those suffering wrong; and preserve the orphan and uphold the widow and wipe out the ways of the wicked.

[64] This phrase is cancelled in the manuscript.

Therefore, Lord, show your mercy to us, that the humble and meek and righteous may rejoice on account of the truth, but the proud and unjust and avaricious be made sorrowful and humiliated until they confess your great and holy name, and the rest acknowledge the name of Lord to you, and you alone most high over all the earth, and your servants may glory in you and praise your name eternally. Amen.

I.iii

Ut supra. Domine. ihesu criste qui regnas in caelis et terris & mirabilis es in omnibus operibus tuis. dominator dominantium. deus angelorum deus patriarcharum prophetarum apostolorum martyrum confessorum uirginum & omnium electorum presta quesumus per

hi rei   sunt

sanctum & admirabile nomen tuum ut si hic reus est huius furti, uel

hi   untur

homicidii aut adulterii, seu maleficii de quo hic requiritur uel in facta aut in conscientia ad adpositam ei per ostensionem ueritatis

eis   a eorum

creaturam panis & casei sanctificati faux ei claudatur, guttur eius

entur   eis

strānguletur & in nomine tuo ante illud reiciatur. quam ab eo deuoretur Sed & spiritus diabolicus cui nulla est communio cum tua criste superna ueritate, in hoc negotio ad subuertendum iudicium, prauis prestrigiorum suorum molitionibus, nichil preualeant, sed qui reus & conscius est rei prefatae, ad hunc pabulum sanctificati panis uel casei, & presertim corporis dominici & sanguinis communionem quam accepit tremat & tremendo palleat & nutabundus in omnibus membris appareat in noxium uero & inscius sobrie ad salubritatem sui cum omni facilitate hanc parte[65] panis uel casei in tuo nomine signatam manducando deglutiat, ut cognoscant omnes quia tu es iudex iustus qui saluos facis sperantes in te. & non est alius praeter qui uiuis.

---

[65] An omitted macron best seems to account for this anomalous form.

As above. Lord Jesus Christ, you who reign in heaven and in the lands and are wonderful in all your works, ruler of rulers, God of angels, God of patriarchs, prophets, apostles, martyrs, confessors, virgins and all the chosen, grant, we pray, through your holy and admirable name, if this/these is/are guilty of this theft or murder or adultery, whether of evildoing in which he/they is/are accused, either in deed or in knowledge of it, that his/their jaw may be closed on this creature of sanctified bread and/or cheese, put before him for the showing of truth, that his/their throat be constricted, and in your name, the same be thrown back up again which was devoured by him/them before. But also the diabolical spirit, for whom there is no communion with your supernal truth, O Christ, may he prevail in no way in this business to overthrow justice, in the depraved labours of his trickeries; he who is guilty and aware of the aforesaid crime, when he has taken this food of sanctified bread and/or cheese, and chiefly through the communion of the body and blood of our Lord, may he tremble, and in trembling grow pale, and may he appear to shake in all his limbs; but if he is unaware of this sin, may he swallow down by eating this piece of bread and/or cheese signed in your name soberly to his health with all facility that all may know you are the just judge who makes whole those hoping in you, and there is none other besides you, who lives [and reigns].

I.iv

De eadem re. Deus cuius scientia senariam circumspectionem angelicis & humanis elongatam sensibus, sola interius penetrat & exterius concludit, quem nulla caelestium uel terrestrium aut infernorum, uota fallere possunt, quantomagis cor unius hominis culpabile, respice ad nostrae humilitatis preces quibus famulatum sacri indidisti ordinis. & presta non nostris exigentibus, meritis sed

                                                                meritis et
tuorum omnium suffragantibus sanctorum precibus. ut quod in hac culpa humanos latet oculos, & sermonum humanae procacitatis obtegitur defensionibus tua caelaesti & superna moderatione sine ullo reueletur obstricamine, & sicut solus es ueritatis auctor

                                                                entes
sententiam elucidare digneris, quatinus innocens sine ulla

nt   ii

difficultate hoc pabulum probationes deglutiat obnoxius autem obtrepidante mentis statu & totius compagine corporis uacillante. quod in tuo sancto nomine consecratur & benedicitur. Nullatenus

N

deuorandi ualitudinem percipiat, sed coram omnibus inualitudine

    si   erunt

confusus quod presumptione in merita suscepit cum irrisione

    N

proiciat.

On the same subject. Oh God, of whose wisdom the providence, far removed from angelic and human understanding, alone penetrates within and confines without, whom no vows in heaven or earth or hell may deceive, however great the guilt in the heart of one human may be, look upon our humble prayers, whose service you have ordained in holy orders, and grant, not through our requests but by favours, merits and prayers of all your saints, that whatever crime lies hidden from human eyes and is concealed by shameless defences of human speech, be revealed without impediment by your heavenly and supernal authority, and just as you alone are the author of truth able to illumine the mind, grant that he/they who is/are innocent may eat the food of this test with no difficulty; however because it has been consecrated and blessed in your holy name, grant that the guilty, through fear of mind joining uncertainty of the whole body, may in no way receive it through eating in good health but, thrown into confusion through infirmity because he/they received it through presumptuous guilt, be exposed to ridicule in front of all.

I.v

ALIA ORATIO. Omnipotens sempiterne deus, cuius sunt iusta iudicia & incommutabilia, agyos, agyos, agyos, sancte pater qui es inuisibilis aeterne deus omnium rerum creator qui archana prospicis, & cuncta cognoscis, qui scrutas corda & renes deus aperi nobis huius rei ueritatem, de qua quaeritur. per.

Another prayer. Almighty, everliving God, whose just judgements are unchangeable, holy, holy, holy father who is invisible, eternal God, creator of all things, who sees secrets and knows everything, who examines hearts and innards, God, open to us the truth of this matter about which we are asking, through.

I.vi

ITEM ALIA. Deus qui liberasti moysen & aaron de terra aegypti & dauid de manu saul regis, Ionam de uentre caeti, Petrum de fluctibus, Paulus uero de uinculis, Teclam de bestiis, Susannam de falso crimine, Danihelem de lacu leonum, Paraliticum[66] de gratbatto, Lazarum de monumento, nunc ostende nobis misericordiam tuam ut qui haec furtum <sacrilegia> quae hic notantur admiserunt panis uel caseus iste, fauces nec guttura eorum transire possit. Per.

Another of the same. God, who freed Moses and Aaron from the land of Egypt, David from the hand of Saul the King, Jonah from the whale's belly, Peter from the waves, Paul from manacles, Thecla from beasts, Susannah from false accusation, Daniel from the lion's den, the paralytic from the pallet, Lazarus from the grave, now show to us your mercy that for those who have committed these hidden <sacrileges>[67] which are here noted, this bread and/or cheese may pass neither their jaws nor throat, through.

I.vii

ORATIO UNDE SUPRA. Exorcizo te maledicte & inmundissime draco & serpens noxie per uerbum ueritatis, per deum omnipotentem iihesum cristum nazareum agnum inmaculatum de altissis missum, de sancto spiritu conceptum ex maria uirgine natum, quem gabrihel angelus adnuntiauit[68] uenturum, quem cum uidisset iohannes[69] clamauit uoce magna dicens, hic est filius dei uiui, ut

---

[66] The Corpus 391 scribe writes "Paraliticus" with a capital in the text, although it appears in the Cracow Pontifical with a small first letter; thus he apparently considered it a proper name and missed the scriptural reference to Matthew 9.2-8.

[67] This word is added into the prayer later.

[68] This material, with its basis in the revelation of the coming of Christ, by Gabriel to Zacharias (Luke 1.13-19), is also resonant of the Creeds.

intro

nullomodo te mittas aliquibus praestrigiis aut maleficius fallaciae tuae ad subuertendum iudicium & iustitiam uel quominus nobis ueritas clarescat neque tuis fraudulentis uersutiis & iniquis indurati ueneficiis ullam potestatem habeant in tuis confidentes maleficiis

de

communicare hunc panem uel caseum istum qui haec furta quae

quibus   inquirimus

litteris ad notauimus admiserunt, & qui de hoc crimine nescii sunt manducent qui uero conscii sunt statim tremebundi euomant. per dominum.

Prayer as above. I exorcise you, cursed and most unclean dragon and noxious serpent, through the word of truth, through the almighty Lord Jesus Christ of Nazareth, the unspotted Lamb sent from the most high, conceived by the Holy Spirit and born of the Virgin Mary, whose advent the angel Gabriel announced, of whom when he saw him John cried in a loud voice saying "here is the Son of the Living God", so that you may in no way send any of your illusions or evil deeds of deceit to subvert the judgement and justice, so that truth may be utterly revealed to us. Nor may those hardened of heart have any power in your crafty tricks and poisonous iniquities, trusting in your evil doings, to share in this bread and this cheese, those who have committed those crimes which we have described and into which we are inquiring; may those who are ignorant of this crime eat, and those who truly know of it, straightway with trembling vomit forth, through the Lord.

I.viii

ALIA ORATIO DE EADEM RE. Suggero[70] tibi domine deus pater omnipotens aeterne qui caelum terramque fundasti, mare liminibus firmasti & magna luminaria solem uidelicet & lunam super iustos &

[69] The reference is to John 1.29-36 and not to Christ's baptism in the Jordan.

[70] Hughes assumes this word to be *supplico*, 1:171; however it stands as *Suggero* in a virtually identical prayer from the Cracow Pontifical: Obertynski, ed., *Cracow Pontifical*, p. 91.

iniustos fulgere iussisti, fac domine signum tale ut omnis mundus omnisque terra intelligat quia tu es deus qui facis mirabilia magna solus. domine ihesu criste fili dei uiui, qui res iam dictas quae hic continentur superscriptae furati sunt & qui ex his conscii & consentientes sunt <u>esse uidetur</u>[71] ut gulae et linguae uel fauces eorum ita fiant constrictae & obligatae ut panem uel caseum istum non possint manducare. per.

Another prayer of the same kind. I beseech you, Lord God eternal Father almighty, who created heaven and earth, made the sea firm in its boundaries, and ordered the great lights of the sun and moon manifestly to shine on just and unjust, give, Lord, a sign such that all the earth and all the land may know that you are God who alone works great miracles, Lord Jesus Christ, Son of the Living God, such that, the aforesaid things inscribed herein[72] which they stole and they having prior knowledge and giving their oath, [grant] that their throats and tongues and jaws thus be constricted and closed up so that they may not eat this bread or cheese, through.

I.ix

POSTEA DICATUR   Hic panis uel hic caseus sit uobis ad probationem hodie ad discernendum uerum dei iudicium, amen.

This bread or this cheese be to you a test today for the discernment of the true judgement of God, Amen.

---

[71] These two words are cancelled by underlining in Corpus 391, but "videntur" appears at this point in the Cracow Pontifical: Obertynski, ed., *Cracow Pontifical*, p. 91.

[72] The key to understanding this section is contained in the rubric from the Cracow Pontifical, "adportetur caseus et panis hordeatius et inscribatur in eo oratio dominica et praesentetur ante altare in patena argente. Res etiam quae furatae sunt inscribantur in breviculo una simul et nomina virorum quibus furata imputantur": Obertynski, ed., *Cracow Pontifical*, p. 89. "Have the cheese and barley bread brought in and on it [I am here assuming *eo* to refer to the loaf of bread] be inscribed the Lord's Prayer and have it offered at the altar in a silver paten. Then let the things that were stolen be inscribed in brief as well as the names of the men accused of having stolen them".

I.x

uos   ines

Coniuro te homo per patrem & filium & spiritum sanctum & per

or

tremendum diem iudicii per iiii evangelistas, per xii apostolorum,

or

per xii prophetas, per xxiiii seniores qui cotidie deum laudant per
illum redemptorem qui pro nostris peccatis in sancta cruce suspendi

es   tis   ta

dignatus est si de hoc furto culpabilis es uel mixtus in aliqua re aut

is   is   tis   is

fecisti aut sciuisti aut baiulasti fraudulentur aut consensisti hoc tibi

tis

ordinatum est de manu dei ut panem uel caseum istum non possis
manducare, nisi inflato ore cum spuma & gemitu & dolore &
lacrimis, fauces uestri ita fiant a iusto iudice constricti, qualiter

mini   nostra

coram omnibus confitearis peccata tua que a te fraudulentur

tes tis

perpetrata sunt //[73] et si innocens es \<h\>uius crimi\<n\>is cum omni
\<f\>acilitate panem \<uel\> caseum in nomini domini \<co\>gnatum

tis

mandu\<ca\>ndo deglutias \<ho\>c omnipotentis dei lar\<gi\>flua
miseratio \<la\>rgiri dignetur \<qu\>i uiuit & \<regnat\> deus, per
omnia//.

I adjure you, man/men, by the Father and the Son and the Holy
Ghost and by the tremendous Day of Judgement, by the four
evangelists, by the twelve apostles, by the twelve prophets, by the
twenty-four elders who daily praise God, and by that redemption
when for our sins He deigned to be hung on the Holy Cross, if you
are guilty of this hidden crime, whether as a result of other things or
committed directly, or if you have knowledge of it or are deceitfully
burdened with it or have consented to it, this trial is appointed for

---

[73] The words bracketed thus // are to be found in the margins of Corpus
391, and do not appear at all in the Cracow Pontifical.

you from the hand of God, that you will not be able to eat this bread or cheese without your mouth being swollen up, with spittle and groaning and pain and tears. Your jaws be thus constricted by the Just Judge, so that before all people you must confess your sins which were fraudulently committed by yourself; and if you are innocent of this crime, you will swallow and eat the bread and/or cheese with facility, known in the name of the Lord, having greatly merited the generous mercy of almighty God, who lives and reigns God, through all things.

Crowds and Power in the
Liber pontificalis ecclesiae Ravennatis

Joaquín Martínez Pizarro

The priest Agnellus, also named Andreas, wrote his *Liber pontificalis ecclesiae Ravennatis* between 830 and 845.[1] The work is an early specimen of *gesta episcoporum*, and consists of biographies of the bishops and archbishops of Ravenna from St Apollinaris, who Christianised the city and founded the Ravennate church, to Agnellus' contemporary and *bête noire*, Archbishop George.[2] In his account of Archbishop Damian, who ruled the see of Ravenna from 692 to 708, Agnellus tells a remarkable story.[3] He introduces it rhetorically as an example of what can happen when

---

[1] Agnellus qui et Andreas, *Liber pontificalis ecclesiae Ravennatis*, ed. O. Holder-Egger, MGH SRL (Hanover, 1878; repr. 1964) [hereafter LPR].

[2] On the genre, see M. Sot, *Gesta episcoporum, gesta abbatum*, Typologie des sources du moyen âge occidental 37 (Turnhout, 1981) and R. Kaiser, "Die Gesta episcoporum als Genus der Geschichtsschreibung", in *Historiographie im frühen Mittelalter*, ed. A. Scharer and G. Scheibelreiter, Veröffentlichungen des Instituts für Österreichische Geschichtsforschung 32 (Vienna and Munich, 1994), pp. 459-80, which also touches on the non-generic aspects of Agnellus' book.

[3] The narrative occurs in chapters 126-29 of the *Liber pontificalis* (pp. 361-63 of Holder-Egger's edition). I discuss this same episode in my book *Writing Ravenna: The Liber Pontificalis of Andreas Agnellus* (Ann Arbor, 1995), pp. 141-58, but the present analysis is quite different from the discussion there, which it is intended to supplement.

Christians are not on guard, like soldiers, against the surprise attacks of the Devil. There is in Ravenna, he tells us, a terrible old custom that has lasted to his own day: every Sunday and on the feast of the Apostles (St Peter and St Paul, June 29), after lunch, the locals come out in groups through the various gates of the city to fight each other. Agnellus points out that all citizens ("Ravennensis cives") take part in this barbarous game: individuals of all ranks and ages, including children and old men. Although he refers to both sexes as participating ("promiscui sexus"), no women are mentioned in the two detailed descriptions of fights that follow. No members of the clergy, of any rank, appear to be involved either. Agnellus deplores this traditional practice, and calls those involved in it mad and raving ("delirati et insani") because they destroy themselves and each other without reason. However, the fights themselves are not the terrible event he has announced, but only the setting for it.

It happens one Sunday in Archbishop Damian's time that the inhabitants of the quarter of the Porta Teguriensis win a crushing victory over those of the Porta Posturulensis, a neighbourhood also known as Summus Vicus. They chase their rivals back to their gate, taunt and mock those who managed to escape, and tear locks and bolts from the gate itself. One week later, this victory is repeated with great carnage and the use of a variety of weapons: spears, swords, clubs, and slings. Agnellus describes children, grown men, and senior citizens bleeding and dying, and mentions a rule that had always been scrupulously observed and that remained in force in his own time: those who begged for their lives could not be slain.

At this point in the story, Agnellus brings back, emphatically, the theme of diabolical inspiration to explain the reaction of the losers, the Posturulenses. The surviving members of that faction get together to bewail their misfortune. They have no doubt that the Tegurienses plan to exterminate them on the following Sunday, and they lament in advance the fate of their wives and children, who will be reduced to servitude, and of their property, which will be seized by their enemies. To prevent this, they decide to kill the Tegurienses by treason. The decision, presented in their own words, is exceptionally clear and deliberate: "Venite, insidiemur illis. Occulte aptemus contra eos dolosa mendacia et improba fingamus verba et decipiamus eos in falsa humilitate".[4] The plan is that on the following Sunday, after mass, each of the Posturulenses will ask one of the Tegurienses to dine at home with him, begging his guest at the same time to keep this invitation a secret. The plan is carried out, and each of the unsuspecting Tegurienses is later murdered by his host with, we assume, the assistance of his family. The murders are carried out in many different ways, and the corpses are hidden away and buried in the various houses.

On the next day, apprehension and dread take hold of the city. Agnellus uses this moment to portray the rich variety of secular urban life brought to a standstill by the disappearance of a large number of citizens. He describes it, as practically everything else in this story, by enumeration:

> Alia vero die fit luctus ingens, moerore undique,
> tota in luctu civitas morabatur. Clausa sunt balnea,
> cessaverunt spectacula publica, mercatores re-
> texerunt pedes, oppilaverunt caupones tabernas,
> nondinatoris reliquerunt negotia ...[5]

This passage is followed by another list, this time of the basic groups of citizens by age, sex, and occupation (priests, elders, youths, married men, married women, virgins, and so on), all of them engaged in different forms of lamentation and in a vain quest for news of their vanished relatives.

When the spontaneous mourning and searching of the population bring no results, Archbishop Damian institutes a three-

---

[4] "Come, let us lay a trap for them. Let us secretly prepare fraudulent lies against them, give out dishonest words, and deceive them with feigned humility": LPR, chap. 128, p. 362.

[5] "On the following day there was great mourning and lamentation everywhere; the entire city was plunged in sorrow. The baths were closed, public theatricals were discontinued, merchants removed their shoes and returned from work, publicans kept their taverns closed, tradesmen abandoned their shops": LPR, chap. 128, p. 362. B. Ward-Perkins, *From Classical Antiquity to the Middle Ages: Urban Public Building in Northern and Central Italy A.D. 300-850* (Oxford, 1984), pp. 108-09, points out the resemblance in phrasing between Agnellus' description and a passage in Eusebius' *Vita Constantini*. This, like other apparent echoes of Byzantine works, remains unexplained, since Agnellus had no access to Greek sources.

day fast together with the septiform or sevenfold litany, which is not a communal prayer, as the name might suggest, but a procession of atonement and penance. Agnellus' source for this ritual is Paul the Deacon's *Historia Langobardorum* 3.24, which describes its use in plague-stricken Rome at the beginning of the pontificate of Gregory the Great.[6] Paul simplified a very full account of the *litania* that he found in Gregory of Tours; Agnellus changes Paul's version slightly and transfers it to Ravenna c. 700. What characterises the *septiformis litania* in Paul and Agnellus' accounts is that the basic social groups mentioned above take part in it separately, in ashes and penitential garments.

> Praesul vero praecepit populo, ut segregatim incederet. Ipse cum clericis et monachis in unam partem, laici vero, senes, adolescentes et pueri unus praecepit ut esset chorus; nuptae vero mulieres et innuptae, viduae et puellae in alteram partem; turma vero pauperum separatim. Non omnes in unum incedebant, sed separatim, quasi medio iactu lapidis.[7]

The weeping of all these groups, to which are added the cries of all the different domestic animals and cattle of Ravenna, fills the city. After three days of these ceremonies, near dusk, a great noise is heard coming from the vicinity of the amphitheatre by the Porta Aurea and all the way to the Porta Posturulensis; a mist rises from the ground and the earth opens, revealing the corpses of the

---

[6] Paul the Deacon, *Historia Langobardorum*, ed. L. Bethmann and G. Waitz, MGH SRL (Hanover, 1878; repr. 1964), pp. 104-05. The passage was borrowed by Paul from Gregory of Tours; see Gregory of Tours, *Libri historiarum x*, ed. B. Krusch and W. Levison, MGH SRM 1.1 (Hanover, 1951), pp. 479-81, which quotes in full Gregory the Great's letter of instructions on the subject, also preserved in Gregory the Great, *Registrum epistolarum libri xiv*, ed. D. Norberg, 2 vols, CCSL 140, 140A (Turnhout, 1982), vol. 2, appendix 9.

[7] "The bishop asked the people to come into the church in separate groups. He stood on one side with the clergy and monks, and ordered that laymen, old men and adolescents as well as children, should gather in one cluster; the women, married and single, widows and young girls, in another place; then the crowd of the poor separately. The groups did not advance together, but a stone's throw from each other": LPR, chap. 129, p. 362.

murdered Tegurienses. Guided by the stench of the dead, the citizens of Ravenna run to the spot and identify the bodies house by house ("per singulas casas"). The Posturulenses together with their families are condemned to various punishments. Their entire neighbourhood is destroyed and their property is offered to the rest of the population, who refuse to take any of it. The area is then named *Regio latronum*, which Agnellus appears to understand as "Quarter of Thieves", and it has kept that name to his own time.

Agnellus' *Liber pontificalis* provides the only record of these events.[8] Two factual aspects of his account deserve our attention. Firstly the text implies clearly that the entire lay population of Ravenna took part in the Sunday fights, and not just the Tegurienses and Posturulenses. This is probably why the practice survived into the ninth century in spite of the murder of one team and the likely execution of all or most members of the other. Secondly Agnellus does not say explicitly that the participating teams represent different neighbourhoods of the city, but this is suggested quite strongly by his characterisation of the Tegurienses and Posturulenses and by his description of the participants in the fights coming out in groups through the various city gates. The teams can therefore be said to represent *demes* or municipal units, unlike the Byzantine circus factions studied by Alan Cameron.[9] That these *demes* were organised as militias of some sort is suggested not only by the variety of weapons they use in the fights, but also by the phrase "contubernalis amicus" ("tent companion") used of the Posturulenses as they sit together lamenting their defeat and by certain pseudo-military features of the fights themselves, in particular the tearing of locks and bolts from the enemy's gates. In an earlier episode, these very locks and bolts are offered as trophies and tokens of victory to an invading army.[10] Seen from this angle,

---

[8] See A. Guillou, *Régionalisme et indépendance dans l'empire byzantin au VIIe siècle*, Studi storici 75-76 (Rome, 1969), pp. 162-63, and T. S. Brown, *Gentlemen and Officers. Imperial Administration and Aristocratic Power in Byzantine Italy A.D. 554-800* (Rome, 1984), pp. 100-01.

[9] A. Cameron, *Circus Factions: Blues and Greens at Rome and Byzantium* (Oxford, 1976).

[10] LPR, chap. 37, pp. 299-302.

the Sunday fights begin to look like an institutionalised wargame, introduced perhaps by troops that had been settled in the area.

This social background of the fights constitutes the most believable part of Agnellus' narrative, and is especially interesting for what it tells us about the organisation of the early medieval city.[11] It has therefore received some attention from historians, while nothing has been said about the remainder of the tale. It is time to approach this episode of the *Liber pontificalis* as a text, for the representations it contains rather than the extra-textual events it may document. In order to do that, we will have to look at the story as a whole.

[11] An important text that has, to my knowledge, not been invoked in interpretations of this incident is Augustine, *De doctrina christiana*, 4:24. Explaining how use of the high style in preaching can on occasion bring forth tears rather than applause from the public, Augustine notes that he has once seen this happen. "Denique cum apud Caesaream Mauritaniae populo dissuaderem pugnam ciuilem uel potius plus quam ciuilem, quam cateruam uocabant – neque enim ciues tantummodo, uerum etiam propinqui, fratres, postremo parentes ac filii lapidibus inter se in duas partes diuisi, per aliquot dies continuos, certo tempore anni solemniter dimicabant et quisque, ut quemque poterat, occidebat": J. Martin, ed., *Sancti Aurelii Augustini De doctrina christiana libri iv*, CCSL 32 (Turnhout, 1962), p. 159. He adds that, having admonished his congregation in the most powerful and dramatic terms, he finally saw them shed tears, "Quas ubi aspexi, immanem illam consuetudinem a patribus et auis longeque a maioribus traditam, quae pectora eorum hostiliter obsidebat, uel potius possidebat, uictam, antequam re ipsa id ostenderent, credidi": Augustine, *De doctrina christiana*, p. 159. According to Augustine, this conversion took place eight years before; the practice of *caterua* in Mauretania should therefore be placed c. 418, as the last book of *De doctrina christiana* was finished in 426.

The report is that of an eyewitness and has high credibility. Like the Ravenna fights, *caterua* is a local custom, based on ancient tradition and practised at an established time. It is also independent of any other contest or competition, and in that sense different from the circus factions of Constantinople, which remained wholly subordinate to the Hippodrome races. Unlike the Tegurienses and Posturulenses, the two sides in the *caterua* cut across family lines, and in this they resemble the circus factions as described by Procopius. The name "caterua" suggests that the custom had a military origin, possibly connected with the settlement of troops in the area.

The most important fact about the narrative is that it appears to be absolutely original: no literary source is known for any part of it except the *litania*, and its connection to the legends and oral traditions of Ravenna is anything but clear. If banquets that end in a massacre of the guests are a standard motif in early medieval histories, the sharing out of the slaughter among a number of households is exceptional, especially in that it makes the event private and thus possible to conceal, and in that it connects it with domestic life. Equally unprecedented is the entirely collective nature of the action: all the protagonists are groups. The archbishop's role in introducing the *septiformis litania* is mentioned in four sentences, but Damian himself is never brought on stage speaking or acting. Even the anonymous member of the Posturulenses shown and quoted as he grieves with his *contubernales*, is not an individual but "unusquisque" ("every single one"), only grammatically singular. Throughout the story, it is groups that fight, kill, and mourn together; relief comes through group prayer and collective ritual, and the episode closes with what would seem to be a scene of mass punishment or execution. Agnellus diverges radically from the traditions of crowd representation that were available to him, all of which use the crowd as a foil for the qualities of outstanding individuals.[12] Classical epic and historiography make the crowd yield to the courage, self-assurance, and eloquence of political or military leaders. The words used for crowds, always strongly pejorative – "vulgus", "multitudo", "plebs", "turba", "populus", – are almost wholly absent here except for one instance of "vulgus" used of the Posturulenses and, interestingly, two instances of the plural "populi" for the teams and the citizens in general, "populi" being – in late antiquity at any rate – the exact Latin equivalent of the Greek "demoi" used in the simple general sense of "people".[13] In the gospels and in Christian hagiographic narrative the *turba* or

---

[12] See E. Auerbach, *Mimesis: The Representation of Reality in Western Literature*, trans. W. R. Trask (Princeton, 1953), pp. 33-40 and 50-60; J. M. Pizarro, *A Rhetoric of the Scene: Dramatic Narrative in the Early Middle Ages* (Toronto, 1989), pp. 92-94, and Pizarro, *Writing Ravenna*, pp. 146-52.

[13] A. Cameron, "Demes and Factions", *Byzantinische Zeitschrift* 67 (1974), 74-91 (p. 79).

multitudo played a less negative part, often serving to confirm the charisma or supernatural powers of a holy man or a bishop by yielding to him, or by witnessing his miracles. Agnellus has simply left out all individual roles. Although the results of his ritual initiative make the archbishop a controller of crowds, which Peter Brown has defined as one of the fundamental roles of late antique bishops, Agnellus carefully avoids making Damian a significant presence in the narrative.[14]

A famous text that shows important similarities to our story is Procopius' account of the Nika riot of 532, and in particular his description of the protagonists of the riot, the circus factions of the Blues and Greens, whose organisation he portrays, very much as Agnellus does with the fighting teams of Ravenna, in terms of the utter diversity of their social makeup, enumerating the groups – diverse in age, rank, occupation, and sex – that forget all other ties and loyalties for the sake of the victory of their team.[15] It is this initial diversity, erased and forgotten once the group takes over, that makes crowds out of the social units described by Procopius and Agnellus.

Even though André Guillou connected Agnellus' teams directly with the Byzantine circus factions, the two are very different, in ways that have been outlined above.[16] In addition, it is unlikely that Agnellus' account is derived from or influenced by Procopius. For one thing, Procopius was not available to Agnellus, who had no direct access to Greek sources and shows no familiarity with the Byzantine historian elsewhere in the *Liber pontificalis*. In addition, Procopius does not keep the focus on the collective that is such an outstanding feature of the Ravennate episode. Having described the circus factions and their *modus operandi*, he moves on

[14] See P. Brown, *Power and Persuasion in Late Antiquity: Towards a Christian Empire* (Madison, 1992), p. 148. See also R. MacMullen, "The Historical Role of the Masses in Late Antiquity", in *Changes in the Roman Empire: Essays in the Ordinary*, ed. MacMullen (Princeton, 1990), pp. 250-76.

[15] Procopius, *De bello Persico* 1.24, in *Opera omnia* 1, ed. J. Haury, rev. by G. Wirth (Leipzig, 1962), pp. 123-24. Cf. Cameron, *Circus Factions*, pp. 276-81.

[16] Guillou, *Régionalisme et indépendance*, pp. 162-63.

to the reactions of Justinian, Theodora, Belisarius, and the usurper Hypatios, placing the leading figures in the attitude of heroic opposition to the seething multitude that characterised great men and women in classical historiography. Finally, there is no moment in Agnellus' narrative that can properly be called a riot: everything his fighting teams do is regulated and planned. Their behaviour shows the chronic, predictable violence that distinguishes sports crowds.

An alternative origin for the narrative of the *Liber pontificalis* might be found in the oral traditions of the city, a possibility supported by the explicit connection of the story to the place-name *Regio latronum*, which according to Agnellus was given to the neighbourhood of the Porta Posturulensis after its inhabitants had been convicted and punished. This place-name, however, introduces a host of new problems. Francesco Lanzoni argued in 1915 that the *latro* in *Regio latronum* bore the older meaning "soldier of the guard" and not "robber, bandit", as Agnellus seemed to believe.[17] The Ravennate place-name closely resembles a *Fossa latronum* in the outskirts of sixth-century Rome: both names refer to areas where soldiers of the guard were presumably housed, and not to a "quarter of thieves" or a "den of malefactors". This suggests also that the place-name is older than Agnellus believes, and was probably in use before the time of Archbishop Damian.

The probability that the story is derived from a local legend remains very high nevertheless, mainly because it is based on a local custom. Clearly, the initial paragraph in which the fights are described in general and roundly condemned was added by Agnellus for expository purposes, thinking of readers who might not be aware of this Ravennate institution. The fights as a real-life custom cannot have been the subject of either the original legend or of Agnellus' retelling, both of which imply and presuppose the tradition of Sunday fighting. If the story revolved around an act of criminal violence, it could only have been one that took place against the background of these mock battles and in violation of their laws, which fits the massacre of the Tegurienses, with its

[17] F. Lanzoni, "La *Regio Latronum* di Agnello", *Felix Ravenna* 20 (1915), 866-67.

aggravating circumstances of treachery and secrecy. And such a story would necessarily have had the discovery of the truth, i.e. the finding of the bodies, as a supplementary focus of interest.

From historical legends we expect a strong and simple sense of motivation as well as transparently clear ideological schemes. These are also the aspects most directly and obviously affected as a legend is handed down and adapted to various literary contexts and aims. The process is very much in evidence here: motivation and ideological coherence are weakened and half-erased at critical points. If the fights were held every week and slayings in the course of them were foreseen and accepted (as implied by the rule of sparing those who begged for their lives), then it is hard to see why two successive defeats should have brought the Posturulenses to such a pitch of despair. Agnellus appears to be aware of this difficulty and skirts it by making the second defeat exceptionally bloody: "Factaque est plaga magna in regione illa, qualis non fuit aliquando a priscis temporibus quam seniores nostri memorare potuissent".[18] This, however, still does not explain the fears expressed by the Posturulenses that their dependants will be made captives and their property confiscated, as if the Sunday fights created a virtual state of war. It also fails to explain why, in a situation of such tension, the Tegurienses were willing to accept invitations to dinner from their enemies. This last motif clearly belongs in a legend, but it has lost its original purpose and makes little sense as it stands.

A further element of uncertainty arises from the collective character of the narrative. It would be surprising if that had no ideological function, but what are we to make of the fact that the crowds in the story only become efficient once they break down into smaller, less spontaneous units that can no longer be perceived as crowds? The Posturulenses only get rid of their enemies when they divide into families and murder the Tegurienses *separatim*, one by one. And the city can only move God to reveal the whereabouts of the bodies when it ceases to mourn communally and spontaneously and divides into the liturgical teams of the *septiformis litania*.

---

[18] "So a carnage took place in that area such as had never occurred in ancient times, as far as our elders could remember": LPR, chap. 127, p. 361.

Finally, it is difficult to imagine the point of the legendary source. If the miracle was attributed to a bishop, Damian or an earlier one, as evidence of his insight and holiness, why would Agnellus, who portrays Damian as a good bishop and ascribes various other miracles to him, have made so little of his role? The other possibility, namely that the episode revolves around the power and efficacy of the *litania*, which is described in some detail, is weakened by the fact that this passage is borrowed from Paul the Deacon, which would hardly have been necessary if the legendary source had also centred on a ritual.

Most of our questions about Agnellus' source, then, cannot be answered with any certainty at present. That is not the case with Agnellus' own interpretation and retelling of the story, the meaning of which can be elucidated from its position in the *Liber pontificalis* and its similarity to other episodes in it.

The *Liber pontificalis ecclesiae Ravennatis* presents itself as (and probably is) a series of *lectiones* or readings on the history of the Ravennate church.[19] The division into *lectiones*, which the author is believed to have held publicly for a disaffected faction of the local clergy, does not belong to the definition of *gesta episcoporum* and is characteristic only of Agnellus' work. The most recent attempt, by Ruggero Benericetti, to number the *lectiones* and identify their beginnings and endings by means of certain conventional phrases and shifts in subject-matter places our story in *lectio* 15, which contains the biography of Damian as well as that of his predecessor Archbishop Theodore, who ruled from 677 to 691.[20] Among other portraits of archbishops as antitypes or negative ideals of the episcopal function, Theodore is perhaps the clearest and most

[19] The presumed origin of the *lectiones* in oral performance is discussed in Pizarro, *Writing Ravenna*, pp. 67-99 and D. Mauskopf Deliyannis, "The *Liber Pontificalis Ecclesiae Ravennatis*: Critical Edition and Commentary", (unpublished doctoral dissertation, University of Pennsylvania, 1994), pp. 190-99.

[20] R. Benericetti, *Il pontificale di Ravenna. Studio critico* (Faenza, 1994), p. 69. A. Testi Rasponi, "Note marginali al *Liber pontificalis* di Agnello ravennate", *Atti e Memorie della R. Deputazione di Storia Patria per le Provincie di Romagna*, 3rd ser., 27 (1908-09), p. 90, posited separate though consecutive *lectiones* for the biographies of Theodore and Damian.

extreme. He had surrendered to the bishop of Rome the prized autocephaly of the church of Ravenna, granted by the Byzantine emperor; he had also burned every copy he could get of the documents that guaranteed the rights of his clergy, and especially their participation in the income of the church. Theodore's biography contains a narrative of ecclesiastical revolt which I will refer to as the Christmas Morning Strike.

Archbishop Theodore loved to sow division in the church by showing favour to the priests and the deacons in turn, always rejecting his former favourites, and turning these two most important ranks of the clergy against each other. In doing so, he was breaking one of the fundamental rules for the behaviour of the bishop, as defined earlier in the *Liber pontificalis*, according to which he must use every opportunity to bring union and harmony to his clergy and, if possible, to all his subjects in the see. Symbols of an ideal community led by its bishop are scattered throughout the *Liber pontificalis*, most often as images of shepherd and flock and, especially, father and children, or as allusions and references to such images.[21] The internal division encouraged by Theodore was eventually brought to an end by the poverty in which he kept all the clergy by withholding from them the share of one quarter of the annual revenues of the church which was theirs by ancient right. Deacons and priests elected representatives, both bearing the name of Theodore and related to each other, and sent them to the archbishop with a list of their joint demands, but Archbishop Theodore met their embassy with curses and threats. At this point, it being Christmas Eve, the two Theodores communicated secretly with the entire clergy of Ravenna and proposed to them that they should all leave the city at dawn and gather in Classe, at the church of St Apollinaris, openly refusing to celebrate Christmas Morning mass with their superior.

The organisation of this unusual ecclesiastical strike is described in some detail. The plotters first had to reassure each other that they would stand together whatever might come and under no circumstances capitulate independently to the archbishop or reach a private settlement with him. This is good evidence that Archbishop

---

[21] See Pizarro, *Writing Ravenna*, pp. 43-52.

Theodore had been able to create distrust and alienation among the ranks of the clergy. In a telling scene, the archpriest Theodore calls on his *cunsubrinus* the archdeacon at home to discuss a collective reaction to the archbishop's tyranny. The archdeacon is at first so full of suspicion and so pessimistic that he declares himself unwilling to speak to his relative. Eventually, however, they agree to work together, and swear oaths before an icon of Christ and St Andrew the Apostle that they will keep their agreement.

On entering his church the following morning, Archbishop Theodore does not find a single member of his clergy to help him celebrate the mass. He is told that they are all in Classe, saying mass by themselves. The archbishop declares himself defeated ("Heu victus sum") and withdraws to his quarters. He later sends men on horseback to Classe to speak to the rebels and try to make them come to terms. Theodore's messengers find all the churchmen of Ravenna gathered in the nave of what is today San Apollinare in Classe. They arise on seeing the messengers come in and, as one man, give voice to a choral *deploratio* in rejection of the archbishop. The gathered clergy are acting without leaders of any sort; Theodore the archpriest and Theodore the archdeacon, who had representative but not protagonistic roles, are not mentioned again. The choral prayer of the clergy is addressed to the great mosaic in the apse of the church, which represents St Apollinaris in the posture of an *orans*, surrounded by grazing flocks. In the strongest terms, they denounce their present shepherd, who is guilty of killing and devouring his sheep, and beg him, Apollinaris, the founder of their church, to celebrate the mass with them on this Christmas Morning. The archbishop's envoys are so deeply moved by what they see in Classe that they return to Ravenna weeping and almost unable to speak. Eventually, with the exarch as mediator, a solution is found and the clergy are once again able to enjoy some of their established rights. Agnellus adds, however, that it was in revenge for this defeat that Archbishop Theodore later surrendered the autocephaly of Ravenna, its ecclesiastical independence from Rome, to Pope Agathon.

The Christmas Morning Strike appears almost immediately next to the story of the Tegurienses and the Posturulenses; if Benericetti is right, these episodes stand side by side in the same *lectio*, separated only by two brief chapters in Holder-Egger's standard division of the text.[22] Although there is nothing that could be properly called a crowd in this account of ecclesiastical in-fighting, the narrative shows a striking parallelism of composition with the adjacent tale of factional violence and secret murder. Here too we have at the beginning a community perversely divided against itself; the influence of the evil Archbishop Theodore is structurally equivalent to that of Satan in the other story. This division and its harmful consequences lead in time to a secret meeting between purely representative figures, in this case the two Theodores, who stand for deacons and priests respectively, and in the other tale the anonymous Posturulenses and their *contubernales*. Though the latter can only be said to represent one faction, we should keep in mind that by the time the two Theodores meet in secret, deacons and priests have been reconciled by economic hardship and form a unified front to resist the archbishop. The nature of the meeting is conspiratorial; a plan is set in motion. Finally, a ritual scene serves to express the restored oneness of the community: the collective *deploratio* at San Apollinare in Classe gives the united clergy of Ravenna a new and fitting shepherd, symbolically replacing the rejected Theodore with the figure of Apollinaris, the immaculate legendary founder. The obvious parallel is of course the *septiformis litania*, in which the entire population of Ravenna, reorganised into liturgical teams by Archbishop Damian's initiative, manages to transcend the divisions created by the Sunday fights.

In addition to this structural sequence of division, conspiracy, and ritual, three common elements can be found in the description and phrasing of the final ceremony. The first is an emphasis on the heterogeneity of the group, marked by enumeration. Just as Agnellus lists the various social subgroups that make up the teams of the *litania*, so the people of Ravenna inform Archbishop Theodore that all the different ranks of his clergy are gathered in Classe celebrating the Christmas Morning mass: "et ibidem missam celebrant presbiteri, diacones, subdiacones, acolithi, ostiarii,

---

[22] LPR, chap. 124-25, pp. 359-61.

lectores, cantoresque, diverso clero, illuc ambulaverunt".[23] A second common feature is collective weeping. As the participants in the *litania* unite in a great outburst of grief, so the ecclesiastics gathered before the great mosaic of St Apollinaris experience a violent paroxysm of sorrow after their choral rejection of Archbishop Theodore, and the emotion is so contagious that it affects the archbishop's emissaries: "In his autem dictis talis lamentatio luctusque ingens ex utrisque partibus fuit, ut illi, qui ad pontificem versi sunt, pro intemperatis lacrimis atque murmurationibus omnium illorum clericorum vix verba dare valuerunt atque legationem explere nequiverunt".[24] Finally, the closing scene represents not a well-established, familiar ceremony, but an instance of ritual creativity, improvised and unprecedented like the choral *deploratio* before the icon of the founder, or else a literary loan like the *litania*, which is documented only once before, for an episode of plague in late-sixth-century Rome.

That similar representations were part of Agnellus' historical narrative long before he got to *lectio* 15 can be shown by a quick look at *lectio* 4, the biography of John I, known as John Angeloptes, a semi-legendary fifth-century bishop. In an episode of this *lectio*, the bishop goes out to meet Attila and his armies in a sort of royal *adventus*. Leading a procession of white-robed citizens of Ravenna, he appears before the Hunnish king and persuades him to spare the city. Attila sets a single condition: there must be a form of surrender by which the Ravennates open the city gates to his troops. The bishop agrees, and this formality is performed the following day at break of dawn. Though they know that they are not in danger, the citizens weep convulsively, "inbecilles facti, trementes gementes-

---

[23] "There priests, deacons, subdeacons, acolytes, porters, lectors, cantors, and all the various ranks of the clergy celebrate the mass; they all went there": LPR, chap. 121, p. 358.

[24] "While these things were said, there was such lamentation and great mourning on either side that those who went back to the bishop could hardly speak on account of the immoderate tears and complaints of all the churchmen, and were unable to carry out their embassy": LPR, chap. 122, p. 359.

que, cum magnis suspiriis celestem Dominum invocantes".[25] Their
diversity is briefly noted when Agnellus describes the rejoicing that
followed these tears: "Fit postmodum ingens alacritas, et maiores
necnon pusilli et mediocres immensa laetitia".[26] It is the oddness of
the occasion, and of the fake surrender in particular, that brings this
account of the deliverance of the city in line with the two other
stories. In all three, collective redemption takes the form of an
emotional crisis brought on, or in any event framed by an unusual
ceremony. Ritual behaviour and the shared outburst of feeling also
have the effect of bringing a diverse community together, although
the Attila episode, unlike the others, does not emphasise hostility
and division before the ceremony.

Agnellus was intensely aware that all threats did not come
from the outside and that a community could fall apart as a result of
its own inner tensions and animosities. In at least three separate
scenes, he shows the people of Ravenna reacting to new
developments with an irrational contentiousness. They disagree
about the miracle by which John Angeloptes is helped to say mass
by an invisible angel: "Intentio magna valde in populo adcrevit; alii
dicebant: 'Non levita dignus', alii adfirmabant 'Non sed visitatio
caelestis'".[27] They quarrel violently about the election of Peter I
(Peter Chrysologus), because he is not a native of Ravenna: "Statim
coepit fremitum dare populus inter se et maximum clamorem ad
caelum. Alii dicebant, quia 'neophitus non recipimus. Non ex nostro
fuit ovile, sed subito invadit cathedram episcopalem quasi latro'.
[...] Alii contra aiebant: 'Iustus est hic homo, non recte dicitis'".[28]

---

[25] "and became stupefied, quivering, sobbing, and praying to God in
heaven with deep sighs": LPR, chap. 37, p. 302.

[26] "Afterwards there was great rejoicing and happiness for the elders of
the city, and also for the children and for those of middle age": LPR, chap. 37, p.
302.

[27] "A great contention arose among the people; some said: 'The acolyte is
unworthy', others maintained: 'No, this is a visitation from heaven'": LPR,
chap. 44, p. 308.

[28] "Instantly the people began to make a rumour and to raise their outcry
to the skies. Some said: 'We will not accept a neophyte. He is not of our fold,
but has usurped the episcopal throne suddenly, like a thief'. [...] Others

Under Archbishop Sergius (744-769), the clergy react to the visit of Pope Stephen II, who comes to plunder the treasures of their church, with an angry debate about different ways to save their property and/or do away with the rapacious pope. Archdeacon Uviliaris finds them "in talis machinamentis sermocinationum sistere et diversa inter se cunsilia volvere. [...] Alii dicebant: 'Suffocemus eum'; alii: 'Non, serventur ecclesiae fortunae'. Erant dispares voces in vulgo".[29] Communities, then, are threatened by the innate quarrelsomeness of their members as much as by foreign conquest, war, or crime.[30]

When Agnellus wrote, the Exarchate of Ravenna had been for several decades under the power of the popes, who already had agents and administrators in the city. This could lead foreseeably to the formation of Roman and anti-Roman parties among the people and the clergy. The power of the Carolingians, to whom the Ravennate clergy had to appeal for support in all their conflicts with

countered: 'This is a righteous man, and you speak mistakenly'": LPR, chap. 49, p. 312.

[29] "caught in a tangle of rumours and diverse projects. [...] Some said: 'Let us choke him;' others said: 'No, but let the property of the church be spared'. There were conflicting opinions among the crowd": LPR, chap. 158, p. 380.

[30] Episcopal elections appear to have been a common occasion for disunion and violence. Early in the *Liber pontificalis*, Agnellus exclaims "Sed vae tibi, Ravenna misera, vicina destructae Classis, quia nunc cum nimia altercatione et controversia pontifex in te ordinatur". ("Woe to you, wretched Ravenna, neighbour to devastated Classe, for now within you the bishop is appointed with excessive tumult and discord"): LPR, chap. 13, p. 284. See also his words on the election of Sergius (744-69): "Quia in tempore istius zelum sacerdotibus et iurgium habentibus, non unitis animo, scissa est multitudo". ("Because in his time the priests were invidious and quarrelsome, not united in spirit, the crowd became divided"): LPR, chap. 154, p. 377.

Benericetti, *Il pontificale di Ravenna*, pp. 103-07 argues that Agnellus' wish to see the frequent scandals at episcopal elections brought to an end may have been his basic motivation in writing the *Liber pontificalis*. Papal elections in the ninth century appear to have been no less riotous and violent: cf. T. F. X. Noble, "The Papacy in the Eighth and Ninth Centuries", in *The New Cambridge Medieval History, Vol. 2: c. 700-c. 900*, ed. R. McKitterick (Cambridge, 1995), pp. 563-86, esp. pp. 574-75.

Rome, only made the threat of division and possible secularisation of the clergy more serious. Agnellus was chiefly concerned with his fellow churchmen and with their right to a fair share of the church revenues, a right he believed to be in greater danger than ever under the government of his former friend and contemporary, Archbishop George. Under the circumstances, every factor of disunion seemed to him potentially fatal, as it weakened the solidarity that the city, and its clergy in particular, needed to preserve at all costs in order to confront George successfully. Hence these images of communities transfigured and healed by shared emotion and ritual invention: they are models to be imitated.[31]

The episode of the Tegurienses and Posturulenses, however, is more complicated than the others. It sets side by side two kinds of solidarity and collective action: the factional spirit of the Posturulenses, which allows them to eliminate their enemies, and the mourning of the entire city under the leadership of the archbishop, which allows them to discover the truth and find the hidden bodies. Could the point be that the crowd is protean and morally neutral, equally amenable to good and to evil? Elias Canetti has useful observations on this point, which may also throw light on the function of ritual in the various episodes we have examined. Great religions (Ger. *Weltreligionen*), as Canetti notes, are historically the chief enemies of crowds.[32] To the deep-set longing to give up all personal distance and dissolve into the multitude they oppose ritual as one of their most powerful weapons. Ritual involves repetition, which is incompatible with the unplanned, uncontrolled character of crowd behaviour. It also reintroduces, almost imperceptibly, the social differences that had to be cancelled and forgotten for the crowd to emerge. Rituals provide a weakened, watered-down equivalent of the crowd experience, and by so doing rob the crowd of its distinctive irrationality and power.

These ideas have particular relevance to Agnellus' description of the *septiformis litania*. His account, as we know, is lifted almost

---

[31] See P. Lamma, "Agnello Ravennate", *Dizionario biografico degli Italiani* 1 (Rome, 1960), p. 429.

[32] E. Canetti, *Masse und Macht* (Düsseldorf, 1960), pp. 22-24 and 175-79.

unchanged from Paul the Deacon. The only significant differences are precisely the words added by Agnellus to emphasise the distances established by Archbishop Damian between the various ritual teams: "... in unam partem ... unus chorus ... in alteram partem ... separatim ... Non omnes in unum incedebant, sed separatim, quasi medio iactu lapidis".[33]

---

[33] "... on one side ... in one cluster ... in another place ... separately. The groups did not advance together, but a stone's throw from each other": LPR, chap. 129, p. 362.

Magic and the Early Medieval World View

Rob Meens

Medieval magic seems to be on the rise. For long tucked away in the margins of history, it now seems to be moving towards the centre of historical attention. Gurevich emphasised the importance of the magical and the miraculous in medieval popular culture and recently Valerie Flint put the subject centre-stage. Whereas for Gurevich magic still has the negative connotations of the primitive and archaic, Flint points to the deep emotional value of magic, still inherent for example in our use of the word as an expression of admiration. Nevertheless, her impressive case for a rehabilitation of the magical in early medieval Europe seems to confirm the view of this period as a "Dark Age", as the title of Alexander Murray's review article indicates.[1]

---

[1] A. Gurevich, *Medieval Popular Culture: Problems of Belief and Perception* (Cambridge and New York, 1988); V. Flint, *The Rise of Magic in Early Medieval Europe* (Oxford, 1991); A. Murray, "Missionaries and Magic in Dark-Age Europe", *Past and Present* 136 (1992), 186-205. For other penetrating criticisms inspired by Flint's book, see R. Kieckhefer, "The Specific Rationality of Medieval Magic", *American Historical Review* 99 (1994), 813-36, G. de Nie, "Caesarius of Arles and Gregory of Tours. Two Sixth-Century Gallic Bishops and 'Christian Magic'", in *Cultural Identity and Cultural Integration. Ireland and Europe in the Early Middle Ages*, ed. D. Edel (Dublin, 1995), pp. 170-96, and I. Wood, "Pagan Religions and Superstitions East of the Rhine from the Fifth to the Ninth Century", in *After Empire. Towards an Ethnology of Europe's Barbarians*, ed. G. Ausenda (Woodbridge, 1995), pp. 253-79.

I do not think Flint's far reaching and original study is conclusive. At times one would wish her analysis to dig deeper, and she does not give sufficient attention to the stereotyped language of her sources. Time and again we meet the same catalogues of superstitions. What does this mean? Were these superstitious practices really rooted so deeply that the prohibitions had to be repeated over and over? Or were these catalogues simply a theoretical list of possible aberrations without much reference to real behaviour?[2] I think both answers are incorrect. While the repetition of superstitious behaviour is an indication that magic was important, it does not mean that the description of a magical rite corresponds with actual behaviour. The description often derives from a literary tradition, though the fact that it is repeated tells us about the enduring need for such legislation. A careful analysis of traditional material sometimes reveals interesting aspects of actual behaviour.[3]

The texts that inform us about magical practices were written by clerics. Most of these texts are of a prescriptive type: sermons, legislation produced by Church councils, penitentials, capitularies, secular law. Except for the Carolingian capitularies and the barbarian laws, the legislation is based on the authority of the Church. Even in the royal capitularies, priests as well as secular lords are addressed as persons responsible for ensuring that nobody performs magical deeds. Motives for the ban on magical behaviour are not as clear as we would like them to be. The ecclesiastical tradition forbidding rival

---

[2] As is stated by D. Harmening, *Superstitio. Ueberlieferungs- und theoriegeschichtliche Untersuchungen zur kirchlich-theologischen Aberglaubensliteratur des Mittelalters* (Berlin, 1979). This point is also raised by Wood, "Pagan Religions and Superstitions", p. 254. Y. Hen also doubts the practical character of these regulations and wants to see them as reflecting only a "mental reality rather than a practical one, and thus [reflecting] first and foremost the fears and worries which preoccupied the author's mind": see Y. Hen, *Culture and Religion in Merovingian Gaul AD 481-751* (Leiden, New York, Cologne, 1995), especially pp. 167-72, citation on p. 171.

[3] See R. Künzel, "Paganisme, syncrétisme et culture religieuse populaire au Haut Moyen Age", *Annales: Economies, sociétés, civilisations* 47 (1992), 1055-69 and R. Meens, *Het tripartite boeteboek. Overlevering en betekenis van vroegmiddeleeuwse biechtvoorschriften (met editie en vertaling van vier tripartita)* (Hilversum, 1994), pp. 267-306.

religious practices certainly plays a role, as well as the concern of secular rulers, especially the Carolingians, for the unity of the realm. Religious unity was a necessary component of political unity. Furthermore rivalries with other persons exploiting religious ideas among the populace seem to have played a role. This is especially clear in the case of the weather magicians, the *tempestarii*, who, according to Agobard of Lyons, were real professionals and earned their living by exploiting the fear of the devastation of crops by bad weather.[4]

Existing side by side with a heroic attitude that tried to abolish all magical behaviour, Flint notices also a favourable attitude towards magical phenomena among the clergy. According to her this favourable attitude was motivated by the recognition of the positive effects of magic. Her argument here is very functional. It is as if the clergy understood that magic could be accommodated for their own purposes if they could take control of it. I wonder if that is the case. Would it not be possible that even clergymen simply believed in magic? We know they sometimes tried to use it in a way that was not in accordance with ecclesiastical legislation.[5] I think that at least some clerics participated to a much greater degree in what we call popular culture, than we tend to admit.[6]

The demarcation between the magical and the miraculous, between the religious and the superstitious is not always that clear, as in the letter from Alcuin to Archbishop Adelard of Canterbury. Alcuin, echoing Caesarius of Arles, criticises the custom that he

---

[4] Agobard of Lyon, "De grandine et tonitruis", in *Agobardi Lugdunensis Opera omnia*, ed. L. van Acker, Corpus Christianorum Continuatio Medievalis 52 (Turnhout, 1981); see K. Heidecker, "Agobard en de onweermakers. Magie en rationaliteit in de vroege Middeleeuwen", in *De betovering van het middeleeuwse christendom. Studies over ritueel en magie in de Middeleeuwen*, ed. M. Mostert and A. Demyttenaere (Hilversum, 1995), pp. 171-94.

[5] Noticed by Flint, *Rise of Magic*, p. 67, see also De Nie, "Caesarius of Arles", p. 183.

[6] Kieckhefer, "Specific Rationality", p. 831; or should we say that magic is part of a "common culture ... not universal or uniform, but sufficiently diffused that it cannot be assigned to any specific subgroup and expressive more of solidarity than of either hegemony or dissent"? Kieckhefer, "Specific Rationality", p. 833.

himself has observed, of people wearing little bags with bones or texts from the Gospels around their neck. According to Alcuin, these relics and holy texts were no more than superstitious amulets. For him it was important to follow the teachings of the saints instead of concerning oneself with their bones; and it was better to preserve the biblical exhortations in one's heart, than to wear them around one's neck.[7] What was perfectly acceptable to some Christians was not acceptable at all for Alcuin. This suggests that questions of authority and power sometimes were more important than what was actually done.

Flint emphasises the positive aspects of a belief in magic. Nevertheless, we tend to regard magic as backward and naive. It is very hard to discuss it from the "native point of view", especially since we have no direct access to ideas of medieval natives about their motives and beliefs, because we only have prescriptive literature. It seems possible however, to see some alternative rationality behind magical deeds. If we want to take medieval men and women seriously, we will have to try to detect this logic, which inevitably brings us to an investigation of their world view.

We tend to believe that people resort to the same kind of magical practices the world over, and in a way this seems to be true. Objectives seem to be alike everywhere: people try to predict the future, to gain economic or sexual success, or to harm their enemies by means of magic. Though in general objectives may be similar, in detail they vary of course, according to the society in which magic is applied. In a hunting society the objectives are different from those in an agrarian society. In the early Middle Ages most of the magic used for economic reasons has to do with crops and cattle. Flint mentions four main objectives for which help from a magician was sought: health, love and death, weather and the planning of enterprises.

---

[7] Alcuin, *Epistola* 290, ed. E. Dümmler, MGH Epistolae 4, Epp. Kar. Aev. 2 (Berlin, 1895), pp. 448-49; cf. Flint, *Rise of Magic*, p. 327. From Alcuin's formulation, it seems that he knew Caesarius of Arles, sermon 50.2 (G. Morin, ed., *Sancti Caesarii episcopi Arelatensis opera omnia nunc primum in unum collecta*, CCSL 103 (Turnhout, 1953), p. 226). See also De Nie, "Caesarius of Arles", p. 185.

Not only do objectives differ between different societies, but so also do the means to achieve these objectives. It has often been noticed that early medieval magic made use of repellent substances. Flint, for example, remarks that magicians deliberately seem to have aroused fear and disgust by their use of creatures and materials.[8] Excrement and bodily remains seem to have been the common stock-in-trade of early medieval sorcerers.[9] A German scholar uses the word "Dreckapotheke" in this context.[10] Theodulf of Orléans alludes to this practice when he forbids the use of sorcery (*maleficium*) or something unclean (*inmundam rem*) for medical reasons.[11]

Indeed, if we look at the substances that are used for magical purposes, this seems to be correct. People in general, not only professional sorcerers, used blood, saliva and semen for magical reasons. Kieckhefer assumes that such repellent substances were especially favoured in non-learned circles.[12] The sixth-century Irish penitential written by Cummeann forbids the consumption of parts of one's skin, that is a scab or lice, and of urine and excrement.[13] Though no motive for such behaviour is supplied here, Burchard of Worms, repeating the same canon some 400 years later, adds that people behave like this for reasons of health (*pro sanitate aliqua*).[14] The penitential of Theodore of Canterbury speaks of women using semen and blood for magical reasons. The former helped to incite a man's lust, the latter was used as a remedy. The same text suggests

---

[8] Flint, *Rise of Magic*, p. 250.

[9] Flint, *Rise of Magic*, p. 249, note 172; Kieckhefer, "Specific Rationality", pp. 834-35.

[10] G. Holtz, "Bussbücher", in *Reallexikon der Germanischen Altertumskunde*, vol. 4 (Berlin, New York 1981), pp. 276-84 (p. 279): "Krätze. Flöhe, Urin und Kot gelten in Krankheitsfällen als heilkräftig; die Dreckapotheke ist bis zum heutigen Tag gefragt".

[11] II Capitulare X 19, ed. P. Brommer, MGH Capitula episcoporum 1 (Hanover, 1984), p. 178.

[12] Kieckhefer, "Specific Rationality", pp. 834-35.

[13] *Paenitentiale Cummeani* (10), 18, in *The Irish Penitentials*, ed. L. Bieler with an appendix by D. A. Binchy, Scriptores Latini Hiberniae 5 (Dublin, 1963), p. 126.

[14] *Corrector Burchardi*, chap. 127, in *Die Bussbücher und das kanonische Bussverfahren*, ed. H. Schmitz (Düsseldorf, 1898; repr. Graz, 1958), p. 437.

the use of a hare's gall as medicine, while at the same time articulating some doubt on the edibility of the animal itself.[15] Though Theodore apparently did allow the consumption of the hare, this permission proves that there existed some doubt regarding the purity of this animal. In the penitential composed by Hrabanus Maurus for Bishop Heribald of Auxerre, the use of menstrual blood in love magic is mentioned, as well as of powder deriving from a dead man's testicles.[16] Menstrual blood also appears to have been used in Montaillou.[17] Another penitential, the *Oxoniense II*, which may have been composed by St. Willibrord, allows people to use honey that is polluted by a mouse or a hen as a medicine if it is at least sprinkled with holy water first.[18] So here we have food that was otherwise regarded as impure being used as a medicine on condition that it is purified by a Christian rite. We may probably infer that the usage of this impure substance as medicine was an established custom and that the purification by holy water served as a subsequent Christianisation of this "superstitious" custom.

We know that blood was also considered to be impure, as it was able to make food unclean.[19] Sexuality was another source of impurity, and this impurity seems to be one of the reasons why such an elaborate calendar of sexual abstinence was worked out in the

[15] *Paeniteniale Theodori U*, chapters 1:14, 15-16 and 2:11, 5, in *Die Canones Theodori Cantuariensis und ihre Überlieferungsformen*, ed. P. W. Finsterwalder, Untersuchungen zu den Bussbüchern des 7., 8. und 9. Jahrhunderts 1 (Weimar, 1929), pp. 308 and 325.

[16] Flint, *Rise of Magic*, p. 235, note 124.

[17] E. Le Roy Ladurie, *Montaillou, village occitan de 1294 à 1324* (Paris, 1982), p. 275; See H. Dienst, "Zur Rolle von Frauen in magischen Vorstellungen und Praktiken - nach ausgewählten mittelalterlichen Quellen", in *Frauen in Spätantike und Frühmittelalter. Lebensbedingungen - Lebensnormen - Lebensformen*, ed. W. Affeldt (Sigmaringen, 1990), pp. 173-94 (p. 186).

[18] R. Kottje, ed., *Paenitentialia minora Franciae et Italiae saeculi VIII-IX*, CCSL 156 (Turnhout, 1994), chap. 54, p. 200. On the possible connection with Willibrord, see R. Meens, "Willibrords boeteboek?", *Tijdschrift voor Geschiedenis* 106 (1993), 163-78.

[19] R. Meens, "Pollution in the Early Middle Ages: The Case of the Food-Regulations in Penitentials", *Early Medieval Europe* 4 (1995), 3-19 (p. 16).

early Middle Ages.[20] So it seems that the substances used in magical rites are not only disgusting to the modern mind, but were also regarded as such in the early medieval period. But whereas for us they are only disgusting, for medieval people they were more than that, for impurity was connected with power. An impure act or substance could have enormous consequences. This is one of the reasons why the royal household had to avoid all impurity. Disorder at the royal household or in royal monasteries could have repercussions throughout the whole kingdom. It could cause battles to be lost, crops to fail, the emergence of famine and other disasters.[21] It seems that this power inherent in polluting substances was used in magic, either for bad or for good; as medicine or poison, as a love potion or as a drink causing impotence.

Magic has to be extraordinary. If it is not, there is no reason to suppose that it will work. This is one of the reasons why polluting substances, the usage of which is forbidden in everyday life, are used in magic. Therefore, the use of things in magic says something of their status in ordinary life. In the episcopal capitularies of Radulf of Bourges and Ruotger of Trier, priests are ordered to watch closely over the chrism, so that nobody can make use of it for medical or

---

[20] J.-L. Flandrin, *Un temps pour embrasser. Aux origines de la morale sexuelle occidentale (VI-XI siècle)* (Paris, 1983), pp. 73-82; and J. Brundage, *Law, Sex, and Christian Society in Medieval Europe* (Chicago and London, 1987), pp. 154-55.

[21] This is especially emphasised in the seventh-century Irish Mirror of Princes known as Pseudo-Cyprian, *De duodecim abusivis saeculi*. For the influence of this text, see H. H. Anton, *Fürstenspiegel und Herrscherethos in der Karolingerzeit*, Bonner Historische Forschungen 32 (Bonn, 1968) and Anton, "Pseudo-Cyprian. *De duodecim abusivis saeculi* und sein Einfluss auf den Kontinent, insbesondere auf die karolingischen Fürstenspiegel", in *Die Iren und Europa im früheren Mittelalter*, ed. H. Löwe, 2 vols (Stuttgart, 1982) 2:568-617. See also M. de Jong, "Power and Humility in Carolingian Society: the Public Penance of Louis the Pious", *Early Medieval Europe* 1 (1992), 29-52 (esp. p. 50); and J. Nelson, "Kingship and Royal Government", in *The New Cambridge Medieval History, Vol. 2: c. 700-c. 900*, ed. R. McKitterick (Cambridge, 1995), pp. 383-430 (pp. 417 and 423).

magical reasons.[22] We may regard this as proof of the enduring existence of magic in early medieval society. The substances used, however, tell us something about the penetration of Christianity. Instead of trying to connect the use of Christian elements with pagan traditions, as Flint tends to do,[23] it seems more useful to regard them for what they are: expressions of the numinous qualities attributed to central elements of the Christian cult. So, in a way, these forms of magic attest to the penetration of Christianity among the populace. The chrism can only be used for magical purposes if it has acquired a special, awesome, significance.

We can observe something similar concerning the regulation of sexual life in this period. Flandrin, Payer and Brundage have shown how early medieval ecclesiastical legislation tried to control sexuality by defining periods and states in which sexual intercourse was taboo.[24] It has often been asked how successful this regulation can have been. I do not wish to exclude the possibility that the mentality from which this regulation sprang is, at least in part, connected to native ideas concerning the appropriateness of certain acts in connection with certain periods of time. In other words, ecclesiastical legislation may have been in keeping with native traditions and may have been influenced by them. Jean-Louis Flandrin plausibly suggested that this was probably one of the reasons why such a detailed sexual calendar was worked out in this period.[25]

---

[22] Ruotger of Trier, *Capitula Episcoporum*, chap. 15: "Ipsum quoque chrisma sub sigillo custodiant et nulli pro aliqua medicina vel maleficio dare praesumant". Radulf of Bourges, *Capitula Episcoporum*, chap. 16: "Presbyteri autem chrisma sub sigillo custodiant, ut nulli sub praetexto medicinae vel alicuius maleficii dare praesumant": both edited by Brommer, MGH Capitula episcoporum, pp. 67 and 244 respectively.

[23] See, for example, the link she tries to establish between wonder-working cloaks of saints and martyrs and the skins of sacrificed animals, or between the use of the cross and holy water on the one hand and the reverence for trees and fountains on the other: Flint, *Rise of Magic*, pp. 188-90.

[24] Flandrin, *Un temps pour embrasser*; P. Payer, *Sex and the Penitentials. The Development of a Sexual Code, 550-1150* (Toronto, 1984); J. Brundage, *Law, Sex, and Christian Society*.

[25] Flandrin, *Un temps pour embrasser*, pp. 153-58.

However, in the so-called Tripartite St. Gall Penitential, a text from the end of the eighth century, probably written in northern France, we come across canons penalising offences of this kind, not in the context of sexual sins, where we would expect them to occur, but in the context of sins concerning magical practices. From this we may infer that people turned to having sexual intercourse during periods that were taboo, for reasons of magic. What these reasons were, the texts do not tell us, although the importance attached to problems of fertility suggests an answer. What these canons do tell us, however, is that the taboo on having sexual intercourse during forbidden periods was already embedded so deeply that a deliberate transgression of it was thought to have magical effects.[26]

We can observe the same thing with regard to the regulation of food. In the St. Gall penitential just mentioned, we also find canons concerning the use of unclean food in the context of magical offences.[27] The same can be observed in the eleventh-century penitential, probably written in the North of France, which I shall call the *Paenitentiale Parisiense compositum*, though this text lacks an explicit rubrication.[28] Gurevich holds that food was regarded as unclean if it was associated with magical rituals.[29] This is at best only a partial explanation of this attitude towards food. I think that the

---

[26] *Paenitentiale Sangallense tripartitum* 2:34a and b, edited by Meens in *Het tripartite boeteboek*, pp. 340-42. On the date and geographical origin of this text, see pp. 73-104.

[27] *Paenitentiale Sangallense* 2:35-38, ed. Meens, *Het tripartite boeteboek*, p. 342.

[28] *Paenitentiale Parisiense compositum*, chapters 18-19, ed. Meens, *Het tripartite boeteboek*, p. 488. This text was formerly known as the *Paenitentiale Parisiense I* (Paris, Bibliothèque nationale, MS lat. 1207). For the reasons for calling it *P. Parisiense compositum*, see Meens, *Het tripartite boeteboek*, p. 177, and see pp. 177-219 for a study of the sources, place and date of origin of this text.

[29] Gurevich, *Medieval Popular Culture*, pp. 91-92. The same explanation, without referring to Gurevich's work, is put forward in the study by J. M. D. de Waardt, *Voedselvoorschriften in boeteboeken. Motieven voor het hanteren van voedselvoorschriften in vroegmiddeleeuwse boeteboeken, 500-100* (Rotterdam, 1996). This study shows insufficient knowledge of early Irish history in general, and of penitentials in particular.

prohibition of certain kinds of food has to be seen in the context of the distinction between the pure and the impure, which seems to have been of great importance in early medieval society. Where the importance attached to this distinction comes from is difficult to say. There are biblical precedents, but these seem to be of secondary importance. Maybe native traditions provided not only a fertile background to these biblical ideas but also an incentive to elaborate on them.[30] As I have indicated before, the power inherent in impure substances made them a perfect vehicle for magical ritual. For this reason we find canons concerned with impure food mentioned in the context of magic. That it is not the other way around is suggested by the date of the texts containing food regulations. Only in later ones do we find the classification of these canons among magical offences; in earlier ones they form a group in itself, which is often called "of pure and impure food". So the notion of impurity seems to be of primary importance in the earlier texts, while the notion of magic only becomes more important in the later texts.

Flint has made valid the claim that magic was of overwhelming importance in the medieval period, especially in the first phase of the process of Christianisation. The repetition of canons forbidding magical practices should not be attributed to the oppressive force of literary tradition, but in fact says something about the importance attached to magic and its suppression. Furthermore, if we look at magical performances and the substances used in them, it becomes clear that these occupy a special position in the mental universe. The use of them is extraordinary and they are often regarded as impure or, in the case of Christian sacraments, as holy. The power inherent in them is used for magical reasons. An analysis of magic along these lines can tell us something of the boundaries of ordinary behaviour and the power safeguarding these boundaries. Thus magic can yield important insights into the world view of early medieval people. The concepts of pure and impure seem to hold an important place in this world view.[31] Christian beliefs in time also played an important role,

---

[30] See Meens, "Pollution in the Early Middle Ages".

[31] See Meens, "Pollution in the Early Middle Ages"; and "Het heilige bezoedeld. Opvattingen over het heilige en het onreine in de vroegmiddeleeuwse religieuze mentaliteit", in *Willibrord, zijn wereld en zijn werk. Voordrachten*

though they were adapted to people's needs in a way that was unacceptable to the clerical supervisors. By proscribing this behaviour the clergy defined what was to be regarded as magic and what as Christian religion. It remains to be seen whether this theoretical distinction was as clearly maintained in people's behaviour.[32]

gehouden tijdens het Willibrordcongres Nijmegen, 28-30 September 1989, ed. P. Bange and A. Weiler, Middeleeuwse studies 6 (Nijmegen, 1990), pp. 237-55.

[32] Cf. Kieckhefer, "Specific Rationality", p. 835 and De Nie, "Caesarius of Arles".

A Cure for a Sinner: Sickness and Healthcare in Medieval Southern Italy

Patricia Skinner

A "tyrant" living in Salerno in the tenth century, chided over his arrogance by St Nilus of Rossano (910-1004), boasted "vitae meae dies anni decem sunt. per octo annos explebo animae meae desideria et inimicos meos subjiciam, sicut volo ego: duobus vero annis poenitentiam agam et recipiet me Deus".[1] But Nilus replied, "nam decem, quos te putas victuram annos ... decem dies tantum sunt".[2] And the tyrant fell ill with a shivering fever which tormented him for nine days. On the tenth he died. And his subjects cut off his head and fed it to the dogs.

This paper attempts to understand stories such as these. The frequent equation in early medieval societies of sickness with sin or ill-doing on the part of the sufferer seems to be a central problem in

I am grateful to the Wellcome Trust for awarding a Research Fellowship to study health in early medieval southern Italy, and to the staff of the Wellcome Institute, especially Professor Vivian Nutton, for providing support and a congenial working environment. I would also like to thank the two anonymous readers of this paper for their acute suggestions for improvements to the published version.

[1] "I have ten years of life left; of these I shall spend eight satisfying my every desire and crushing my enemies, then for the final two I shall repent, and God will wait for me": *Vita sancti Nili abbatis*, 2.9, AASS Sept. vol. 7, ed. J. Stiltinger et. al. (Antwerp, 1760), p. 289.

[2] "Your years are only days": *Vita sancti Nili*, 2.9, p. 289.

the social history of medicine. I shall investigate whether this association was in fact always made, if so whether it was constant throughout the Middle Ages, and finally explore some reasons.

The area under consideration, southern Italy between the ninth and thirteenth centuries, provides an ideal locus of investigation, conserving as it does a wide variety of sources. It is not difficult to find examples in this evidence of the association of sickness with sin. The Lombard laws, issued in the sixth and seventh centuries in the Lombard kingdom to the North but still current in many parts of the South in our period, are explicit in attaching guilt for sin to the occurrence of leprosy and madness.[3] Paul the Deacon's *Historia Langobardorum*, written at Montecassino in the duchy of Benevento in the late eighth century, also provides examples of such a correlation.[4] The anonymous tenth-century Chronicle of Salerno is even more replete.[5] From the Byzantine part of the South, the lives of

[3] Rothari's law 180 ascribes the madness, going blind or leprosy of a bride-to-be explicitly to "peccatum eminente et egritudine superveniente" ("her weighty sins and resulting illness"); a later law of Rothari, no. 323, restates the connection of madness with the victim's "peccatis eminentibus" ("weighty sins"): F. Bluhme and A. Boretius, eds, *Leges Langobardorum*, MGH Leges 4 (Hanover, 1868), pp. 42, 74. See also R. I. Moore, *The Formation of a Persecuting Society* (Oxford, 1987), p. 48: Rothari's leprosy laws were not a response to any change in disease pattern, but continue the late antique tradition of laws on leprosy.

[4] Paul the Deacon, *Historia Langobardorum*, ed. G. Waitz, MGH SRL (Hanover, 1878), pp. 12-187, 3.11: Emperor Justin became mad "cum a divinis mandatis aurem cordis averteret, iusto Dei iudicie amisso rationis intellectu amens affectus est" ("when he turned away the ear of his heart from the Divine commands ... having lost the faculty of reason by the just judgement of God"); 4.47: a man who opened the sepulchre of King Rothari in church of St John was subsequently hit in the throat by the saint whenever he tried to enter the church; 6.5: pestilence in Rome stopped when an altar of St Sebastian was set up in the church of St Peter in Chains. Cf. D. Harrison, "The Invisible Wall of St John: On Mental Centrality in Early Medieval Italy", *Scandia* 59 (1992), 177-211, which highlights similar examples of supernatural barriers being set up against sinners.

[5] U. Westerbergh, ed., *Chronicon Salernitanum* (Stockholm, 1956). For example, chap. 14, the tale of a woman who, having been unfaithful with a priest, gave birth to a child without bones. This is ascribed to her having asked

local saints teem with miscreants being struck down, allowing the saint to enter and provide a cure in return for repentance.[6] Alongside these sources, however, there are others. A huge archive of medieval charter material exists from almost every major settlement.[7] And southern Italy was also a prime locality for the copying and preservation of ancient medical texts in this period.[8]

Much (although by no means all) of the ancient material was written before the rise of Christianity, which is often seen as the key point at which attitudes changed. The association of illness with sin derived from the patristic writings of the first six centuries of the

---

for pardon without being truly penitent. In chap. 56 a murderer, Agelmond, has a vision of his victim, who cuts him with a sword between his shoulder blades. He begins to vomit blood and dies three days later of his mortal wound. In chap. 71 one Roffred, having obtained the death of an abbot, is struck with paralysis in one leg which never heals.

[6] For example, *Vita sancti Nili*, 7.52, a *domesticus*, Leo, was struck down with a pain in his head after fooling around with a monk's cowl, and died. The most detailed episode of this type, 8.54-56, concerns the imperial judge Eufrasius. Arriving in southern Italy in 968, he was incensed that Nilus did not come out to fete him. His threats against the saint were punished with a grave illness, gangrene of his genitals. This, relates the *Vita* with relish, "medicorum quidem sollicitudinem frustra esse ... poenas autem exigebat ab instrumento luxuriae, per quod ille naturae legibus intemperanter abusus erat" ("resisted the doctors' care, and punished in him the organs of dissoluteness, with which he had intemperately violated the laws of nature"). Nilus, having ignored the man's pleas to visit him, left the judge in this state for three years, until his genitals were eaten away. Then, as the affliction threatened to affect the judge's internal organs and kill him, Nilus, the "spiritual doctor", went to his bedside, and tonsured the unhappy man, who found some relief from wearing the poor clothes of a monk before dying three days later. Of course, hagiography was not confined to this part of the South, as the *Vita Barbati*, a ninth-century biography of the seventh-century bishop of Benevento illustrates: MGH SRL, pp. 555-64.

[7] All numbers, unless stated, relate to documents in the published editions.

[8] A guide to these is A. M. Ieraci Bio, "La trasmissione della letteratura medica greca nell'Italia meridionale fra X e XV secolo", in *Contributi alla Cultura Greca nell'Italia Meridionale*, ed. A. Garzya (Naples, 1989), pp. 133-255.

Christian era, which connected sickness with the Fall.[9] In compilations produced in the early medieval period, therefore, one might have expected that commentaries on the texts copied would introduce a note of blame, particularly since the most likely translators and copyists were churchmen.[10] This does not appear to have happened.

In the charter evidence, perhaps the most reliable mirror of large parts of people's everyday life, absolutely no direct association of illness with sin can be found. The formulaic preambles to pious gifts and to some wills do mention the awareness on the part of the author of his or her imperfection, and the need to compensate for this in some way with a donation or bequest to a local church, but even when illness is mentioned the two are not linked up at all. Given that neither medical texts nor charters seem to support the correlation in narratives and legislation between disease and sin, how can these two very different pictures be reconciled?

Bachrach and Kroll have already examined the problem of whether sin really was believed to cause sickness. Using a wide variety of narrative texts from medieval Europe, they reached the conclusion that this equation only arose out of enmity between the author/protagonist of the text and the person afflicted. Such an association was more often a rhetorical device used to condemn the writer's adversaries than a reflection of actual beliefs about illness. Whilst sin was an important part of explanations of illness, it was not the primary part except in this specific context of animosity.[11] A man

---

[9] N. Siraisi, *Medieval and Early Renaissance Medicine* (Chicago, 1990), p. 8.

[10] For example, Alfanus I, archbishop of Salerno, translated and composed works; his close contemporary Constantine the African, a monk at Montecassino, undertook translations from the Arabic; and it is likely that many of the surviving ninth- and tenth-century codices originated in southern monasteries. We have very little evidence of this activity, and what we have comes from difficult sources: the *Vita* of the tenth-century Calabrian St Fantinus the Younger describes him undertaking calligraphy: *La Vita di San Fantino il Giovane*, ed. E. Follieri (Brussels, 1993), chap. 21.

[11] J. Kroll and B. Bachrach, "Sin and the Etiology of Disease in Pre-crusade Europe", *Journal of the History of Medicine and Allied Sciences* 41 (1986), 395-414.

or woman who injured or offended the subject of the narrative, for example a saint, or a political enemy, was then deemed deserving of some pain. Their action, rather than their character as a whole, was what was being judged. They compounded their wrong by turning to doctors. This theory, however, rests upon the selective reading of a limited number of texts and would seem to be relevant only in cases where the author of the text was a close contemporary of the protagonists: even in this limited scenario, the model does not work for southern Italian hagiographic texts.

Nevertheless, the faith of ordinary people in the power of divine healing is illustrated by a document issued by Risus, son of Maraldus of Terlizzi, in 1182. In it, he promises that if he recovers from his present (unspecified) illness, he will give all his property to and enter the church of St Angelus.[12]

More informative still is the case of Constantine son of Leo, of Fondi in Lazio. In 1039 he records that whilst at the house of his father-in-law at Terracina he fell ill and could neither drink nor speak. A miracle of the cross in the local church allowed him to make a will. Then John, the bishop of Terracina, came with holy water for Constantine to drink. The "wound" in his throat broke and he vomited *fracidume*[13] and spoke, vowing to make an offering to the church in thanks for his cure. After a period at home convalescing he returned to Terracina and made the gift.[14]

Whilst we may or may not believe the miracle that occurred to cure Constantine, some comments on his document are possible. The notable absentee in the entire proceedings is any kind of medical care, despite the fact that the illness sounds extremely serious. Perhaps we should not expect to see such care, since the document is about Constantine's gratitude to his actual healer. He perhaps had already consulted doctors in vain before the events he describes.

---

[12] F. Caraballese, ed., *Codice Diplomatico Barese, III: Le pergamene della cattedrale di Terlizzi* (Bari, 1899), p. 134.

[13] It has proved impossible to translate this term exactly from Latin; given the context, it would appear to have connections with the term *fraces*, "grounds, dregs", or the modern Italian adjective *fradicio*, "rotten".

[14] *Codex diplomaticus Cajetanus* 1 (Montecassino, 1887), doc. 172.

It is striking that even though these charters make pious gifts in the hope of, or in thanks for, a cure, they do not reveal any guilt or attach any judgement to the author's sickness. This is a crucial point: just because there was a high level of belief, for which there is much evidence, in the efficacy of saintly cures, this does not mean that the medieval southern Italian mind automatically associated these with personal salvation. Indeed, the charter material illustrates a population whose *habitus* or logical response was to purchase a cure with a pious gift, rather than seek the reason for their illness in their personal conduct.

This too is important, for another major theme in the narrative sources is the rapaciousness of doctors and their ineffectiveness in the face of disease. The scene of a sick person coming to a saint having been failed by the doctors is a common one in medieval hagiography throughout Europe.[15] The fact that he or she had seen a doctor in the first instance has been taken as crucial evidence that such were available.[16] Valerie Flint argues that the existence of doctors was essential to the viability of saints' cults, since their "failure" provided the opportunity for the saint to shine. The doctor was, in her words, an "esteemed fall-guy".[17] In order for his failure to be credible, she

---

[15] As well as those episodes discussed here, other southern Italian *vitae* contain the same pattern. St Fantinus the Younger, when he travels to Thessaloniki, cures a certain Antipas whose mother has had no success with the doctors and a man with a painful head and teeth "who had placed all hope in the doctors to no avail" ("τὴν δὲ ἐλπίδα πᾶσαν εἰς ἰατρους ἀναθέμενος, μᾶλλον τὸ ἄλγος ἐπηύξησε"): *Vita di San Fantino*, ed. Follieri, chap. 44, p. 452. Other, *post mortem*, miracles occur in the same pattern. We must, of course, be more wary of this *Vita*, since it was written in Greece and may reflect local norms of hagiography and practice rather than Italian ones.

[16] B. Baldwin, "Beyond the House Call: Doctors in Early Byzantine History and Politics", in *Symposium on Byzantine Medicine*, ed. J. Scarborough, Dumbarton Oaks Papers 38 (Washington DC, 1984), pp. 15-20 (p. 19). See also H. J. Magoulias, "The Lives of the Saints as Sources of Data for the History of Byzantine Medicine in the Sixth and Seventh Centuries", *Byzantinische Zeitschrift* 57 (1964), 127-50, for a rather uncritical view of the evidence to be gleaned from these sources.

[17] V. J. Flint, "The Early Medieval *medicus*, the Saint – and the Enchanter", *Social History of Medicine* 2 (1989), 127-45 (p. 136).

argues, the technical details of treatment administered had to be accurate, and thus hagiography, in particular, can provide far more information about medical skills in the early Middle Ages than has previously been thought.[18]

This assertion must be treated with some caution: accuracy in medical treatment was probably not a major concern of the average consumer of hagiography, even assuming that he or she would have the knowledge to recognise it. Nor does all hagiography contain the detail which Flint has found in the Frankish sources. However, to discredit the local doctor too much might lead to a devaluation of the powers of the saint. A creative tension had to exist between the two, and both might be called in to help. Recent research has demonstrated a lenient attitude on the part of patristic writers to the role of medical practitioners. Sickness as a judgement from God meant that there was little use in consulting a human healer. Christ was the true physician, one who unselfishly succoured the ill and, crucially, took no fee. However, all healing ability, according to Origen, was a gift from God, as were the herbs used by practitioners.[19] Sickness might be punishment for a sin, but doctors could be consulted so long as the patient did not place faith entirely in their skills.[20]

The tension between saints and doctors in hagiographical texts has also formed a subject of some debate, particularly within the Byzantine sphere. Alexander Kazhdan focuses on the southern Italian hagiography to support his assertion that hostility towards physicians in Byzantine hagiography reached a peak towards the end of the tenth century, before softening to the more common accommodation of them in the eleventh and twelfth centuries. The *Vita* of St Elias Speleotis, for example, describes "an ignorant and inexperienced

[18] Flint, "Early Medieval *medicus*", pp. 135-36. See also Magoulias, "Lives of the Saints".

[19] Quoted from D. Amundsen, "Medicine and Faith in Early Christianity", *Bulletin of the History of Medicine* 56 (1982), 326-50 (p. 333). On the issue of saints and doctors, see also P. Horden, "Saints and Doctors in the Early Byzantine Empire: the Case of Theodore of Sykeon", in *The Church and Healing*, ed. W. J. Sheils, Studies in Church History (Oxford, 1982), pp. 1-12.

[20] Amundsen, "Medicine and Faith", p. 341.

iatros [doctor]".[21] Kazhdan also uses an episode between St Nilus and the Jewish doctor Domnulus to support his case. Whilst Nilus is in Rossano, Domnulus offers to prescribe a drug to alleviate the saint's recurrent illness and keep him from falling sick throughout his life. The saint indignantly refuses this offer, saying that God is his doctor, that he has no need of the doctor's drugs, and that furthermore he is not going to boost Domnulus' business by allowing the doctor to boast that he has treated the holy man![22] Of course, this tale is edifying in its promotion of faith in God, but has added impact in that the person at fault is also Jewish. Domnulus is mentioned later as the physician who had failed to cure the imperial judge Eufrasius. Kazhdan does not posit any particular reason for this peak in hostility. Further investigation of the southern Italian milieu in which the saints lived, however, may provide some clues.

A precious piece of information provided by the charters is a rough distribution of those titled *medici*. None is seen in a practising context, and indeed their main function in many documents appears to have been as respected witnesses or as writers of the documents themselves. However, it is fairly safe to take these men (and one woman) as medical practitioners of some sort. In the tenth century, several Jewish practitioners are documented, one of whom, Shabbetai Donnolo of Oria in Apulia (913-post 982), has left evidence of his work.[23] Donnolo has been identified, erroneously I feel, with Domnulus, the Jewish doctor in the *Vita* of St Nilus. But his herbal does provide evidence of actual practice by a Jewish doctor in this period.

The antagonism between saint and doctor might perhaps be explained in two ways. It would be tempting to ascribe Nilus' refusal to the Christian nature of the text – that is, that Domnulus, as a Jew, was to be despised. This does not work for southern Italy, however. Here the Jewish community was numerous and, from what evidence

---

[21] "ἄπειρος ἰατρὸς": AASS Sept. vol. 3, ed. J. Stiltinger et al. (Antwerp, 1750), p. 852. Quoted in A. Kazhdan, "The Image of the Medical Doctor in Byzantine Literature of the Tenth to Twelfth Centuries", in *Symposium on Byzantine Medicine*, pp. 43-52 (p. 48).

[22] *Vita sancti Nili*, 7.50.

[23] A. Sharf, *The Universe of Shabbetai Donnolo* (Warminster, 1976).

survives, did not attract hostility as such.[24] And, crucially, Domnulus' faith is not at the core of Nilus' rebuttal. In fact, what bothers Nilus is the fact that the doctor will be able to charge higher fees and gain prestige in the community if he goes around boasting that he cured the saint. Nilus' hostility, therefore, may not be to Domnulus as doctor, but to Domnulus as fee-charger, as the text to some extent makes clear. An almost contemporary source from northern Italy reflects this view: Ratherius of Verona thought that doctors should help the poor free of charge.[25] In the case of St Elias, too, the criticism seems to be more of an individual letting down an otherwise respected tradition of medical practitioners, rather than condemning *iatroi* as a group.

The issue, then, was not simply one of a competition between faith in the doctor's skills and those of the saint. As we have seen, a choice of healer was accompanied by a transfer of assets: a successful healing saint or shrine could bring in a great deal of revenue to the church.[26] Nilus, with his direct reference to Domnulus' ability to raise

[24] Although it may be possible to see discrimination against Jews in the prices charged for land in some Salernitan documents, for example a lease of 1012 appears to charge a much heavier rent to Jews than in similar leases to Gentiles: P. Morcaldi. et al., eds, *Codex diplomaticus Cajetanus*, 1-8 (Milan, Naples, Pisa, 1873-93), vol. 4, doc. 651. See also P. Delogu, *Mito di una Città Meridionale* (Naples, 1977), p. 150. The only clear-cut persecution came from outside the peninsula in 943, a brief period of intolerance under Emperor Romanus; a more obscure episode of book-burning took place at Bari around 952: J. Mann, *Texts and Studies in Jewish History and Literature* 1 (Cincinnati, 1931), pp. 11, 13. It is unlikely that the stance of the Byzantine Church, which forbade Christians to be doctored by Jews, had very much influence in southern Italy, although the *Vita* of Nilus may be an attempt to enforce such a policy. Indeed Magoulias, "Lives of the Saints", pp. 132-33, cites the episode between Nilus and Domnulus to illustrate the prohibition.

[25] J.-L. Goglin, *Les Misérables dans l'occident médiéval* (Paris, 1976), p. 42.

[26] Even if, as Peregrine Horden convincingly argues, "we have perhaps taken the hagiographers too much at their word, failing to question their recurrent implication that saints were readily available to those in need", it is still true to say that access to a church, in which to pray to that saint and offer gifts, was rather easier: P. Horden, "Responses to Possession and Insanity in the Earlier Byzantine world", *Social History of Medicine* 6 (1993), 177-94 (p. 181).

his prices, is not (or at least, not only) criticising the doctor's avarice, but is acknowledging the drop in offerings to the church that might ensue. In southern Italy, the competition from *medici* was strong – the charters provide evidence of a substantial number (and there must have been many more who offered cures but were not designated with the title *medicus*) – and so it might be expected that competition in this region might be expressed in the texts with particular acuteness. That is, the sharpness noted by Kazhdan is a regional rather than a chronological one.

A further cause of conflict here may have been the opportunity for patronage. If we examine the distribution of *medici* in relation to what we know of the political history of the area, we find clusters of them around centres of power. For example, the principate of Salerno and the duchy of Naples both had stable, strong rulers in the tenth and early eleventh centuries, and these appear to have attracted *medici*. When, after the Norman conquest, the focus of power was in Sicily, *medici* are documented there too.[27]

All medieval rulers were keenly aware of their duty to patronise their local church and churchmen, and to attract or bring holy relics to their city, but in terms of their own health they were also the ones with most access to doctors.[28] If, therefore, they favoured these over the powers of a local shrine, the poor example set to their people (among whom most lived in cities), could be potentially very damaging to the church's prestige and/or income.[29]

---

[27] This picture must, of course, take account of the production and survival of the charters themselves: where there was a ruler, more charters would be produced, making it statistically more likely that *medici* would be recorded if they were present.

[28] For example, the *Chronicon Salernitanum*, chap. 163, tells of one Peter, a cleric and medic who was very dear to Prince Gisolf (943-78), and later became bishop of Salerno.

[29] Paul the Deacon provides an example of each type of recourse by Lombard kings. King Grimoald ruptured the vein of his arm. "Cui, ut ferunt, medici venenata medicamina supponentes, eum ab hac funditus privarunt luce" ("The doctors, as they say, administered poisoned medicines and totally withdrew him from this life"): *Historia Langobardorum*, 5.33. Paul's disapproval, as a cleric, is obvious. King Liutprand's nephew was injured with an arrow during hunting, and the king sent to a holy man, Baodolinus, for

It is possible to argue, however, that in southern Italy the clergy were conscious of and determined to control the activities of medics. The first thing to consider is the almost monopolistic position that the clergy exerted over the transference of medical texts. Admittedly this was a region where the level of lay literacy was probably higher than any other part of medieval Europe,[30] but there is little evidence of laymen copying texts.[31] Even if many *medici* appear to have been valued for their writing skills, clerics maintained a measure of control over the dissemination of texts. And if, as seems likely, the activities of the Salernitan "medical school" began in the eleventh century with the work of clerics like Archbishop Alfanus, it would appear that the clergy were keen to confine scientific knowledge within a firm framework of Christian faith as well.

It is no coincidence that the advance of scientific medicine in the late eleventh and early twelfth centuries was accompanied by the development of a notion of personal salvation much stronger than had existed before, and the beginning of the systematic attack on Jews, major providers of medical care, among other things, in canonist literature.[32] From the mid-twelfth century, several church councils began to forbid monks and canons to study medicine for the sake of temporal gain or to leave their cloisters to practice medicine elsewhere, and eminent churchmen such as John of Salisbury and Bernard of Clairvaux reacted against consulting doctors.[33] This type

prayers, but the boy had died before the messenger reached the holy man: *Historia Langobardorum*, 7.8. The implication is that something effective might have been done had Baodolinus reached the scene in time.

[30] I have summarised the evidence for this assertion in "Women, Literacy and Invisibility in Medieval Southern Italy", in *Women, the Book and the Worldly*, ed. L. Smith and J. Taylor (Cambridge, 1995), pp. 1-11.

[31] For example, despite the apparent concentration of lay *medici* in Naples, the only documented "book of the arts of medicine" is listed among the possessions of a church, that of St Euthimius in the city: "Regesta Neapolitana", in *Monumenta ad Neapolitani historiam pertinentia*, 2.1, ed. B. Capasso (Naples, 1885), docs 162 and 179.

[32] Moore, *Formation of a Persecuting Society*, p. 7. Already, in 1063, the Jews had been expelled from Benevento: Moore, *Formation of a Persecuting Society*, p. 32.

[33] Siraisi, *Early Medieval and Renaissance Medicine*, p. 13.

of evidence suggests that the nub of clerical objections was really the monetary aspect, and the real progress made in medicine in these centuries probably inflated the fees that doctors could charge. The keenness of rulers like Frederick II in Italy to exercise control over medical practitioners may also have been motivated by financial considerations: licensing was an easy way to increase fiscal revenue.[34]

If finding a cure had been a matter of faith to the church fathers, I believe that it soon became far more important to clerics to ensure that the income from pious donations in the hope of cures was not damaged by the activities of medical practitioners. It may not have been a clear-cut case of the patient seeking help from one or the other: any number of sources may have been tapped for help.[35] In an area like southern Italy, where medical learning was carefully preserved, and medical practitioners were relatively numerous, the need for an aggressively vigilant stance on the part of saints and their biographers, as well as that of the keepers of holy relics and Christian cult centres, was especially felt. Clerics responded by constructing, and maintaining, a distinction between "good" payments to saints and ecclesiastical institutions, and "bad" payments to avaricious doctors.[36] And their success in maintaining belief in the efficacy of divine intervention is expressed by the charter evidence from this region. *Medici*, it is clear, were respected members of their communities, to judge by their numbers and their appearances as proprietors, witnesses and redactors of documents. But the surviving evidence for pious donations in the context of illness shows that they

[34] D. Abulafia, *Frederick II: a Medieval Emperor* (Oxford, 1988), p. 264.

[35] A point made by Flint, "Early Medieval *medicus*", and Horden, Responses to Possession".

[36] An essential aspect of this difference appears to be the strong expectation of a positive outcome in the case of gifts offered to the church, although there is no parallel in southern Italy to the ritual humiliation of saints (or their effigies) who had not performed, highlighted recently by Patrick Geary, "Humiliation of Saints", in his *Living with the Dead in the Middle Ages* (Ithaca, NY, 1994), pp. 95-115. Payments to doctors, on the other hand, were characterised by clerical writers as a waste of money. It is interesting, nevertheless, to find no mention in hagiography of any sanctions against a doctor who failed to perform a cure that had been paid for.

had strong competition from supernatural sources, who might command exactly the same levels of payment.

Scandinavian Law in a Tenth-Century Rus'-Greek Commercial Treaty?

Martina Stein-Wilkeshuis

During Viking times and indeed long before, groups of people travelled by ship from Northern Europe along the Russian rivers in a southern direction in pursuit of trade, booty, asylum, or adventure. Often their goal was Constantinople, in Old Norse called *Mikligarðr*, the great city. Their name was Rus'.

The debate concerning the identity of these Rus' seems to be closed now: linguistic, especially onomastic,[1] and archaeological evidence,[2] and results of investigations into the political structure

The translations of the Scandinavian articles of law are my own. I would like to thank Dr J. Schaeken of Groningen University and Dr W. Vermeer of Leiden University for their help with the translation of the Old Russian text of the Nestor Chronicle. Although references are given to the primary texts, in this article the Old Russian material will only be given in translation.

[1] V. L. P. Thomsen, *The Relations Between Ancient Russia and Scandinavia and the Origin of the Russian State* (Oxford, 1877; repr. 1965), lectures 2, 3, and Appendix.

[2] I. Jansson, "Communications Between Scandinavia and Eastern Europe in the Viking Age", in *Abhandlungen der Akademie von Wissenschaften in Göttingen*, Philologisch-Historische Klasse 3, 156 (Göttingen, 1987). J. Graham-Campbell et al., eds, *Cultural Atlas of the Viking World* (New York, 1994), pp. 184-98.

including tax system,[3] indicate the short-lived but rather influential presence of Scandinavians, especially Swedes, in the area. Information on these journeys and the development of important commercial and political centres en route, Staraia Ladoga, Novgorod and Kiev, is given by the twelfth-century Old Russian Nestor Chronicle.[4] The remarkable thing about this chronicle is that three tenth-century charters have been included, treaties between Rus' and Greek after Russian attacks on Constantinople.[5] The 911 treaty in particular, signed by Rus' princes and merchants bearing Scandinavian names, was favourable for the Rus'. Besides all kinds of commercial privileges it provides articles regarding the legal position of merchants with respect to the procedure in cases of manslaughter, injury, theft and robbery.

So far, hardly any attention has been paid to the origins of the legal articles, and those few scholars who have studied them have assumed the influence of Byzantine law.[6] However, a close reading of the original text reveals the possibility of other interpretations. In this paper I shall look at the articles from a different perspective and compare them with medieval Scandinavian legal institutions. For this comparison many Scandinavian lawbooks are available, all of them written down in the twelfth and thirteenth centuries, after the

[3] S. Mikucki, "Etudes sur la diplomatique russe la plus ancienne, les traités byzantino-russes du Xe siècle", *Bulletin international de l'Académie polonaise des Sciences et des Lettres* (1953), Suppl. 7.

[4] Named after the Kievan monk Nestor, the supposed author. It is also known as the *Povest' Vremennych let* and the Primary Chronicle. Text: D. Cizevskij, ed., *Die Nestor-Chronik* (Wiesbaden, 1969); translations: S. H. Cross and O. P. Sherbowitz-Wetzor, trans, *The Russian Primary Chronicle* (Cambridge, Mass., 1953); R. Trautmann, trans., *Die altrussische Nestorcronik. Povest' Vremennich let* (Leipzig, 1931).

[5] G. Ostrogorskij, "L'expédition du Prince Oleg contre Constantinople en 907", *Annales de l'Institut Kondakov* 11 (1939), 47-61; A. A. Vasiliev, *The Second Russian Attack on Constantinople*, Dumbarton Oaks Papers 6 (Washington DC, 1951).

[6] For instance I. Sorlin, "Les traités de Byzance avec la Russie au Xe siècle", *Cahiers du monde russe et soviétique* 2 (1961), 313-60 and 447-75.

introduction of writing in the northern countries.[7] Important new regulations on the Christian religion and politics, and traditional laws and customs stand side by side, and disentangling old and new is often a risky enterprise. Because of this situation we cannot be satisfied with pointing out a few accidental parallels between our tenth-century source and the later Scandinavian material. Only clear traces and fundamental resemblances, both with regard to system and details, will make a reasonable case for the possible Scandinavian origin of the legal articles preserved in the Nestor Chronicle.

I begin with the procedure:

> With regard to the prescriptions on offences we agree the following: as far as something has been publicised by way of public statements of witnesses made according to the rules, it is to be believed. But if it is not believed, the party who wants to deny has to do so by way of an oath. After having taken the oath in accordance with his faith, the punishment has to be in conformity with the offence.[8]

This states that publication of offences and charges by way of witnesses is a prerequisite, and if this has been done in the prescribed way, the charge is considered to be well-founded. The basis of the early Scandinavian jurisdiction, and indeed of several continental early medieval *leges* too, was the principle of public knowledge: facts and agreements had to be well-known, as had the legal position between individuals. In a largely illiterate society the law, therefore, required not only important contracts involving marriages,

---

[7] C. J. Schlyter, ed., *Samling av Sweriges Gamla Lagar* (Stockholm, 1827-77); R. Keyser, P. A. Munch, G. Storm and E. Hertzberg, eds, *Norges gamle Love indtil 1387*, vols 1-5 (Kristiania [Oslo], 1846-95); English translation in L. M. Larson, trans., *The Earliest Norwegian Laws. Being the Gulathing Law and the Frostathing Law* (New York, 1935); V. Finsen, ed., *Grágás Konungsbók, Staðarhólsbók* and *Skálholtsbók* (Copenhagen, 1852, 1879 and 1883); English translation in A. Dennis, P. Foote and R. Perkins, trans., *Laws of Early Iceland, Grágás I* (Winnipeg, 1980); J. Brøndum-Nielsen and P. J. Jørgensen, eds, *Danmarks gamle Landskabslove med Kirkelovene*, vols 1-8 (Copenhagen, 1933-61).

[8] Cizevskij, *Nestor-Chronik*, p. 33.

inheritance, selling and buying land to be publicised, but also conflicts and injuries.[9] Thus, a man who killed someone or inflicted injury on somebody should publicise it as his work, and the offended party should publicise it as a charge against him. A Swedish lawbook puts it thus: "Uärþär maþer dräpin ok af daghum takin, þa skal uighi a þingi lysä".[10] Public knowledge could be achieved by calling certain facts to the attention of assembled men, usually at the Assembly, or an ale-feast, or by making an official appeal to at least two "good men", free men who had come of age, the witnesses, who had to remember what was settled. A "witness" is defined as a person who on the basis of what he has seen and heard, knows something about the matter involved, so that he is able to make a reliable statement in court. His testimony served to fix the existence of a legal situation only, not to find out the truth or the cause of a case. An unpublicised crime was considered worse than one which had been given public notice: a secret and unpublicised killing with the body being hidden, for example, would be legally treated as murder, and secretly taking away somebody's property, with the loot hidden and the tracks covered up, as theft. For the offender this meant the loss of all rights. As a Norwegian lawbook says: "en ef lýsir eigi svá vígi þá er hann mordinge réttr. oc bæði fyrirgort löndum oc lausum eyre oc koma hann alldri í land aptr".[11]

The prescription on taking an oath shows that in our articles the right of proof usually rested with the defendant: if the case was not self-evident, or had not been properly publicised by the plaintiff, the defendant was entitled to prove his innocence by taking an oath. All Scandinavian lawbooks are familiar with this institution and provide detailed prescriptions on the purgatory oath, sometimes taken alone,

---

[9] E. Hertzberg, *Grundtrækkene i den ældste Norske proces* (Kristiania [Oslo], 1874); *Kulturhistorisk Leksikon for Nordisk Middelalder*, 2nd ed. (Copenhagen, 1980), articles on "Rettergang", "Straff", "Vitne".

[10] Schlyter, ed., *Samling av Sweriges Gamla Lagar*, Äldre Västgötalagen, Af Mandrapi 1: "If a man is assaulted and deprived of his life the killing shall be published at the Assembly". See also Keyser et al., eds, *Norges gamle Love*, Frostathings-Lov, 4.7.

[11] Keyser et al., eds, *Norges gamle Love*, Frostathings-Lov, 4.7; "And if he (the killer) does not report the slaying this way, he is in the highest degree a murderer and has forfeited land and chattel, and shall never return to the land".

sometimes also with the help of so-called "oath-helpers". If the defendant did not succeed in clearing himself, the charge was considered to be well-founded, and judgement was passed.

Punishment, according to the Nestor Chronicle, had to be in accordance with the offence. In early Scandinavian sources as also in various medieval continental *leges*, punishments were directly related to the crime and meant to compensate the victim, they were neither dependent on the circumstances of the offence, nor meant to educate the offender.

The article on manslaughter states:

> If a Rus' kills a Christian, or a Christian a Rus', he has to die on the spot where he commits this manslaughter. If the one who committed manslaughter flees, and if he owns property, the nearest relative of the man killed must take his share, that is to say what is legally due to him, but the wife of the person who killed has to keep as much as rests with her legally. If the person who committed manslaughter and fled, is poor, the charge against him must remain until he is found, then he has to die.[12]

The first sentence suggests that revenge is to be executed on the scene of the offence, at the moment it happened, and on the offender personally. It is not clear which person is entitled to take revenge.[13] In general, the law of the Nordic countries allowed revenge in cases of serious crimes, such as manslaughter, injury, theft, verbal or other insult, or sexual offences committed against close kinswomen. In cases of killing the Swedish laws stipulate: "Dræpær maþær man varþær han siþen dræpin a fotum hanum liggi a værkum sinum. böti huarti konungi ellær hæræþi".[14] In other words: revenge was to be

---

[12] Cizevskij, *Nestor-Chronik*, p. 33.

[13] M. Stein-Wilkeshuis, "Legal Prescriptions on Manslaughter and Injury in a Viking Age Treaty Between Constantinople and Northern Merchants", *Scandinavian Journal of History* 19 (1994), 1-16.

[14] Schlyter, ed., *Samling av Sweriges Gamla Lagar*, Äldre Västgötalagen, Af Mandrapi 6; "A man kills somebody else. If he is killed then at the dead man's

taken on the offender only, and preferably on the same spot as the offence. Compare "at the dead man's feet" with "on the spot" of the Russian article.

The next part of the legal article deals with a killer who has fled. If this happened, the relative had to take his legal share. This shows that it was the next of kin who was entitled to receive compensation. We may assume that this compensation was paid from the property of the offender and/or his next of kin. Apparently his wife's possessions were excepted from this payment; she was allowed to keep as much as rested with her legally. In Scandinavian sources a similar attitude is seen: paying and receiving compensation, a "mangeld", was a matter for the kin, depending on the grade of relationship. Contrary to the articles under discussion, it was not restricted to cases where the killer had fled, but it was always possible to compensate killings by an amount of money, although there is evidence that this was despised: "I do not want to carry my brother in my purse", is a well-known Old Icelandic saying. Usually compensation was paid from the yield of confiscation of the offender's property. All lawbooks provide detailed information on the convening of a special court of confiscation. Excepted from confiscation was the property of the offender's wife: "En allt þat er kononne er golldit með vitum oc með váttom eða í öðro fé. þá á hon þat allt".[15]

The Nestor Chronicle article on injuries is as follows:

> If somebody strikes another person with a sword or hits him with some pot, he must according to Russian law, pay five pounds of silver for this stroke or blow. If the person who did this is poor he has to pay as much as he can, and even take off the clothes in which he walks around, and in addition take an oath according to his faith that he has

feet, he lays there by his own deed and no compensation is to be paid for him to the king or the country". See also Östgötalagen, Drapa Balkær 2.

[15] Keyser et al., eds, *Norges gamle Love*, Frostathings-Lov 5.13; "But whatever has been paid to the man's wife with wit and witness or given her in other forms of property, all that she shall keep". See also Finsen, *Grágás*, Konungsbók 49.

nobody to help him. After that the charge against
him is not to be continued.[16]

This shows that, like manslaughter, inflicting injuries was seen as a
violation of personal integrity. Unlike manslaughter, injury demanded
a fixed compensation for the victim: five pounds of silver. Although
Norwegian and Icelandic law acknowledge the right of revenge in
case of injuries,[17] in general Scandinavian law required payment of a
weight of precious metals (a mark) as a compensation to the victim.
Distinction was thereby made between the respective categories of
wounds, the fines being adapted according to their seriousness or
size.[18] The legal articles under discussion here do not make this
distinction: in theory a wound is a wound, and a blow a blow and the
standard-tariff is five pounds of silver.

Although the insistence that the offender should "even take off
the clothes in which he walks around" may seem somewhat curious,
undressing a person is also found in Icelandic saga literature as a way
of humiliating defeated enemies, and in some Scandinavian lawbooks
as a means of compensation for theft of food. Danish and Swedish
laws issued a prohibition on stripping dead bodies.[19] With regard to
the words "take an oath", our discussion of the procedure has shown
that oaths formed part of the normal legal practice. The words "that
he has nobody to help him" recall the collective responsibility as an
important element of Scandinavian law, postulating that compen-
sations were to be yielded by the kin. In practice, the situation of
travelling merchants caused a break-up of family ties, and made an
appeal to help from relatives not feasible. This may be the reason
why the offender would have "nobody" to help him.

---

[16] Cizevskij, *Nestor-Chronik*, pp. 33-34.

[17] Keyser et al., eds, *Norges gamle Love*, Gulathings-Lov 189; Finsen,
Grágás, Konungsbók 86.

[18] Schlyter, ed., *Samling av Sweriges Gamla Lagar*, Äldre Västgötalagen,
Af särämalum bolkar, pp. 1-6 and Östgötalagen, Uaþa mal ok sara mal, hor, ran
ok styld, pp. 5-26. T. Wennström, *Brott och Böter: Rättsfilologiska Studier i
Svenska Landskapslagar* (Lund, 1940).

[19] K. E. Gade, "The Naked and the Dead in Old Norse Society",
Scandinavian Studies 60 (1988), 219-45.

The Nestor Chronicle's legal articles dealing with theft are as follows:

> If any Rus' steals something from a Christian man,
> or the other way round a Christian man from a
> Rus', and the thief is caught by the victim at the
> moment he is committing the theft, or when
> preparing himself to commit a theft, and if he is
> killed thereby, no compensation is to be required
> for his death, neither by Christians nor by Rus'.
> And first of all the victim has to recover his
> properties. If the one who stole surrenders, he shall
> be taken and bound by the one against whom the
> theft was committed, and he has to return whatever
> he dared to steal, making a threefold restitution for
> it at the same time.[20]

There is a question here of the right of revenge; the victim is personally entitled to kill the thief at the time and the place of the action. It is clear that by the offence the thief loses his legal protection, is a man without rights who may be slain with impunity, and for whom no compensation can be claimed.[21]

How does Scandinavian law handle thieves? One article states: "Ef maðr tekr fe manz oc vinnr þiofscap at. enda standi hin hann at þvi er fe þat á. sva at hand numit verðr. oc fellr sa oheilagr er fe hefir tekit fyrir þeim manne er fe þat atte er þiofstolit var a þeim véttvangi oc sva fyrir þeim öllum er honom veita lið at þvi",[22] showing that in this system too, theft was, like murder, considered one of the most detestable crimes, as it was committed secretly. Because of this, a thief lost his legal protection and revenge could be taken on him

[20] Cizevskij, *Nestor-Chronik*, p. 34.

[21] M. Stein-Wilkeshuis, "A Viking-age Treaty Between Constantinople and Northern Merchants, with its Provisions on Theft and Robbery", *Scando-Slavica* 37 (1991), 35-47.

[22] Finsen, ed., *Grágás*, Staðarhólsbók 367; "If a man takes another man's property and commits theft thereby, or if he is found with the stolen goods in his hands, then the one who took the property falls at that place of action with forfeit immunity if killed by the man who owned that property and by all those who give him help in this". See also Keyser et al., eds, *Norges gamle Love*, Frostathings-Lov, Indledning Hakon Hakonsson 9.

without legal redress. The laws permitted the injured person or his helper to exact revenge at the place of the offence and at the moment the thief was caught red-handed. Some lawbooks also acknowledge the right of revenge on someone who was preparing a theft.[23]

The second part of the Russian article stipulates that if the victim of a theft decides not to make use of his right to revenge, he has to bind the thief, and probably take him to court, where the offender will be sentenced to return the stolen property and pay three times its value to the owner.

There is a Swedish legal article which similarly shows that the possibility was left open that a victim might not wish to employ his right to revenge: "Nu stial man inne unde lase ok uarþær takin uiþær: þa skal þiufnaþ a bak hanum binda ok til þingxs föra".[24] Apart from restitution of the stolen goods the thief then had to pay two or three times their value to the victim of the theft.

The next article in the Nestor Chronicle deals with the theft, escape or illegal sale of a slave:

> In addition, if a Russian slave is stolen, or escapes, or is sold under compulsion, the Rus' have to institute a claim, and a statement of witnesses is made regarding the slave, then they take the slave back with them. Also, if merchants lose a slave and institute a complaint they have to search, and when he has been found, take the slave back to Rus'. If somebody does not permit this search operation, the occupant shall forfeit his right.[25]

Slaves were valuable articles of commerce, and to a merchant the loss of a slave meant serious damage. This prescription for the institution of an official claim with witnesses is in accordance with what has been said above with regard to the rules of procedure, both in Scandinavian law and in the Nestor Chronicle.

---

[23] See Keyser et al., eds, *Norges gamle Love*, Gulathings-Lov 160.

[24] Schlyter, ed., *Samling av Sweriges Gamla Lagar*, Östgötalagen, Uaþa mal etc. 32.1; "if someone steals something from a locked house and is caught red-handed, then one shall tie the stolen goods on his back and take him to the Assembly".

[25] Cizevskij, *Nestor-Chronik*, pp. 35-36.

The last sentence of the article has been something of a puzzle for the translators of the Nestor Chronicle.[26] I have presented here the literal translation, and my suggestion is that the words "somebody", "occupant" and "his" denote one and the same person, and that the stipulation is to be interpreted as a house search: if the merchant did not get back his slave he was entitled to organise a house search at the home of the one whom he suspected of the theft, after having performed the necessary formalities, and if the occupant did not permit this he lost his right to domestic peace, and the search operation was to be undertaken with violence.

In Scandinavia, the house search was widely applied for all sorts of theft, all law books devoting a special chapter to the institution; it was subject to strict rules and to be undertaken on the initiative and under the leadership of the person who had fallen victim to theft: "Ef þeir vilia eigi láta hafa lucla at lúka lásom upp. oc verða lóc þeirra oheilog við brote".[27] Medieval Frisian law also preserves traces of the institution.[28] Danish laws show that a stolen slave could be looked for in the same way: "Ransak skal ængin man syniæ andrum, þær ær han uil ransakæ æftir hiona sinu".[29]

Finally the Nestor Chronicle's article on robbery states: "If any person whether Greek or Rus', forcibly extorts something from somebody and appropriates with open violence some articles of his property, he shall repay three times their value".[30] This stipulation deals with violently taking away other people's property, an offence considered to be less punishable than theft; revenge is not applicable

---

[26] Trautmann, *Die altrussische Nestorcronik*, p. 22; Cross, *The Russian Primary Chronicle*, p. 68; Sorlin, "Les traités de Byzance", p. 335.

[27] Finsen, *Grágás*, Konungsbók, Rannsókna-þattr, 230 (p. 167); "If they will not let them have the keys, the locks forfeit their immunity when being prised off".

[28] Martina Stein-Wilkeshuis, "Frisian Law and the 'Forbidding Northern Countries Overseas'", *Journal of Legal History* 18 (1997), 17-29.

[29] Brøndum-Nielsen, *Danmarks gamle Landskabslove*, Skånske Lov, chap. 134; "No one shall refuse to allow someone else to undertake a house search for a stolen slave". Also Skånske Lov, Anders Sunesøns Latinske Parafrase, chap. 79, and Schlyter, ed., *Samling av Sweriges Gamla Lagar*, Skånelagen 136b.

[30] Cizevskij, *Nestor-Chronik*, p. 34.

here, and the robber has to compensate three times the value of the robbed goods to the victim.

In Scandinavia too, robbery, contrary to theft, was regarded as a fair crime because it was committed openly and the victim had a chance to defend himself. A well-known Old Icelandic saying illustrates this attitude: "Vikings have the habit of gathering booty by robbery, thieves on the contrary conceal it afterwards". Robbery in its unqualified form was punished relatively mildly by the payment of a three-marks fine as a compensation to the victim, revenge not being applicable.

Our comparison of the legal articles of the 911 treaty with Scandinavian medieval law has demonstrated that the basic principles of Scandinavian law and the 911 treaty are similar: with regard to the procedure, both focus on the publication of offences, by the offender and/or the offended party. The role of witnesses is prominent, their public statements forming an essential part of the procedure. The right of proof rests with the defendant who, in dubious cases, is entitled to prove his innocence by taking an oath. Unpublicised offences are the worst: theft, a secret crime, is more serious than robbery. Offences were legally considered private insults, the victim or his next of kin being entitled to receive compensation. Revenge after a killing and theft also belonged to the basic principles, it was ito be taken on the offender personally, at the time and the place of the action.

Moreover, some striking parallel details are evident. First, the exceptional position of the wife's goods with the confiscation of her husband's properties; the taking off of clothes as a means of compensation in case of insolvency is another such common feature; and finally, the house search operation, enabling the victim of theft to look for his lost belongings, are found in both sources.

To conclude: the law included in the articles of the 911 Rus'-Greek treaty, bears definite resemblances to Scandinavian law, both in procedure and in detail. It fits perfectly well into the picture of onomastic, archaeological and political evidence, indicating the presence of Scandinavians in Kievan Rus'. If this conclusion is accepted, these legal articles may represent the earliest testimony of Scandinavian law known so far, dating from a period when the latter was still orally transmitted, and provide interesting data on the legal history of early Scandinavia.

IV   DEATH, BURIAL AND COMMEMORATION

Burial, Ritual and Merovingian Society

Guy Halsall

Frederick Paxton has written that:

> Archaeological finds are rich but anthropologists
> and archaeologists have not solved the vexing
> problems of the relations between ritual behavior
> and mortuary remains, or between religious
> change and forms of burial. In neither case is there
> an easy way to derive the former from the latter.[1]

Identifying religious change from burial forms is indeed a thankless
task as numerous studies have shown,[2] although these have not yet
made much impact on early medieval archaeology. However, if we
turn to the first of Paxton's problems, the relationship between
mortuary remains and ritual behaviour, then there are greater
grounds for optimism, and it is on this subject that some ideas will
be proposed in this essay.

The paper is grounded primarily in the data of the
Merovingian region of Metz.[3] The relevant evidence almost

---

[1] F. S. Paxton, *Christianizing Death: The Creation of a Ritual Process in
Early Medieval Europe* (Cornell, 1990), p. 3.

[2] See especially B. K. Young, "Merovingian Funeral Rites and the
Evolution of Christianity: a Study in the Historical Interpretation of
Archaeological Material" (unpublished PhD dissertation, University of
Pennsylvania, 1975).

[3] G. Halsall, *Settlement and Social Organization: The Merovingian
Region of Metz* (Cambridge, 1995), contains the empirical basis for this paper:

exclusively comprises archaeological data: burials with grave-goods. Written descriptions of funerals come mainly from further south, where different burial styles were in use, and this makes it difficult to match up the plentiful archaeological data from north of the Loire with what we know about funerals from written sources. Nevertheless, general comparisons can be suggested. Study of Anglo-Saxon and Alamannic cemeteries also suggests that this paper's general points might be more widely applicable in "grave-good-burying" regions.

The advantage of the archaeological evidence is that it allows us to study a ritual over two hundred years of development, permitting us to introduce both the temporal element which is all too often absent in anthropological studies of ritual, and to look at practice, rather than what people periodically said should be done, something rarely possible in documentary historical analyses. In the early medieval period it is very rare, too, to be able to follow the workings of a frequent ritual over two centuries.

Burial north of the Loire can be divided into a number of constituent components, all of which are visible in the excavated evidence. It should be stressed that each of these components represents the outcome of particular, active choices. First of all, the body seems to have been dressed for its burial. The funerary clothing could be elaborate, or extremely simple (maybe just a shroud), leaving no archaeological trace; it is extremely unlikely that anybody was actually interred naked. The body was, however, dressed in a very deliberate way, as will be seen. At about the same time, the grave was dug at the cemetery site. A number of variables were, again, open: the grave's shape and size, the means, if any, of revetting its sides; the possible construction of chambers within the grave for the deposition of particular grave-goods.

see chapters 3-4 for discussion of cemetery sites, the problems of the data, and references, and chapters 8-9 for interpretation. This paper develops some aspects of that interpretation. Some elements also derive from a paper, "Burying the Author? Graves as Texts in the Study of Gender in Sixth-century Merovingian Society", given to the Gender and Medieval Studies Group's annual conference in Cardiff in January 1992.

Then the body was transported to the cemetery. As far as one can tell, sixth-century Merovingian cemeteries, like Roman grave-yards, lay away from the centres of habitation, so the transportation of the body must have processed at least a few hundred metres. The body was then interred. Like the clothing of the body, its positioning appears to have been another variable, resulting from conscious choices. Any grave-goods could include other dress adjuncts, like belts and purses or pouches, not worn but placed by the body, and it is important to note the difference between these options. Other accessories to costume, such as weaponry, could, in the case of swords or scramasaxes, be worn in their scabbards, or deposited next to, or otherwise on the body. Finally, there was an array of other grave-goods, such as pottery, glass-ware, other vessels, and so on, deposited around the body. The positioning of the grave-goods was, again, deliberate and meaningful.

A final element of the funeral process was feasting by the grave. This is suggested by a number of archaeological features: pits on cemetery sites containing ashes, bones and broken pottery; similar traces in the fills of graves; and pottery and other food offerings in the grave itself. The latter evidence and the position of other elements in the grave's fill suggest that the feasting was done before the grave was filled in.

The key to understanding grave-good deposits like these is to see the funeral as an important space for the writing of a symbolic "text".[4] The artefacts placed in the grave were significant vessels for the storage and transmission of social information. It seems that an artefact's size and material could be used to convey important information. Not only that, but pottery and metalwork provide surfaces which were frequently decorated. This decoration has only recently begun to be studied as a form of iconography[5] but one thing

---

[4] On interpreting material culture as text, see C. Tilley, ed., *Reading Material Culture. Structuralism, Hermeneutics and Post-Structuralism* (Oxford, 1990); D. Miller, *Artefacts as Categories. A Study of Ceramic Variability in Central India* (Cambridge, 1985).

[5] D. Leigh, "Ambiguity in Anglo-Saxon Style. I Art", *Antiquaries Journal* 64 (1984), 34-42; T. M. Dickinson, "Material Culture as Social Expression: The Case of Saxon Saucer Brooches with Running Spiral Decoration", *Studien zur*

which has been remarked upon is the apparently deliberate ambiguity of its symbolism. This leads to an important point; even at the most basic level, objects are polysemic. The example used by Ellen-Jane Pader,[6] perhaps the first person to reveal the fact that burials were texts which had to be read in much more sophisticated ways than had hitherto (or, for that matter, since) been the case, is that of the straw hat or boater. As an item of clothing it could symbolise an Etonian, a Vaudeville performer or a gondolier. To decide which of these is the case we need more contextual information. To be "translated" at a basic level, all symbols, no matter how elaborate or technical, have to be incorporated into sets with other symbols. This is true not only of items of clothing, but of all the other variables mentioned above. It is surely unreasonable to suppose that crossing the deceased's arms on his or her chest, or digging a grave with bowed sides or rounded ends, always meant exactly the same thing. All the elements listed earlier form individual symbols, or "words". Some may relate to different things; others may add emphasis or clarification. But it is the burial itself which combines these into an overall coded message. To understand this message, then, we need to look at all the variables and study closely their correlations and combinations. This would seemingly give an almost endless array of possibilities, and this study is limited by the fact that excavators of Merovingian cemeteries do not yet observe or publish all the necessary information. In this paper I should like to pursue this symbolic, linguistic interpretation by analogy with ritual language.

Sachsenforschung 7 (1991), 39-70; H. Härke, "Changing Symbols in a Changing Society: The Anglo-Saxon Weapon Burial Rite in the Seventh Century", in *The Age of Sutton Hoo. The Seventh Century in North-Western Europe*, ed. M. O. H. Carver (Woodbridge, 1992), pp. 149-65; J. D. Richards, "Anglo-Saxon Symbolism", in *The Age of Sutton Hoo*, ed. Carver, pp. 131-47.

[6] E.-J. Pader, "Material Symbolism and Social Relations in Mortuary Studies", in *Anglo-Saxon Cemeteries 1979*, ed. P. A. Rahtz, T. M. Dickinson and L. Watts, British Archaeological Reports, British Series 82 (Oxford, 1980), pp. 143-59. See also E.-J. Pader, *Symbolism, Social Relations and the Interpretation of Mortuary Remains*, British Archaeological Reports, Supplementary Series 130 (Oxford, 1981).

It is, furthermore, important to note that the precise meaning of a statement or symbol, or its "tone", is also created by the context in which it is made or seen. The early medieval cemetery, a shared ritual site away from the settlement and reached by a funerary procession, "frames" the statement made by the burial; it is the context which clarifies the precise meaning of the symbolic language employed in the burial.[7] In other words, the meanings of symbols which might, in everyday life, have been employed in diverse and imprecise ways are focused into a particular semantic range by the clear context in which the symbols are employed. The best way to see the sixth-century cemetery is as the field for a frequently competitive discourse, with individual graves as the (albeit lacunose) texts of statements within that discourse, and the elements of the burial as the symbolic language used to make the statement.

There is another important element to be understood here: time. This text was intended to be read, and understood, very briefly. As soon as the grave was filled in, seemingly at the end of the rite, the message would no longer be visible. It therefore needed a large audience of people present during the ritual. Sixth-century cemeteries appear to be large, and apparently served a number of local settlements. This, of course, allowed the funeral to incorporate and unify, at least potentially, all the elements of a dispersed rural community in a shared ritual.[8] The procession with the body from the settlement to the cemetery would also help display certain elements of the message to an audience. We can confirm that all this did constitute a public field of display, if confirmation is felt necessary, from the fragmentary written sources. Gregory of Tours, for example, refers to people following a royal funeral procession in Soissons "as though dressed up for the burial of their spouses".[9] To be understood by this large but transient audience, the display

---

[7] For a discussion of framing, see Miller, *Artefacts as Categories*, pp. 181-83.

[8] This, of course, is a standard element of ritual.

[9] Gregory of Tours, *Libri historiarum X*, 5.34, ed. B. Krusch and W. Levison, MGH SRM 1.1, 2nd ed. (Hanover, 1951); *Gregory of Tours. The History of the Franks*, trans. L. Thorpe (Harmondsworth, 1974).

needed clear rules, the "grammar" discussed above, and the clarification of the symbolism by its "framing" within the cemetery.

Some of this grammar becomes visible in the course of closer analysis. There are some correlations between the grave-goods, their type and their number, and the age and sex of the deceased. This shows that the clothing of the corpse, as well as the other artefacts placed in the grave with the body, was deliberately chosen to transmit information about the deceased. There were other correlations suggested, between skeletal positioning and grave-type, between the lay-out of the grave-goods and grave-type, and between grave-size and grave-type, but on the whole all the variables seemed fundamentally independent.[10] One thing which should be noted is that the people who received the most lavish interments, in terms of grave-goods at least, were those who will have played an important public role: young women; young male adults; and especially some mature adult males. This seems to be mirrored in the public nature of their burial.

How does all this work as ritual?[11] The first point is that it deals with cosmology. We do not know what was said over the grave as part of the "funeral service" or feasting, and our evidence gives us but few clues in this. Funerals obviously involved a supernatural element, but the evidence we have is concerned with other elements of cosmology. This, I think, is fundamental to our understanding. If we recognise that ritual is about the definition and redefinition of cosmology then the common misconception that ritual has to incorporate some kind of supernatural element is side-stepped; cosmology, as Tambiah says,[12] involves man's relations with man (or woman), child with adult, young with old, man's

[10] See Halsall, *Settlement and Social Organization*, chapters 3-4.

[11] On the nature of ritual, I have been most heavily influenced by the concise and pertinent comments of J. Black-Michaud, *Feuding Societies* (London, 1975), pp. 209-17; and by the work of S. J. Tambiah, *Culture, Thought and Social Action. An Anthropological Perspective* (Cambridge, Mass., 1985).

[12] S. J. Tambiah, "A Performative Approach to Ritual", *Proceedings of the British Academy* 65 (1979), pp. 113-69, reprinted in Tambiah, *Culture, Thought and Social Action*, pp. 123-66. I cite the 1985 reprint. The article contains a splendid bibliography of ritual studies.

relation with nature, as well as man's relations with the supernatural, the gods.

The clothing and other grave-goods make a display of the deceased person's identity. They set out how a person of that age and gender was to be seen, setting out symbols of the role of people of that station in life. I have interpreted these statements of roles elsewhere,[13] and do not intend to go into them here. But, like all ritual, this involves the use of what might be termed "heightened" language. All the evidence suggests that the grave-goods, even the contents of purses and pouches, were deliberately chosen. A comparatively restricted array of objects is employed to give an idealised depiction of the deceased's social identity. A wide range of things which may well have been very important in everyday life are not interred on all sites, or are only employed in very specific circumstances.

The use of a restricted range of artefacts brings with it a concomitant aspect of ritual "language": repetition. The repeated use of particular types of grave-goods in association with particular groups of people serves to reassure the participants; it superimposes what is recognised, familiar, or "safe" on circumstances which are potentially critical, threatening and unknown. By the use of well-understood symbols or references the ritual "remakes" comparable scenes from the past. It links the current burial to previous burials of the same kind, telescoping time in the minds of the observers.[14]

---

[13] Halsall, *Settlement and Social Organization*, chapter 8; G. Halsall, "Female Status and Power in Early Merovingian Central Austrasia: The Burial Evidence", *Early Medieval Europe* 5 (1996), 1-24.

[14] I originally came to this view via a phrase of Virginia Woolf: "I find that scene-making is my natural way of marking the past", "A sketch of the past", in *Moments of Being: Unpublished Autobiographical Writings*, ed. J. Schulkind (New York, 1985), p. 122 (and I am grateful to Felicity Riddy for putting me onto this trail). This concept of "scene-making", however, equates with very commonly held notions of how memory is "stored" and "accessed". In this paper, rather than looking at individuals' means of recalling the past, or at "ritual" enactments of "social memory", I wish to suggest how ritual functions by creating "memorable" scenes. On memory in the middle ages, see M. Carruthers, *The Book of Memory. A Study of Memory in Medieval Culture* (Cambridge, 1990); J. Fentress and C. Wickham, *Social Memory* (Oxford,

Thus a time of potential change in local social relations is masked by the emphasis laid on "continuity", things which are "the same". The cemetery itself acts as a clear "place of memory". Like the commonly used grave-goods, it brings to the minds of the participants previous occasions of the same kind. This "scene making", or reconstructing the past, in ritual is very important. One of the reasons why is that it permits a certain flexibility, to which I will return.

Whilst such memories as were evoked by ritual "scene-making" would likely be of grief and loss, they would serve to unite the participants with the bereaved family. At the same time, the evocation of the remembered past is, or at least often can be, comforting when compared with the insecurities of the future; after all, previous crises of this kind had been endured. The "telescoping" of time could be significant in other ways. If, as is very likely, the distribution of food and drink at funerary feasts represented one form of reciprocal gift-giving, it would bring to mind the occasions when the family hosting the feast was itself the recipient of such gifts.[15]

Scene-building is strengthened by the use of several media, another key element of ritual performance.[16] We may be able to suggest this if we make the not unreasonable supposition that the deposition of the grave-goods placed around the body was accompanied by some spoken statement, thus heightening the symbolism, in much the same way as, in some Christian ceremonies,

1988); P. Geary, *Phantoms of Remembrance. Memory and Oblivion at the End of the First Millennium* (Princeton, 1994); see also B. M. Ross, *Remembering the Personal Past. Descriptions of Autobiographical Memory* (New York, 1991).

[15] On the role of time in strategies of gift-giving, see P. Bourdieu, *Outline of a Theory of Practice*, trans. R. Nice (Cambridge, 1977), pp. 4-9; P. Bourdieu, *The Logic of Practice*, trans. R. Nice (Oxford, 1990), chapter 6. This telescoping of time does not, however, quite "abolish the interval" (Bourdieu, *Outline of a Theory of Practice*, p. 6). In examining the role of time in such strategies, as well as considering methods of employing "real time" we need to look at means by which lived time can be distorted.

[16] Tambiah, "Performative Approach to Ritual", pp. 128, 142-43.

the spoken "ashes to ashes, dust to dust" motif is accompanied by the physical act of throwing dirt onto the coffin.

The meaning of the "language" is underlined further by the fact that all these things would connect with other rituals. Other rites would have made use of the very symbols also played with in funerary ritual. Some of these are themselves suggested in the burial evidence: the acquisition of weapons, for example, as part of the entry into manhood; the dressing up of young women in their jewellery by their mothers; the cutting of hair as another part of the rites of passage associated with socialisation[17] is referred to in the deposition of shears and combs in burials. The burial was then part of a constant sequence of public rituals related to the life cycle, cross-referring with them.

Those burials which involved the greatest display were, as mentioned, those of people who led the most "public" lives, and therefore those whose deaths were likely to cause the greatest threat to the maintenance of the status quo: young adult males, seen symbolically at least as warriors, certainly as potential heirs, probably served to some extent as lynch-pins in local politics if, as has been suggested,[18] their rites of passage to manhood involved alliances between families; young women, the betrothed and the married, were certainly extremely important in joining families in alliance, and if there were children, then the potential tension between a woman's family and that of her husband would be increased;[19] and above all, mature adult males who had died before their sons had established their own local position, and thus their right to succeed to their father's social status: hence the need to spend resources on playing down the crisis which is brought by the death, by constructing a ritual "scene" which presents a picture of normality.

[17] See K. A. Eckhardt, ed., *Pactus legis Salicae* 24.2-3, 67, MGH LNG 1.4.1 (Hanover, 1962); K. Fischer Drew, trans., *The Laws of the Salian Franks* (Philadelphia, 1991).

[18] J. H. Lynch, *Godparents and Kinship in the Early Medieval Europe* (Princeton, 1986), chapter 6.

[19] See Halsall, "Female Status and Power", for full discussion.

All this underlines that grave-good deposits are a symptom of precariously and expensively maintained local power and status. Tensions are eased, and relationships remade or reaffirmed in ritual display and the attendant gift-giving in the form of feasting. But this itself suggests an element of conflict. Although the norms which governed grave-goods deposits can be reconstructed, they are of course fuzzy to some degree, probably partly as a result of the nature of the evidence and partly because, as Bourdieu has written,[20] these schemes tend to be fuzzy anyway. Nevertheless, some graves are better furnished than others. In the sixth century, this competitive display takes the form of exaggeration of the norms. The appropriate grave-goods are multiplied. This might take the form of placing multiple objects of the same type in the burial; it can also be effected by placing more of the types of object generally appropriate. In the latter case, returning to the linguistic analogy, we can make a comparison with the repetition of different synonyms or metaphors in elaborate ritual language: what one anthropologist calls "stacking".[21]

These funerary displays probably can be read as those of members of families of local prestige, of families who needed to maintain their position by particular manifestations of their ability to bury the dead appropriately. But, again, the possible tension in social relations is eased by a form of ritual "scene-making" which emphasises the familiar. A certain element of competition is nevertheless permitted. All these ritual "statements" taken together form a sort of ritual dialogue or discourse. A family may try to enhance its standing as well as maintain it by a particularly stylised burial display, accompanied of course by lavish feasting.

Finally I would like to return to the chronological dimension of our evidence: the creation, around 500 AD in this region, of this type of burial ritual, its florescence between c. 525 and the end of the sixth century, and its gradual decline through the seventh century. The rite first appears in the last quarter of the fifth century, probably beginning with the celebrated grave of Childeric I in

---

[20] Bourdieu, *Outline of a Theory of Practice*, chapter 3.

[21] G. Gossen, cited in Tambiah, "Performative Approach to Ritual", p. 142.

Tournai, c. 480, and giving rise to the lavish burials of the "Flonheim-Gültlingen Group", in this region represented by Lavoye, grave 319. The appearance of these graves is doubtless related to the end of the Roman Empire in the West, and to the creation of the post-Roman political units based on Frankish and Alamannic kingdoms. The changed power structures were symbolised by the deposition of material culture, including symbols of power, of new, particularly Germanic types, as well as of old Roman ones. The uncertainty and instability of the times was also represented by these graves, mainly of mature adult males, the age-group where death could call into question current local socio-political relationships. But these graves also frequently found new cemeteries, or new phases on cemeteries. Obviously, to encourage people to follow suit and use a new burial ground would require an altogether exceptional display. This makes it a mistake to compare these founder graves with later burials and to derive significance from the lack of similar burials in later phases.[22]

The problem of how such new rites were created is extremely interesting, but requires more space than is available here. Some suggestions might nevertheless be made. We should note that, though furnished burial had been sparse in the middle decades of the fifth century, after the phase of lavish late Roman burials in northern Gaul in the late fourth and early fifth centuries,[23] inhumation itself

---

[22] F. Stein, "Les tombes d'un chef franc et de sa famille à Güdingen: Considérations sur la role de l'aristocratie dans l'implantation franque entre la Meuse et la Sarre", *Saarbrücker Studien und Materialen zur Altertumskunde* 1 (1992), 117-44; B. K. Young, "Quelques réflexions sur les sépultures privilégiées, leur contexte et leur évolution dans la Gaule de l'Est", in *Inhumations privilégiée du IVe au VIIIe siècle en occident*, ed. Y. Duval and J-C. Picard (Paris, 1986), pp. 69-88; B. K. Young, "Example aristocratique et mode funéraire dans la Gaule mérovingienne", *Annales: Economies, sociétés, civilisations* 43 (1986), 379-407.

[23] On the interpretation of these, see G. Halsall, "The Origins of the *Reihengräberzivilisation*: Forty Years on", in *Fifth-Century Gaul: A Crisis of Identity?* ed. J. F. Drinkwater and H. Elton (Cambridge, 1992), pp. 196-207. I briefly discuss possible reasons for the absence of lavish burial in the mid-century in "Towns, Societies and Ideas: The Not-So-Strange Case of Late

continued and there were occasional burials with grave-goods (for example at Haillot, Krefeld-Gellep, Mainz-Kostheim, Rhenen and possibly Furfooz). The new phase of burials can be read, rather than as completely new "intrusive" rites, as particularly elaborate variations on a theme which had only been played pianissimo for thirty or forty years. The theme itself, fundamentally a late Roman provincial theme, was, however, recognisable. The new variation used different elements, especially those which proclaimed the ascendant power of the Germanic kingdoms.

By c. 525, what may have begun as the burial ritual for local magnates had spread to other local families; entire communities were burying their dead with grave-goods, engaging in this ritual discourse. But the ritual, like all rituals, did not remain static. New elements were introduced, sometimes relating to dress. Women began to be buried with some forms of artefact which had earlier been reserved for men, for example. As just intimated, for all their norms, rituals remain "performances", with the norms as the "score", which can be elaborated or trimmed down.[24] Another element enabling flexibility within this discourse is the fact that this "scene-making" will never entirely reproduce the past; certain elements will be left out; by stressing the main elements the important link is made, but the opportunity is left for the incorporation of subtle changes. This is important in understanding how rituals change and develop.

Around 600 AD a wide-ranging set of transformations taking place in north Gallic society, and largely connected to an increase in aristocratic power,[25] had a profound effect on the ritual. Some families made displays in their funerals which, rather than exaggerating the old norms, broke with them, burying, for example, old women with quite lavish displays of jewellery, although, again, some of these burials are "founder graves" and so are atypical. In the seventh century new cemeteries appear, they are smaller, they

Roman and Early Merovingian Metz", in *Towns in Transition*, ed. N. Christie and S. T. Loseby (Aldershot, 1996), pp. 235-61.

[24] A commonly expressed view of ritual, but see, for example, Tambiah, "Performative Approach to Ritual", passim.

[25] See Halsall, *Settlement and Social Organization*, pp. 262-70.

serve smaller communities, the audience is smaller. The display, perhaps not surprisingly, becomes correspondingly simple. The number of artefact-types used diminishes; the specific symbolism decreases in direct relation. Associations between grave-goods, gender and age are much more difficult to discern. This constitutes another aspect of "ritual language": condensation. The array of weaponry of different forms, deployed in different combinations, in the sixth century to transmit information about the deceased's identity, becomes reduced to single weapons, usually scramasaxes or spears, probably just meaning male, maybe "free male". Jewellery becomes very rare; pottery deposits very rare indeed, on newly founded sites. The grave-goods cease to be those connected with gender and age, and seem to relate mainly to elaborate dress, and thus more nearly to the "wealth", for want of a better word, of the family.[26] The amount of "meaning" is reduced. It is not difficult to see how the possibilities for playing with the ritual, to construct new messages, are reduced concomitantly. The use of such elements in ritual becomes decreasingly important, until by 675 the only elements attested are items of the corpse's clothing, themselves apparently reduced to the simplest, standardised form. The focus of display, at least in terms of surviving material culture, seems to shift from the transient display of grave-goods and feasting during the funeral itself, to permanent, above-ground markers.

To conclude, previous interpretations of grave-goods have been unsatisfactory because they have failed to take the performative, ritual aspects of the practice (including time and audience) into account. Due acknowledgement of those aspects serves above all to underline that grave-goods displays are symptomatic of insecure power. The elaboration of the transient ritual display stands in direct relationship to the potential threat to social relationships posed by the death in question. Lavish grave-goods displays are therefore certainly not "expression[s] of personal

---

[26] Compare, for example, the distribution of sixth- and seventh-century grave-goods with adult males at Lavoye (Meuse): Halsall, *Settlement and Social Organization*, figs 4.19 and 4.28.

and/or dynastic power",[27] or at least not in any straightforward way. Recognition of the performative and ritual aspects of furnished burial, and of the way in which material culture is employed as "heightened" ritual language, creating, and being created by, social categorisation, also allows us to side-step traditional archaeological debates about the extent to which burial customs reflect or obfuscate "real" social relationships. What I hope to have suggested is that archaeological cemetery evidence does permit a way into considering the rituals of early Merovingian society, and a way which allows us to look in detail at specific local practices and at temporal developments. It also allows us to see something of how rituals contain within them their own dynamic for change. And in that dynamic for change lie important aspects of the ways in which early medieval society itself changed. In these customary societies, social relationships, often themselves ritualised, were similarly performative, playing with, as well as within, the norms. Merovingian rituals were not static and neither was Merovingian society.

---

[27] L. Webster, "Death's Diplomacy: Sutton Hoo in the Light of Other Male Princely Burials", in *Sutton Hoo: Fifty Years After*, ed. R. Farrell and C. Neuman de Vegvar (Oxford, Ohio, 1992), pp. 75-81 (p. 75).

The Early Medieval Inscriptions of Western Britain: Function and Sociology

Mark Handley

This paper will deal with the corpus of 242 inscriptions from western Britain that date to the period of roughly AD 400-700.[1]

---

[1] Most of the inscriptions are found in either *CIIC*, or *ECMW*. For new finds see K. H. Jackson and R. P. Wright, "A Late Inscription from Wroxeter", *Antiquaries Journal* 48 (1968), 296-300; *An Inventory of the Ancient Monuments in Glamorgan, Vol. 1: Pre-Norman, part III: The Early Christian Period*, The Royal Commission on Ancient and Historical Monuments in Wales (Cardiff, 1976) [hereafter *RCAHM Glamorgan*], pp. 38-39; W. J. Hemp and C. A. Gresham, "A New Early Christian Inscribed Stone from Trawsfynydd, Merioneth", *Archaeologia Cambrensis* 110 (1961), 154-55; D. P. Webley, "The Nant Crew Stone: A New Discovery", *Archaeologia Cambrensis* 108 (1958), 123-24; R. S. O. Tomlin, "A Sub-Roman Gravestone from Aberhydfer near Trecastle", *Archaeologia Cambrensis* 25 (1975), 68-72; R. B. White, "Excavations at Arfyn, Bodedern, Long-cist Cemeteries and the Origins of Christianity in Britain", *Transactions of the Anglesey Antiquarian Field Club* (1971-72), 15-27; K. A. Steer, "Two Unrecorded Early Christian Stones", *Proceedings of the Society of Antiquaries of Scotland* 101 (1968-69), 127-29; C. Thomas, "The Early Christian Inscriptions of Southern Scotland", *Glasgow Archaeological Journal* 17 (1991-92), 1-10. For the South-West now also see E. Okasha, *Corpus of the Early Christian Inscribed Stones of South-West Britain* (Leicester, 1992). All of the post *CIIC* inscriptions from the South-West are assigned a 1200 or 1400 number in C. Thomas, *And Shall These Mute Stones*

These inscriptions range in location from the Isles of Scilly in the south, to Scotland in the north, with none further east than those at Wareham in Dorset.[2] The vast majority of the inscriptions are in Latin, but 28 are bilingual, that is in both Latin and Primitive Irish. The Irish is written in the linear alphabet known as ogam. Twenty-two are solely ogam inscriptions, and one inscription is in Old Welsh. I will attempt to argue that the accepted interpretation of the function of these inscriptions as personal memorials is only a part of the answer, and that instead we should be seeing these inscriptions as something very similar to charters. If such a conclusion can be shown to be correct, then we find ourselves in the presence of a source that can shed a great deal of light upon the socio-economic nature of early medieval western Britain.

The surviving literature from early medieval western Britain is notoriously sparse; in spite of this we still find in it many references to standing and inscribed stones. Moreover, the sources from western Britain can be greatly supplemented by evidence from Ireland. The first of the sources is the Book of Llandaff.[3] In the last few years renewed interest in the Book of Llandaff has been occasioned by linguistic work on the charter material by both John Koch and Patrick Sims-Williams.[4] A combination of these results, along with the internal consistency of the witness lists and diplomatic evidence, points to a conclusion that the charter

---

Speak? Post-Roman Inscriptions in Western Britain (Cardiff, 1994), pp. 330-31, and this is how they will be referred to.

[2] On the Wareham stones see *An Inventory of the Historical Monuments in the County of Dorset, vol. II, South-East*, RCAHM (London, 1970) [hereafter *RCAHM Dorset*], pp. 304-12, and most recently D. A. Hinton, "The Inscribed Stones in Lady St. Mary Church, Wareham", *Proceedings of the Dorset Natural History and Archaeological Society* 114 (1992), 260.

[3] This text has been re-introduced as a source for early Wales by the work of Wendy Davies, see *The Llandaff Charters* (Aberystwyth, 1979) and "The Orthography of the Personal Names in the 'Liber Landavensis'", *Bulletin of the Board of Celtic Studies* 28 (1978-80), 553-57.

[4] J. T. Koch, "When was Welsh Literature First Written Down?", *Studia Celtica* 20/21 (1985/86), 43-66, and P. Sims-Williams, "The Emergence of Old Welsh, Cornish and Breton Orthography, 600-800: The Evidence of Archaic Old Welsh", *Bulletin of the Board of Celtic Studies* 38 (1991), 21-86.

collection has a great deal of earlier material within it, much of which can be dated to the seventh and eighth centuries.

In the Book of Llandaff all of the references to stones come from boundary clauses. Recently the dating of these clauses has been thrown into doubt, with it being argued that their dates fail "dramatically to correlate with the ostensible dates" of the charters.[5] The basis for this argument is the orthography of the word "to", or *di>i* in Welsh, yet the *d*-form, generally regarded as the older version, appears about 420 times, compared to the 65 *d*-less forms. Thus whereas Armstrong argued that the *d*-form was an archaising spelling,[6] it is perhaps equally possible to suggest that the *d*-less forms were instead a modernising spelling. In short the orthography of *di* gives us little reason to suspect the boundary clauses of being later than the charters themselves.

From twenty-one boundary clauses, thirteen of which are dated to before AD 760, we find twenty-seven separate references to boundary stones.[7] Some of these stones are named, such as "Lybiau's stone", "the stone of Oudocui", "Maen Tyllog", or "petram Onnbrit".[8] Others point to a relationship between the owner of the land and the stones, or a relationship between the erection of a stone and a burial. Charter 187 records a gift of land by one Conhae to Llandaff. The boundary of this land is said, at one point, to run "downwards as far as Maen Cinahi". The difference between *Cinahi* and *Conhae* is not that great, representing no more than syncope, or the loss of unstressed medial vowels, in the latter version, whilst the interchangeability of *Cin* and *Con* need not

---

[5] J. Armstrong, "On some Middle Welsh Relative Constructions", *Studia Celtica* 22/23 (1987/88), 10-28 (p. 23).

[6] Armstrong, "Relative Constructions", p. 23.

[7] J. G. Evans and J. Rhys, eds, *The Text of the Book of Llan Dav* (Oxford, 1893; repr. Aberystwyth, 1978) [henceforth *Book of Llan Dav*], pp. 74, 122, 123, 128, 142, 145, 156, 173, 188, 189, 191, 196, 197, 207, 208, 213, 224, 240, 242, 260, 272, 383. In Davies, *Llandaff Charters*, their numbers are 73a, 121, 122, 127b, 140, 145, 156, 171b, 187, 188b, 190b, 195, 206, 208, 212, 223, 224, 239, 240, 259, 271.

[8] Numbers 140, 156, 188b and 195.

trouble us.[9] The owner appears then to have had a stone on his boundary named after him.

Charters 190b and 176a form a doublet, both recording the gift of the "villa in qua sepulcrum est Gurai".[10] The boundary clauses of these charters are very similar except in one respect, the boundary of 190b starts with the "Maen Brith", that of 176a with the grave of Gurai.[11] The possibility presents itself therefore that these two features were sited next to each other, with the "Maen Brith" perhaps marking the grave of Gurai. The Book of Llandaff is therefore a very important source for our perception of standing stones in early medieval western Britain. It paints a picture of their use as boundary stones, as well as of their association with burial and ownership.

The Gospel Book known as the Lichfield Gospels, or The Book of Chad, which was at Llandeilo in southern Wales from the very early ninth century, contains eight marginal notes.[12] The notes known as Chad 4 and Chad 6 contain references to stones in their boundary clauses. The stone in Chad 4 is "hirmain guidauc", or "the long stone of Guidauc".[13] It is likely that Chad 3 and Chad 4 are speaking of the same land,[14] and indeed in Chad 3 the land being given away is known as "Treb Guidauc".[15] Both the farm and the stone are named after the one person, perhaps a former owner of the

---

[9] For other examples of this from the Book of Llandaff, see the index entries under the names Cinan, Cinblus, Cinbran, Cingual, Cinuchan, Cinuelin, Conguarui and Congual, in Davies, *Llandaff Charters*, pp. 153-58.

[10] Davies, *Llandaff Charters*, pp. 108, 113.

[11] *Book of Lan Dav*, pp. 176, 190.

[12] D. Jenkins and M. Owen, "The Welsh Marginalia in the Lichfield Gospels. Part 1", *Cambridge Medieval Celtic Studies* 5 (Summer 1983), 37-66.

[13] Facsimiles and texts of these marginalia were printed in *Book of Lan Dav*. For Chad 4 see p. xlvi.

[14] G. R. J. Jones, "Post-Roman Wales", in *The Agrarian History of England and Wales, Vol. I, Part II, A.D. 43-1042*, ed. H. P. R. Finberg (Cambridge, 1972), pp. 312-13.

[15] *Book of Lan Dav*, p. xlvi.

land.[16] In Chad 6, on the other hand, we find reference to an unnamed "bir main", or "short stone" in its boundary clause.[17]

The poem known as the *Gododdin* and ascribed to the poet Aneirin also contains references to stones. There has been some debate as to the authenticity of this poem and its dating, but it is now being seen to have been composed and quite probably written in the mid-seventh century.[18] The three references to stones in the poem come from three variants of the one stanza eulogising the fallen warrior Grugyn.[19] Two of these are from the archaic text B and one from text A.[20] The lines speak of "a slab of rock in cleared land", and may refer to a standing stone.

The collection of poems known as the "Stanzas of the Graves", or the "Englynion y Beddau", which has been dated to the ninth or tenth century is a list of the sites of the graves of fallen warriors.[21] Stanza 51 speaks of a warrior who has become "speechless under stones"; stanza 63 of a "four-sided grave with its four stones at its head", and Stanza three from another collection of *englynion* of "The grave of Gwydion son of Don on Morfa Dinlleu under the stones of Defeillon".[22] An Irish poem in the same genre, composed after AD 972, speaks of the graves of the men of Leinster. Within this poem we find "the grave of Fergus Long-head at the pillar-stone of the Plain of Duma", as well as "the grave of

---

[16] *Book of Lan Dav*, p. xlvi.

[17] *Book of Lan Dav*, p. xlvii.

[18] Koch, "When was Welsh Literature First Written Down?", and J. T. Koch, "The *Cynfeirdd* Poetry and the Language of the Sixth Century", in *Early Welsh Poetry: Studies in the Book of Aneirin*, ed. B. F. Roberts (Aberystwyth, 1988), pp. 17-41; also see P. Mac Cana, "On the Early Development of Written Prose in Irish and Welsh", *Etudes Celtiques* 29 (1992), 59-66.

[19] These variants have been used to posit that the text we have is a collation of three different manuscripts of the *Gododdin*. See G. R. Isaac, "Canu Aneirin Adwl LI", *Journal of Celtic Linguistics* 2 (1993), 65-91.

[20] A translation can be found in K. H. Jackson, ed., *The Gododdin: The Earliest Scottish Poem* (Edinburgh, 1969) of stanzas 3 and 24 of Text B and stanza 48 of Text A.

[21] T. Jones, "The Black Book of Carmarthen 'Stanzas of the Graves'", *Proceedings of the British Academy* 53 (1967), 97-100.

[22] Jones, "Stanzas of the Graves", pp. 127, 131 and 135 respectively.

red-faced, Mael Duin in the locality of the pillar-stones of Mac Carthind", and a further reference to "a pillarstone like Lic Tullida".[23]

The Medieval Welsh laws survive from the late twelfth or thirteenth century onwards. All of these laws are known collectively as "The Law of Hywel Dda", a tenth-century Welsh king.[24] The exact antiquity of much of these laws is unknown, although comparison with the Irish laws has led Thomas Charles-Edwards to posit that many of the stipulations on land and inheritance date from what he terms the "Common Celtic period".[25] Within the Book of Iorwerth we find reference to the crime of removing "a boundary stone, which is notorious between two townlands".[26] Although we cannot date this stipulation, it is clear that the laws of medieval Wales contain a reference to boundary stones erected between estates.

Evidence from the early Irish laws can also further our picture of standing-stones and monumental inscriptions in early medieval western Britain. Quite apart from any similarity between Irish and Welsh law, the main reason for this is that the type of inscription referred to in the Irish Laws, namely ogam inscriptions, are also found in those areas of Britain that were settled by the Irish in our period. The bilingual inscriptions where ogam and Latin texts appear in translation also point to the relevance of the ogam model. In early Irish law the ogam stones were seen as one of the ways of proving ownership of land. Indicative of this is the gloss on the phrase "the ogam on the pillar-stone" which reads "it is like a

---

[23] M. E. Dobbs, "On the Graves of Leinster Men", *Zeitschrift für Celtische Philologie* 24 (1953-54), 139-53, especially p. 139 and stanzas 5, 10, 53.

[24] D. Huws, "The Manuscripts", in *Lawyers and Laymen. Studies in the History of Law presented to Professor Dafydd Jenkins on his Seventy-fifth Birthday*, ed. T. M. Charles-Edwards, M. E. Owen and D. B. Walters (Cardiff, 1986), pp. 119-36.

[25] T. M. Charles-Edwards, *Early Irish and Welsh Kinship* (Oxford, 1992), p. 213.

[26] D. Jenkins, ed., *The Law of Hywel Dda. Law Texts from Medieval Wales* (Llandysul, 1986), p. 128.

witness".[27] Furthermore one of the means of "testifying that it is one's land" is, "the testimony ... which is in the land, the ogam in the pillar-stone".[28] A further passage states that "the inheritance has been...engraved in ogams",[29] moreover in answer to the question "How is truth (with regard to land ownership) to be found in Irish law?", one of the answers is the "ogam in stones".[30] In another passage "ogam stone" and "boundary stone" appear synonymous,[31] whilst in an archaic legal poem we find reference to "stone pillars of contest, fighters who fasten title", a passage which the editor sees as referring to ogam stones.[32] The early Irish legal texts make it perfectly clear that the ogam stones served as recorders of landed title.

The Irish Sagas are another source which contains references to inscribed stones. From recension I of the *Tain Bo Cualinge* we find the statement that "Etarcomol's grave was dug and his headstone was planted in the ground; his name was written in ogam and he was mourned".[33] In the *Aidedh Ferghusa* we find that on Fergus' death "his grave was dug, his name was inscribed in ogam and his funeral games were performed".[34] There are more than twenty references within the Ulster Cycle of Tales to the erection of either standing-stones or ogam inscriptions over the dead thereby providing further evidence of the function of these inscriptions.[35]

---

[27] *CIH*, p. 1566, lines 6-7. For the translations see D. McManus, *A Guide to Ogam* (Maynooth, 1991), pp. 163-66.

[28] *CIH*, p. 754, lines 39ff.

[29] *CIH*, p. 746, lines 37ff.

[30] *CIH*, p. 596, lines 6ff.

[31] *CIH*, p. 2199, lines 8-10, and p. 2143, lines 21-22.

[32] D. A. Binchy, "An Archaic Legal Poem", *Celtica* 9 (1971), 152-68, especially pp. 157, 160.

[33] C. O'Rahilly, ed., *Tain Bo Cualinge Recension I* (Dublin, 1976), pp. 43, 163.

[34] S. H. O'Grady, ed., *Silva Gadelica*, 2 vols (Dublin, 1892), 1:252. For this translation see McManus, *Guide*, p. 154.

[35] See J. Mallory, "The Disposal of the Dead in the Ulster Cycle of Tales", Paper read at the 10th International Congress of Celtic Studies, Edinburgh, 1995.

When we combine the information supplied by all of these references we find ourselves facing three distinct functions for standing stones within early medieval western Britain. The charter evidence points towards them serving as boundary stones, the sagas and the poetry point to them as marking burial, whilst the Irish laws and the occasional charter point to them serving as proof of ownership of land. That we have three different functions does not, however, require us to have three different types of stone. For the sagas the ogams marked a hero's burial, for the laws they provided proof of ownership and demarcation of a boundary; the one stone could serve all three of our functions. The situation in western Britain need not be seen as any different; each stone could be multi-functional, as an analysis of the inscriptions will show.

The inscriptions of western Britain can, for ease of analysis, be divided into four types. Group 1, the largest of the groups, consists of inscriptions with no nominative, with the main and usually first word of these inscriptions being a name in the genitive. Group 2 contains those inscriptions that carry a memorial formula and a name in the nominative. Group 3 is a mixture of the first two in that it is made up of inscriptions with both a memorial formula and a name in the genitive. Group 4 is something of a miscellany and is made up of those inscriptions which are either too fragmentary to be read properly or which have a name in the nominative but no memorial formulae, or which have an explicitly religious function.

The second of these groups is regarded as representative of the inscriptions, with the result that the entire corpus has been seen by most commentators as being inscribed personal memorial stones. Of the 242 early medieval western British inscriptions the total number of Group 2 stones is 38. If we add to this figure the Group 3 inscriptions, which total 43, we are still only left with a grand total of 81 inscriptions with any sign of a memorial function inscribed upon them and upon which the assumptions for the rest of the corpus have been based.

The problem with the memorial hypothesis for the inscriptions is that it does not answer many of the questions relating to the corpus. One such question is the uneven gender representation on the inscriptions. If the stones were simply memorials, why do we find women under-represented, when presumably just as many women as men died?[36] One could posit that women were not considered to be as socially significant as men, as was surely the case, but this merely makes those women that are found on the inscriptions even more puzzling. Another problem is to be found in the limited use of the *hic iacit* formula.[37] Given that this formula has been found from all regions of western Britain, why, if all the stones were memorials, did not all the stones use this most obvious of memorial formulae? Or, to put it another way, why did only 81 of the 242 stones say they were memorials if all 242 were? Another question that the memorial hypothesis leaves unanswered is why so many Christian graves were situated outside ecclesiastical enclosures, and placed instead upon upland heath, or on fords and pathways? If an hypothesis could be found to answer all these questions, and more, then this hypothesis would be preferable.

The largest of the groups is the first, that in which a word in the nominative case is lacking, the first word being in the genitive. One such stone is that from Cornwall which reads "CUMREGNI FILI MAUCI".[38] The name Cumregni is in the genitive, meaning that a word in the nominative is implied at the beginning of the inscription, thereby giving the meaning of "(The something) of Cumregnus son of Maucus".[39] Within the corpus there are 94 such inscriptions in Latin,[40] as well as 22 inscribed in ogam,[41] thereby making a total of 116 inscriptions within Group 1.

---

[36] See figs 2 and 3 below.

[37] The correct spelling would be *iacet* but this is very rare.

[38] *CIIC*, no. 486.

[39] Such a translation is contrary to the arguments of Thomas Charles-Edwards, who sees the use of the genitive as being indicative of bad Latin. Yet that the ogam inscriptions follow the same genitive pattern would seem to preclude this, unless we want to see the use of the Primitive Irish genitives as a pointer to the loss of "good Irish". See T. M. Charles-Edwards, "Language and Society among the Insular Celts 400-1000", in *The Celtic World*, ed. M. Green (London, 1995), pp. 703-36 (pp. 716-17).

[40] *CIIC*, nos 458, 460, 461, 468, 469, 471, 472, 473, 477, 481, 484, 485, 486, 488a, 489a, 489b, 490, 491, 492, 493, 499, 509, 511, 1060; *ECMW*, nos 6, 40, 44, 66, 68, 71, 75, 84, 89, 96, 136, 140, 141, 142, 144, 148, 149, 160, 166, 169, 170, 171, 172, 174, 175, 176, 177, 198a, 238, 271, 272, 279, 282, 286, 297, 298, 299, 306, 307, 308, 312a, 312b, 314, 315, 320, 335, 345, 349, 352, 353,

A good example of the Group 3 inscriptions (those that combine the genitive with a memorial formula) is that found on a stone from Anglesey which reads "CUNOGUSI HIC IACIT".[42] From this we get "(The something) of Cunogusus; he lies here". Group 3 consists of 45 inscriptions,[43] which can be added to Group 1 making a total of 161 inscriptions in the genitive. Just as importantly, the Group 3 inscriptions make up more than half of the 81 memorial inscriptions.

The word implied at the beginning of these inscriptions is normally assumed to be "stone" or "memorial" giving the meaning of, in the above example, "(The stone or memorial) of Cunogusus, he lies here". Such a "translation" is the result of two assumptions, that the inscriptions had only one function and that this function was that of a memorial. We have already seen that it is perhaps more likely that the inscriptions served a number of different functions, two of which had more to do with the ownership of land than with marking a burial. It is a possibility then that the word implied at the beginning of the genitive inscriptions was "land" rather than "memorial". This would give the meaning of "The land of Cumregnus son of Mauci" and "The land of Cunogusus, he lies here" to the two above inscriptions respectively. It is also a possibility that the inscriptions were consciously left vague precisely because of their multi-functional nature. Just as the written sources point towards inscriptions serving more than one function, so too do these Group 3 stones; the one inscription could serve as

354, 384, 390, 399, 400, 402, 403, 404; White, "Bodedern"; *RCAHM Glamorgan*, no. 2; *RCAHM Dorset*, no. 2, and Thomas, *Mute Stones*, nos 1202, 1205, 1209, 1210, 1400, 1401, 1402, 1403, 1404.

   [41] *CIIC*, nos 488b, 489c, 489d, 501, 502, 503, 504, 506; *ECMW*, nos 67a, 74, 110, 150#2, 198b, 228, 296, 300, 301, 346#2; Thomas, *Mute Stones*, no. 1207 and Aberhydfer-b. All the Irish stones follow this pattern, see McManus, *Guide*, p. 51.

   [42] *ECMW*, no. 9.

   [43] *CIIC*, nos 457, 462, 466, 467, 470, 474, 478, 500, 505, 514, 515; *ECMW*, nos 9, 26, 34, 39, 41, 42, 43, 70, 73, 92, 94, 95, 97, 103, 105, 122, 126, 138, 150, 183, 214, 215, 229, 268, 277, 278, 284, 305, 313, 316, 370; Webley, "Nant Crew Stone"; *RCAHM Glamorgan*, no. 1; Thomas, *Mute Stones*, no. 1206.

the marker of a grave as well as something very much akin to a charter.

Charles-Edwards has argued for a similar dual function for the ogam stones of Ireland,[44] whilst Goodier has pointed to the number of burials that are to be found on parish, and therefore probably estate, boundaries in southern England,[45] indeed many Anglo-Saxon charters speak of burial sites along their bounds.[46] Thus it may be significant that in Cornwall many of the stones lie on or near parish boundaries, and about 50% by trackways or fords.[47]

The Group 4 inscriptions are lumped together despite the fact that they differ greatly from each other. Leaving aside the lost and irrecoverable inscriptions the group is dominated by those which seem to have had a primarily religious function. One such inscription is that from Whithorn which reads "LOCI PETRI APUSTOLI", which has been translated as "(The sign) of the *locus* of Peter the Apostle".[48] The other inscription from Whithorn translates as "We praise Thee Lord! Latinus, of 35 years, and his daughter, of four years, here made a *sinus*. He was a descendant of Barrovadus",[49] and has also be seen as having had a primarily religious function. From North Wales we have an inscription which reads "SENACUS PRSB HIC IACIT CUM MULTITUD(i)NEM

---

[44] T. M. Charles-Edwards, "Boundaries in Irish Law", in *Medieval Settlement: Continuity and Change*, ed. P. H. Sawyer (London, 1976), pp. 83-87 (p. 84).

[45] A. Goodier, "The Formation of Boundaries in Anglo-Saxon England: A Statistical Study", *Medieval Archaeology* 28 (1984), 1-21 passim.

[46] D. Hooke, "Burial Features in West Midland Charters", *Journal of the English Place-Name Society* 13 (1980-81), 1-40 and L. V. Grinsell, "Barrows in the Anglo-Saxon Land Charters", *Antiquaries Journal* 71 (1991), 46-63.

[47] A. Preston-Jones and P. Rose, "Medieval Cornwall", *Cornish Archaeology* 25 (1986), 135-85 (p. 157).

[48] *CIIC*, no. 519. Also see Thomas, "Early Christian Inscriptions", p. 3.

[49] *CIIC*, no. 520. "TE DOMINUM LAUDAMUS LATINUS ANNORUM XXXV ET FILIA SUA ANN IV IC SINUM FECERUTN NIPUS BARROVADI". The most in-depth discussion of this inscription can be found in C. Thomas, *Whithorn's Christian Beginnings*, First Whithorn Lecture 1992 (Whithorn, 1992), in which the argument is made that this inscription records the founding of a church by the layman Latinus.

FRATRUM", which Nash-Williams translates as, "Senacus the Priest lies here with the Multitude of the Brethren".[50] Such inscriptions should be seen as amongst a minority for which the delineation of ownership was by no means an intended function.

One objection that could be voiced against the inscriptions acting as something akin to a charter is that within a generation or two an inscription would cease to be a useful tool in providing proof of ownership. There are two arguments against such an objection. Firstly, the Irish law codes make it perfectly clear that the comparable ogam inscriptions did serve as charters. Indeed the law codes that we have post-date the time when the inscriptions were being erected, yet this was not seen as an objection to their usefulness in providing evidence of ownership.

The other argument against such an objection is that we find quite a large number of stones being re-used at a later date for another inscription. One such example is that from Buckland Monachorum in Devon which has an ogam inscription which reads "ENABARR" and a Latin inscription that reads "DOBUNNI FABRI FILII ENABARRI".[51] This is a clear example of a stone being used by one generation and then again by the next. With the passing of one generation a new inscription was added, and the information was kept up-to-date. The Aberhydfer stone from the former county of Brecknockshire is another example of the re-use of a stone, although this time the Latin inscription was scoured to make way for a later ogam inscription.[52] The Fardel stone from Devon is an even better example in that there are a total of four inscriptions on the stone, two in ogam and two in Latin.[53] From Llandawke, in the former county of Carmarthenshire, we have another re-used stone which carries both Latin and ogam inscriptions.[54] The Latin

---

[50] *ECMW*, no. 78.

[51] *CIIC*, no. 488.

[52] Tomlin, "Sub-Roman Gravestone", p. 72.

[53] *CIIC*, no. 489, but also see Okasha, *Corpus*, pp. 103-08. Thomas has tried to see this stone as consisting of two bilingual inscriptions, but his means of making "FANONI" equivalent to "SVAQQUCI" seems overly fraught, see Thomas, *Mute Stones*, pp. 267-68.

[54] *ECMW*, no. 150.

reads "BARRIVENDI FILIUS VENDUBARRI HIC IACIT", and the ogam "DUMELEDONAS MAQI M[UCOI.....]". We cannot know which of the two came first, or if the people recorded were in any way related, and for our purposes we do not need to. The inscription was re-used and a new name added. From St Clement in Cornwall we find another example of a stone being re-used for a second inscription.[55] The first inscription reads "VITALI FILI TORRICI". The second, inscribed further up the stone and in a noticeably different script reads simply "IGNIOC". Again any relationship is unknown. There are a number of other stones that also appear to have been re-used,[56] and which further contradict this argument that the inscriptions could not have been akin to charters. That these stones were re-used would also argue against them being a grave-stone, in any specific sense. They may have marked a burial ground, but as we have seen this need not be incompatible with the inscriptions acting as charters.

A few of the inscriptions make it explicit that they were acting as charters, or at least records of generosity. From Llanllyr in Dyfed we have an inscription which reads "TESQUITUS DITOC MADOMNUAC OCCON FILIUS ASAITGEN DEDIT". This has been translated as "The small waste plot of Ditoc which Occon, son of Asaitgen, gave to Madomnuac".[57] There is also a later inscription from Ogmore which reads "Be it known to all that Arthmail has given a field to God and to Glywys, and to Netrat and to Fili the Bishop".[58] The already discussed *Latinus* inscription from Whithorn may record the granting of land to found a church, whilst an inscription from the monastery of Maughold on the Isle of Man records that "Branhui led off water to this place".[59]

---

[55] *CIIC*, no. 473.

[56] *ECMW*, nos 198, 287, 312, 346.

[57] *ECMW*, no. 124. For a fuller discussion of this inscription, and a different translation, see M. A. Handley, "Isidore of Seville and 'Hisperic' Latin: The Epigraphic Culture of Llanllyr and Llanddewi-brefi", in *Roman, Runes, Ogham*, ed. K. Forsyth, J. Higgitt and D. Parsons (forthcoming, 1998).

[58] *ECMW*, no. 255.

[59] For the Latinus stone see note 49 above. For the Man inscription see B. R. S. Megaw, "The Monastery of St. Maughold", *Proceedings of the Isle of Man Natural History and Antiquarian Society* 5 (1950), 169-180 (pp. 170-71).

We should not be surprised by the use of stone as a medium for recording information: indeed it has recently been written of the early medieval period that "as an alternative to papyrus or parchment, stone has certain obvious advantages as a medium in which records may be made and preserved".[60] Other areas of early medieval Europe, such as Italy, Armenia and Scandinavia also utilised stone charters in this way.[61] In the British Isles however the practice appears to have been more the norm than the exception with the Class I Pictish Stones being seen by some as "acting as a form of property charter",[62] in much the same way as the inscriptions of western Britain and Ireland. That many of the charters of Anglo-Saxon England contain references to stones in their boundary clauses may also point to the practice in at least some parts of England.[63] The use of inscribed charters in western Britain is not therefore abnormal or exceptional; indeed within an Insular context one could argue that it would have been more abnormal for western Britain not to have used inscriptions in this way. The early medieval western British inscriptions seem then to have fulfilled all the functions alluded to by the written sources. They served as burial and boundary markers and as recorders of title. All three of these functions could, and probably did, overlap in the one inscription.

[60] R. Collins, "Conclusion: The Role of Writing in the Resolution and Recording of Disputes", in *The Settlement of Disputes in Early Medieval Europe*, ed. W. Davies and P. Fouracre (Cambridge, 1986), pp. 207-14 (p. 207).

[61] For Italy see E. Diehl, ed., *Inscriptiones latinae christianae veteres*, 3 vols (Berlin, 1925-31), 2:264-79; for Armenia see A. Ter-Ghewondyan, *The Arab Emirates in Bagratid Armenia* (Lisbon, 1976), p. 13; for Scandinavia see B. Sawyer, *Property and Inheritance in Viking Scandinavia: The Runic Evidence* (Alingsås, 1988).

[62] S. Foster, "The State of Pictland in the Age of Sutton Hoo", in *The Age of Sutton Hoo: The Seventh Century in North-Western Europe*, ed. M. O. H. Carver (Woodbridge, 1992), pp. 217-34 (p. 231), and R. Samson, "The Reinterpretation of the Pictish Symbols", *Journal of the British Archaeological Association* 145 (1992), 29-65 (pp. 30-33, 59-61).

[63] For a few such references see D. Hooke, *The Anglo-Saxon Charter Bounds of Worcestershire* (Woodbridge, 1990), pp. 53, 54, 65, 76, 127, 128, 172, 306, 364, 380, 382, 402, 414.

Nonetheless, if we look at the inscriptions over time we can note quite significant changes in the type of inscription being erected. It should be noted that the dating of these inscriptions is notoriously problematic, suffice it to say, however, that the broad divisions – such as "the sixth century" – which I will use are more than likely to be accurate and thus that we can be relatively confident that any analysis which uses such broad divisions will be largely representative of any chronological trends.[64]

Of the ten Latin inscriptions ascribed to the fifth century that refer directly to an individual, five have the formula *hic iacit*.[65] A further inscription carries the pagan memorial formula "DIS MANIBUS".[66] On the other hand only two fifth-century inscriptions have the first name in the genitive, and both of them combine the genitive with *hic iacit* and, moreover, are dated to the late fifth-century.[67] The fifth-century inscriptions, few as they are, appear to have had a primarily memorial function. Graph 1 clearly shows that this was not the case amongst those inscriptions assigned to the "fifth-sixth century" or to the "sixth century".

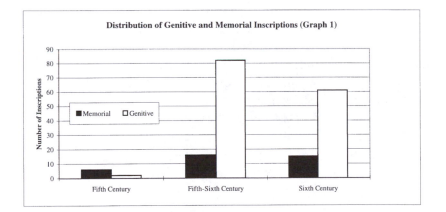

[64] This has also recently been argued by Thomas, *Mute Stones*, p. 116.

[65] *CIIC*, nos. 479, 498, 500; *ECMW*, no. 27; *RCAHM Glamorgan*, no. 1.

[66] *ECMW*, no. 285.

[67] *CIIC*, no. 500; *RCAHM Glamorgan*, no. 1.

The nature of the inscriptions appears to have changed towards the end of the fifth century with the memorial inscriptions ceding their primacy to the "akin to a charter" genitive-type inscriptions.

What took place in western Britain in the late fifth century that could have brought about such a change? One event dating from this time was the migration to western Britain of people from southern Ireland,[68] the distributional centre of the Irish ogam inscriptions.[69] We have already seen that the ogam inscriptions in Ireland served a charter-like function; it may be therefore that the settlement of the Irish in western Britain brought about a change in the nature and function of the western British inscriptions.

Such a conclusion is further supported by the relationship between the inscriptions in the genitive and those with vertical lettering, an epigraphic trait usually thought to be the result of the influence of the verticality of the ogam script. Of the 139 Latin inscriptions in the genitive, 116, or 83.4%, have vertical lettering. Of the remaining 81 Latin inscriptions only 47 or just over 58% are vertical. The correlation between the vertical lettering and the genitive formula is not merely a function of the overall percentage of vertical inscriptions. The inscriptions in the genitive are linked to those with vertical lettering. If the vertical inscriptions are seen as indicative of Irish influence, then the genitive inscriptions can also be seen in such a light. Indeed inscriptions in the genitive are the norm among the Irish ogam stones.[70]

This conclusion is supported by the geographical distribution of the genitive inscriptions. Of the 38 inscriptions from the old county of Pembrokeshire, the main centre for Irish settlement in Britain, 33 are in either ogam or the genitive.[71] In Carmarthenshire,

---

[68] B. Copplestone-Crow, "The Dual Nature of the Irish Colonization of Dyfed in the Dark Ages", *Studia Celtica* 16/17 (1981/82), 1-24. See now Thomas, *Mute Stones*, pp. 27-162.

[69] McManus, *Guide*, pp. 45-46.

[70] McManus, *Guide*, p. 51.

[71] *ECMW*, nos 296, 297, 298, 299, 300, 301, 305, 306, 307, 308, 312a, 312b, 313, 314, 315, 316, 319, 320, 335, 345, 346#2, 349, 352, 353, 354, 370, 384, 390, 399, 400, 402, 403, 404.

which bordered Pembrokeshire, 18 of the 22 inscriptions are ogam or genitive,[72] whilst in Devon and Cornwall, another area of Irish settlement, 42 of the 62 inscriptions carry either ogam or the genitive.[73] In southern Scotland on the other hand, where there was minimal, if any, Irish settlement, the figures are very different: only three of the seventeen inscriptions are in the genitive.[74] Those areas that came into contact with the Irish were the areas where the form and function of the inscriptions changed the most. It can be argued therefore that it was the influence of the Irish ogam stones, brought to western Britain by Irish settlers, which was responsible for a change in the function of the western British inscriptions.

That the majority of the early medieval western British inscriptions were, to a certain extent, erected to provide a record of land-title implies that the people recorded on the inscriptions were themselves land-owners. We are thus presented with an opportunity to analyse the social make-up of the land-owning classes in early medieval western Britain. One of the means of doing so is to look at the names of the people recorded. Analysis of these names and the elements they contain can serve as a pointer towards the status of the individuals recorded. Fig. 1 clearly shows that just under half the inscriptions contain a name which appears to be aristocratic or heroic. However, such an interpretation of the evidence is made problematic by the fact that names need not have been class-specific.[75] Any particular name could (as far as we know) have been

[72] *ECMW*, nos 136, 138, 140, 141, 142, 144, 148, 149, 150, 150#2, 160, 166, 169, 170, 171, 172, 174, 175.

[73] *CIIC*, nos 457, 458, 460, 461, 462, 466, 467, 468, 469, 470, 471, 472, 473, 474, 476, 477, 478, 481, 484, 485, 486, 488a, 488b, 489a, 489b, 489c, 489d, 490, 491, 492, 493, 499; Thomas, *Mute Stones*, nos 1202, 1205, 1206, 1207, 1209, 1210, 1400, 1402, 1403, 1404.

[74] *CIIC*, nos 506, 509, 514.

[75] D. Ellis Evans has however argued that dithematic names were more prevalent amongst the nobility of Ancient Gaul and that monothematic names were more prevalent amongst the lower classes, thereby making it a possibility that the dithematic names which we find on our inscriptions are a further indicator to the status of the individuals recorded; see D. Ellis Evans, *Gaulish Personal Names. A Study of Some of the Continental Celtic Formations* (Oxford, 1967), p. 42.

held by a person from a number of different social strata, whilst the nature of our sources does not allow us to see the naming patterns of those tied to the land.[76] This having been said, the specific nature of so many of the names on the inscriptions would seem to indicate a person who, at the very least, was attempting to claim high status for themselves. Few other explanations seem plausible for people who were named such things as "Kingly Raven" or "Great in Judgement".[77] There are other names within the corpus, which appear only once, that also have specific connotations of lordship or martial valour, such as "NETTASAGRI"; the champion of Sagri,[78] "TOVISACI"; prince,[79] as well as "TRIBUNI" and "CUMREGNI".[80] From an inscription at Llansadyrnin in the former county of Carmarthenshire we have the name "TOTOVALI" which could mean something like "kingdom or tribe worthy".[81]

[76] By the tenth and eleventh centuries, however, when we have the evidence from the names of the Bodmin manumissions, we find that there appears to be little difference between the names held by the slaves and those of the witnesses and manumittors, see W. Stokes, "The Manumissions in the Bodmin Gospels", *Revue Celtique* 1 (1870-72), 332-45, and H. Jenner, "The Manumissions in the Bodmin Gospels", *The Journal of the Royal Institution of Cornwall* 21 (1922-25), 235-60.

[77] These are the translations offered for "RIALOBRANI" and "MOBRATTI" respectively, see Thomas, *Mute Stones*, pp. 285-86.

[78] *ECMW*, no. 300.

[79] *ECMW*, no. 176, see K. H. Jackson, *Language and History in Early Britain. A Chronological Survey of the Brittonic Languages from the First to the Twelfth Century* (Edinburgh, 1952), pp. 186-87.

[80] These are *CIIC*, nos. 476 and 486 respectively.

[81] *ECMW*, no. 166. The Welsh word *tud*, here found in an early form, can mean either tribe or kingdom, whilst *valos has the meaning of "worthy". See Jackson, *Language and History*, p. 648, and Thomas, *Mute Stones*, p. 286.

Breakdown of "Aristocratic" Name-Elements (Fig. 1)

	No. of Names	No. of Inscriptions
*rix – king[82]	25	24
*maglos – prince[83]	18	17
*tigernos – lord[84]	10	9
*cun – hound/lion[85]	27	25
*catos – battle[86]	17	16
*iud – lord[87]	2	2
*dunon – fortress[88]	7	7
Total	106	100

We cannot know if such names were given at birth or if they were bestowed or chosen later in life. Either way, however, the giving or taking of such names appears as a conscious attempt to

---

[82] *ECMW*, nos 6, 26, 27, 34, 41, 84, 103, 104, 138, 140, 140, 284, 315, 349, 353, 403; *CIIC*, nos 458, 461, 468, 470, 473; Thomas, *Mute Stones*, no. 1205, *RCAHM Glamorgan*, no. 1, and the inscriptions from Wroxeter and Trawsfynydd. For the name see K. H. Jackson, "*Varia*: II. Gildas and the Names of the British Princes", *Cambridge Medieval Celtic Studies* 3 (Summer 1982), 30-40 (p. 38).

[83] *ECMW*, nos 103, 121, 127, 157, 177, 177, 183, 214, 297, 301, 353, 369; *CIIC*, nos 477, 498, 501; Webley, "Nant Crew Stone" and *RCAHM Glamorgan*, nos 1 and 2. For the name see Jackson, "*Varia*: II", p. 34.

[84] *ECMW*, nos 33, 54, 108, 229, 270, 284, 312b; *CIIC*, no. 477; Thomas, *Mute Stones*, no. 1403, 1403. For the name see Jackson, "*Varia*: II", p. 36.

[85] *ECMW*, nos 9, 34, 70, 70, 105, 105, 142, 144, 172, 301, 353, 369, 384, 402; *CIIC*, nos 468, 469, 477, 479, 487, 490, 493, 501, 504, 511 and 1048; the stone from Wroxeter and *RCAHM Glamorgan*, no. 1. For the name see Jackson and Wright, "A Late Inscription from Wroxeter", p. 297.

[86] *ECMW*, nos 13, 43, 54, 66, 127, 170, 175, 229, 297, 346, 352; *CIIC*, nos 457, 461, 500, 500; *RCAHM Dorset*, no. 3; Thomas, *Mute Stones*, no. 1202. For the name see Jackson, "*Varia*: II", p. 37.

[87] *ECMW*, no. 116 and *RCAHM Dorset*, no. 2. For the name-element see K. H. Jackson, "The Idnert Inscription: Date, and Significance of Id-", *Bulletin of the Board of Celtic Studies* 19 (1960/62), 232-34.

[88] For the name see Jackson, "*Varia*: II", p. 33. The stones are *ECMW*, nos 43, 71, 150#2, 307, and *CIIC*, nos 457, 503, 504.

proclaim the status of, or claim a status for, the bearer.[89] Some of the inscriptions also mention the occupation of the person recorded. Within the corpus we have physicians,[90] priests,[91] a sub-deacon,[92] bishops,[93] kings,[94] a "protector",[95] princes,[96] a magistrate and a holy woman.[97]

The cost of quarrying the stone and moving it to where it was to be erected, as well as the cost of hiring a lapidary to cut, dress and carve the stone almost necessitate that the people for whom the stones were erected had at their disposal an ample agricultural surplus that could be used to pay for such services; such a surplus would have required a sizeable amount of land. The use of a surplus in this manner also indicates a willingness to indulge in conspicuous consumption, an activity usually restricted to members of élites who were in constant need of maintaining the image of their own status. It seems reasonable therefore to argue that the inscriptions belong to a class of landowner that could best be described as aristocratic.

There are a few possible exceptions to this rule. An inscription from North Britain and another from Dyfed record men described as "medicus"; that is, they were physicians of some kind.[98] From Devon an inscription survives which reads "DOBUNNI FABRI FILII ENABARRI",[99] "(The land of) Dobunnus the smith, the son of Enabarr". Dobunnus was not an aristocrat, but rather an artisan. That an artisan should have a sufficiently high status to own land should not surprise us given the status of smiths and artisans in

---

[89] Thomas, *Mute Stones*, pp. 76-77.

[90] *ECMW*, no. 92, and *CIIC*, no. 509.

[91] *ECMW*, nos 77, 78.

[92] Thomas, "Early Christian Inscriptions", p. 3.

[93] *CIIC*, nos 459, 516, 517; *ECMW*, nos 33, 83, and Thomas, "Early Christian Inscriptions", p. 4.

[94] *ECMW*, nos 13, 272.

[95] *ECMW*, no. 138.

[96] *CIIC*, nos 491, 515.

[97] *ECMW*, no. 103 (magistrate), no. 33 (holy woman).

[98] *CIIC*, no. 509, and *ECMW*, no. 92.

[99] *CIIC*, no. 488.

British and indeed Celtic society.[100] The implication is that members of the professions could own land, with ownership, presumably, being the result of the largesse of a wealthy patron. Members of the professions should not therefore be seen as exceptions to the general rule that the people recorded on the western British inscriptions were of high status.

The evidence seems to point to the conclusion that the inscriptions were erected by members of the élite. The status of the people who erected the inscriptions would have been recognisable to their contemporaries. To a certain extent the inscriptions asserted the distinction between the land-owning élites and the rest of the population; they were a means by which the status of the aristocracy was proclaimed. This one-way social discourse between the few and the majority may have been part of the process by which a new post-Roman aristocracy was established within western Britain. By erecting these proclamations of ownership within the landscape the aristocrats of early medieval western Britain appear to have been asserting their right, and ability, to dominate society. The significance of the inscriptions, for both erector and observer, was their proclamation of power; they were a means by which hierarchical social differentiation was both created and maintained within early medieval western British society.

We can also look at the representation of women on the inscriptions of western Britain. Discussions of the role and status of women in early medieval Celtic society have not, to date, included an analysis of the epigraphic evidence, yet if these inscriptions were the charters of the landed élites, then the representation of women upon them becomes significant indeed. Fig. 2 gives the extent of the representation of women on the western British inscriptions,[101] and it quite clearly reveals that women are drastically under-represented on the inscriptions; fifteen out of 242 is an insignificant proportion. The number of women who shared rights with their husbands or siblings is even smaller, representing only 2.4% of the corpus.

---

[100] See for example Jenkins, ed., *The Law of Hywel Dda*, pp. 37-38, 40, where the rights of the court smith are outlined, including the right to hold land.

[101] No equivalent table would be worthwhile for the Irish ogams in that not a single ogam inscription from Ireland records a woman.

Gender Breakdown of Western British Inscriptions (Fig. 2)

Inscriptions recording men:	208	(86.0%)
Inscriptions recording women:	15	(6.2%)[102]
Inscriptions recording both genders:	6	(2.4%)[103]
Gender not available/applicable:	13	(5.4%)[104]
Total number of inscriptions:	242	

The sheer extent of the gap in the genders cannot be explained away, and should be seen as a function of the extent to which women could inherit land in early medieval Wales. To put it in the simplest of terms, few women are found on the inscriptions because few women inherited land.[105] If we look at just the genitive and ogam inscriptions of Britain we find that the discrepancy between the genders is even more pronounced.

Gender on the Genitive and Ogam Inscriptions (Fig. 3)

Inscriptions recording men:	152	(94.5%)
Inscriptions recording women:	5	(3.1%)[106]
Inscriptions recording both genders:	4	(2.4%)[107]
Total Number of Genitive and Ogam Inscriptions:	161	

The previous evidence for the ownership of land by women during the fifth, sixth and seventh centuries was very sparse indeed,

[102] *CIIC*, nos 479, 511, 512; *ECMW*, nos 33, 40, 75, 102, 121, 132, 142, 184, 294, 401; Trawsfynydd and Thomas, *Mute Stones*, no. 1401.

[103] *CIIC*, no. 520; *ECMW*, nos 26,183, 271, 284, 287.

[104] *CIIC*, nos 518, 519, 1069; *ECMW*, nos 69, 76, 124, 317, 322, 409; Thomas, *Mute Stones*, nos 1201, 1203, 1204, 1208.

[105] See for example D. Jenkins, "Property Interests in the Classical Welsh Law of Women", in *The Welsh Law of Women*, ed. D. Jenkins and M. Owen (Cardiff, 1980), pp. 69-92.

[106] *CIIC*, no. 511; *ECMW*, nos 40, 75, 142; Thomas, *Mute Stones*, no. 1401.

[107] *ECMW*, nos 26, 183, 271.

with only one of the Llandaff charters from this period referring to a female landowner, this being Onbraust the wife of King Meurig.[108] There is a further, slightly later, charter in which we find King Ffernfael giving land to his wife Ceingaer who then gave it to the church with his consent,[109] but even so this is little evidence upon which to base any theories. The inscriptions are a very welcome extension to the sources. Nonetheless the testimony of the inscriptions appears to reinforce the picture presented in the Laws and the Book of Llandaff, leaving us with an image of women as a largely subject group within early medieval Celtic society.[110]

The corpus of early medieval western British inscriptions changed in its function from being primarily memorial to demarcating the boundaries of, and providing evidence for the ownership of, landed estates. This change came about as a result of the introduction of the example of the Irish ogam stones and should be linked to the various Irish settlements in western Britain that date to the fifth century. The old theory of the inscriptions simply being memorials appears difficult to maintain. This changed interpretation provides us with a new source of information on such issues as land-ownership, kinship structures, inheritance, gender relations, the rural economy, the resolution of disputes and the creation of the post-Roman élite, only some of which has there been space to touch on here.

---

[108] Davies, *Llandaff Charters*, no. 17, p. 97.

[109] Davies, *Llandaff Charters*, no. 97, p. 117.

[110] This phrase is taken from W. Davies, "Celtic Women in the Early Middle Ages", in *Images of Women in Antiquity*, ed. A. Cameron and A. Kuhrt (London, 1983), pp. 145-65 (p. 160). Also see the papers collected in *Welsh Law of Women*, ed. Jenkins and Owen.

Treasure Bequest: Death and Gift in the Early Middle Ages

Dominic Janes

High value movables are conveniently symbolic of élite status. Such objects played a prominent role in social communication within high society during the early Middle Ages.[1] Gift-giving was carried out not only in the context of life, but also in that of death. Grave goods bear witness to offerings to the deceased, but presents were also received from them via the agency of wills. These documents are especially valuable in that they derive from one of the few circumstances in which such exchanges of items were systematically recorded in writing. Roman law made extensive provision for the bequest of such tokens of esteem. A whole chapter of the Digest of Justinian is devoted to legacies of gold, silver, jewellery and perfumes, clothing and statues.[2] The evolution of late antique judicial procedures in the post-Roman West provides a context in

For their considerable help with the preparation of this paper, I would like to thank Dr Rosamond McKitterick, Dr Greg Woolf and Dr Patricia Skinner. References are given not only to Latin texts but also, where possible, to English translations.

[1] D. Cheal, *The Gift Economy* (London, 1988), p. 16, on "transactions that are used in the ritual construction of social worlds". See also C. A. Gregory, *Gifts and Commodities* (London, 1982).

[2] Justinian, *Digesta*, 34.2, Latin text edited by T. Mommsen and P. Kreuger with English translation by A. Watson, 4 vols (Philadelphia, 1985), 3:148-58.

which to understand the development of relationships between the living, the dying and the dead.

It must be admitted that the evidence is not especially abundant or easy to interpret. Roman survivals are limited to fragmentary inscriptions, papyri and literary references. However, in the Christian West, various ecclesiastical centres preserved wills for their value as land grants. This has ensured that a small corpus of testaments has been preserved from Merovingian Gaul.[3] Although forgery or adaptation of estate donation clauses was far from uncommon, it is less easy to imagine the reason for fabrication of details of gifts of single items which might well have had no meaning for later generations. It is instructive to consider Patrick Geary's comments in his study of Abbo's will as evidence for the seventh-century aristocracy of Provence. He wrote that, although "if the form is genuine, the content was probably interpolated ... [nevertheless] at most the interpolations may have added certain place names to those actually bequeathed by Abbo": land, of course, was very much a matter of ongoing concern.[4] There are about twenty texts from before AD 750, the authenticity of which is fairly secure. Of these, about one third mention individual treasure items such as silver bowls and chalices, while others include bequests of small amounts of gold coin (*solidi*). The current study will present selected case studies from that material, with the aim of illustrating the early medieval construction of relationships expressed through the publicly witnessed transfer of treasures.

Edward Champlin has made an excellent attempt to re-animate the Roman testament in its social context. Most Romans did not make a will. The illiterate poor had little to give and less access to

---

[3] I. Wood, *The Merovingian Kingdoms, 450-751* (London, 1994), pp. 206-13, provides a general introduction to the evidence, while for more detail see U. Nonn, "Merowingische testamente: Studien zum Fortleben einer römischen Urkundenform im Frankreich", *Archiv für Diplomatik* 18 (1972), 1-29.

[4] P. Geary, *Aristocracy in Provence*, Monographien zur Geschichte des Mittelalters 31 (Stuttgart, 1985), p. 31.

the legal processes of the empire.[5] The rich, by contrast, often (but not invariably) had drawn up complex legal agreements of the sort that survive from Merovingian Gaul. In the nobles' world of *amicitia* and other social networks, the will was a public and social act "tempered with a strong sense of duty, mixed with self-esteem".[6] The frequent mention of wills in literary sources such as Pliny's letters illustrates how the bequests of notables were a matter of popular interest. The power of the gift was magnified by its public nature. Constantine adjusted the laws of gift and donation so as to ensure that the legal acts were performed as publicly as possible.[7] Even if the item given was small and worth but a tiny fraction of its owner's income its treasured nature (being made of gold, say) ensured that its style was fitting for its élitist ritual context. Such presents were measured against general conventions of decorum. All treasures of this kind would, of course, pass to a person's heirs, unless there was made specific provision for legacies of movables. There was clearly the belief that along with a legacy of land, a wife's personal items, her jewellery, clothes and toiletries, should be specifically assigned to her.[8] Secondly, to friends went token bequests in the form of coin or crafted goods such as silver plate.[9] This can be illustrated by the will of Augustus: Dio records that the emperor dictated that many articles and sums of money should be given to relatives of his and to friends and dignitaries.[10]

[5] J. Crook, "Intestacy in Roman Society", *Proceedings of the Cambridge Philological Society*, new ser., 19 (1973), 38-44.

[6] E. Champlin, *Final Judgements: Duty and Emotion in Roman Wills, 200 B.C. - A.D. 250* (Berkeley, 1991), p. 17.

[7] E. Levy, *West Roman Vulgar Law*, Memoirs of the American Philosophical Society 29 (Philadelphia, 1951), pp. 138-39 and W. Davies, "The Latin Charter Tradition in Western Britain, Britanny and Ireland in the Early Medieval Period", in *Ireland in Early Medieval Europe: Studies in Memory of Kathleen Hughes*, ed. D. Whitelock, R. McKitterick and D. Dumville (Cambridge, 1982), pp. 258-80 (p. 275).

[8] Champlin, *Final Judgements*, pp. 122-24.

[9] Champlin, *Final Judgements*, pp. 148-50.

[10] Dio, *Roman History*, 56.32.2, ed. and trans. E. Cary, Loeb Classical Library, 9 vols (London, 1924), 7:72-73. The passage refers to AD 14.

Other individuals in turn made customary gifts to the emperor in their wills.[11] It is in this context that Dasumius' AD 108 legacy of a few pounds of precious metal to Trajan should be understood.[12] The will has furthermore been reconstructed as mentioning table-silver and gold and silver figures.[13] Gifts of such personal items as plate must have represented a distinct degree of (at least desired) intimacy in the relationship. On the other hand, cash had the advantage of allowing easy equality of gifts amongst friends. In addition, at a lower social level, where men and women did not own hoards of plate, cash could play the same role in marking out relationships outside the immediate circle of inheriting relatives. This is just what we find in the surviving, albeit fragmentary, papyri from the civic archive of late antique Ravenna, in which there are frequent references to the giving of *solidi*.[14]

The nature of Roman inheritance is illustrated by a wide variety of textual evidence. The same cannot be said for the early Germanic peoples. Tacitus, in the *Germania*, paints a picture of communal tribal existence. Ploughlands were divided up yearly amongst the community.[15] Despite the unsatisfactory nature of the evidence, it seems clear that by the time of the invasions, the power of royalty and of family units had considerably eroded the enormous power held by the kin in early tribal culture.[16] The settlement of barbarians by the Roman government was achieved under a system

[11] D. Braund, "Royal Wills and Rome", *Papers of the British School at Rome* 51 (1983), 16-57 (p. 54).

[12] V. Arangio-Ruiz, *Negotia*, Fontes Iuris Romani Antejustiniani 3 (Florence, 1943), no. 48, "Testamentum P. Dasumii Tusci Nobilis Viri", pp. 132-42 (an edition of Corpus Inscriptionum Latinarum 6.2 (Berlin, 1882), no. 10229) at pp. 141-42 and Champlin, *Final Judgements*, p. 152.

[13] Arangio-Ruiz, *Negotia*, no. 48, p. 135, line 38, "... item argenti es]CARI ET POTOR[i] EX MEO QUOD E[ligerit ...", and p. 138, lines 74-75, "... item signa mea aure[A ET ARGENTEA OMNIA ET IM[agines argentias meas omnes".

[14] J.-O. Tjäder, ed., *Die Nichtlitterarischen Lateinischen Papyri Italiens aus der Zeit 445-700*, 1 (Lund, 1955) and 2 (Stockholm, 1982), nos 4-6.

[15] Tacitus, *Germania*, chap. 26, in *Tacitus Opera*, trans. M. Hutton, Loeb Classical Library, 5 vols, rev. ed. (London, 1970), 1:168-71.

[16] M. Todd, *The Early Germans* (Oxford, 1992), p. 32.

of allotment. The nature of the system of *hospitalitas* has been a matter of huge controversy. Suffice it to say that even if barbarians merely enjoyed tax-revenues rather than actually receiving land themselves, with that money they were then able to enter the world of Roman land-owning, with its associated legal forms.[17] For example, it has been stated that "as far as the records allow us to look, we find Gothic nobles buying and selling in the traditional and often archaic Roman legal forms".[18]

The appearance of the codes notwithstanding, there was no precise distinction between Romans and barbarians in legal practice. There were separate law codifications stemming from very different traditions, but in the situation of Burgundy, for instance, these have been seen as applying to individuals according to their political and social role, rather than their cultural or ethnic community.[19] Indeed, the *Lex Burgundionem* says that if a *barbarus* wishes to give or to make a will, either Roman or German custom may be observed.[20] The barbarian law-codes themselves are enigmatic documents which, moreover, are far from informative on the topic of inheritance. With regard to the Celtic evidence it has been remarked that the rules of inheritance are "assumed rather than expounded" in the laws, a remark which fits many passages of Germanic law.[21] So, for example, there is no mention of wills in the *Lex Salica* and it has been explained that the chapter *de alodis*, "gives only a partial statement of Frankish inheritance ... [because] it is a statement of the

[17] Levy, *West Roman Vulgar Law*, p. 87, expresses this view, "private ownership ... constituted the basis of the law of property in the early kingdoms on Roman soil, for the Germanic population as well as the Roman".

[18] T. S. Burns, *A History of the Ostrogoths* (Bloomington, 1991), p. 125.

[19] P. Amory, "The Meaning and Purpose of Ethnic Terminology in the Burgundian Laws", *Early Medieval Europe* 2 (1993), 1-28 (p. 26).

[20] R. J. R. Goffin, *The Testamentary Executor in England and Elsewhere* (London, 1901), pp. 14-15, compares the various codes and gives references, including one to the *Lex Burgundionem* text which states that either Roman or barbarian customs ("consuetudines") of donation and testation may be followed.

[21] T. Charles-Edwards, *Early Irish and Welsh Kinship* (Oxford, 1993), p. 61.

peculiar 'Frankishness' of Salian practice": it lists the ways in which the scheme for intestate inheritance differs from Roman practice.[22]

The practice of distributing lands primarily among sons was displayed in the repeated divisions of the Merovingian kingdom between brothers. The position of women, with regard to early Germanic land-holding practice, is difficult to determine. They were especially associated with movable goods, above all the ownership of dowries.[23] If early Germanic practice can be thought of as concentrating on socially accepted norms in the handing on of goods, the Roman tradition offered the formal opportunity to set out in writing the transfer of specific items to specific individuals, as witnessed by a chosen group of people. This ability was clearly seen as advantageous in the early medieval world, as witnessed by the continuation of that late antique tradition. Nevertheless, such means of social construction did not always work smoothly. Gregory of Tours, in his *Liber vitae patrum*, gives a splendid description of the reading of the will of Nicetius of Lyons in AD 573: "huius antestitis testamentum in foro delatum, turbis circumstantibus, a iudice reseratum recitatumque est".[24] A priest then exploded with anger when he found that Nicetius had left nothing to the church of the Holy Apostles (later St Nizier) in which the bishop was to be buried. The etiquette of polite communication through the agency of donation had clearly broken down in this case.

How such social worlds were built up through witnessed promises to give, and, we can presume, the ensuing transfer of

---

[22] K. A. Eckhardt, ed., *Pactus legis Salicae*, MGH LNG 1.4.1 (Hanover, 1962), chap. 59, "On inheritance", pp. 222-24 and *Laws of the Salian and Ripuarian Franks*, trans. T. J. Rivers (New York, 1987), pp. 106-07. Quotation from A. C. Murray, *Germanic Kinship Structure: Studies in Law and Society in Antiquity and the Early Middle Ages*, Pontifical Institute of Mediaeval Studies, Studies and Texts 65 (Toronto, 1983), pp. 211-12.

[23] S. F. Wemple, *Women in Frankish Society: Marriage and the Cloister 500-900* (Philadelphia, 1981), p. 46.

[24] Gregory of Tours, *Liber vitae patrum*, ed. B. Krusch, MGH SRM 1 (Hanover, 1885), "Nicetius", pp. 661-744, chapter 8.5 (p. 695). "The document was brought to the forum where, before crowds of people, it was opened and read out by the judge": E. James, trans., *Life of the Fathers*, Translated Texts for Historians, Latin Series 1 (Liverpool, 1985), p. 68.

treasures, will now be illustrated by reference to examples of the testaments themselves. The first piece which I wish to introduce, the will of Ermintrude of Paris, has been dated to the early seventh century.[25] The testament, an original copy on papyrus, is untidy, idiosyncratic and with some very obscure vocabulary. In addition to gifts of land to the north-east of Paris to family members and Parisian churches, there were donations of workers, farm animals, equipment, clothing and also items of precious metal. The treasures were given to relatives and to churches. Thus, Ermintrude gave to her son a silver pot ("canna") valued at twenty-five *solidi* and a silver goblet ("caucus") worth thirty.[26] A grandson, Bertigisilus, received a silver pitcher ("ichrarius").[27] A grand-daughter, Deorovara, was given a dish ("scutella") decorated with crosses.[28] The church of St Peter in Paris got a silver pitcher or pot ("urceus") worth twelve *solidi* together with a gold clasp with gems on it. To the church of Lady Mary went a silver bowl ("gabata") worth twelve *solidi* and a gold cross valued at seven. To St Stephen's went a nielloed ring, valued at four *solidi*, and another with Ermintrude's name upon it went to St Gervase's.[29] The cathedral of Paris, as was

[25] Ermintrude, "Testamentum", in *Diplomata, chartae, epistolae, leges aliaque instrumenta ad res Gallo-Francicas spectantia nunc nova ratione ordinata* 2, ed. J. M. Pardessus (Paris, 1849), no. 451, pp. 255-58. J.-P. Laporte, "Pour une nouvelle datation du testament d'Ermenthrude", *Francia* 14 (1986), 574-77. Note however, that J. Mabillon, *De liturgica Gallicana* (Paris, 1685), pp. 462-66, no. 5 and J. Vezin and H. Atsma, eds, *Chartae latinae antiquiores* 14 (Zurich, 1982), pp. 72-79, would put the date twenty-five to seventy-five years earlier.

[26] Ermintrude, "Testamentum", p. 255: "dono tibi canna argentia, valante plus minus sol. xxv, et a parte mea dono tibi cauco argentio, valante sol. xxx".

[27] Ermintrude, "Testamentum", p. 256: "Item dulcissimo nepoti meo Bertegisilo, ichrario argentio".

[28] Ermintrude, "Testamentum", p. 256: "Nepoti meae Deoravarae, scutella argentea cruciclata ... dari constituo".

[29] Ermintrude, "Testamentum", p. 256: "Baselicis constitutis Parisius id est basilicae Sancti Petri, urcio argentio valente soledus duodec, et fibla aurea gemmata ... [text damaged] ... manto dario constituo. Basilicae domane Mariae gavata argentea valenta sol. duodece, et cruce aurea valente sol. septe, dari jubeo. Basilicae domni Stephani anolo aurea nigellato, valente sol. quattuor, dari

perhaps only fitting, got an especially grand silver platter ("missorium") valued at fifty *solidi*. St Vincent's obtained ten silver spoons.[30]

This evidence is partly at odds and partly accords with what is known of classical Roman practice. The gifts to relatives in the absence of friends represent a different practice, as at first sight do the token offerings to the churches. If however, the saints thereby represented are understood as powerful friends, then the Roman pattern of treasure gifts is here nicely replicated in the context of a Christian society.[31] The gift of single items of treasure appears as the prominent means of the bestowal of tokens of personal recognition. The witness list of Ermintrude's will included two high ranking officials, a "spatharius" (royal sword-carrier) and a "defensor" (high city official) of Paris. As Nonn has pointed out, she was an important woman and her inscribed finger ring was a significant token. She was thus communicating both within her family and amongst the high society of her region.[32]

Perhaps the most famous Merovingian will is that of Remigius, bishop of Rheims, who, according to Gregory of Tours, baptised Clovis.[33] The testament has been the centre of controversy, partly because it is presented to us in different forms by two later authors. The first "short" version is included by Hincmar in the

---

volo. Basilicae domni Gervasi anolo aureo, nomen meum in se habentum scribtum, dari praecipio".

[30] Ermintrude, "Testamentum", p. 257: "Sacrosancte Ecclesiae civitatis Parisiorum, missorium argentio, valente sol. quinquagenta, dari praecipio. Basilicae Sanctae-Cruces vel domni Vincenti, cocliaria argentea dece, dari jubeo".

[31] There is, of course, a vast literature on this topic. Good introductions are P. Brown, *The Cult of the Saints* (Chicago, 1981), and R. Van Dam, *Leadership and Community in Late Antique Gaul* (Berkeley, 1985), both with extensive references and bibliography.

[32] U. Nonn, "Erminethrud – eine vornehme neustriche Dame um 700", *Historisches Jahrbuch* 102 (1982), 135-43.

[33] Gregory of Tours, *Libri historiarum X*, ed. B. Krusch and W. Levison, MGH SRM 1.1 (Hanover, 1951), 2.31, pp. 76-78 and *The History of the Franks*, trans. L. Thorpe (Harmondsworth 1974), pp. 143-44.

ninth-century *Vita Remigii episcopi Remensis*.[34] The second version, which includes additional passages, is furnished by Flodoard in his mid-tenth-century *Historia Remensis ecclesiae*.[35] The editor of Hincmar, Krusch, did not approve of either version since he reasoned that if the latter was an adaptation, why should the former not be so as well. However, Jones, Grierson and Cook subjected his formal criticisms to severe scrutiny and judged, after lengthy deliberations, that "the case against the [Hincmar] will is, it is submitted, very weak".[36] Since it is not an original copy it can never be so secure as the will of Ermintrude, but the language and style of both documents fit well together.

The Hincmar version of the will of Remigius is undated and its origin can only be measured against the year of Remigius' death which took place in AD 533. His heirs were the church of Rheims, Lupus (the son of Remigius' deceased brother), and his nephew, the priest Agricola. To his successor bishop he left his white Easter chasuble, two dove-coloured rugs, and three curtains.[37] To the archdeacon Ursus there went several specified items of clothing including "the best tunic I leave at my death".[38] A silver pot ("*vasa*") of eighteen pounds in weight was to be divided between the churches of Rheims and Laon for the making of patens and chalices. Another silver pot ("vasa"), which had originally been given by Clovis for Remigius to do with as he wished, was to go to Rheims for the making of a thurible and chalice.[39] To a further

---

[34] Remigius of Rheims: Hincmar's version, *Testamentum s. Remigii*, ed. B. Krusch, MGH SRM 3 (Hanover, 1896), pp. 336-41, with summarised additions of Flodoard, *Addimenta amplioris Testamenti s. Remigii*, pp. 341-47.

[35] Remigius of Rheims: Flodoard's version, *Testamentum s. Remigii*, ed. J. Heller and G. Waitz, MGH SS 13 (Hanover, 1881), pp. 428-43.

[36] A. H. M. Jones, P. Grierson and J. A. Crook, "The Authenticity of the 'Testamentum s. Remigii'", *Revue belge de philologie et d'histoire* 35 (1957), 356-73 (p. 368-69).

[37] Hincmar, *Testamentum s. Remigii*, p. 337: "Futuro episcopo successori meo amphibalum album paschalum relinquo: stragola columbina duo, vela tria".

[38] Ibid., p. 339: "tunicam quam tempore transitus mei reliquero meliorem".

[39] Ibid., p. 337: "Alius argentium vas, quod mihi domnus illustris memoriae Hludovichus rex, quem de sacro baptismatis fonte suscepi, donare

nephew, Praetextatus, were granted a number of slaves, four spoons, a cup, a cloak and a crozier. Praetextatus' son, Parorius, was bequeathed three spoons, a cup and a cape. The woman, Remigia, received three spoons with Remigius' name on them, a cloth and "a bowl about which I have spoken to Gundobad".[40] A series of donations of *solidi* (gold coins) were made to various ranks of clerics in the church. The deacons and priests of Rheims were given between them twenty-five *solidi*. The subdeacons, readers, door-keepers and poor on the register, were to receive two *solidi* amongst each group; eight in total.[41] The priests of Laon were left eighteen *solidi*, whilst the subdeacons, readers and door-keepers shared four in total and the poor were allotted one *solidus*.[42] The church at Sissiones got eight *solidi*; Chalons, six; Mouzon, five; Chery, four and Porcien, four. Vancq was left a convenient field, as an equivalent token.[43] Six "viri clarissimi" subscribed, then there was appended, "after the completion and signing of this will, it occurred to me that a silver dish weighing six pounds should go to the church of the lord martyrs Timothy and Apollinaris, from which may be made provision for the future resting place of my bones".[44]

The provisions appear in a rather jumbled order, not as given above. But when classified, the gifts show coherence. The next bishop and the present archdeacon are given vestments. Cash sums are donated in graded amounts to the staff of the main two churches and to the smaller churches in the area. In addition to land and slaves, most of his relatives have treasures given to them. Three times this is in the form of spoons, a dish and a garment or cloth. These are specifically personal items, given according to a repeated formula, which suggests a desire for equality of symbolic gift.

dignatus est, ut de eo facerem, quod ipse voluissem, tibi, heredi meae aeclesiae supra memoratae, iubeo turibulum et imaginatum calicem fabricari".

[40] Ibid., p. 338: "hichinaculum quoque dono illi, de quo Gundebado dixi".

[41] Ibid., p. 337 passim.

[42] Ibid., pp. 338-39 passim.

[43] Ibid., p. 339 passim.

[44] Ibid., p. 340: "Post conditum testamentum, immo signatum, occurrit sensibus meis, ut basilice domnorum martyrum Timothei et Apollinaris missorium argentium VI librarum ibi deputem, ut ex eo sedes futura meorum ossuum componatur".

Praetextatus is to get a cloak given by Friaredus, and Remigia is to get back the cloth she had given to Remigius. Presumably, his heirs and relatives Lupus and Agricola would have known the particular objects he was talking about. Remigius made extensive use of cash gifts, but only for the politely impersonal purpose of a general allotment to clergy and churches. Specific items were given out to churches with instructions for them to be broken up, especially for the making of liturgical vessels. The friendship of the saints was therefore paid heed to, albeit with a rather more patronal style than was the case with Ermintrude and her granting of her ring and brooch, her most personal treasures. The lack of donation to worldly superiors (the equivalent of "friends" such as Trajan) is notable. Remigius appears here in the context of providing ritualised fulfilment of the dictates of duty and emotion as bishop of the local church and head of his family.

As has been remarked, it is impossible to know precisely how reliable the text is. However, the intricate provisions of specific items would hardly appear to have been necessary for an eloquent forgery, and they would have been quite unsuitable if such provisions were unexpected in old documents. A comparison of the Hincmar and Flodoard versions of Remigius' will is illuminating. The longer text is made up of the shorter plus additions. There are a number of major interpolations. There is included a new and lengthy list of estates which are to go to Rheims, some of which, we are carefully and repeatedly informed, were given by the lord king Clovis of illustrious memory.[45] This section makes clear sense as a forgery, as it adds land endowments and emphasises relations with Clovis referred to in the Hincmar version only in connection with a silver dish. That very passage itself may seem potentially suspect, but it closely parallels a reference in the same text to a cloak given by the far from famous Friaredus: items were thus partly defined by those who gave them. Besides, the Clovis dish is ordered to be broken up; it is to be made into church plate, not at the request of the king, but of Remigius. These details would hardly have been

---

[45] Flodoard, *Testamentum s. Remigii*, p. 341, line 27 to p. 343, line 16 passim.

inserted by a later writer with the aim of magnifying the position of Clovis.

This text contrasts with the situation in Flodoard's version, where the dish given by Clovis in the Hincmar version is the subject of a localised alteration. The rather dowdy "other silver dish" ("aliud argentium vas"), in this text is made of gold and weighs ten pounds.[46] In addition to the chalice to be made with images ("imaginatum calicem") there was to be an inscription.[47] One wonders if there was a certain well-known object kept as a relic of the saint to which this addition referred? As for the presence of the original dish, if it was a gift from the king, it would have been a prominent item for Remigius and his family. By remaking it into church plate it would, appropriately enough, receive its own baptism.

An additional major interpolation builds up the donation of quantities of *solidi* into a statement of benefaction to all the ecclesiastical institutions in Rheims.[48] The will is thus aggrandised, as is Remigius' reputation for charity and patronage to the church. The third addition is a homily on the subject of the powers of the bishop, including in it biblical quotations and ending with an "amen".[49] In addition, further aggrandisement is achieved in the Flodoard text by the augmentation of the unsuitably secular six "viri clarissimi" of the Hincmar subscription-list, by no less than eight bishops and three presbyters.[50] These differences between the Hincmar and Flodoard versions highlight the fact not simply that alterations in documents were made, but also that such interpolations would tend to follow patterns which can be extrapolated. Symbolic treasure gifts were more associated with immediate social links and had little relevance, in comparison with the ownership of land, for future generations. The presence of small, individual gifts of treasure items in Merovingian documents, it is

---

[46] Ibid., p. 343: "vas aureum decem librarum".
[47] Ibid., p. 343, lines 20-21.
[48] Ibid., p. 343, line 24 to p. 344, line 23.
[49] Ibid., p. 345, line 6 to p. 346, line 36.
[50] Ibid., p. 346, line 37 to p. 347, line 17.

contended, only appears intelligible when understood in the context of the practices of symbolic gift in the immediately post-Roman age.

These individual single gifts should be put in the context of the huge treasure hoards held by early medieval magnates, thus emphasising the symbolic nature of these individual gifts. Gregory of Tours wrote of the dowry brought together in AD 584 for Rigunth, daughter of the Merovingian king Chilperic, that "tanta fuit multitudo rerum, ut aurum argentumque vel reliqua ornamenta quinquaginta plaustra levarent".[51] Treasure was, on occasion, provided *en masse* as part of church endowment, and recorded in inventories, as can be seen from the Constantinian donations in the *Liber pontificalis*.[52] One such treasure list, attributed to Desiderius, bishop of Auxerre from AD 605 and AD 623, is contained in the ninth-century *Gesta pontificum Autissiodorensium*, which was modelled on the *Liber pontificalis*.[53] The relevant section is attributed to the monks Heric, Alagus and Raingala who were active in the years following 870, but it includes material which Rouche refers to as evidently extracted from Desiderius' will.[54] He refers to an extraordinary list which takes up two pages of printed text. Important for the dating of these lists is the repeated use of the word "anacleam" to indicate relief decoration. The only close parallel is "anacleta", which is found in the treasure lists of Leodbod's "will" (the donation charter of Fleury), from a neighbouring diocese only thirty years or so later (c. AD 650).[55] The remainder of the

---

[51] Gregory of Tours, *Libri historiarum x*, 6.45, p. 318. "There was such a vast assemblage of objects that the gold, silver and other precious things filled fifty carts": *History of the Franks*, trans. Thorpe, p. 378.

[52] *Liber pontificalis, pars prior*, ed. T. Mommsen, MGH Gesta pontificum Romanorum 1 (Berlin, 1898), "Silvester", pp. 42-72, and *The Book of Pontiffs (to AD 715)*, trans. Raymond Davis (Liverpool, 1989), pp. 14-26.

[53] *Gesta pontificium Autissiodorensium, de Desiderio*, in *Bibliothèque historique de L'Yonne*, ed. L. M. Duru (Auxerre, 1850), pp. 332-40. The treasure list runs from the top of p. 334 to line 7 of p. 336 and cannot here be given in full.

[54] M. Rouche, *L'Aquitaine des Wisigoths aux Arabes 418-781: naissance d'une région* (Paris, 1979), p. 200, note 111.

[55] Leodbod, "Testamentum", in *Diplomata, chartae, epistolae* 2, ed. Pardessus, no. 358, pp. 142-47 (p. 143): "vasa dono argentea, anacleta,

somewhat obscure vocabulary mirrors that in other Merovingian documents. It certainly appears to represent a genuine inventory of the period. It is carefully noted that to St Stephen's church went in total 420 pounds, seven ounces of silver, whilst St Germanus' got rather less, 119 pounds and five ounces. These totals do not quite add up to the listed weights, which, in modern terms equal about 137 kg. One of the greatest hoards ever found in Britain, the Mildenhall treasure, is dwarfed in comparison. Buried around AD 360, its items could easily be described using the language of the Auxerre list. A catalogue entry notes that "though many (late Roman) families possessed silver plate, a set of this quality would have belonged to a person of outstanding wealth and status".[56] At 26 kg it comes to less than a sixth of what is listed as donated by Desiderius.

The evidence of lists and inventories such as these shows that items of élite culture were collected into vast hoards by those able to do so. Treasure items circulated between such accumulations in early medieval Europe in a variety of ways, one of which appears to have been the socially determined individual testamentary gift. Single treasure items, in the context of hoarding, can be seen to have been employed as tokens of admiration, affection, or duty, in a ritual practice based on Roman precedent. There is, however, the important difference that symbolic giving of individual items is strongly focused in the later period toward relatives and saints rather than friends. Since gift-giving was a social and not just a personal act, this may reflect the fact that the "audience" for Merovingian wills was more restricted and the kin more important than was the case in a world of Roman empire-wide networks of *amicitia*.

Classical practice was associated with the maintenance of social correctness. As Veyne has written, the Roman will "was a kind of confession in which social man revealed himself fully and

pensantea libris VIII et uncias duas". ("I give a decorated silver vessel weighing eight pounds and two ounces").

[56] J. P. C. Kent and K. S. Painter, *Wealth of the Roman World, AD 300-700* (London, 1977), p. 33.

by which he would be judged".[57] This desire had not atrophied in Merovingian Gaul, although changes had by then taken place in the composition of a testator's social obligations. The importance of the earliest medieval wills to religious houses can be judged from the fact that it has been argued that "most gifts to the church in the fifth century actually came by bequest".[58] Of the present significance of such testaments, Rosamond McKitterick has noted that "these documents show us not only how wealthy these magnates were in terms of their movable and immovable property, but also what they considered to be precious among their possessions".[59] Not only that, but as has been shown, these wills provide valuable evidence for the ritual expression of social relations. The witnessing of wills and their subsequent public reading displayed these formal friendships in high society, including those between the aristocracy and the church, each of which desired the favour of the other. Such was the continuing power and potential of testamentary gift, which early medieval notables exploited in the manner of their own culture to provide public social links in life and in death.

[57] P. Veyne, "The Roman Empire", in *A History of Private Life, vol. 1, From Pagan Rome to Byzantium*, ed. P. Veyne, trans. A. Goldhammer (Cambridge, Mass., 1987), pp. 5-233 (p. 31).

[58] Davies, "The Latin Charter Tradition", p. 276 note 69.

[59] R. McKitterick, *The Carolingians and the Written Word* (Cambridge, 1989), p. 158.

Vikings Deceased in England – Commemorated by Whom? Runic Memorials in Sweden

Bertil Nilsson

There is in Sweden a small but unique and important collection of source material, dating from the Viking Age, which makes it possible to ask questions about the connection between England and Sweden during the decisive period of Christianisation: mainly the first half of the eleventh century. Among the inscriptions on twenty-eight of the erected rune-stones, the name "England" is found. It is therefore appropriate and interesting to ask questions, on the one hand about Christian influence in certain Swedish regions and, on the other, to say something about Viking activity in England. Who were the Swedish Vikings who travelled to England? Furthermore, where did they come from? What did they do? And where are they buried and commemorated respectively? Finally, what do the answers to these questions tell us about the English impact during the period when the Church was established in the provinces which later became Sweden?

The purpose of this paper is not to debate the inscriptions from a linguistic point of view, but rather to give an account of present opinion among scholars in Sweden and to pose some new questions about the implications of the inscriptions for church history. The primary material on which this study is based is interpretation of the texts by runological scholars.

The Material

The erecting of rune-stones during the Viking Age is, generally speaking, connected with the transition from paganism to Christianity; the rune-stones thus constitute very important primary material from a period which, in Sweden, lacks other written sources. The primary documentation on these stones of parts of the Christianisation process in Sweden is not limited to the inscriptions; the whole monument, as such, is an original record. Therefore many other aspects must be taken into consideration when forming an opinion about a rune-stone, such as ornamentation, and the placing of the stone.[1] What I am about to present is thus merely one layer of the evidence.

Generally, the inscriptions on the rune-stones are short and in lapidary style. This is quite natural. Stone is not a material on which to carve very long stories, and therefore it is usually a matter of just a couple of sentences. Difficulties can arise in interpretation of the texts, particularly when the actual stones have been destroyed and transcriptions must be relied upon. Even when the text has been securely established, varying interpretations are still possible. It should also be noted that some of the stones to which I refer are fragmentary; parts of the inscriptions are missing and therefore, of course, the reading of the text as a whole is uncertain.

As is well known, it is in Sweden that we find the majority of memorial inscriptions on rune-stones from the period of Christianisation – mainly from the eleventh century. That the custom of erecting rune-stones ceased so relatively suddenly has caused scholars to talk about a short period of prosperity and a period of fashion. The rune-stone fashion is considered to have ended when the custom was established of burying the dead in a churchyard.[2] Accordingly, an approximate dating is arrived at; the rune-stones belong to the missionary era and they are unique in the sense that

---

[1] See H. Williams, "Vad säger runstenarna om Sveriges kristnande?", in *Kristnandet i Sverige. Gamla källor och nya perspektiv*, ed. B. Nilsson, Projektet Sveriges kristnande 5 (Uppsala, 1996), pp. 45-83.

[2] Cf. O. von Friesen, *Runorna i Sverige. En kortfattad översikt*, 3rd ed. (Uppsala, 1928), pp. 74-76.

they belong to a period in Swedish history when other, domestic, written source-material is lacking. The position of current research, in opposition to scholars who wrote during the first part of the twentieth century, is that rune-stones dating from the eleventh century which do not expressly have elements from the pre-Christian Scandinavian religion should also be viewed in a Christian context.[3]

The rune-stones are generally Christian. Of course, stones cannot be Christian in the strict sense of the word, but it is used here in the sense that they contain prayers for the soul and the spirit of the deceased and have crosses, sometimes both. Sometimes, however, they have neither and the evaluation of such stones is considerably more difficult.[4] These variations may be local but may also be seen in a chronological perspective related to the gradual establishment of the Church. However, as regards those inscriptions in which England is mentioned, there are no problems of linguistic interpretation, in so far as it is a question of establishing that it is indeed England that is referred to.

It should also be mentioned that the rune-stones may have had several functions at the same time, serving, for example, as boundary markers, or as documents relating to the inheritance of estates.[5] However, the main reason why the rune-stones were erected was to commemorate the dead; the custom is thus a part of the Christian *memoria* tradition.[6] Some may have been cenotaphs, commemorating people who had died in England, for example, who were therefore not in the place where the stone was located. There are, however, obvious examples where the rune-stones were gravestones in the usual sense of the word, marking the grave itself. This can be seen from the inscription "Here X is buried".[7] The number of such stones

---

[3] H. Williams, "Runstenstexternas teologi", in *Kristnandet i Sverige*, ed. Nilsson, pp. 291-312.

[4] Williams, "Runstenstexternas teologi", pp. 292-96.

[5] B. Sawyer, *Property and Inheritance in Viking Scandinavia. The Runic Evidence* (Alingsås, 1988).

[6] R. Palm, *Runor och regionalitet. Studier av variation i de nordiska minnesinskrifterna*, Runrön 7 (Uppsala, 1992), pp. 45-48.

[7] Palm, *Runor och regionalitet*, p. 144; see also B. Nilsson, *Kvinnor, män och barn på medeltida begravningsplatser*, Projektet Sveriges kristnande 3 (Uppsala, 1994), p. 60, and note 21.

is not very great, but, as Anne-Sofie Gräslund has pointed out, the real number may be greater, since other stones without this particular inscription may have been placed in burial grounds of the Viking Age or in churchyards.[8] The original placing of the rune-stones is, however, a complex problem and it is evident that many of them have been moved, for example, those which have been built into the walls of stone churches dating from the high and late Middle Ages.[9]

Among the approximately 2,500 rune-stones in Sweden, there are twenty-eight in which the name "England" is found in the inscription, and there is one such stone from Norway.[10] This is not very much to build upon and not sufficient data from which to make statistical calculations. Some other inscriptions on rune-stones may have an oblique reference to England but this cannot be known for certain. These are the inscriptions which refer to voyages westwards without any information being given about the destination. This is the case on thirteen stones from Svealand, where the custom of erecting rune-stones was most intensive, and on only one stone from the rest of Sweden.

The Travellers to England

Who were the Swedes who went to England in the Viking Age? First of all, it can be seen that all of them in this material are men. This fact is not very surprising, since the majority of rune-stones are erected in memory of men, even though a great many women too have been

[8] A.-S. Gräslund, "Runstenar, bygd och gravar", *Tor. Tidskrift för nordisk fornkunskap* 21 (1986-87), 241-62.

[9] L. Wilson, *Runstenar och kyrkor. En studie med utgångspunkt från runstenar som påträffats i kyrkomiljö i Uppland och Södermanland*, Occasional Papers in Archaeology 8 (Uppsala, 1994), pp. 7-8.

[10] For the recording of material from Svealand, see M. G. Larsson, *Runstenar och utlandsfärder. Aspekter på det senvikingatida samhället med utgångspunkt i de fasta fornlämningarna*, Acta archaeologica Lundensia, Series in 8°, 18 (Stockholm, 1990), pp. 44-59; for the province of Småland, see P. Stille, *Småländska englandsfärder i runstenarnas belysning* (B-uppsats i arkeologi, ht 1988, Uppsala universitet). I have also used the computer-text database, Department of Scandinavian Languages at Uppsala University.

commemorated in this way.[11] It also seems to have been usual that men to a greater extent than women should make long voyages, whether they were taking part in peaceful trading expeditions, violent pillaging or more systematically organised warfare.

There is, however, a very famous example of a woman who at least wanted to travel. She lived in the province of Uppland, and her name was Ingirun. On a rune-stone we can read that she intended, as the text runs, "to travel eastwards", namely to "go on a pilgrimage to Jerusalem".[12] We do not know whether her plan was carried out, but Gräslund has called attention to the fact that a woman from eastern Sweden at this time in history did not regard it as a complete impossibility to make such a long journey.[13] But, as already stated, no women are mentioned among the travellers to England.

Let us look a little more closely at who these men were. Since the material is meagre, it is difficult to get a clear view of the differences between the Swedish provinces with regard to the number of people who went England. As it is, eleven examples come from Götaland, the southern part of Sweden. Seventeen examples are found in Svealand, of which eight are in the province of Uppland, where more rune-stones were erected than in all the other provinces. The Swedish traveller who came from the furthest distance known to us is one Åsmund, who is mentioned on a fragment from the parish of Torsåker in the province of Gästrikland, inland about 200 kilometres north of Uppsala.[14] As already mentioned, I do not regard it as meaningful to try to produce any detailed statistics in this case, though some scholars have done so. But still it should be emphasised that these inscriptions are an important source of information about the connections between England and Sweden during the Viking Age and for our knowledge of English Christian influence in different

---

[11] On this specific topic see A.-S. Gräslund, "'Gud hjälpe nu väl hennes själ': Om runstenskvinnorna, deras roll vid kristnandet och deras plats i familj och samhälle", *Tor. Tidskrift för nordisk fornkunskap* 22 (1988-89), 223-44.

[12] *Sveriges runinskrifter* (Stockholm, 1900-) 8, *Uppland*, no. 605, pp. 4-10.

[13] Gräslund, "'Gud hjälpe'", pp. 231-32.

[14] *Sveriges runinskrifter* 15, *Gästrikland*, no. 8, pp. 71-78.

ways in certain regions of Sweden. Obviously, the fact that one had visited England was something worth remembering.

In taking a few examples, I start in the south with the stones in the province of Småland, where the inscriptions, in my view, seem to differ somewhat from the others. These stones have been analysed by Per Stille.[15] First, we may note that the number of inscriptions mentioning travellers to England is relatively high in this province, higher than in any other. If we also include those mentioning travellers westwards and one uncertain stone, we reach a total of eleven, which, according to Stille, is nine per cent. Why is that? One may at least ask if these stones were erected at a time when more people went to England than the times when stones in other provinces were erected; one may also ask if more people actually went from Småland than from the other provinces.

In following the order in the Swedish corpus of runic inscriptions, the first person we meet is a son called Ketil.[16] About him, we learn that he "ended his days in England", and probably he was buried there as well. But something else is also related about him, which may be used as an illustration of the difficulties of textual interpretation. The text says, according to one interpretation, that "he was smallest among men", followed by a word which has been deciphered as *niding*. A *niding* was a miser, a skinflint, an avaricious person. Rightly, Stille has asked in what type of society such qualities could be regarded as praiseworthy, but he leaves this question unanswered.[17] The reading of the last word is, as far as I can see, not certain, but would it not be strange if his father had erected an expensive memorial stone with this judgement carved on it for posterity? And furthermore the text continues: "not greedy about food or quick to revenge". According to Sven B. F. Jansson, we should instead read "among men the greatest *oniding*".[18] *Oniding* is the opposite and stands for an excellent, wealthy and generous man, which probably fits better with such people as were able to go to

---

[15] See above, note 10.

[16] *Sveriges runinskrifter* 4, *Småland*, no. 5, pp. 41-44.

[17] Stille, *Småländska englandsfärder*, p. 6.

[18] S. B. F. Jansson, *Runes in Sweden* (Stockholm, 1987), p. 128.

England and belonged to families which honoured them at home with huge monuments when they learned about their deaths.

For the rest of those who went from Småland, we are told that they died in England. However, there is no information about what they had done in England, with one exception, nor are any prayers written on the stones. About Helge it is said that he buried his deceased brother Gunnar "in a stone coffin in Bath in England". There is also a so-called stave cross on the edge of the stone.[19] These personal names were common ones during this period and for a long time during the Middle Ages[20] and thus do not indicate what type of people they were, although it has been assumed that they were in the service of the Danish king.[21] In any case, does the expensive stone coffin in Bath indicate that Gunnar and Helge had lived in England for quite a long time and under permanent conditions?[22]

The rest of the inscriptions from Götaland, two from Västergötland[23] and two from Östergötland,[24] have the same character as those from Småland in that only one deceased person is mentioned on each stone and all of them died in England. About two of them we learn that they were killed and one of them was "a good warrior". Clearly there is no easy way of placing the stones from Götaland in a pattern, at least not to any great extent. This is true also of the inscriptions from Svealand.

The stones from the province of Södermanland in Svealand sometimes have information which we have not met with so far, but with regard to some persons, we still have only the information that they had gone to England and had died there. About one of them we learn that he drowned,[25] about another that he died in the so-called *tingalidet*, i.e. the army which King Knut kept in England after the

---

[19] *Sveriges runinskrifter* 4, *Småland*, no. 101, pp. 232-34.

[20] Stille, *Småländska englandsfärder*, p. 8.

[21] Stille, *Småländska englandsfärder*, p. 6.

[22] Cf. Stille, *Småländska englandsfärder*, p. 5.

[23] *Sveriges runinskrifter* 5, *Västergötland*, no. 20, pp. 36-37; no. 187, p. 335.

[24] *Sveriges runinskrifter* 2, *Östergötland*, no. 104, pp. 104-05; S. B. F. Jansson, "Några nyligen uppdagade runstenar", *Fornvännen* 45 (1950), 330-44, especially pp. 341-42.

[25] *Sveriges runinskrifter* 3, *Södermanland*, no. 83, p. 61.

last hostile taxation (*gäld*). This army is supposed to have existed until 1066, although this cannot be said to be certain.[26] One person who is said to have gone to England was "manly".[27] What did he do in England? We do not know, but the word in question has to do with boldness and capability. He probably went on duty, as we would put it today. Here, we have an inscription which leaves us in uncertainty as to whether the person in question had died in England or had just been active ("manly") there. That he had died is clear from the prayer for his soul.

In the provinces of Svealand, there are also inscriptions commemorating men who had visited England but had obviously left the country and died somewhere else. The fact that they had visited England is regarded on these stones as something praiseworthy or maybe even sensational. Sometimes it is more precisely stated what the person had done abroad. A "good" father is said to have taken part in the so-called *danagäld*, the Danish hostile taxation of England, and later on to have invaded the towns in Saxland.[28] Another man was perhaps less successful. He had gone to England as "a young warrior", but "he died at home to great sorrow". His father was still alive when this happened; he was the one who erected the memorial.[29]

We can also read about visitors to England on three stones from the province of Västmanland. One of them is said to have died in England.[30] About another the text relates that he "died in Spjallbode's ...". The rest of the text is missing, but Spjallbode is a man's name, here in the genitive, and this has led to speculation that the word or words missing mentioned that he had participated in Spjallbode's army or the like and would thus indicate the existence of an otherwise

---

[26] *Sveriges runinskrifter* 3, *Södermanland*, no. 160, p. 122; Larsson, *Runstenar och utlandsfärder*, p. 103.

[27] *Sveriges runinskrifter* 3, *Södermanland*, no. 207, p. 184.

[28] *Sveriges runinskrifter* 3, *Södermanland*, no. 166, pp. 127-29.

[29] *Sveriges runinskrifter* 3, *Södermanland*, no. 55, pp. 41-42.

[30] *Sveriges runinskrifter* 13, *Västmanland*, nos 9 and 10, pp. 24-29.

unknown Viking raid westwards. The stone is Christian; we read: "May God help his soul".[31]

It is in Uppland that we find recorded the greatest number of travellers to England and on three of the rune-stones we can read about persons who had participated in hostile taxations in England. One of them had taken part in three such events, one in two and one of them in one. The stones in question are located very close to each other. As Larsson has pointed out, these persons had obviously returned from England as wealthy warriors, and only later, when they died at home or elsewhere, were they commemorated in this way. According to Larsson, we have here men who took part in voyages to England before the year 1018, when Knut had definitely conquered England and had carried out the final taxation. However, these rune-stones cannot be as old as that, and this once again, points to the fact that the visits to England, hostile or not, were regarded as something impressive and enhancing one's status. Probably this was the case not only in connection with one's memorial but also in one's life at home. These inscriptions all have prayers for the deceased.[32]

A final category to be mentioned consists of people who had themselves erected stones. As regards the memorial inscriptions on rune-stones the erectors generally play an important role, sometimes more important even than the one to be remembered. The custom of mentioning the person who undertook the erection or paid for the monument disappears gradually on the monuments in churchyards, where only the deceased is commemorated. In one case, the person in question has erected the memorial stone for his father and, in the other, for himself. However, they are described as travellers to England.[33] Accordingly, it is not only the commemorated person who is described in this way, in contrast to all the other inscriptions that I have analysed. This fact emphasises the importance of the visits to England even more. For the returnees also, it was thus important to preserve for posterity the memory of their journeys, and it was not

---

[31] *Sveriges runinskrifter* 13, *Västmanland*, no. 5, pp. 16-20; cf. no. 18, pp. 55-57.

[32] Larsson, *Runstenar och utlandsfärder*, pp. 100-03.

[33] Larsson, *Runstenar och utlandsfärder*, p. 102.

only those who died abroad who were commemorated with this in mind.

Let me finally summarise some of the conclusions which can be drawn from the material discussed above. Firstly, and once again, it is important to stress the fact that only men are to be found among those who went to England and have been commemorated on rune-stones. This is not particularly remarkable, since women are not known to have played an important part in the voyages of different types to England. Secondly, the deceased were commemorated by close relatives; quite a lot of the stones were erected for sons, on three or four occasions for a father and sometimes for a grandfather. However, this does not necessarily mean that the grandfather was old when he started out on his voyage, nor even that he had grandchildren at that time since the memorial may have been erected later. Accordingly, we do not know for sure how long a time had passed between the death in England or in Sweden and the moment when the stone was erected. It may be that mainly young men took part in these voyages.

This assumption leads on to the question of where they were buried. In just one case, we are informed on this point: that of the Gunnar who was buried in Bath.[34] It has been assumed that he was buried in a Christian way "with dignity" and this seems likely. Fragments of a coffin with runic inscriptions dating from the first part of the eleventh century have been found not very far from St Paul's Cathedral in London, thus indicating a Scandinavian burial there.[35] Such coffins, though from the second part of the eleventh century, can still be seen in some Swedish churchyards. They are undoubtedly part of Christian burial customs.[36] As regards the other people mentioned, we are ignorant of the place of burial, nor do we know whether the deceased men were Christian or were buried in a Christian manner. This reflection is particularly relevant to the inscriptions from Götaland, because I think that they differ from those in Svealand with regard to the content and the way of

[34] See above, note 19.

[35] *Sveriges runinskrifter* 4, *Småland*, p. 234.

[36] Regarding these monuments, see T. Neill and S. Lundberg, "Förnyad diskussion om 'Eskilstunakistorna'", *Fornvännen* 89 (1994), 145-59.

expressing their message. In all these cases, the men commemorated had died in England. We do not meet with any returnees, and all the inscriptions lack prayers for the souls of the deceased, even though four of the ten stones have crosses carved on them and are therefore clearly of Christian character. Is it possible that these stones are older, belonging to a time when those who went to England were not Christians to the extent which soon became the case? This may be the reason why there are no prayers. We do not know anything about whether they were buried in England, and one may ask whether heathen Vikings who took part in pillage and warfare would be buried in a Christian environment, in English churchyards.

The stones from Svealand, on the other hand, all give the impression of being in the Christian memorial tradition. Here, we find crosses and, above all, prayers for the dead, which was one of the most important means of helping the deceased and which also could and should be used by everyone, not just priests. Here, we also meet with the fact that the voyages to England brought material wealth, something to boast about to those at home and to posterity. That is probably the reason why some inscriptions have just the laconic phrase "he had been in England"; everyone knew what that meant. Going to England was something memorable and was probably also connected with the admiration of those living at home, especially, of course, in the case of returnees who had come back with acquired wealth. Their social status was thus enhanced. It probably also meant that ordinary people in the Swedish countryside learned about Christian cult and customs in their English versions long before any parishes were organised or any churches were built on Swedish soil.

The most important knowledge of the conditions in England was, of course, brought back by the returnees, but we should not forget that the memorials to persons who remained permanently in England must have aroused curiosity on a local level in Sweden. Both categories thus played an important role in the English contribution to the Christianisation of Sweden at a very early time when we do not have any actual knowledge of English influence in other ways, but only legendary traditions for liturgical use about missionary bishops coming from England, written down a long time after the people lived and the events which they tell about took place. The rune inscriptions thus convey, though in lapidary style, direct information

about connections between Sweden and England during the first half
of the eleventh century.

On Broken Letters Scarce Remembred: Nash-Williams and the Early Christian Monuments of Wales

Mark Redknap

Early medieval inscribed and decorated stones form one of the principal archaeological sources for early medieval Wales and include contemporary records of its people. As has been stated before, the study of the inscribed stones contributes valuable information to the disciplines of archaeology (in their functions as tombstones, grave markers, memorials and boundary markers), history (in that the early inscribed stones constitute written records reflecting the social structure and provide the names, kinship and status of persons, some independently attested in other historical sources),[1] and linguistics (as the inscriptions may reflect both

I would like to thank John M. Lewis, Jeremy Knight and Carlo Tedeschi for their valued comments on the manuscript of this paper, and Tom Daly of the Department of Archaeology and Numismatics, National Museums & Galleries of Wales for the line drawings.

[1] For example, that of Cantiori, who was VENEDOTIS CIVE, and cousin of MAGLI MAGISTRATI ("Penmachno", Caernarfonshire, originally alongside the Roman road from Tomen y Mur to Caerhun, near Beddau y Gwyr Ardudwy; Gwyn Thomas papers, RCAHM in Wales archive; *ECMW* 103); that of Melus who was a MEDICVS (Llangian, Caernarfonshire; *ECMW* 92); that of the wife of Bivatig(irnus) who was a SACERDOS (Llantrisant, Anglesey; *ECMW* 33) and Guadan, also a SACERDOS (Llandetty, Brecknockshire; *ECMW* 46); that of Senacus, PRESBITER (Aberdaron, Caernarfonshire; *ECMW* 78). Historically

contemporary stages of Irish and British, and the interaction of Insular Celtic and contemporary spoken and written Latin).[2] The *Early Christian Monuments of Wales* by Victor Erle Nash-Williams remains a landmark in the study of the period.[3] It is nearly fifty years since publication of this authoritative work, and this brief paper will examine both its impact and recent developments in the study of the stones.

Nash-Williams was born in 1897 at Fleur-de-Lys, Monmouthshire (fig. 1). He passed his entire professional career in the service of the National Museum of Wales and of the University College of South Wales and Monmouthshire, as it was then known. He went to the Front in 1916, but was invalided out because of rheumatic fever. Following demobilisation he gained first class honours at Cardiff University College, and in 1924 he was appointed Assistant Keeper in Archaeology in the National Museum of Wales, and two years later succeeded Sir Cyril Fox as Keeper (and also lecturer in Archaeology at University College).[4]

Nash-Williams was by no means the first scholar to take up the subject of the early inscribed stones of Wales: their study is traceable as early as the seventeenth century, with the publication of many of the more notable examples in Camden's *Britannia*, for the new edition of which Edmund Gibson had enlisted Edward Lhuyd (1660-1709) to revise the Welsh entries. Other antiquaries to record stones include Robert Vaughan (the "Antiquary of Hengwrt", 1592?-1667) and Theophilus Jones (1759-1812). Lhuyd included inscriptions and sculptures in the questionnaire upon which his *Parochialia* is based, and described inscriptions and ogam (without understanding the significance of "Ye Stroaks"). Robert Vaughan recorded the

---

attested persons include Vortepor, Gildas' "tyrant of the Demetae", on the monument from Castell Dwyran (Carmarthenshire; *ECMW* 138) and Cadfan (CATAMANVS REX; Llangadwaladr, Anglesey; *ECMW* 13).

[2] These have been highlighted recently by C. Thomas, *And Shall These Mute Stones Speak? Post-Roman Inscriptions in West Britain* (Cardiff, 1994).

[3] V. E. Nash-Williams, *The Early Christian Monuments of Wales* (Cardiff, 1950). Individual monuments are cited by catalogue number.

[4] H. R. Randall, "Obituary Notice – V. E. Nash-Williams 1897-1955", *Archaeologia Cambrensis* 105 (1956), 150-51.

inscription on the Bedd Porius stone used in Gough's *Britannia*,[5] and that on the linguistically important Towyn stone, Merionethshire, described by the late Sir Ivor Williams as the earliest example of the Welsh language inscribed in eighth-century half-uncial on stone.[6] It has been suggested that Henry Vaughan "the Silurist" (1621-1695) may have been describing the early Christian monument from Scethrog (Brecknockshire)[7] in his "Vanity of Spirit":

> A peece of much Antiquity
> with Hyerogliphicks quite dismembred
> And broken letters scarce remembred.[8]

Theophilus Jones' *History of the County of Brecknock* illustrates the cross of Briamail Flou,[9] as well as seven other stones,[10] while Fenton's *A Historical Tour through Pembrokeshire* (London, 1811) illustrates the Carew cross[11] and E. Donovan's *Descriptive Excursions through South Wales and Monmouthshire in the year*

---

[5] See C. A. Gresham, "Bedd Porius", *Bulletin of the Board of Celtic Studies* 32 (1985), 386-92 for a recent account of this stone, which is now displayed in the National Museum & Gallery, Cardiff.

[6] I. Williams, "The Towyn Inscribed Stone", in *The Beginnings of Welsh Poetry. Studies by Sir Ifor Williams*, ed. R. Bromwich (Cardiff, 1980), pp. 25-40. The earlier inscription begins with a cross, and has been read "tengrui cimalte(d) gu/ adgan" ("Ceinrwy, wife of Addian (lies here)"), which continues on another side "ant erunc du but marciau" ("close to Bud and Merchiaw"). A footnote may be inscribed "mc / er tri" ("Memorial of the three"). Another inscription, considered to be later, reads "Cun Ben Celen" ("Cun, wife of Celyn") and on another side "tricet/ nitanam" ("the grief and loss remain"), with a footnote "mort/cic pe/tuar" ("memorial of the four"). This revision of the reading by Williams post-dates the publication of *ECMW*.

[7] *ECMW* 68, now in Brecon Museum. G. C. Boon, "Tretower Court and Castle", in *Programme and Notes of the 137th Annual Meeting of the Cambrian Archaeological Association, August 13 - 17*, ed. G. C. Boon (Cardiff, 1990), pp. 36-39.

[8] Lines 22-24. From *Silex Scintillans: Sacred Poems and Private Ejaculations* (London, 1650).

[9] T. Jones, *A History of the County of Brecknock, containing the Antiquities and Sepulchral Monuments and Inscriptions*, vol. 2, part 1 (Brecknock, 1809); the cross is *ECMW* 49.

[10] *ECMW* 43, 54, 65, 66, 68, 73, 74.

[11] *ECMW* 303.

1804 (published in 1805 for the benefit of those on the Welsh Tour) describes and illustrates the stones at Llantwit Major, including the Houelt stone.[12] One engraving shows the Ilci and Ilquici stones from Margam in use as a footbridge.[13] Growing interest in the stones is reflected in watercolours by R. Franklen dated 1816, copying plates in Meyrick's history of Cardiganshire.[14]

By 1853 a large proportion of the most important inscriptions had been discovered and recorded by J. O. Westwood, who published many notes on early Christian inscribed stones. His *Lapidarium Walliae and the Early Inscribed and Sculptured Stones of Wales* brought together for the first time descriptions of most of the Welsh examples then known.[15] Sir John Rhys, a subscriber to Westwood's *Lapidarium Walliae*, who returned to Wales in 1871 to pursue philological research was appointed to the Celtic Chair in Oxford in 1877. An early fruit was his *Lectures on Welsh Philology* and his contributions to *Archaeologia Cambrensis* on the early inscribed stones of Wales gave the journal a leading position in this area of research. J. Romilly Allen (1847-1907), from a landed Welsh family of some distinction in church and legal circles, was by 1877 a member of the General Committee of the Cambrian Archaeological Association, and brought sculptured stone to the public eye with his comparison of Celtic art in Wales and Ireland.[16] It was to these and others that Nash-Williams paid homage in the introduction to his Corpus.

The growth of the early Christian monument collection held by the National Museums & Galleries of Wales mirrors the growing interest in early medieval visual art in Wales in the late nineteenth

---

[12] *ECMW* 220, and 223-24.

[13] *ECMW* 236 and 237.

[14] S. R. Meyrick, *The History and Antiquities of the County of Cardigan* (London, 1808). The watercolours copy plates opposite pp. 192, 238 and 252, and are in the archive of the Department of Archaeology and Numismatics, National Museum & Gallery, Cardiff.

[15] Issued by the Cambrian Archaeological Association in annual parts between 1876 and 1879, and then as a single volume: *Lapidarium Walliae. The Early Inscribed and Sculptured Stones of Wales* (Oxford, 1876-79).

[16] *The Monumental History of the Early British Church* and articles on Welsh stones in *Archaeologia Cambrensis*.

century. It began in 1892 with the gift to the Cardiff Free Library and Museum (as it then was) of the tenth-century stone from Bryn Cefneithin (Cwm Gwenffrwd, Neath; fig. 2, *ECMW 265*).[17] It was twenty years before it acquired another, and during this time the Council of the Cardiff Museum and Art Gallery[18] agreed on a programme of commissioning plaster casts of pre-Norman stones from all over Wales, the first in 1894 being the late ninth- or tenth-century Conbelin stone[19] (figs 3 & 13, top right) and the late ninth-century cross of Enniaun at Margam.[20] Ward's definition of an ideal collection was of complete casts of all the stones, but he accepted that in some cases just the inscriptions and markings would suffice. He thought that every inscription, no matter how illegible, at least should be cast. Such a cast could invariably show "lettering more distinct than in the original stone ... The carvings and other markings are more accentuated through the stronger contrast of the lights and shadows and in consequence many details are now rendered visible which before were unnoticed".[21] By the time this forward-looking policy of casting "campaigns" was brought to an end in 1914 by the outbreak of war, the Museum had acquired casts of most of the principal stones. W. Clarke of Llandaff had been commissioned not only to continue with the casting, but also to search for any as yet undiscovered or forgotten. Several more casts have been added since, most recently in fibreglass,[22] their lightness and durability making them useful for travelling displays. Between the wars the Museum acquired most of its present collection of originals, largely through

[17] *ECMW* 265.

[18] From 1902, known as the Welsh Museum of Natural History, Art and Antiquities.

[19] *ECMW* 234.

[20] *ECMW* 231. The work was undertaken by Brucciani and Co., in the employ of the British and South Kensington Museums.

[21] J. Ward, "Pembrokeshire Casts – General Observations" (unpublished manuscript notes in the Department of Archaeology and Numismatics archive, 1913), p. 2.

[22] Fibreglass replicas of stones were made by the National Museum of Wales in conjunction with the Welsh Arts Council for exhibition at the National Eisteddfod at Bangor in 1971.

the efforts of Nash-Williams, including the monumental Similinus[23] and Tegernacus stones[24] and the splendid, if incomplete, tenth-century cross of Eiudon (fig. 9).[25] Replicas have been installed to replace some monuments which have been moved into improved environments: for example, the shaft fragment with inscription from Ogmore castle, Glamorgan,[26] and the slab with incised cross from the site of Capel Gwladys, Gelli-gaer, Glamorgan.[27]

Before the publication of *ECMW*, R. A. S. Macalister's *Corpus inscriptionum insularum Celticarum* was the only attempt at a full catalogue of the inscribed and commemorative stones in Britain,[28] and he had provided a valuable review of earlier work in this field in the Centenary Volume of the Cambrian Archaeological Association.[29]

The Nash-Williams Corpus

It was recognised at an early date by John Ward (Curator of the Cardiff Free Library and Museum as it had become known in 1892) and others that while Westwood's *Lapidarium* was a notable achievement, it was "a very unsatisfactory work", frequently including monuments later than pre-Norman, lacking definite and

---

[23] *ECMW* 176 from Clocaenog, Denbighshire.

[24] *ECMW* 270 from Tirphil, Capel Brithdir, Glamorgan.

[25] *ECMW* 159 from Llanfynydd, Carmarthenshire.

[26] *ECMW* 255; *An Inventory of the Ancient Monuments in Glamorgan Vol.1: Pre-Norman part III, The Early Christian Period,* The Royal Commission on Ancient and Historical Monuments in Wales (Cardiff, 1976) [hereafter *RCAHM Glamorgan*], no. 926, pp. 55-56.

[27] V. E. Nash-Williams, "An Inventory of the Early Christian Stone Monuments of Wales, with a Bibliography of the Principal Notices", *Bulletin of the Board of Celtic Studies* 8 (1936), 161-88, esp. p. 162; *RCAHM Glamorgan*, 44.

[28] A work which has been criticised as lacking in meticulousness, with many inaccurate and, at times, imaginative drawings and readings.

[29] R. A. S. Macalister, "The Early Christian Period", in *A Hundred Years of Welsh Archaeology: Cambrian Archaeological Association Centenary Volume 1846-1946,* ed. V. E. Nash-Williams (Gloucester, 1947), pp. 105-28.

systematic terminology, lacking information on the size and shape of early inscribed stones, and having faulty illustrations.[30]

Nash-Williams saw the opportunity of bringing together in one volume all the available evidence on the monuments, as contemporary records of the conversion of Wales to Christianity and the establishment and development of the "Celtic" church.[31] The first edition of *ECMW* was published by the University of Wales Press in 1950 on behalf of the National Museum of Wales and the University of Wales' Board of Celtic Studies, and it formed the first systematic illustrated corpus of the early medieval inscribed and decorated stones in Wales. Composition of the book was the result of the best part of twenty years of study, and it demonstrated his ability to analyse, condense and arrange diverse materials. The fieldwork was often accomplished with the assistance of his 1200cc motorbike, in particular in the pre- and post-war years.

Nash-Williams has been described as a stickler for the chain of command through which every project had to be filtered to higher authority, and this characteristic may be a reflection of his experience on enlistment.[32] He was, above all, deeply religious and a high Anglican, "one to whom religion was the foundation of life",[33] and this in part accounts for his single-minded devotion to and love for the production of the Corpus. It is of interest that he took particular pride in his membership of the Governing Body of the Church in Wales, and to some extent the practising churchman in him motivated his research. As others have pointed out, this background was important: he saw the inscriptions as evidence of the way in which his countrymen had developed into literate Christian people, seeing a

---

[30] Ward, "Pembrokeshire Casts".

[31] Also as a reflection of "racial and cultural movements", *ECMW*, p. 1.

[32] G. C. Boon, "An Apprenticeship and its consequences: W. F. Grimes at the National Museum of Wales 1926-1938", *The Monmouthshire Antiquary* 6 (1990), 78-87, esp. p. 84. During the latter part of his military service (1940-45) he was seconded to the Historical Section (Military), War Cabinet offiices.

[33] Randall, "Obituary Notice", p. 150.

direct link between the churches of Lyon and of Britain, an idea with origins in the history of the Victorian church.[34]

The Corpus was preceded by "An Inventory of the Early Christian Stone Monuments in Wales", published in two parts in the *Bulletin of the Board of Celtic Studies* in the 1930s. These are useful as they contain extensive bibliographies on which his Corpus depended. Nash-Williams died suddenly in 1955. For his Corpus, he was posthumously awarded the G. T. Clark prize by the Cambrian Archaeological Association in 1956.

Nash-Williams' Classification of the Stones

Nash-Williams' scheme of classification and chronology remains highly influential in mediating our understanding of the primary material. His chronology relied heavily on both epigraphical and art-historical arguments, based on form, decoration and epigraphy (fig. 5),[35] and comparisons with Irish, Anglo-Saxon, Scottish and Continental sculpture. This succeeded in putting epigraphic and language studies back on an equal footing with sculptured art,[36] and was followed by Kenneth Jackson's masterly *Language and History in Early Britain*.[37] Only recently have attempts been made to re-evaluate his scheme.

Nash-Williams was the first scholar to divide the early Christian monuments of Wales into four main types, and this simple classification remains an extremely effective system for describing and presenting the stones to both students and the general public.

[34] J. K. Knight, "The Early Christian Inscriptions of Britain and Gaul: Chronology and Context", in *The Early Church in Wales and the West*, ed. N. Edwards and A. Lane, Oxbow Monograph 16 (Oxford, 1992), pp. 45-50, esp. p. 45.

[35] His "elegant" scheme was also applied to monuments outside Wales, such as Dumnonia (C. A. R. Radford, "The Early Christian Inscriptions of Dumnonia", 1974 Holbeche Corfield Lecture (Truro, 1975)).

[36] C. Thomas, *Mute Stones*, p. 259.

[37] K. Jackson, *Language and History in Early Britain: A Chronological Survey of the Brittonic Languages, First to Twelfth Century AD* (Edinburgh, 1953).

Half a century on, the general scheme remains valid, though individual exceptions to the rule have now been recognised. *Group I* (not *Class*, as has often been mistakenly repeated) was defined as inscribed, unshaped, or roughly shaped pillar stones bearing inscriptions in Latin and ogams, or, commonly both (figs 6-7),[38] and *Group II* as cross-marked stones (fig. 8). *Group III* included both inscribed and uninscribed slab-crosses and freestanding sculptured crosses (fig. 9), and *Group IV* was defined as "a miscellaneous series of late monuments of early Romanesque types, found sporadically throughout Wales".[39] He subdivided *Group III* into (a) freestanding stone crosses and (b) slab-crosses. Some stones, such as the tenth-century hogback from Llanddewi-Aber-Arth, Cardiganshire,[40] did not fall easily into any of these categories. The monuments were grouped by pre-1974 county and numbered consecutively up to 415, but not grouped within county by Group or type. Nash-Williams had never been able to draw well,[41] and the Corpus was illustrated largely by photographs,[42] backed up by simple line drawings, most of which had been prepared by others. One criticism of the volume was the use of photographs of casts, rather than the original stones, and the liberal use of chalk to define letters or designs.

Some Recent Developments in the Study of the Early Christian Monuments

The earliest inscribed stones may be seen as principally visible monuments, forming a symbolic presence, reinforced on occasions by legible messages. The earlier inscriptions on stones in themselves do

---

[38] *ECMW*, pp. 3-16.

[39] *ECMW*, p. 47.

[40] In the form of a recumbent, house-shaped grave cover with a curving roof ridge (*ECMW* 114). For a discussion of the house representation with its impression of a clinkered roof, unpatterned by shingles, see H. Schmidt, *Building Customs in Viking Age Denmark* (Denmark, 1994), p. 140.

[41] Boon, "An Apprenticeship", p. 84.

[42] A hundred years ago, J. Romilly Allen advocated setting up a photographic archive of early medieval inscribed stones, intending them for scholarly and educational purposes.

not represent acts of worship, but are essentially commemorative. The significance of the archaeological classification and of the occurrence of cross markings on pillars in the eyes of the early medieval population, and the relationship of literate and non-literate communication, form the subject of continuing research.[43] Excavations since 1950 of early medieval cemeteries such as Plas Gogerddan (Dyfed), Llandegai (Gwynedd), Tanderwen (Clwyd) have shed light on their layout and development, and future work on cemeteries with associations with early Christian monuments may contribute to this understanding of belief and burial practice. This is evident from recent excavations at Llandough (South Glamorgan), where some 858 burials have been excavated by the Cotswold Archaeological Trust (with a further 152 groups of disarticulated bones) from an area adjacent to the churchyard of St Dochdwy, in which can still be found the late-tenth/eleventh-century cross of Irbic (*ECMW* 206: fig. 12, bottom right). The burials, which range in date from Roman to eleventh-century, form part of the early Christian cemetery associated with the church of St Dochdwy (historically attested in the *Vita Cadoci*), and the skeletal material forms a unique sample of the population of early Christian Wales.[44] Assessment of the association between the freestanding cross and the later development of the cemetery will provide information not available to Nash-Williams.

In *ECMW* many *Group I* stones fell into distinctive shapes, but tended to be treated as texts; the physical form of the stone was sometimes overlooked. The majority of Welsh monuments are decorated with nothing more elaborate than a cross incised into the surface of the stone which generally fall into a few broad categories (for example Latin crosses, linear equal arm crosses, cross potent, outline equal-armed crosses with ring). In *ECMW* some of the line drawings, which show the styles of several hands, were necessarily

---

[43] For example, K. Dark, "Epigraphic, Art-Historical and Historical Approaches to the Chronology of Class I Inscribed Stones", in *Early Church in Wales*, ed. Edwards and Lane, pp. 51-61, esp. p. 52; P. McDonald (personal communication).

[44] For an interim statement, see A. Thomas and N. Holbrook, "Llandough", *Current Archaeology* 146 (1996), 73-77.

schematic, and as Radford and Hemp recommended in 1961, many now receive more detailed illustration, while some require correction in the light of recent re-examination. Photography with oblique lighting would now be recommended for all stones as a basic level of illustration, with line drawings complementing the plates either as interpretations or reconstructions.

Most of the sculpted monuments, related as many of them are to more elaborate Merovingian, Anglo-Saxon, Irish or Scandinavian traditions, are capable of more precise classification,[45] with formal decoration represented by classes such as plaitwork (plain or broken), interlace, and straight-line key or fret patterns (fig. 10). Nash-Williams used the system devised by Romilly Allen in his *Early Christian Monuments of Scotland* (1903), based on the belief that manuscript interlace was based on a diagonal grid. In recent years it has been shown that a horizontal/vertical grid of squares was employed in the layout of abstract ornament, and this has led to a reconsideration of the possible methods employed in their construction.[46] Nash-Williams was also of the opinion that "masterpieces" were lacking in tenth- and eleventh-century Wales – a phase of "artistic sterility and technical ineptitude, expressed in

---

[45] R. Bailey's work on Viking-Age monuments in the north and northeast, *Viking Age Sculpture in Northern England* (London, 1980), S. Margeson's analysis of the iconography of the Manx crosses, "On the Iconography of the Manx Crosses", in *The Viking Age in the Isle of Man*, ed. C. Fell et al., Viking Society for Northern Research (London, 1983), pp. 95-106, and the data published in the *Corpus of Anglo-Saxon Stone Sculpture*, ed. R. Cramp et al. (Oxford, 1984-) can now be applied to Welsh examples.

[46] Dark, "Epigraphical, Art-Historical and Historical Approaches"; N. Edwards, "Some Observations on the Layout and Construction of Abstract Ornament in Early Christian Irish Sculpture", in *Studies in Medieval Sculpture*, ed. F. H. Thompson (London, 1983), pp. 3-17, esp. p. 15. J. Clarke discusses the decoration on later stones, comparing the decorative patterns on those from Llanfynydd (Brecs.), Llantwit Major (the "Samson" stone), Carew and Nevern: "Welsh Sculptured Crosses and Cross-Slabs of the Pre-Norman Period" (unpublished PhD dissertation, University College, London, 1981). This shows that they use identical dimensions, suggesting that they might be the work of the same craftsman. If true, this has implications for their chronology (Samson conventionally tenth-century, Carew c. 1035).

grotesque monumental forms and mere travesties of ornamentation"[47] – but his own harsh view is not supported by the fine designs evident in fragmentary sculpture such as Bulmore, Caerleon and St Davids.[48] There are grounds for proposing a reassessment of the comparisons made with sculpture outside Wales, and more specifically for comparisons to be sought for the Welsh abstract ornament.

Epigraphic styles and the techniques of carving employed have been the subject of recent study by K. Dark and C. Tedeschi,[49] who have also looked at the chronology of the stones, though the classification and firm dating have remained largely unchanged. The most significant attempt to revise the 1950 classification has been the late Gwyn W. Thomas' addition of new "classes" for the Royal Commission survey of the early medieval monuments of Glamorgan, which updated all the entries for the county.[50] The Royal Commission survey redefined the previous groups according to the form of the monument and its decoration.[51] This chrono-typological revision took little account of the various functions of the monuments and has yet to be universally adopted. Gwyn Thomas recently provided an important descriptive catalogue of the monuments of Cardiganshire for the County History.[52]

---

[47] *ECMW*, p. 31.

[48] *ECMW* 221, 290, 291 and 377 respectively; M. Redknap, *The Christian Celts* (Cardiff, 1991), p. 68.

[49] C. Tedeschi has examined the evolution of letter forms from fifth-century Roman capitals strongly dependent on third/fourth-century models (for example Carausius, Penmachno *ECMW* 101) to fully developed half-uncials at the other end of the chronological spectrum: "Osservazioni sulla paleografia delle iscrizioni britanniche paleocristiane (V-VII sec.). Contributo allo studio dell'origine delle scritture insulari, *Scrittura e civiltà* 19 (1995), 66-121; also C. Tedeschi, "Osservazioni sui formulari delle iscrizioni britanniche dal V al VIII secolo", *Romanobarbarica* 13 (1994-95), 283-95.

[50] *RCAHM Glamorgan*, p. 22.

[51] *Class A*, Inscribed Stones of the Early Period; *Class B*, Pillar-stones with Incised Cross; *Class C*, Recumbent Grave-slabs with Incised Cross; *Class D*, Standing Sculptured Slabs; *Class E*, Pillar-crosses; *Class F*, Other Decorated Stones; *Class G*, Headstones and Grave-slabs of the Late Period.

[52] G. W. Thomas, "The Early Christian Monuments", in *Cardiganshire County History Vol.1, From the Earliest Times to the Coming of the Normans*,

Dating

Individual minor errors in Nash-Williams have been recognised, such as the alleged internal dating of specific memorials (his chronological benchmarks) and on those inscriptions linked to textual sources.[53] Criticisms of the chronology have focused on the refuting of the internal dating of specific memorials, and inscriptions which can be linked to textual sources. Nash-Williams listed twelve inscriptions which he dated by external evidence. Of the early stones, two have clearly acceptable historical associations: the stone from Castell Dwyran[54] and that from Llangadwaladr.[55] The former, inscribed "Memoria Voteporigis Protectoris" (fig. 6), is probably a royal commemorative stone to Vortepor, Gildas' "tyrant of the Demetae", c. 540-50. The stone from Llangadwaladr inscribed "Catamanus rex sapientissimus opinatissimus omnium regum", commemorates Cadfan, ruler of Gwynedd who died c. 625, and illustrates the use of Insular half-uncial at this time. There is no reason to see this stone as the latest in Nash-Williams' *Group I* sequence, though it displays the most evolved system of script (later than, for example, that of the Penmachno Carausius inscription, *ECMW* 101).

It is clear that many inscriptions provide *termini post quos* for monuments. For example, Knight has clarified aspects of the chronology on the inscription on the Penmachno stone which Sir John Rhys and Nash-Williams took to refer to a stone set up in the time of the consul Iustinus (i.e. in the year 540). The stone bears two inscriptions: one vertical inscribed FILI AVITORI, and a second horizontal inscription, now viewed as the text end of a lengthy vanished inscription on the right, having a post-consular date some

ed. J. L. Davies and D. P. Kirby (Cardiff, 1994), pp. 407-20. The dating of some parallels may have changed – the Linlithgow cross cited under the pillar cross from Silian (*ECMW* 129) should read Abercorn, which may be later, of ninth-/tenth-century date (R. B. K. Stevenson, personal communication).

[53] M. L. Jones, *Society and Settlement in Wales and the Marches 500 BC-AD 1100*, 2 vols, British Archaeological Report 121 (Oxford, 1984), esp. pp. 259-68.

[54] *ECMW* 138.

[55] *ECMW* 13.

time after the 540s.[56] Nash-Williams attempted to identify some names inscribed on stones with saints or rulers whose dates are documented, assuming that such *emminenti* would be commemorated both in literature and on monuments, and that their names would be rare. For example, the person commemorated on the slab at Cynwyl Gaeo (Carmarthenshire)[57] in metrical hexameter was identified by Nash-Williams as Paulinus, reputed teacher of St David, who may have died c. 588 and was reputed to have been present as an old man at the Synod of Llandewi-Brevi held perhaps in 545. However, the name is common in hagiographical literature up to c. 600, and may even be earlier.[58] Instances of later dated stones include the cross of Hywel ap Rhys, subject of Alfred and ruler of Glwysing, who died in 884 (Llantwit Major ; *ECMW* 220; fig. 13); the pillar of Eliseg, Valle Crucis, Denbighshire, the base of a cross of Mercian type inscribed with at least thirty-one lines of Insular text, set up in memory of great-grandfather Eliseg by Cyngen ap Cadell, last of the Powys kings, who died in 854 while on pilgrimage to Rome (*ECMW* 182); and the Carew cross (Pembrokeshire), inscribed in abbreviated

[56] J. K. Knight, "Penmachno Revisited: The Consular Inscription and its Context", *Cambrian Medieval Celtic Studies* 29 (1955), 1-10. The inscription may show the use of two hands, perhaps one sculptor following on where another finishes, or inscriptions of different date. G. Thomas provided an alternative reading INTEP(IDI)/IVSTISSI(MI)/CON(IVGI), "of a most loving and righteous husband (or wife)", citing two occurrences in Anglesey inscriptions of CONIVX, but this depends on whether one reads an O after INTEP. Professor Sims Williams and Knight have both cast doubt on this alternative, which does not appear to be supported by a close examination of the lettering on the inscription.

[57] Now in Carmarthen Museum: *ECMW* 139.

[58] As noted in a *Times Literary Supplement* review of 22 September, 1950. See also Jones, *Society and Settlement*. C. Thomas, *Mute Stones*, p. 104 has pointed out that the saintly Paulinus in *Vita Beati Davidi* was buried at St Pol de Leon in Brittany, and suggests that the Welsh Paulinus may have been a prominent and noble layman buried on his own estates. A letter from J. F. Jones, curator of Carmarthen Museum (9 June, 1951), refers to a missing stone mentioned by Tho. Morgan to Edward Lhuyd in 1694 from Maes Llanwrthwl. In his presidential address to Carmarthen Cymreigyddion Society in 1826, Archdeacon Beynon gave the inscription as HIC IACIT PALVS/FILIVS PAVLINI.

Insular letters "Margit/eut.re/x.etg(uin).filius" (possibly Meredudd ap Edwin, who died in 1035; *ECMW* 303). It is possible that some texts demonstrated continuity with the past in order to legitimise contemporary territorial rights, status and influence.

Nash-Williams' dating of the *Group I* stones was largely epigraphic, and his scheme, while having the merit of being generally applicable to large groups of stones, does not necessarily hold out for individual examples. Dark has argued for a different approach, recognising that while the epigraphy may contribute a broad *floruit* for many inscriptions, and a series of *termini post quos* dates, it cannot enable close-dating. Nash-Williams divided non-capital scripts into half-uncial and rounded half-uncial, and estimated date by the percentage of half-uncial forms present. While this is now considered unreliable, the introduction of non-capital forms is clearly a chronological benchmark from the mid-seventh century, if not earlier. In the light of recent palaeographical study, Dark has argued for a contextual rather than a purely epigraphic analysis, taking account of regional variability, external contacts and varying educational backgrounds for the commissioners of work. He also sees a much narrower range of letter forms with fewer variants than those recorded by Nash-Williams, taking account of technical aspects of their formation, though in fairness it is clear that Nash-Williams recognised "variant forms, due to these stylistic diversities as well as to the idiosyncrasies of the local (Celtic) lapidaries"[59] (for example, six forms of the letter *A*: fig. 5). In an appendix Nash-Williams presented his analysis of letter forms as an alphabetic concordance, cross-referenced to illustrated examples, with foreign examples cited when considered applicable. The horizontal *I* and reversed or inverted letters are epigraphically solely Insular and common in West Wales and Cornwall, while the angular *A* appears from the fifth century. Dark has rightly pointed to the weakness of end-dates and that, according to Nash-Williams' criteria, stones exist which would refute a seventh-century date for the end of the sequence of *Group I*.

However, Nash-Williams was not unaware of the limitations of his classification (hence *Group* rather than *Class*), and recognised that the "simple monuments of this character continued to be used

---

[59] *ECMW*, p. 11.

locally to the end of the Early Christian period, especially in outlying regions".[60] The reviewer in the *Times Literary Supplement* astutely stated that, in view of the overlap between *Groups I* and *II*, "it would be wiser to regard the two series as parallel, just as the simple inscribed headstone of modern times continues alongside the elaborate architectural memorial". John Lewis has noted an absence of *Group II* and *Group III* stones from sites with *Group I* stones in Pembrokeshire, and suggested that those sites with *Group I* stones in this area may consequently have been disused prior to the currency of *Group II* stones.[61] It is now recognised that some *Group II* stones with a seventh- to ninth-century date bracket should be given a later tenth- to twelfth-century date (such as Llanddowror, Carmarthenshire,[62] Llanegryn, Merionethshire,[63] Llanwnda, Pembrokeshire[64] and Whitford, Flintshire[65]) and that function was a determining feature.

Charles Thomas' recent study of the stones from three counties in Dyfed now proposes a hypothetical typology of the visible shape of the messages, regardless of individual names and words, on the premise that the *Group I* inscribed memorials are a monument type introduced to Demetia by Irish settlers and not previously invented in Demetia.[66] Nash-Williams chose cautiously not to perceive such a sequence, being less specific about the date of individual stones within his *Group I* (fifth-seventh century) on grounds of epigraphy, physical shape or formulaic character.

---

[60] *ECMW*, p. 20; examples are stones from Heneglwys, Anglesey (*ECMW* 5) and Llangorse, Powys (*ECMW* 60), dating to the twelfth century. Dark mistakenly assumed that Nash-Williams arbitrarily decided on a *Group I* or *II* grouping for cross-marked pillars, and would place all the inscribed pillar stones in *Group I*, and all the uninscribed cross-marked stones in *Group II*.

[61] J. M. Lewis, "A Survey of the Early Christian Monuments of Dyfed, West of the Taf", in *Welsh Antiquity*, ed. G. C. Boon and J. M. Lewis (Cardiff, 1976), pp. 177-92.

[62] *ECMW* 151 and 152.

[63] *ECMW* 280.

[64] *ECMW* 328, 329.

[65] *ECMW* 189.

[66] C. Thomas, *Mute Stones*; the three counties studied are Pembrokeshire, Cardiganshire and Carmarthenshire.

A number of extended Latinate inscriptions exclusively in Latin differ from other Insular inscriptions in being derived from external models; Nash-Williams recognised the expanded and differing vocabulary and the existence of models in fifth- or sixth-century epitaphs from Gaul. He noticed the likely Gaulish background of the HIC IACIT formula, but in the absence of evidence, avoided the question of how a fashion centred around Vienne and Lyon could appear in South Wales. As has been pointed out, he needed to explain the apparent discontinuity between Romano-British Christianity (the lack of fourth-century monuments) and the appearance of Insular inscriptions in the fifth century, in particular of the HIC IACIT type and Lyonnais and the Rhône valley were reasonable candidates in the face of contemporary evidence. This view has been challenged, the source area being extended now to "Atlantic Gaul".[67]

Okasha has recently published her valuable survey of stones from south-west Britain, which has a direct bearing on the relationships of the Welsh stones to their neighbours. Her *Category I* (pillar stones, pieces of undressed or roughly dressed stone usually without any carved decoration, bearing inscriptions) shares characteristics in script, layout, language and formulae with Nash-Williams' *Groups I* and *II*, to form in her view a south-west tradition "akin to but not identical to that of Wales" and subject to similar influence.[68]

[67] Knight, "The Early Christian Inscriptions"; C. Thomas, "The Early Church in Wales and the West: Concluding Remarks", in *Early Church in Wales*, ed. Edwards and Lane, pp. 145-49, esp. p. 146. As Knight has pointed out, since 1950 the study of Insular imported wares has added a ceramic dimension to sixth-century Insular contact with Gaul and the Mediterranean.

[68] E. Okasha, *Corpus of Early Christian Inscribed Stones of South-west Britain*, Studies in the Early History of Britain (London, 1993), p. 42. Okasha writes of the influence of Welsh inscriptions on those found in the south-west of England; Tedeschi has suggested that consideration should be given to south-west influence on South Wales (as a British phenomenon).

Ogam and Runes

Nash-Williams worked within the constraints of the views then held about the chronology of ogam script. Kenneth Jackson's *Language and History in Early Britain* proposed invention of ogam by an immigrant from Ireland becoming familiar with Latin and the structures used by grammarians in Britain, before returning to Ireland. This 1953 view, one Nash-Williams understood ("invented in Ireland before the fifth century"[69]), has now been superseded by the theory of invention in southern Ireland, close to Latin-speaking Roman Britain, perhaps in the late third century.[70]

The churchyard cross at Corwen was thought by Nash-Williams to have incisions as transverse bars which may represent a vestigial "key-pattern" or similar design,[71] but it has been suggested that the shaft bears the name I Th FUS (Idhfúss) in runes, possibly of tenth- or eleventh-century date. Nash-Williams possibly thought the cross of too late a form to bear runes, whereas the shaft may in fact be a medieval reshaping of an earlier cross.[72]

Revised Readings and Schools

Some readings have been revised, such as that on the sixth-century Bedd Porius stone, inscribed in Roman capitals from Pen-y-stryd, Ardudwy, Merionethshire (fig. 6), whose various readings have

[69] K. Jackson, *Language and History in Early Britain*, pp. 137-38.

[70] C. Thomas has suggested the existence of trading establishments under Roman control near the outflow of large rivers such as the area around Cork, modern Youghal, or Waterford, and its export to SW Wales not long after c. 400: *Mute Stones*, p. 34. D. McManus' *A Guide to Ogam* (Maynooth, 1991) examines both the nature of writing and position of ogam within it, and the history of the many theses concerning its origin, and he corrects many readings.

[71] The runes were originally published by Macalister as a note in the report on the 89th Annual Meeting of the Cambrian Archaeological Association at Llangollen, *Archaeologia Cambrensis* 90 (1935), 248-49. *ECMW* 276.

[72] R. Moon, "Viking Runic Inscriptions in Wales", *Archaeologia Cambrensis* 127 (1978), 124-26. If the marks are runes (unclear), they could be English.

included the word PLANVS (leper: flat-faced, wnepclawr). Gresham's comparisons of antiquarian recordings and the condition of the stone support a version PORIVS HIC IN TUMVLO IACIT HOMO XRIANVS FVIT, whereas Nash-Williams read PLANVS, following archdeacon Thomas ("He was a plain (simple) man").[73] The interpretation of the Towyn inscription by Sir Ifor Williams (1949) was too late to be incorporated into *ECMW*.

Reassessment by Ralegh Radford of the Samson crosses at Llantwit Major in *Archaeologia Cambrensis* suggested a dating earlier by several centuries or more than previously accepted,[74] a view not accepted by Gwyn Thomas for several reasons, one being similarities in decorative patterns with the crosses at Carew and Nevern observed by Clarke.[75] Paradoxically, it was Radford who reinterpreted the inscription on the Carew cross in 1949, revising Nash-Williams' earlier 1939 reading of the inscription in the left-hand panel.[76]

The South Wales schools have been further defined by Knight (upon whose work fig. 13 has been based), while Edwards has drawn

---

[73] Gresham, "Bedd Porius", pp. 388-92. The Lhwyd MS (Aberystwyth, National Library of Wales, Llansteffan MS 185) and a record by Robert Vaughan do not support Gresham's solution (Gwyn Thomas papers). A charter of 1209 from Llywelyn ab Iorweth to Cymer names a place Bedd yr Esgob close to the findspot, suggesting a possible context for the stone.

[74] C. A. R. Radford, "Two Datable Cross-shafts at Llantwit Major", *Archaeologia Cambrensis* 132 (1983), 107-15.

[75] Yet the Samson stone, perhaps referring to a head of the house and Llantwit Major, was dated by Thomas to the tenth century: W. G. Thomas, "Inscribed and Sculptured Stones", in *RCAHM Glamorgan*, pp. 50-51. Both the decoration and the top mortice also occur on the cross of Eiudon stone from Llanfynydd, now in the National Museum & Gallery, Cardiff, and the Carew cross.

[76] C. A. R. Radford, "The Inscription on the Carew Cross", *Archaeologia Cambrensis* 100 (1949), 253-55: MARGIT/EUT.RE/X.ETG(uin). FILIUS (*ECMW* 303). This ingenious reading was eagerly accepted by Nash-Williams as another bench-mark (Maredudd ap Edwin, d.1035), and has increasingly been used, but the inscription is difficult to read to the point of being cryptic (unlikely to have been deliberate).

comparisons to parallels between many north Welsh freestanding crosses and the Chester school and Northumbria.

Revising Nash-Williams

While many may have initially felt that, following publication of *ECMW*, there was little left to do, there have been many new discoveries (over 100) since 1950. Additions to the Corpus include the Pen-y-fai stone from near Bridgend, Glamorgan, possibly reused in the twelfth century as a boundary marker;[77] a fragment of pillar cross from Llangynwyd, Glamorgan;[78] stones found at Walton West, Pembrokeshire,[79] and at Nant Crew, Brecknockshire;[80] and new *Group II* stones from Caernarfonshire.[81] Elisabeth Okasha has published the interesting inscription in Anglo-Saxon lettering from Ramsey Island near St David's of Saturnbiu, a possible reference to Saturnbiu Hail (the generous), Bishop of St Davids who died in 831.[82] More recent discoveries include a *Group II* stone with outline ring cross from Bryngwyn Farm, Cards. (near St Dogmaels, Pembs.) (fig. 11) and the head of a late freestanding cross of late tenth- or eleventh-century date found in 1992 during grave-digging in the churchyard of St Stephen and St Tathan, Caerwent (fig. 12).[83]

---

[77] This illustrates functions for early Christian monuments other than tombstones: see J. M. Lewis, "An Early Christian Stone from Pen-y-fai, Glamorgan", *Archaeologia Cambrensis* 119 (1970), 71-74.

[78] J. M. Lewis, "A Fragmentary Pillar Cross from Llangynwyd, Glamorgan", *Archaeologia Cambrensis* 129 (1980), 158-59.

[79] R. E. Kay, "An Early Christian Monument from Walton West (Pembs.)", *Archaeologia Cambrensis* 107 (1958), 122-23.

[80] D. P. Webley, "The Nant Crew Stone: A New Discovery", *Archaeologia Cambrensis* 107 (1958), 123-25.

[81] C. A. R. Radford and W. J. Hemp, "Some Early Crosses in Caernarfonshire", *Archaeologia Cambrensis* 110 (1961), 144-53.

[82] E. Okasha, "A New Inscription from Ramsey Island", *Archaeologia Cambrensis* 119 (1970), 68-70.

[83] M. Redknap, "A pre-Norman Cross from Caerwent and its Context", *The Monmouthshire Antiquary* 10 (1994), 1-6. A fragmentary head from another freestanding cross which had fallen out of the churchyard wall at St Michael's

When the stock of *ECMW* was exhausted in 1980, the Director of the University of Wales Press asked the Board of Celtic Studies about reprinting or revising *ECMW*. Editorship was taken up by John M. Lewis, then Assistant Keeper, Medieval and Later Antiquities, National Museum of Wales and the late Gwyn W. Thomas, formerly of the Royal Commission in Aberystwyth. Lewis covered counties in South and East Wales (Brecknockshire, Glamorgan, Monmouthshire and Radnorshire) with outliers in Herefordshire and Shropshire, while Thomas was to cover West and North Wales (Anglesey, Caernarfonshire, Cardiganshire, Carmarthenshire, Denbighshire, Flintshire, Merionethshire, Montgomeryshire, Pembrokeshire). The original primary aim of updating the original book was to include the many new discoveries and identifications made since 1950, and to modernise the presentation to make the work more serviceable in several respects. The topographic basis of the Corpus, the historic counties, was retained. The revised edition was still to be Nash-Williams' in concept and, as far as is possible, content.

A revision is also needed in order to update the present location of the monuments: no less than seventy have been moved to new locations, some under protective cover in accordance with recommendations made by the Ancient Monuments Board for Wales in 1956. The main threats to monuments in the open are natural (lichen and human agency in the form of vandalism, graffiti, theft and accidental damage), and anthropogenic in the form of air pollution. More precise findspots can now be given for some stones, as a result of individual place-name studies and a more systematic examination of early records such as those associated with Edward Lhuyd: for example, the stone of Brohomaglus Iattus and his wife Cauna, listed in *ECMW* under Pentrefoelas in Denbighshire, was associated with a long-cist cemetery only a few metres into that county across the

church, Llanfihangel Ysgeifiog, Anglesey, was found in 1991: N. Edwards, "St Michael's Church, Llanfihangel Ysgeifiog (SH 478 734)", *Archaeology in Wales* 33 (1993), 65. This is similar in style to the tenth- or eleventh-century example from Penmon, Anglesey. A *Group I* stone inscribed VERE was found some time after 1977 during preparations for ploughing at Bryn Gwylan, Llangernyw, Denbighshire: N. Edwards, "Bryn Gwylan, Llangernyw (SH 892 699)", *Archaeology in Wales* 27 (1987), 58.

Conwy, just outside Penmachno parish (*ECMW* 183), and consequently has a possible relationship to the two high-status churches at Penmachno.[84] Another instance is the tenth-/eleventh-century decorated font provenanced in the 1950 edition at Beaumaris, Anglesey (*ECMW* 1) which should now be placed under Penmon (church), having been recorded by Fenton: "In the Nave a font with some old sculpture on the stone, too much blunted by daubings of whitewash to be traced".[85]

Modernisation of the Corpus format will result in the inclusion of bibliographies, the introduction of metric measurements and National Grid references, and greater standardisation of format for entries with a new system of numbering within the historic counties. A system of classifying the types of decoration has been devised, which is in line with that recently published by the British Academy.[86] Over seventy relocations and corrections have been recorded, together with revisions suggested since 1950. It was initially accepted that the Introduction was more personal, and problematic; that it should still be primarily Nash-Williams' text, but that it would need revision and updating. Sound grounds now exist for modifying this approach, and for the revision to be published either as one volume or in several parts. In the case of the latter, the first volume could provide the revised Corpus catalogue, which was primarily utilitarian, with the addition of a completely new introduction which provides the background to the 1950 edition and the rationale and systems adopted for the new Corpus entries. The editors' first aim has been and should remain to turn the existing work into a more serviceable tool for further research, rather than to

[84] Knight, "Penmachno Revisited", pp. 8-9.

[85] R. Fenton, *Tours in Wales (1804-1813)*, ed. J. Fisher (London, 1917), p. 257.

[86] R. Cramp, *Grammar of Anglo-Saxon Ornament. A General Introduction to the Corpus of Anglo-Saxon Stone Sculpture* (Oxford, 1984). The descriptions in the revised Nash-Williams Corpus follow a standardised format – dimensions (h x w x d) followed by a more detailed account of the inscription and/or decoration. Where the surface is divided, these are described under separate numbered sections (1, 2, 3), and each surface is identified by a letter (A, B, C).

expand into areas which would now be expected within any synthetic work.[87]

It is, nevertheless, important that the revision promotes rather than inhibits further study, in the way that the 1950 edition did for some time. A companion text would be needed to address the necessity of updating Nash-Williams' original discursive introduction with a series of new chapters by specialists which examine key issues, such as the historical background to the sculpture; the regional geology;[88] the sequence of forms; the abstract pattern analysis; the constructional principles, sizes and standards in monument design; the iconography; analysis and comparison of monument groups, such as those at Llantwit Major and Margam. The purpose of the inscriptions – whether in vernacular or formulaic, whether addressing a secular audience or the redeemer – could also be covered.[89] Any newly discovered stones not included in Part 1 could also be included in companion volumes. Jeremy Knight has recently considered the precise location of the monuments of parts of South Wales and their geographical relationship to patterns of pastoral care.

Public awareness of this early medieval artistic legacy has increased dramatically in recent years. In 1975 the National Museum

---

[87] A number of topics certainly deserve more detailed appraisal, such as the detailed topography of the monuments and their position in the landscape, the lithology of the stones, and the schools of carving.

[88] Re-examination of the Carew cross by R. Turner of Cadw: Welsh Historic Monuments included geological examination by R. E. Bevins of the National Museums & Galleries of Wales. The main shaft is a microtonalite (igneous lava) found 40 km away in the Preseli Mountains, while the upper stone is a Carboniferous sandstone, most probably from the Carmarthen coalfields (R. Turner, Cardigan lecture, 15 June 1991; Turner, *Cadw Guide to Lamphey Bishop's Palace, Llawhaden Castle, Carswell Medieval House, Carew Cross* (Cardiff, 1991), pp. 49-52). In Cardiganshire, the stones were largely local, one exception being Llanbadarn Fawr pillar cross (*ECMW* 111), a granitic rock possibly from north Caernarfonshire: G W. Thomas, "Early Christian Monuments", p. 408.

[89] For an overview of much of the Welsh evidence, see J. Higgitt, "Words and Crosses: The Inscribed Stone Cross in Early Medieval Britain and Ireland", in *Early Medieval Sculpture in Britain and Ireland*, ed. J. Higgitt, British Archaeological Report 152 (Oxford, 1986), pp. 125-52, esp. pp. 137-41.

of Wales opened an Archaeological Gallery devoted solely to early Christian monuments, bringing together twenty-three stones and fourteen casts from its extensive cast collection, arranged in three main groups in accordance with Nash-Williams' Corpus (fig. 4).

Saunders Lewis' perception of Welsh history as a comparison of Classicism and Barbarism, with Wales as the final repository of classical learning in the West through the Christian Church, coincided with that of Nash-Williams, who said, half in jest, that "the Welsh were already Christians when 'those English' were still a gang of pagans".[90] The Corpus of early Christian monuments by Nash-Williams, though now out of print, continues to draw public attention to the artistic achievements of the people of Wales.[91] The database of stonework of the period has expanded since 1950, but Nash-Williams' work remains a cornerstone of any such evaluation, and has provided a benchmark in the study of early medieval Wales. His obituary described the work as "a successor to Westwood's *Lapidarium Walliae* (1876-79) and itself never likely to be superseded at all".[92] His own comment in 1950 was that it would probably serve for twenty-five years.[93] It would indeed be a fitting tribute if the appearance of the first fascicule of the revision coincided with the fiftieth anniversary of the original work.[94]

---

[90] Quoted in Knight, "Early Christian Inscriptions", pp. 45-50 (p. 45).

[91] The present-day resurgence of an interest in Celtic visual art has led to a wide-ranging craft movement freely adapting Celtic designs. This has resulted on occasions in the use of the ringed cross as a symbol of identity within a form of nationhood which is specifically non-Saxon. A few are specifically Welsh, such as the icon for Cadw: Welsh Historic Monuments, and the design appearing on one side of the medal struck in 1988 to commemorate Gerald of Wales' journey through the country in 1188, both based on the head of the Carew cross (Pembrokeshire, *ECMW* 303).

[92] Randall, "Obituary Notice", pp. 150-51.

[93] Gwyn Thomas papers.

[94] Since this paper was given (1994), Dr Nancy Edwards has been appointed by the Board of Celtic Studies to complete the revision initiated by Gwyn Thomas; John Lewis and Mark Redknap are completing the first fascicule.

Fig. 1 V. E. Nash-Williams (1897-1955), shown here at Caerwent.

Fig. 2 Tenth-century sandstone panelled cross from Cwm Gwenffrwd, near Neath, Glamorgan (*ECMW* 265). The incomplete half-uncial inscription reads: PROP/ARAVI/T GAI[ ] C/[...("Gai prepared ..."). Recorded as "having been taken from a small holy-well", at *Bryn Cefneithan*, a farm north of Blaenavon.

Fig. 3 Pencil drawing by Thomas Henry Thomas of the "Cross of Conbelin" at Margam Abbey, Glam., made prior to its removal to the Stones Museum (*ECMW* 234). Thomas was a collector of antiquities, Herald of the Gorsedd of Bards, and friend of Goscombe John.

Fig. 4 Nash-Williams *Group III* stones on display at the National Museum & Gallery, Cardiff. The Carew Cross stands in the centre.

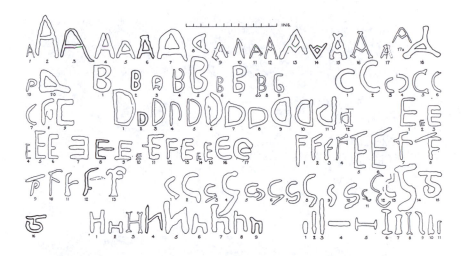

Fig. 5 *Above*: letter forms, reproduced from *ECMW*.

Fig. 6 *Group I* stones. *Above*: memorial from Llangadwaladr, Anglesey, to CATAMANVS REX, Cadfan king of Gwynedd who died c. 620-30 (*ECMW* 13). The lettering is characterised by letter forms close to full Insular forms, such as the R to miniscule R, and M, and the date of the inscription accords with the first examples of Insular script (Tedeschi, "Osservazioni sulla paleografia delle iscrizioni britanniche"). *Below*: the Porius stone from Trawsfynydd, Mer. (*ECMW* 289). The inscription shows ligatures directly comparable with later Romano-British lapidary script. Nash-Williams argued for a re-introduction of Roman epigraphic practice from Gaul in the fifth century. (Not to same scale).

Fig. 7 *Group I* stones: (a) the SIMILINI TOVISACI stone with ogam S[I]B[I]L[I]N[I]// [TO]VISACI from Clocaenog, Denb. (*ECMW* 176); (b) the TRENACATVS stone with ogam from Capel Wyl, Llanwenog, Cards. (*ECMW* 127); (c) the late fifth-/early sixth-century stone from Maes-Llyn farm, Llangwyryfon, Cards., inscribed DOMNICI/IACIT FILIVS/ BRAVECCI (*ECMW* 122); (d) the partly half-uncial sixth-century POTENINA MALIIER stone ("Potentina, the wife of ...") from Tregaron, Cards. (*ECMW* 132). Photographs: National Museums & Galleries of Wales. (Not to same scale).

a

b

c

d

Fig. 8 *Group II* **pillar-stones: (a) Pont-rhyd-y-fen, Glam. (*ECMW* 257); (b) slab with equal-armed ring cross inscribed in half-uncial script ENEVIRI on side, from Tregaron, Cards. (*ECMW* 133); (c) Carn Caca (Vale of Neath, Glam.), found in 1953; (d) Pen-lann-wen, Tirabad, Llanddulas, Brecs. (*ECMW* 48). Photographs: National Museums & Galleries of Wales. (Not to same scale).**

Fig. 9 *Group III* stones: (a) cast of the tenth-century stone of "Briamail Flou", from Llandyfaelog Fach, Brecs. (*ECMW* 49); (b) the tenth-century cross-slab from Nash farm, Glam. (*ECMW* 250); (c) the freestanding "Eiudon" cross from Llanfynydd, Carms. (top missing; *ECMW* 159); (d) the incomplete shaft with inscription commemorating a grant of land by Artmail to the church, from Ogmore, Glam. (*ECMW* 255). Photographs: National Museums & Galleries of Wales. (Not to same scale).

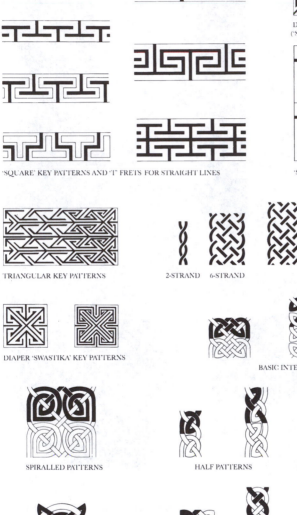

DIAGONAL KEY PATTERNS
('SWASTIKA' TYPE)

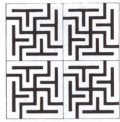

'SQUARE' KEY PATTERNS AND 'T' FRETS FOR STRAIGHT LINES

'SWASTIKA' T-FRETS

TRIANGULAR KEY PATTERNS

2-STRAND   6-STRAND

22-STRAND   PLAIN PLAITS

DIAPER 'SWASTIKA' KEY PATTERNS

BASIC INTERLACE PATTERNS

SPIRALLED PATTERNS

HALF PATTERNS

ENCIRCLED PATTERNS

SIMPLE PATTERNS

RING-CHAIN

Fig. 10 Selection of patterns found on Welsh *Group III* stones. The revision seeks to formalise their description (drawing by T. Daly).

Fig. 11 New discoveries: pillar stone with lightly carved outline cross, found at Bryngwyn Farm, near St Dogmaels (now in the National Museum & Gallery, Cardiff). The second cross-inscribed stone to be found on this farm, it is probably associated with the pre-Norman monastery at Llandudoch/St Dogmaels, about 800m to the north-west of the findspot.

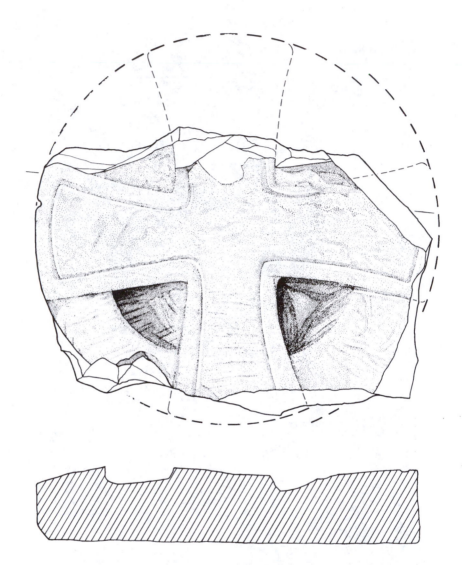

Fig. 12 New discoveries: the incomplete late tenth- or eleventh-century cross found in 1992 within the churchyard of St Stephen and St Tathan, Caerwent (drawing by T. Daly). This find, together with the intramural cemetery nearby, support identification of St Tatheus' *clas/monasterium* in the vicinity of the present church. (Scale 1:8).

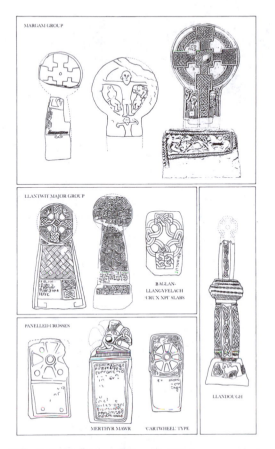

Fig. 13 Simplified drawings of South Wales crosses, grouped into local styles (from left to right). *Top*: ninth-century disc-headed slab from Mynydd Gellionen, Pontardawe (*ECMW* 210); late ninth-/tenth-century disc-headed slab from Llan-gan with Crucifixion; the late ninth-/tenth-century "Conbelin" stone, Margam (*ECMW* 234). *Middle*: the "Enniaun" stone, Llantwit Major (*ECMW* 231); the "Houelt" stone, Llantwit Major (*ECMW* 211); the late ninth-/early tenth-century stone from Baglan (*ECMW* 191). *Bottom*: the ?tenth-century slab cross from Eglwys Nynnid, near Margam (*ECMW* 200); eleventh-century cross from Methyr Mawr (*ECMW* 240); the tenth-/eleventh-century "Ilquici" stone from Margam (*ECMW* 236); the late tenth-/eleventh-century Llandough cross (*ECMW* 206) (drawing by T. Daly).